A Chanticleer Press Edition

PACIFIC COAST

By Bayard H. McConnaughey and Evelyn McConnaughey

Birds
Miklos D. F. Udvardy, Professor of Biological Sciences,
California State University, Sacramento

Fishes, Whales, and Dolphins
Daniel W. Gotshall, Senior Marine Biologist, California
Department of Fish and Game; and David K. Caldwell and
Melba C. Caldwell, Research Scientists, University of Florida

Mammals
John O. Whitaker, Jr., Professor of Life Sciences, Indiana
State University

Seashells
Harald A. Rehder, Zoologist Emeritus, Smithsonian
Institution

Seashore Creatures
Norman A. Meinkoth, Professor Emeritus of Zoology,
Swarthmore College

Wildflowers
Richard Spellenberg, Professor of Biology, New Mexico State
University

Alfred A. Knopf, New York

Prepared and produced by
Chanticleer Press, Inc., New York.

Printed and bound by Dai Nippon, Tokyo, Japan.
Typeset in Garamond by Dix Type Inc., Syracuse, New York.

Second Printing.

Library of Congress Cataloging in Publication Data
McConnaughey, Bayard Harlow, 1916–
The Audubon Society nature guides. Pacific Coast.
Includes index.
1. Natural history–Pacific Coast (U.S.)–Handbooks,
manuals, etc. 2. Natural history–Pacific Coast (B.C.)–
Handbooks, manuals, etc. 3. Coastal ecology–Pacific Coast
(U.S.)–Handbooks, manuals, etc. 4. Coastal ecology–Pacific
Coast (B.C.)–Handbooks, manuals, etc. 5. Zoology–Pacific
Coast (U.S.)–Handbooks, manuals, etc. 6. Zoology–Pacific
Coast (B.C.)–Handbooks, manuals, etc. 7. Botany–Pacific
Coast (U.S.)–Handbooks, manuals, etc. 8. Botany–Pacific
Coast (B.C.)–Handbooks, manuals, etc. 9. Coastal flora–
Pacific Coast (U.S.)–Identification. 10. Coastal flora–Pacific
Coast (B.C.)–Identification. 11. Animals–Identification.
I. McConnaughey, Evelyn, 1927–   II. National Audubon
Society. III. Title. IV. Title: Pacific Coast.
QH104.5.P32M37 1986   574.5'2635'0979   84-48673
ISBN 0-394-73130-1 (pbk.)

CONTENTS

ACKNOWLEDGMENTS

Credit first must go to the editors of Chanticleer Press for the vision of a guidebook encompassing the entire panorama of our Pacific shores and seas, as well as for the final shape of the written contributions and the selection of the marvelous photographs. We gratefully acknowledge assistance from friends and family, including our sons Ted and John, who provided firsthand information and compositions about Alaska. At the University of Oregon Institute of Marine Biology, staff members Dan Varujean, Mike Graybill, and Jan Hodder, along with Jean Hanna, librarian, provided valuable assistance in selection and description of marine birds and mammals.

We also wish to thank James Nybakken of Moss Landing Marine Laboratories, California State University, for his careful review of the manuscript. Others who loaned important reference material and made many valuable suggestions were Joel Hedgpeth, Larry McQueen, Herb Wisner, Barbara Koser, Peggy Robinson, Phillip Johnson, Andrea Coffman, and several state and federal wildlife agencies in the Pacific coastal states and British Columbia.

Bayard McConnaughey
Evelyn McConnaughey

Cover photograph: Over many centuries, the forces of water and wind have sculpted Elephant Rock on Washington's Tunnel Island.

Bayard H. McConnaughey
Specialist in marine biology, Bayard McConnaughey is a
professor of biology at the University of Oregon, where he has
taught since 1949. He received his B.A. from Pomona College
in California, his M.A. from the University of Hawaii, and a
Ph.D. from the University of California at Berkeley. During
World War II he served in the bacteriology-parasitology
section of the Central Pacific Area Laboratory of the U.S.
Army. The author of numerous articles in his field, Dr.
McConnaughey has also written *Introduction to Marine Biology*,
a widely used college text. Formerly he was the acting director
of the Oregon Institute of Marine Biology in Charleston,
Oregon.

Evelyn McConnaughey
An expert on seaweeds, Evelyn McConnaughey received her
B.A. in zoology at the College of Idaho and M.A. in biology
at the University of Oregon. She conducts workshops on how
to collect and cook with marine algae, and is completing a
book on foraging, which includes recipes and information on
many applications of marine algae.

The McConnaugheys have lived in Eugene, Oregon, since
1949. They are active in local environmental affairs and in the
Eugene Natural History Society.

HOW TO USE THIS GUIDE

This guide is designed for use both at home and in the field. Its clear arrangement in four parts—habitat essays, color plates, species descriptions, and appendices—puts information at your fingertips that would otherwise only be accessible through a small library of field guides.

The habitat essays enable you to discover the many kinds of habitats on the Pacific Coast, the relationships among the plants and animals found there, and highlights not to be missed. The color plates feature coastal scenes and over 600 photographs of different plant and animal species. The species descriptions cover the most important information about a plant or animal, including a description, the range, specific habitat, and comments. Finally, the appendices include a bibliography, a glossary, and a comprehensive index.

Using This Guide at Home

Before planning an outing, you will want to know what you can expect to see.

1. Begin by leafing through the color plates for a preview of the Pacific coast.
2. Read the habitat section. For quick reference, at the end of each chapter you will find a list of some of the most common plants and animals found in that habitat.
3. Look at the color plates of some of the animals and plants so that you will be able to recognize them later in the field. The table called How to Use the Color Plates provides a visual table of contents to the color section, explains the arrangement of the plates, and tells the caption information provided. The habitats where you are likely to encounter the species are listed in blue type so that you can easily refer to the correct habitat chapter. The page number for the full species description is also included in the caption.
4. Turn to the species descriptions to learn more about the plants and animals that interest you. A range map or drawing appears in the margin for birds, mammals, and many of the wildflowers. Poisonous seashore creatures, fishes, and dangerous whales are indicated by the danger symbol $\otimes$ next to the species name.
5. Consult the appendices for definitions of technical terms and suggestions for further reading.

Using This Guide in the Field

When you are out in the field, you will want to find information quickly and easily.

1. Turn to the color plates to locate the plant or animal you have seen. At a glance the captions will help you narrow down the possibilities. First, verify the general habitat by checking the blue type information to the left of the color plate. Next, look for additional information in blue type—for example, when wildflowers bloom or the specific habitat of fishes and seashore creatures. To find out whether a bird or mammal is in your area, check the range map or range description next to the color plate.
2. Now turn to the species description to confirm your identification and to learn more about the species.

First frontispiece: Near the shore off the coast of Baja California, a bull elephant seal displays its prominent snout.

Second frontispiece: California Sea Lions, afloat on their backs, take a rest off the California coast near Monterey.

Third frontispiece: A Killer Whale, displaying its distinctive, long dorsal fin, swims along the California coast.

Fourth frontispiece: Winter view of Jalama Beach on the rocky coast near Point Conception, California.

Fifth frontispiece: A Black Turnstone looking for its next meal among a bed of sea anemones exposed at low tide at Monterey Bay, California.

PREFACE

Where sea meets land at the continent's edge, the forces of wind, waves, currents, and continental movements, together with runoff from the land, combine to form a dynamic, constantly changing and demanding environment. The jagged 4000 mile long coastline from Alaska to Baja, if straightened, would measure over 56,000 miles—more than twice around the world. A series of headlands and beaches, glaciers and fjords, river mouths and tidelands, provide distinct habitats for communities of plants and animals, each uniquely adapted to meet the rigors of their special environment.

A visit to the coast provides an exhilarating panorama of sights, sounds, and smells—storm-tossed waves of cliffs, pleasant sandy beaches, and occasional glimpses of spectacular marine mammals, fishes, and birds. The more curious and persistent observer also discovers fascinating creatures clinging to rocks as the intertidal zone is revealed by changing tides.

From Sea to Land

It has been aptly said that life is a marginal affair. Most of it occurs at or near boundaries or interfaces—at the interface between air and land or in the thin, illuminated layer of water at the surface of the oceans. Similarly, physical and biotic boundaries within the earth's thin living biosphere are of special interest and commonly contain more species and more dynamic interactions than do the central parts of biotic communities. Such boundaries are termed ecotones. Familiar examples are the transitional zones between forest and prairie, between grassland and sagebrush, between wet lands and dry lands.

Of all these transitional zones, those between the land and the sea are the sharpest, most varied, richest, and most subject to change. The incessant daily movements of the tides subject the intertidal zone to submersion in salty waters, to exposure to air, to drying and warming in sun and wind, to exposure to fresh water in rain, to different sets of predators when covered with water and when exposed, and to wave shock during incoming high tides and storms.

Organisms living here must be adapted to, or able to protect themselves from, sharp and sudden changes in temperature, osmotic relationships, the availability of food and oxygen, waste removal, wave impact, predation, and a host of other changes in addition to the slower seasonal changes to which all terrestrial forms are subjected. Somehow they must manage to establish themselves, live, reproduce, and disperse themselves in the face of all these problems.

Moreover the land/sea interface is itself constantly changing due to changes in the relative levels of sea and land, to erosion and sediment deposition, sediment transport, and other geological and oceanographic processes. One might suppose that all this would impose so many, and such contrasting, stresses upon organisms that few would be able to survive and flourish there, yet intertidal areas all over the world are teeming with rich and varied forms of life, many of them unlike anything found anywhere else.

In North America we are fortunate in having long and varied coastlines extending through latitudes with very different climatic regimes, including all the major types of intertidal habitats to be found from the warm tropics to the frigid north. In this book we consider the coasts of western North America, from the Arctic to the temperate waters off southern California.

Several kinds of habitats, shaped by the various landscapes of the Pacific Coast, grade into each other in the West. These include the rocky intertidal; beaches; sand dunes; protected marine environments (estuaries, salt marshes, and wharves and pilings); and offshore waters.

Although these habitats are described separately, we will see that they intergrade, overlap, and influence each other. Similarly, many of the plants and animals, although predominantly associated with a particular habitat, may range between several.

Within each of the habitats are distinct zones with different microclimates determined by wind, tide, exposure, and other factors. The animals and plants within each habitat are described according to the particular zone that they occupy.

Equipment

A visit to any one of these habitats offers a marvelous opportunity for learning about nature first-hand. It is best for the amateur naturalist to take little along in the way of equipment. For starting out, a pencil and a notebook (preferably waterproof), a pair of binoculars, and perhaps a small magnifying lens will be sufficient.

Use the notebook to describe accurately the animals and plants that you see; record the time of day, the kind of weather, the season, and any other particulars, such as behavior or place of growth, that may be helpful in confirming your identification later on.

A small magnifying lens will help you take a closer look at some of the fascinating tiny life forms that can be seen clinging to rocks when the tide is low. Binoculars, of course, are essential to bird identification, especially along the coast, where many birds flying out over the open water can be recognized by their style of flight or other characteristics visible only at a distance. Binoculars will also be handy for spotting whales, dolphins, Sea Otters, and other playful marine mammals.

A camera is also a welcome bit of equipment at the seashore. Much of the Pacific Coast is magnificently photogenic, and it is comparatively easy to learn to take snapshots or slides that will add to your enjoyment after your trip to the beach is over. If your camera has a telephoto lens, you will be able to take better identification shots of marine birds and mammals.

Some Cautions

The plants and animals of the intertidal regions of the seashore depend on each other for survival. Each is equipped to live within a particular niche, and if a careless visitor starts turning over rocks, digging up sands, and carting off specimens, many animals will needlessly die, and the area will take a long time to recover. So investigate the plants and animals in their habitats and enjoy them, but do not destroy them. When turning a rock over to see what lives under it, do so gently; try not to crush animals, and be sure to turn the rock back the way it was. Return animals to protected damp places such as under rocks or seaweed. After digging for burrowing animals, fill in the holes, because piles of mud and sand may smother small clams or worms whose burrows can no longer reach the surface. Avoid crushing animals by stepping on them.

Don't run, both for the sake of the animals and your own safety—some rocks that are coated with seaweed will be very slippery. It is helpful to stay low in the cracks between rocks to avoid falling. Do not collect live animals such as shells, starfish, and sea urchins. For one thing, such activities may be against the law. In any case, marine animals are difficult, if not impossible, to keep alive in a home aquarium—such experiments are the province of scientists and specialists. It's better just to take a photo; these keep their colors far better than preserved or dried specimens, and are much easier to keep and share.

Some Rules for Your Own Safety
First, know your area. Check guides and maps, and talk to local people. Go to safe, protected bays, inlets, and estuaries. Avoid cliffs, caves, and sandbars. Consult tide tables and plan to arrive well before the incoming tide so that there will be plenty of time to see the plants and animals at low tide. Keep your eye on the ocean, and check frequently to see that a turning tide doesn't cut you off from retreat. Wave height is unpredictable, so don't turn your back. If you are caught in an unexpected wave, hunker down like a barnacle or starfish and hang on to the rock. It is a good idea to watch out for the wake of passing motor boats or ships. Wear a life jacket when near deep water. Don't climb cliffs, as they often are of unstable materials, and when facing the ocean may be cut off by incoming tides. Never walk on floating logs, and use caution on beached logs, as they may roll unpredictably. Stay with someone for safety; in case one person gets hurt, the other can go for help. Have fun, but don't fool around!

An Invitation
This guide is for the genuinely curious, who want to understand the forces that, over the ages, have shaped our spectacular coastline, to see the many creative ways plants and animals have adapted, and why they live, eat, behave, and protect themselves as they do. It is hoped that with better understanding of the ocean communities we will see how all life is interrelated, and how what we do can protect this marvelously integrated but vulnerable planet.

INTRODUCTION

Ours is a watery planet. The seas, which cover more than seventy percent of the earth's surface, shape the world, moderate its climate, and are the cradle of life. Everything in the seas is in a state of constant flux and change. Yet there are striking uniformities and an overall stability, which are of utmost importance to living things.

Stretching for more than 4000 miles as the crow flies and encompassing a staggering 56,000 miles of shoreline, the Pacific Coast of North America is a region of great diversity. Along these shores, the interested visitor can encounter hundreds of thousands of life forms, ranging from the tiniest microorganisms, which float by the millions in the water, to the mighty whales, whose unlikely relationship to humans has intrigued investigators since time immemorial.

With a little study and some attention to detail, it is possible to learn about the seashore and about its fascinating history and inhabitants. Whether you are a scientist or just a casual visitor, the Pacific Coast offers a variety of sights and discoveries. It includes rocky shores, wide, flat beaches, and massive dunes, as well as protected bays and estuaries, salt marshes, and the mysterious, deeper waters offshore.

Although the habitats are described separately, in reality they intergrade, overlap, and influence each other. Similarly, many of the plants and animals, although predominantly associated with one particular habitat, are sometimes found in several of them. Within each habitat, distinct zones with different microclimates are determined by wind, tide, exposure, and other factors; animals and plants are described according to the particular zone in which they live.

Description

The coast of southern California is bordered mostly by low sea cliffs. A few terraces occur alongside coastal plains and deltas, as, for example, in the Los Angeles area and near Ventura. A series of ridges and terraces extend inland from the coast, such as Point Loma, the Soledad Mountains, and the San Pedro Hills. The Santa Monica Mountains follow the coast north of Los Angeles. Many unstable cliff areas exist along the southern portion of the state; indeed, old maps show that entire blocks of property on the terraces adjoining cliffs in the San Diego area have disappeared since the 1800s.

A somewhat different kind of coastline extends north of Point Conception, and the difference is reflected by a change in plant and animal forms. This coastline is quite straight, despite rugged mountain ranges that cut across in a north-northwest trend. Sediment from the broad river valleys has resulted in large dunes.

There are large embayments at Monterey and San Francisco, the latter at the mouths of rivers draining the great Central Valley. North of San Francisco, some of the smaller bays— Bolinas, Bodega, and Tomales—follow the San Andreas Fault, which goes to sea just south of Cape Mendocino. Along the central and northern California coast, high cliffs and elevated terraces rise up out of the sea.

The storm-exposed coast of northern California continues
through Oregon to the entrance to the Strait of Juan de Fuca,
off the coast of Washington. The coastline alternates between
relatively low mountainous tracts with rocky headlands and
outcroppings and a few large river estuaries.

Sand dunes are found along the entire West Coast, but they
attain their greatest development along the coast of Oregon
and southern Washington. Nearly all of Oregon's coast is
owned by the public, including a spectacular forty-five-mile
extent of dunes between North Bend and Florence. This
stretch has many coastal freshwater lakes and streams, so that
it is possible to wade in salt water with one foot while the
other foot is in a fresh rivulet. Dunes, lakes, streams, woods,
and sea all join at Honeyman Park, near Florence.

Downwarping of the land has created drowned (or submerged)
river mouths and a large estuary at Coos Bay. Many of the
region's rivers, including the giant Columbia, enter the sea via
such estuaries.

The long estuaries of southern Washington have a geologic
history similar to the estuaries south of New York: Such areas
are located just south of land that was once glaciated. During
glaciation, an upfolding of the coast occurred south of the
glacial pack. As the ice melted, this bulge subsided, lowering
and flooding the river mouth. In Washington, the twenty-
mile strand guarding Willapa Bay is the longest sand beach on
the entire coast.

Puget Sound, the giant estuary that extends south along the
western side of Seattle, marks a significant change in the
character of the Pacific Coast. To the north, the coastline
breaks into an assortment of islands, channels, and fjords that
cut deeply into a rugged coastal mountain range; broad sandy
areas and extensive sand or mud flats are rare. These
mountains were built when dozens of crustal fragments were
plastered onto the western edge of North America by the slow
convections of the earth's interior; most of these scrambled
pieces now lie more or less parallel to the coastline. The
intertidal areas in Puget Sound tend to be narrow and rocky,
because frequent storms and heavy surf erode sand and other
loose material from the beaches and deposit it in deeper
water.

The Strait of Juan de Fuca, at the border between Canada and
the United States, is a typical glacial trough with straight
sides and deep basins. To the east, other troughs—notably
Puget Sound—trend in various directions. The glacial troughs
in the Puget Sound area are bordered by glacial deposits. From
the San Juan Islands northward, glaciated rock islands are
interwoven with many passageways. These coastal waters are
extremely rich in plant and animal life.

The coast of British Columbia and the adjacent parts of
southern Alaska are very different from the coastal areas farther
south. Along the rugged, mountainous 500-mile-long coast of
this Canadian province, numerous islands and fjords cut deep
into the land, creating a jagged coastline 16,000 miles long.
Some of the mountains are still glaciated; snow and ice

blanket their upper slopes throughout the year, and all levels in the winter. The great variety of temperatures and salinities in this area results in an abundant and diversified assemblage of plants and animals. Vancouver Island is by far the largest island along the Pacific Coast. Its civilized southeast rests in the calm waters of Puget Sound, while its wild northwestern cape receives the full force of open ocean waters. The Queen Charlotte Islands lie farther north off the coast of British Columbia. This region, the home of the Haida tribe, was a haven of life during the period when glaciers covered the continent. Glacial peaks and rain forests come down to the sea all along the Queen Charlotte Sound, which funnels into the straits of the Inside Passage.

The same type of coast continues into southeastern Alaska, but in this area many glaciers still exist at sea level. The Malaspina Glacier, the largest in North America, occurs just beyond the place where the Alaskan coast bends to the west. Mountains in this area include the St. Elias Range, which has the highest peaks in North America, next to Mt. McKinley. The chief populated areas occur along the fjords west of the St. Elias Range, where faulting, volcanism, upheavals, and glacial erosion have together formed a rugged topography. The volcanic Aleutian Islands extend 1300 miles out from the mainland and provide another productive area for plant and animal growth.

West and north of the Alaska Peninsula, in the Bering Sea and arctic Alaska, extensive coastal plains are intersected by lakes and winding stream channels. A few mountains extend down to the sea. A large delta formed by the Yukon River forms a vast plain, on which the delta formed by the drowned mouth of the Kuskokwim River occurs. This coastal area was largely free of ice during the Pleistocene Epoch, but permafrost has greatly increased the abundance of depressions that fill with water in the summer. North of the Yukon delta, Norton Sound represents a deep indentation of the coast. Nome, which is located on the northern shore of the sound, has no harbor; this city was developed when gold was found in beaches at various elevations. The Seward Peninsula, on which Nome is situated, is mountainous: a barrier coast extends north to Kotzebue Sound. The northern coast of Alaska is also bordered by barriers, including the unusually shaped forelands of Point Hope, as well as Point Barrow, the most northern spot of Alaska.

The Shoreline Takes Shape

To understand the habitats of the Pacific Coast, it is helpful first to have an understanding of the forces that have shaped it over the course of geologic history.

During the last great Pleistocene ice age, which occurred about 20,000 years ago, most of northern North America and much of northern Eurasia were covered by an immense ice sheet. The formation of this ice sheet resulted in the removal of approximately fourteen million cubic miles of water from the oceans. This process lowered the sea level by 425 feet, and

**Pacific Ocean Currents
and Winds**

currents

winds

thus exposed formerly submerged coastal areas all over the
world. Along the West Coast, some of the newly emerged
coastal plains in nonglaciated areas south of the great ice sheet
extended more than sixty miles beyond the current shorelines.
Mammoths and small bands of early people roamed these low
coastal plains. Rivers cut channels through them and created
new deltas and estuaries along the coast. Broad beaches were
formed. Some of the old river channels are now submarine
canyons.

The melting and retreat of the glaciers 12,000 years ago
gradually returned much of the water to the oceans, causing
generally rising sea levels and releasing the northern portion of
the continent from most of the immense weight of ice. In
Alaska and British Columbia, the level of the land rose; in
Washington, Oregon, and California, it became lower. As a
result, along the coastlines of British Columbia and southern
Alaska, offshore islands are numerous, and the coastline is
highly dissected by many rivers and streams, which plunge to
the sea in fjordlike canyons.

Immense ice sheets still covered the region as recently as
10,000 years ago. Rivers of ice flowed down from the coastal
mountains and merged, becoming a continuous ice sheet from
Puget Sound to the Alaska Peninsula. In the Puget Sound
region, the ice attained thicknesses of more than a mile; since
the sea level was then some 200 to 300 feet lower than it is
now, the ocean met this ice sheet well out on what is now the
continental shelf. The retreat of the ice sheets opened up vast
areas of new and still evolving coastal habitats from Alaska to
Washington.

South of British Columbia, the situation was very different.
The general lowering of the land and the rising sea level
caused extensive flooding of low valleys and river mouths and
the formation of large, marine-dominated estuarine areas,
especially in the Puget Sound and San Francisco Bay areas.
Numerous broad beaches were formed as rivers brought sand
to the coast and the rising waters eroded the coastal cliffs.
Shales, siltstones, sandstones, and other uplifted marine
sedimentary materials make up the bulk of the land around
Puget Sound, while harder rocks are more abundant to the
north. The softer materials weather and erode rapidly, creating
spectacular cliffs and bluffs. Basalts that have erupted beneath
the sea have been forced to the surface in some places, such as
Dosewallips Falls near Hood Canal in Washington. The lava
visible there is similar to the basalts erupting more than a
mile below sea level along the Juan de Fuca Ridge, offshore.
Where hard rocks—such as granite or intrusions of basalt—
occur along the coast, they resist erosion longer than do softer,
sedimentary, calcareous rocks, sandstone, consolidated clay, or
shale. The hard rocks form rocky headlands and promontories,
which alternate with stretches of recessed shoreline bordered
by sand beaches, giving the shoreline a scalloped aspect.
Storms are less frequent along the southern half of the coast,
and the offshore waters are shallower; thus the sand eroded
from beaches by winter storms is not lost, but is instead

deposited at the breaker line offshore and is pushed up onto the beach again by the smaller waves of summer.

Life in the Waters

The many different plants and animals that live at sea or along the coastline must be adapted to survive a variety of hazards and challenges, many of which terrestrial organisms do not have to face. Creatures at sea and in the intertidal zone—the region along a shoreline that is affected by the rising and falling of the tides—must cope with the stresses presented by currents, strong wave action, and tides. In addition, different levels of light, changes of temperature, and the amount of oxygen and salinity, and nutrients in the water also affect marine life. Animals and plants that live in areas where freshwater and saltwater mix must adjust to changes in salinity; and creatures of the intertidal area must also be adapted to live with a certain amount of exposure to air and wind.

The presence and distribution of every plant and animal that survives in these marine habitats is determined by a combination of these factors. Organisms that survive best in a particular kind of environment form communities of interdependent plants and animals; these communities are called ecosystems.

Currents

The Pacific Ocean contains almost half of the earth's 340 million cubic miles of salt water. The North Pacific and California currents are part of a great planetary current, or gyre, that is pushed by winds around the North Pacific basin. These cool waters move down the West Coast from the polar regions to the Equator, bringing life-sustaining nutrients from the ocean's depths. Coastal currents and waves sculpt rocky headlands, piling sands that form peaceful beaches and mighty dunes. Currents merge, ceaselessly moving, pushing waters off the continental shelf and out again into the great expanses of the sea.

Large-scale surface currents moderate the world's climate, warming western and northern regions and cooling eastern and tropical areas. Lesser currents result from differences in salinity and temperature in different areas; such differences are caused by massive evaporation, heavy precipitation, runoff from large rivers, and changes in barometric pressure. Temporary, large-scale currents are also brought about by storms and gales. Although deep-water currents usually move far more slowly than surface currents, they are also very important. Their vertical movements bring nutrient-rich subsurface waters to the surface, and oxygen-rich surface waters into the depths. Interactions of all these factors produce patterns of ocean circulation that, on the grand scale, can be seen to have certain overall regularities, which also display constantly changing, complex details.

Along coasts, the edge of a continent is partially submerged, forming a gradually sloping area known as the continental shelf. This shelf extends out to where the water reaches a depth of about 150 fathoms—a little over 600 feet—and then gives way as the ocean bottom declines steeply into the abyssal depths. In some regions the continental shelf is narrow, while in others it is broad.

The waters above the continental shelves are known as neritic, or coastal, waters. They are almost always much richer in dissolved plant nutrients than the waters of the open ocean; because additional nutrients are washed into them from the land. In addition, when winds move surface water offshore, an upwelling occurs as deeper water moves in to replace it. The great planetary gyres, such as the California Current along western North America, bring cool, high-latitude waters, which are nutrient- and oxygen-rich, to the outer shelf areas, and upwelling along the landward borders of the shelves brings these nutrients to the surface. They are carried over the rest of the shelf by eddies and countercurrents, winds, and gales. Because of the action of waves and tides, as well as the interaction of coastal and wave currents with irregularities of the shelf topography, the shelf waters generally circulate more actively than do open ocean waters at the same depth. For these reasons, coastal waters are far more productive than most oceanic areas; they contain more than ninety percent of the world's productive fisheries.

Wave Action

The effect of wave action varies from spot to spot, depending on the height of the waves, the aspect and character of the rock, the degree of protection afforded by rock outcroppings, local topography, the vegetation on the sea bottom, and other factors. The strong winds of the Pacific can produce some of the most powerful waves in the Northern Hemisphere. These waves can rapidly and dramatically change beaches and wear down rocky headlands along the Pacific Coast.

There are few sights more awe-inspiring than the crashing of waves on a storm-blown shore. Their enormous force can devastate the shoreline, tearing plants and animals from the rocky substrate or blasting them with sand and stones. Thus the presence of loose rocks along a wave-battered coast may greatly increase the destructiveness of storm waves. The degree of wave shock is an important factor in determining the distribution of plants and animals in the rocky intertidal and subtidal zones of an unprotected coast.

Waves usually approach a beach obliquely rather than head-on. As water within a breaking wave is set in motion, it runs up the beach at an angle—the angle of incidence—and recedes in the opposite direction at an equivalent angle—the angle of reflection. This action sets up a current just seaward of the breakers; known as a longshore current, it moves parallel to the shore, transporting sand as it moves.

Longshore currents can both strip areas of all their sand and build up beaches. Where the source of the sand carried by a longshore current is altered—for instance, when a river that empties into the ocean is diverted—the current may transform a sandy beach into a rocky or gravelly shoreline. In contrast, when a current meets an embayment, it may deposit its sediment load as the waves lose some of their force. In this way, it may create a spit of land or a sandbar along the outer side of the channel where none had existed before. Such action may eventually move the mouth of the bay miles from where it had originally been; this is in fact what happened at Coos Bay, Oregon, where North Spit extends six miles from the original river mouth.

When a longshore current comes to the edge of the continental shelf or to a steep submarine canyon, it may cascade a great deal of sand down the steep slopes. This cascading sediment, called a turbidity current, can be extremely forceful.

Along the coast of the Pacific Northwest, the direction of wave trains is seasonally reversed. Thus, in the winter, sand will accumulate at the southern end of a beach, and at the northern end in summer. Where a bay occurs, a sandbar may close both sides of the bay's mouth alternately, according to the time of year.

Tides

In their influence on coastal morphology, tides are second only to waves; in some places, tides are even more important because they are the primary forces shaping and transporting sediment. The largest tidal ranges are associated with wide continental shelves and narrow straits or semiconfined seaways, which have a funneling effect. Since these conditions are prevalent along the Pacific Coast, tidal ranges of ten to fifteen feet are not unusual in this region. The largest tidal ranges on the West Coast—fifteen to twenty feet—occur in the upper reaches of Puget Sound and in Cook Inlet, Alaska. The most extreme tidal ranges along the North American continent are found in the Bay of Fundy in eastern Canada, where they may reach forty-five feet.

Along the Pacific Coast, there are usually two high tides of unequal height and two low tides of unequal height each day. Such tides are called mixed semidiurnal tides. (By contrast, the tides along much of the Atlantic Coast are the same height each day.) When the moon and sun are aligned, as they are during a new moon and a full moon, the gravitational pull on the earth is combined. As a result, the tides are more extreme; that is, the highest tide is higher, and the lowest tide is lower. These tides are called spring tides. During a half moon, on the other hand, when the sun and moon are at right angles with respect to the earth, their attractive forces partially cancel each other out rather than reinforce each other; the resulting tides, called neap tides, are less extreme. Because of the timing of the lunar month, spring and neap tides follow each other in alternate weeks. In addition, because of the speed at which the moon revolves around the rotating earth, the tides come a little later each day; thus there is a regular progression of high and low tides, which come at different times of the day during different seasons.

The movement of tidal waters near the shoreline causes tidal currents that can reach speeds of a few miles per hour. As the tide rises, the water flows toward shore as a flood tide, moving into shallow coastal marshes and up streams. During ebb tide, the water moves out, exposing low-lying coastal areas. These tidal currents may cut channels in mud flats. They may also build up and tear down barrier islands, sandbars, and deltas.

Erosion and Geological Factors

Other factors that affect shorelines include salt spray, wind, and ice. Salt spray plays an active role in sculpting coastal shrubs. The pitting that develops on limestones and calcareous sandstone in the spray zone of rocky shores is called alveolar weathering, or fretting.

At high latitudes and on cold-climate coasts, such as those of western Canada and Alaska, ice can alter the shoreline dramatically. It may take the form of frozen wave swash and snow at the shoreline, or floes, freezing of the sea, glaciers, and icecaps. The presence of ice in the water limits wave generation and action. Sediment or transport may be reduced, but redistribution may occur as a result of ice push or ice rafting. Melting ice leaves behind such features as kettles, dirt cones, and ridges. The effect is most marked on a vegetated tidal flat, where the freezing and rafting process can create a pitted surface that is characterized by numerous water-filled pans. The deposition of rafted blocks can contribute to the extension of a marsh, since vegetation quickly takes root. The gouging action of ice floes on a tidal flat produces characteristic scars, grooves, and striations. Ice also affects the bottom sediment by gouging, constricting the bottom currents, and scouring.

Isostatic adjustment—the slow response of the earth to erosion, deposition, water loading, desiccation, ice accumulation, and deglaciation—also causes dramatic changes in shorelines. In March 1964, in the vicinity of Prince William Sound in Alaska, an earthquake measuring between 8.3 and 8.6 on the Richter scale damaged an area of 216,000 miles. Undersea avalanches created local tsunamis (or "tidal waves"), which—together with a large tsunami caused by the major crustal upheaval—extensively damaged harbors, leveled coastal forests, and dumped silt on salmon grounds. Some freshwater lakes were inundated with seawater; others were drained by the tilting of land and by landslides. Tsunamis swept the length of the Pacific shores to Antarctica and caused extensive damage and loss of life as far south as California. Many miles of new beaches were created along Prince William Sound by the upward thrust. These new beaches markedly changed the shape of the coast and subjected inshore marine life to great stresses. At MacLeod Harbor on Montague Island, which lies at the entrance to the sound, the uplift destroyed the entire intertidal zone and twenty feet of subtidal sea bottom. This cataclysm provided scientists with an excellent opportunity to observe the survival of displaced species and the recolonization of damaged areas.

Light, Temperature, and Oxygen

The most basic of the forces that limit and define life along the shore is light. Photosynthesis—the conversion by green plants of energy from the sun into carbohydrates, which provide useful energy for every other form of life—is the origin of life as we know it. Photosynthetic plants are the foundation of all other living things; in one way or another, every animal that lives on the earth depends on this process of conversion. At certain depths, and depending on the amount of turbidity, water is a barrier to sunlight. Thus certain regions of the seashore are more productive than others.

In most places, only a thin surface film of the water, known as the photic zone, is illuminated during the day. Most of the ocean lies in the aphotic zone of eternal blackness. Since the depth to which light penetrates also depends upon the angle at which the light enters the water and is greatest when the sun is directly overhead, the deeper parts of the photic zone are illuminated only very briefly and very dimly each day. The depth of the photic zone varies from place to place and from time to time in the same place—depending on such factors as cloud cover, roughness of the surface water, amount of plankton and other matter in the water, and the season of the year. Thus the photic zone is further subdivided into an upper part—the euphotic zone—which receives enough light to support photosynthesis, and a dysphotic zone, which does not. By far the greater part of oceanic life is found in the euphotic zone, especially in coastal waters, which are usually rich in dissolved plant nutrients.

Below the euphotic zone, there is a sharp drop-off in living biomass and in the amount and variety of available food. There are no growing plant cells, and the animals here must depend upon organic matter coming down from above, as well as upon each other.

Adaptations enabling organisms to live in total darkness, to find mates and reproduce under these conditions, and to live at great hydrostatic pressures have produced fantastic, otherworldly animals.

Temperature is another of the critical factors determining the distributions of animals and plants in the coastal regions of the Pacific. In general, ocean water becomes colder with increasing depth and distance from the equator. In the tropical zones, warm water—which is less dense than cold water— remains at the surface during the summer. This warm water is separated from the colder water below by a thermocline, a zone in which the temperature changes relatively rapidly with depth. At more northern latitudes, the surface water becomes so cold during the winter that it sinks below the next level of water, breaking down the thermocline and forcing water of intermediate depths up to the surface. In Arctic and Antarctic waters, the surface waters are so chilled all year that they sink to the bottom and spread out slowly along the ocean floor toward the equator, displacing bottom water upward.

Most organisms live near the upper limits of their thermal tolerance; they are more quickly killed by abnormal warming than by the same degree of cooling. Thus, intrusions of cold-water organisms into warm waters are very rare, whereas warm-water organisms carried by currents into cooler areas may survive for some time and even continue to grow, though they may not successfully reproduce and establish permanent populations there.

Certain elements vital to plant growth, such as nitrogen and phosphorus, are commonly in short supply in the surface waters of the open ocean. Thus, the total biomass, or amount of living substances, that can be produced in a given time is limited by the quantities of the plant nutrient that is locally in shortest supply. When most of a nutrient is contained in the bodies of living organisms, new plant growth depends upon release of that nutrient through excretion or by the death and decomposition of existing organisms.

Plant nutrients are lost from the euphotic zone when dead organisms, fecal pellets, crustacean shells, and other organic matter sink away before decomposition is complete. The surface waters of the open ocean thus tend to become so depleted of nutrients that they become, in effect, biological deserts; this occurs in the tropics and subtropics. However, in some areas, such as along most of our Pacific shores, vertical circulation and seasonal overturn ensure a renewal of nutrients. Plant growth is limited at high latitudes by the lack of light in winter. In addition, many plant cells are carried below the shallow euphotic zone because the chilling of surface waters causes them to become dense and sink—and to be replaced by nutrient-rich water from below. In early spring, when the water begins to stabilize and more light is available each day, these nutrient-enriched waters support massive blooms of tiny plant life, or phytoplankton. These blooms in turn stimulate the proliferation of animals that graze on phytoplankton, and eventually of other animals higher in the food chain. Thus the far northern reaches of the Pacific provide the basis of the food web that sustains the life along all of the Pacific shores.

Marine Plants

Since the animal inhabitants of the ocean's vast expanse are dependent on photosynthetic plants, marine plants in one sense represent the most important of all groups of organisms on earth. Yet ninety-five percent of the sea's vegetation is invisible: the free-floating, mostly microscopic algae, which are the "meadow grass" of the sea and the primary food source for life on earth. All algae contain the green pigment chlorophyll, which enables them to use energy from the sun to manufacture energy-rich plant foods from inorganic substances. Millions of planktonic creatures eat algae, and in turn are eaten by larger and larger animals, thus forming a food web that culminates in the great marine fishes and mammals.

In the sea, extremes of temperature are modulated by the water medium. Although the sunlit shores provide rich and complex habitats, the vast depths of the sea are monotonously dark and cold. Accordingly, on the whole, there is less diversity of living things in the sea than on land. Only a few seed plants and fungi, and no mosses or ferns, occur in the ocean. With the exception of bacteria and a few parasitic and saprophytic fungi, marine plants are independent, providing their own food by photosynthesis. For this they primarily need water, carbon dioxide, and sunlight. Because most of the vast ocean depth lacks the sunlight needed for photosynthesis, plants are restricted to the upper reaches—the euphotic zone. This zone may be 200 to 300 feet deep in clear waters, but is much shallower in the turbid, turbulent waters off much of the Pacific Coast.

The larger marine plants fall into two main groups, algae and marine grasses. The grasses are descendants of seed-producing land plants, while the algae constitute an extremely ancient and diverse group and are the ancestors of land plants. The evolutionary relationships among the algae are not clear; the complex life histories of many species remain to be worked out. Comprising more than 20,000 species—both freshwater and marine—the algae range from microscopic, one-celled forms to giants that rival the redwoods in size. Seaweeds—the larger marine algae that grow attached to the bottom—occur mostly in the intertidal and continental shelf areas, which make up less than eight percent of the ocean area.

The edge of the sea is one of the best habitats for plant growth in temperate latitudes. It has been estimated that the large marine algae and sea grasses growing in a narrow belt on only five percent of the earth's surface represent over one third of the ocean's productivity. For example, the Perennial Giant Kelp, a marine alga that is commercially harvested off the coast of California, has a standing crop productivity estimated to be between twenty-five and forty tons, and an average annual yield of four to six tons per acre. It regenerates remarkably quickly after proper harvesting and grows eighteen inches or more each day—faster than any other plant known.

Because they are surrounded by the nourishing ocean, algae have evolved few of the specialized structures that terrestrial plants require such as roots to absorb nutrients, stems to conduct and provide support, and leaves to conduct photosynthesis. Although seaweeds have structures that resemble these organs, the entire plant has a very simple structure, with the bulk of the plant serving both photosynthetic and reproductive functions.

Seaweeds produce no flowers, seeds, or fruits, but reproduce by a bewildering variety of alternating single-celled and leafy forms, which are both asexual and sexual. Seaweeds come in every conceivable form and texture and may be broad, narrow, leafy, tough, soft, flat, tubular, encrusting, branched, or composed of fine filaments. To make matters more confusing, there are numerous marine animals that closely resemble some seaweeds.

In terms of abundance, tiny photosynthetic algae—diatoms, dinoflagellates, and other types of minute plants—are the most important of the planktonic plant forms. Diatoms are the main contributors to primary productivity in the sea's economy, as they are eaten either directly or indirectly by everything that feeds in the sea. These little plants are encased in cell walls composed of silica; the ornate cases consist of two halves of a tiny box, which fits around the cell. The phytoplankton drift in clouds in the sunlit upper waters of the sea, providing grazing for copepods, krill, and, eventually, tremendous baleen whales.

Under certain conditions, including the influx of nutrient-rich waters, these clouds burst into frantic fertility, resulting in a magnificent feast for fish, whales, and all. Such a bloom may become so dense that its members color the sea.

Blooms of one dinoflagellate, *Gymnodinium breve,* breed death. At the peak of a "red tide" bloom, concentrations of these dinoflagellates may reach six million plants per liter, coloring the water red. These tiny organisms excrete waste that includes powerful toxins; these toxins affect the nervous system of fishes, immobilizing their gills. Massive decomposition of the dead fishes fuels the bloom until the oxygen content of the water is exhausted; then the fishes that have not yet taken in the toxin suffocate. Such occurrences result in severe losses to the fishing and tourist industries, and annoyance to residents in areas where large numbers of dead fishes wash onto the beaches and into the bays. Moreover, people can be poisoned by eating the toxin-bearing fish.

Seaweeds fall into three main groups based on their chemistry and presumed relationships. Although these classifications are made on the basis of the pigments contained in the plants, seaweeds are not readily identified by the apparent colors alone. The bright green algae of the group Chlorophyta include many familiar plants, large and small, freshwater and marine. The red algae, or Rhodophyta, have, in addition to chlorophyll, water-soluble red or blue pigments. These algae range in color from all shades of red, green, and gray to almost black. Members of the Phaeophyta, or brown algae, have green chlorophyll masked by golden or brown pigments; these give the seaweeds a brown to olive color. They flourish in cool temperate to arctic marine waters.

The only strictly marine flowering plants are submerged sea grasses, Eelgrass, and surfgrasses. Ruppia occurs along the upper edges of estuaries, mud flats, and in the channels and along the lower edge of salt marshes. Several other sea grasses, such as turtle grass (*Thelassia*), are important in tropical waters. Many other vascular plants occur as conspicuous elements of the high beach, dune, and coastal saltmarsh flora.

Although the majority of marine plant forms are algae and sea grasses, a few other kinds of plants are associated with coastal habitats. In the spray zone, lichens—such as *Verrucaria*—and blue-green bacteria, such as *Calothrix,* are found. Filamentous blue-green algae are sometimes grouped with seaweeds; these algae often form the dark band on high intertidal rocks and extensive mats on estuarine mud flats. Blue-green algae are particularly important because, like bacteria, some have the ability to transform atmospheric nitrogen into chemical forms that can be used by other plants. Mixed with microscopic green algae, they frequently give intertidal rocks and shells a greenish hue.

The bright orange *Trentepholia,* a microscopic terrestrial green alga, adds a spectacular color to rocks, cliffs, and even trees that are exposed to coastal salt spray. These are sometimes mistaken for lichens, another group of generally terrestrial plants that occasionally form a colorful part of the vegetation on rocks immediately above the high intertidal zone. One moss, *Grimmea maritima,* is found in the spray zone.

No truly marine mushrooms exist, but microscopic fungi are important components of marine communities. Similarly, liverworts, mosses, and ferns do not occur in strictly marine habitats, although they can be found on back dunes, sea cliffs, and in high marshes.

Marine Food Webs

In most marine habitats, the primary source of food for animals is plankton—the clusters of small to minute animals and plant cells drifting in the water. The photosynthetic organisms of the plankton constitute the phytoplankton, or plant plankton. The rest is composed of animals (zooplankton) and bacteria (decomposers).

A secondary food source is detritus—minute, nonliving particles of organic or inorganic materials that either drift in the water or accumulate at the bottom of the sea. Detritus consists of decomposed plant and animal remains, fecal particles, and crustacean exoskeletons, as well as inorganic particles such as clay and volcanic ash. When such inorganic particles are exposed to marine water, they are quickly coated with a film of organic molecules; they may then serve as a food source for filter feeders and other detritus consumers.

Phytoplankton, or plant plankton, can only grow at the top of the ocean in the euphotic zone, where there is enough light for photosynthesis to occur. Zooplankton graze upon the phytoplankton. Thus most ocean life occurs in the relatively thin upper strata of the water.

Marked changes in the plankton can occur from time to time. Varying seasonal conditions favor particular species because of interactions within the population (the intensity of grazing by zooplankton, for example), because of changes in the levels of nutrients and metabolic products in the water, and because of water movements that may carry away the resident plankton and replace it with different forms.

On the bottom of shallow coastal waters, where there is substrate to attach to or to burrow into, most of the dominant animals live as plants do on land—as attached organisms, filtering or straining the water for food and oxygen. Here, they compete for space, access to the water, and protection from predation, rather than for food.

All of the major kinds of invertebrates—protozoans, sponges, coelenterates, bryozoans, worms, mollusks, and crustaceans—have evolved numerous intertidal and subtidal forms that are modified for a sessile, or attached, existence. Some of them look so bushy and plantlike that early biologists classified them as plants. Many of these sedentary animals are dominant members of their communities. If you try to imagine how sessile land animals could ever survive, you will have a picture of how different an environment the sea is.

The eggs or larvae of such sedentary animals are generally carried into the sea in great numbers and form a conspicuous, often seasonal, part of the coastal plankton population. Other animals hide in or near the bottom during the day and enter water closer to the surface only in the evening or at night.

The presence of great numbers of sedentary animals and of many drifting and swimming animals means that many of the creatures that prey on them can also be sessile or slow-moving. Many hydroids, sea anemones, gorgonians, and other creatures grow attached to the substrate; they sting and entrap their prey as it brushes against their tentacles. Starfishes, whelks, nudibranchs, and numerous other slow-moving animals prey upon sedentary creatures such as barnacles, mussels, and sponges.

In coastal waters, detritus is a more important food source than it is in the upper waters of the open ocean. This is because of the vastly greater amounts of organic detritus produced in coastal waters and because of the large amounts of organic and inorganic particles washed out from the land. Where the bottom consists of soft sediments such as sand, mud, or silt, a wide variety of detritus feeders utilize these sediments to filter particles of particular sizes or densities. Other detritus feeders, such as many worms and sea cucumbers, are nonselective: these filter feeders simply take in quantities of mud or sand, digest the small organisms together with the organic matter in it, and excrete the indigestible particles.

Where the substrate is rocky or firm, it becomes coated with a film of organic molecules, diatoms, bacteria, and small algae, together with minute animals such as protozoans and tiny worms. This coating, known as algal film, quickly coats all surfaces frequently or regularly exposed to marine waters. It is an important food source for another rather specialized group of animals: the algal-film scrapers. Certain molluscs—chitons, limpets, periwinkles, and others—feed by moving slowly over the surface and scraping off the algal film with their filelike tongues, or radulae. This group is especially prominent in the fauna of rocky intertidal and subtidal areas.

Human Impact

In recent years, human activities have increasingly contributed to the alteration of shores, coastal ocean bottoms, and the quality of ocean waters. Agricultural practices have often resulted in extensive soil erosion and the subsequent filling in of estuaries. Artificial islands have been created as sites for disposal, electrical power-generating facilities, and deep-water ports. Mineral extraction and fuel production industries in coastal areas have altered the ocean environment. Dredging for sand and gravel has changed waves, currents, and nearby beaches, and has thus displaced many marine life forms. Measures designed to protect shorelines include the building of dikes, rubble mounds, sea walls, and jetties, as well as the fencing off of particularly valuable parts of the coast. Many of these methods result in unwanted beach changes, because they alter currents and the sedimentation process. Seawalls and jetties jutting out into the sea can obstruct sediment drifts, and thus destroy long stretches of beach.

The use of coastal lands and shallow ocean bottoms for waste disposal has increasingly become a problem. The prime example of mismanagement in this regard is the spoiling of productive wetlands by dumping solid refuse and garbage in them. In addition, deep ocean basins have been used for the disposal of toxic or radioactive wastes. Phosphates and nitrates in municipal and agricultural wastes may change the local ecological balance and can sometimes result in oxygen depletion, as well as odor or aesthetic problems.

It is clear that coastal areas have reached their capacity. If these areas are to remain good sites for recreation, shell fishing, sport and commercial fishing, seaweed production, waterfowl hunting, and navigation—and to continue supplying industrial and municipal water—we must all realize that the health of our oceans is essential to the survival of all life on the planet.

We have discussed some of the factors that shape, limit, and define life in the seas and along the coast. These powerful forces have created distinct habitats, each harboring certain kinds of plants and animals that find life in these spots congenial. Let us now take a closer look at the relationships of life forms in these different ecosystems—along rocky shores, beaches, and dunes, in protected estuaries and bays, salt marshes, and the deeper waters just a short distance offshore.

THE ROCKY INTERTIDAL HABITAT

The rocky promontories and reefs along the unprotected coast
from Point Barrow, Alaska, to Point Conception, California,
bear the full brunt of storms at sea and are battered by great
waves—the products of long ocean swells generated far out at
sea. The force of the waves and the wind is so great that on all
but the calmest days—and at the lowest tides—even the
higher intertidal zones are drenched with spray.
These are the most dangerous places along the open coast.
Large waves can unexpectedly sweep a person to sudden death.
When exploring or fishing, you should know an exposed area
—or at least observe it for a while from a safe vantage point
before venturing out—and you should avoid dangerous-
looking places, especially if you are alone. If caught by a large
wave, don't try to run from it; it is better to lie flat, face the
wave, and cling to a rock as tightly as possible.
Such an experience makes you appreciate the great clinging
power required of plants and animals that live in these areas.

Sea Palm
Postelsia palmaeformis
496

Here there are plants, such as the Sea Palms, that have
exceptionally strong holdfasts and strong, flexible stalks. Here
also are animals, such as barnacles, that fasten firmly to the
rock and are protected from wave impact by their strong
shells. Mussels fasten to the rock and to each other by
filaments, called byssus threads, that are stronger than steel
thread. The chitons, limpets, and snails found here each have
a broad muscular foot, with which they cling to the rock
surface. The shells of all animals living on exposed rock
surfaces subject to direct wave impact are shaped to deflect
water and to resist the shock of the waves.
Not all rocky sites are equally exposed to the elements. Some
provide protected microhabitats for numerous organisms that
would be unable to survive if exposed to the full fury of the
waves.

The Nature and Formation of Rocky Areas

Rocky areas occur in several types of settings: wherever there
are hard rock outcroppings along the coastline; in coastal
waters where there is sufficient water movement to prevent the
rock from being buried by soft sediment; and where the rock
face is too steep to allow sediment to collect.
No two rocky sites are alike, since many factors go into the
shaping of each. Some of the more important factors are the
following:

1. The composition, consolidation, and degree of hardness of
the parent rock materials.
2. The orientation of the rock strata (layers) to the coastline.
3. The direction and size of the waves.
4. The direction and speed of inshore currents.
5. The frequency, direction, and force of storms and gales.
6. The nature and rate of erosion and drainage from the
adjacent land.
7. The steepness of the slope at sea–land interface.
8. The recent geologic history of the region, especially any
changes that have taken place in the relative heights of the
land and the sea level.

The Forces That Shape Rocky Shores

Areas where the sedimentary rock is stratified, or layered, are particularly interesting. The strata vary greatly in degree of consolidation and hardness, some eroding more readily than others. The orientation of such layers of sediment with respect to the coastline gives the resulting exposure its particular appearance and character. For example, if the strata are nearly horizontal and slope toward the sea, the intertidal and subtidal rock forms broad, relatively smooth platforms. If the strata slope more steeply and the waves cut a platform across several strata, the backwash from the waves may erode the softer sediment layers and form channels that parallel the coastline. If the strata slope toward the land, their exposed edges face the full brunt of the waves; then deeper, more irregular, seaward-facing crevices form parallel to the shore. Erosion is accelerated by the direct impact of the waves and the compression of air in the crevices as the waves hit. Rock layers that meet the land at a sharp angle are said to have a steep dip; where such layers are lined up edgewise to the sea, long, deep channels and parallel ridges of rock may extend seaward from the shore. A cliff at the upper edge of the intertidal area may be undercut by the waves; this sometimes produces sea caves, or it may cause severe erosion, calving, and rock slides, especially during storms. Such forces create loose boulders of various sizes and shapes.

Most rocky areas are not the clear-cut result of one or another of these processes, but are instead complex combinations of types. This is because the rock strata are subject to bending, warping, erosion, resedimentation, faulting, and tilting. Where faults trend inland from the coastline, they often create areas of weakness that can ultimately result in wave-cut embayments.

During heavy surf, rocks that are near sand may undergo severe sand scouring. Those that are frequently scoured or buried by sand tend to be worn smoother and to have far less life attached to them than rocks at the same tidal level that remain exposed most or all of the time.

Beaches that are commonly exposed to heavy surf tend to be steep, and often the sand is washed away. Sometimes they develop into shingle or cobble beaches; these are covered with stones of a similar size that move against each other as large waves crash into them, grinding them down and smoothing them. Such beaches support far less life than most others. During periods when, very slowly, the sea level rises or land subsides, broad wave-cut platforms may be formed as the sea erodes the adjacent land. Old wave-cut platforms that have been raised above present sea level are called marine terraces. Ancient marine terraces have been found far inland and at considerable elevations. Their existence attests to the great changes in the relative levels of sea and land over geologic time.

Another type of shoreline erosion is alveolar weathering, also known as salt-spray fretting. This occurs above the usual high-tide level in places where the rocks are subjected to infrequent but periodic wetting by the highest spring tides or spray, and are exposed to direct sunlight much of the time. The water in these areas penetrates between the rock granules and in microscopic cracks. When the water is dried up by the sun and wind, small salt crystals are left in the rock matrix. As the rock warms in the sunshine, the expansion of these crystals causes adjacent rock granules to pop out or loosen. Depending on the fineness of the rock matrix and the degree of exposure to wetting, drying, and warming, complex patterns of fretting may occur in rock surfaces that face the sun.

In areas where an embayment has formed along a fault, the rock on the northern side of the embayment (i.e., rock facing south) often retreats. As the rock retreats, a shelf may be formed a little above mean high-tide level, where frequent washing by tidal waters prevents the rock from heating and drying in the sunshine. The rock on the southern, shaded side plunges more directly and steeply into the embayment. Offshore rock islets usually show more erosion and gentler slope on the southern aspect than on the northern side.

At somewhat lower levels, erosion by living things may be a prominent factor. Purple Sea Urchins commonly make bowl-like excavations in the rock, into which they fit snugly, protecting themselves from the surf; where sea urchins are abundant, they may completely occupy the bottoms and sides of tide pools and surge channels. Rock surfaces may be denuded of larger seaweeds by the grazing of sea urchins; when this happens, the rocks become coated with encrusting coralline algae, which gives them a reddish or purplish appearance.

Purple Sea Urchin
Strongylocentrotus purpuratus
434

Sandstone or mudstone—especially that along the vertical ledges and walls of the channels—may be honeycombed with the burrows of rock-boring clams. These clams, called piddocks, begin to create their burrows when in the tiny postlarval stage; as they grow, they continue to scrape out the burrows to conform to their changing size. A piddock does this by affixing its broad foot to part of the anterior wall of the burrow and moving its hard, serrated shell backward and forward against it. The result is a club-shaped hollow at a right angle to the rock's surface.

Another type of rock-boring clams, known as chemical borers, have an acid gland in the foot. When the foot is pressed against rock, especially limestone, this acid gradually eats out a burrow. A chemical borer is prevented from dissolving its own shell because the acid is secreted in small amounts, is held against the rock by the animal's fleshy foot, and is mostly neutralized before the foot is released, so the entire burrow doesn't fill with acid. The shells of these clams are also protected by a thick, horny covering, called a periostracum.

Like other bivalves, rock-boring clams feed and breathe by circulating seawater into the mantle cavity, through the gills, and out again through the posterior siphons. The ends of these siphons can be seen at burrow entrances when they are covered with water.

Even the daily scraping of rock surfaces by the filelike tongues (radulae) of countless limpets, periwinkles, and chitons has a detectable—although very slow—erosive result. The action of such animals may have some significance over very long periods of time, although in most areas, other, more rapid erosive processes have a greater effect on the shoreline.

Zonation

The positions that different organisms occupy in the intertidal zone depend on both biological and physical factors. The tides progress in approximately fortnightly cycles: Moderate, or neap, tides alternate with more extreme tides, which are called spring tides. (Spring tides come every other week, when the alignment of the sun, moon, and earth causes the gravitational forces of the sun and moon to reinforce each other. The name has nothing to do with spring as a season.) This pattern of alternating tides results in a division of the intertidal zone into roughly three parts.

The central portion is submerged by almost all high tides and exposed by most low tides—that is, it is alternately covered and uncovered by both neap and spring tides. This area is called the middle littoral zone.

Above the middle littoral zone is an area submerged only by spring tides; this area is designated the upper littoral zone. Below the middle littoral zone is an area that remains submerged in water most of the time, being exposed only by the low spring tides; this is the lower littoral zone.

Seasonal progressions of the tides change, to some degree, the heights of all tides at different times of the year; moreover, wind and waves also influence the actual height attained by the water during any given tide. These factors may also be very different in different regions and at different seasons of the year. Thus the boundaries of these zones are not sharp. And although tidal levels provide one helpful way to distinguish areas along a rocky shore, such definitions are arbitrary, since numerous other factors also play important roles in determining the actual distribution of organisms. Some of these factors are the degree of exposure to direct sunlight and wind, the relative humidity and temperature of the air, exposure to fresh water (e.g. rain, fog, snow, ice, or runoff), wave impact, and sand scouring or abrasion by wave-carried objects (such as loose stones or logs). The ability of larvae or plant spores to settle and establish themselves in a given place and the adults' ability to survive there are of great importance, as is interaction with other organisms.

Thus the actual vertical distribution of a given organism or community of organisms may vary from place to place. In discussing the zones of life in the intertidal region, it is safer to rely on the actual distribution of the plants and animals in a given area than on the absolute vertical height of tides above or below mean sea level, or on calculated times of exposure and submergence.

Zonation is most clearly seen on vertical or steep, fairly uniform rock surfaces extending throughout the tidal range.

Here communities of organisms are banded together in narrow, horizontal strips, and demarcation between them is often amazingly sharp. Where the slope of the coastline is more gentle and where rocky areas are highly irregular—with many channels, pools, higher rocks, and even loose boulders of various sizes and shapes—the situation is more complex. Because such an area provides many different microhabitats, more kinds of animals and plants are usually present, and organisms that usually live in quite different intertidal zones are often found in close proximity to each other.

In general the upper limit of the distribution of any particular intertidal organism is largely determined by physical factors, such as the amount of exposure it can withstand. The exposure it gets on a given site is determined by the amount of sun and shade, coolness and warmth, moisture and dryness in the area. The lower limit of an organism's distribution is usually determined by its interactions with other animals and plants —that is, by predator-prey relationships, competition for space, and the possibility of being overgrown and smothered by other organisms.

Vegetation

In the northern regions, along rocky slopes that face the sea, Rock Tripe—a type of large lichen—grows closer to the sea than most other large plants of terrestrial origin. During clear, warm weather, it dries out and becomes thin and scaly. When wet, it absorbs water and becomes thicker and pliable.

The tops of some sea cliffs—especially north-facing cliffs, which do not get much direct sunlight—are marked by a bright orange band of algae. These algae, called *Trentepholia*, get their bright color from carotenoid, a pigment that masks the green chlorophyll within them.

Blackish patches of another lichen, *Verrucaria*, sometimes occur slightly lower on the rock. Immediately below the lichens, the rocks are usually relatively barren, home to perhaps only a few flies or an occasional sea roach (*Ligia* spp.). In many parts of the world, the mark that most distinctively signifies the junction of land and sea is "the black zone."

Above this zone, everything is essentially terrestrial; below it, marine. The black zone occurs at the level where spray wets the rock on a fairly regular basis and looks more like a dark stain on the rock than a band of living organisms.

Microscopic blue-green algae, minute lichens, green algae, and bacteria grow in this zone. Many of these organisms have gelatinous or mucuslike sheaths that absorb water and protect them from drying out during long periods of exposure to sun and wind. Small periwinkles sometimes graze here.

Where the middle and lower littoral zones meet, several characteristic larger seaweeds can be found. These include species of *Iradaea, Cystoseira,* and *Sargassum,* as well as the long, straplike *Egregia,* which looks like a feather boa.

Seaweeds such as *Alaria,* Bull Kelp, and the giant kelp *Macrocystis*—or beds of *Laminaria*—occur in the lower part of the lower littoral zone and also extend into the sublittoral.

Bull Kelp
Nereocystis luetkeana
493

Surf Grass
Phyllospadix spp.
509

Beds of Surf Grass, a seed plant that flowers and pollinates itself underwater, may be found in this zone in areas where the rock is partially covered with sand.

Animal Life in Rocky Areas

Rocky intertidal or subtidal areas provide a firm substrate to which animals and plants can cling or attach themselves. These areas also contain innumerable microhabitats where animals and plants can be protected from waves, sun, and wind. The water circulation in such places also allows for respiration, plankton feeding, and the removal of waste products.

The food supply here—as in most marine habitats—consists mostly of plankton, which are small to microscopic organisms and minute particles of detritus drifting in the water. Therefore most of the dominant animals are filter feeders: They are able to strain small particles from the water, as well as to transport desired food particles to the mouth and to reject unwanted ones. The fineness or coarseness of an animal's filtering apparatus determines the sizes and shapes of the particles retained. Animals with very fine filters subsist on minute phytoplankton (plant plankton) cells or tiny detrital particles, while those with coarser filters consume zooplankton (animal plankton). All abundant small organisms or particles are utilized by at least some of the animals.

Because food is all around them in the water, many animals don't have to go anywhere to get it. They live as sessile (attached) organisms. Competition is not primarily for food, but is instead for favorable attachment sites. Such animals commonly crowd together as closely as possible, often growing over each other; some of them display such bushy, plantlike growth habits that early biologists classified them as plants. Where wave action is direct and strong, most of these animals have developed a low, encrusting form, which minimizes the impact of the waves. Erect or bushy types of animals also flourish in more protected places or in deeper water.

A second major food source in intertidal and subtidal rocky areas is algal film, which is a thin coating of minute algae, protozoa, microscopic metazoa, and larger oganisms in their early stages. This film covers all surfaces that are regularly or continuously submerged in seawater. A group of animals—made up mostly of mollusks—has evolved to exploit this resource; these animals cling tightly to the rock surface, moving slowly over it and scraping the algal film with their filelike tongues (radulae). This group includes such familiar animals as limpets, periwinkles, and chitons.

Feeding Styles

Wherever many animals and plants exist, some of the animals will evolve as herbivores; some, as carnivores; and yet others, as scavengers. Some limpets and snails have taken to rasping the tissues of seaweeds or seagrasses rather than the algal film on the rock surfaces. Several of the larger gastropods and chitons, such as abalones and Giant Pacific Chitons, tear off and ingest larger pieces of seaweed. Sea urchins also are largely

Giant Pacific Chiton
Cryptochiton stelleri
180

herbivorous. Where they dominate the sea floor, they may destroy kelp beds by chewing off the kelp stems near their holdfasts and consuming new plants as soon as they begin to form.

Direct grazing is not the only, or perhaps even the main, way that seaweeds contribute to the food supply of animals. Large amounts of seaweed are ripped from their moorings by storm waves and are cast up on nearby shores. Once they begin to decompose, they are fed upon by hordes of sand fleas, kelp fly larvae, and other scavengers. In addition, seaweeds and seagrasses lose parts of their bodies during growth; they may also undergo some dieback and disintegration in the fall or early winter. They thus contribute to the food web both by way of the detrital cycle and by the release of soluble organic matter into the water.

In marine rocky areas, where many of the animals are sedentary, there is no need for most of the carnivores to develop speed or agility. Indeed, with little change in structure or habits, some algal-film scrapers have evolved into carnivores that graze on colonies of polyps, bryozoans, or sponges.

Starfishes prey upon slow-moving or sessile animals. Sea anemones rely on their practice of stinging and entrapping their prey instead of actively seeking it out. Other, related carnivores—such as hydroids—have tentacles equipped with stinging cells, with which they capture zooplankton that brush against them.

In whelks and other carnivorous gastropods, the radula, or tongue, has been adapted for boring holes through the shells of mussels, barnacles, and other shelled prey. In still other carnivores, it is used as a spear, and is often made more effective by the presence of a poison gland.

The behavior of many of these predators and scavengers is like that of their terrestrial counterparts. This category includes many crustaceans—such as crabs and shrimps—worms, mollusks, and fishes. And during low tide, birds such as oystercatchers and gulls also prey on the intertidal fauna.

The Barnacle Zone

Below the black zone is an area frequently dominated by acorn barnacles (*Balanus* spp.), and tufts of the red alga *Endocladia*. When crowded together, barnacles create a white zone that is visible from a considerable distance. Among the barnacles are small Checkered Periwinkles and Fingered Limpets and, in southern parts of the coast, the Rough Limpet. In the lower part of the barnacle zone is a band of larger algae called fucoids, or rockweeds. These are readily recognized by their branches, which end in gas-filled bladders containing the reproductive structures. *Fucus distichus* is the most prominent of these rockweeds along most of the coast; along the central California coast, *Pelvetia* and *Pelvetiopsis* are equally abundant.

It is a testimony to the abundance of phytoplankton in the coastal waters that the dominant animals of this largely exposed upper zone are barnacles. These sessile phytoplankton feeders are unable to feed, respire normally, or rid themselves of waste except during the relatively brief periods during which they are submerged. In the top parts of the upper littoral zone, the periods of submergence are especially brief, occurring for only a few days every other week, during spring tides. Yet barnacles thrive. Another curious feature of barnacles is that, although they are hermaphroditic, they require cross-fertilization by copulation in order to reproduce (in marked contrast with most sessile marine animals, which simply shed vast numbers of reproductive cells into the water, where fertilization occurs). This means that barnacles must settle in crowds, within reach of each other. Those that grow up isolated cannot reproduce.

When the spring tides rise and the surf is strong, the barnacle zone may take a heavy beating from the waves. Animals living in this zone are able to cling very tightly and are shaped so as to minimize the waves' impact. They often cluster in crevices, depressions, or between more firmly attached forms—where there is some protection from the full force of the waves. Smoother rock surfaces in this zone—especially those that are likely to receive a trickle of fresh water—may develop a seasonal coating of the green algae *Cladophora* and *Enteromorpha,* which form bright green areas. When they dry out, they may lose this color and become white, thus giving the rock a patchy appearance. Black patches of the tar spot alga, *Ralfsia,* are also frequent in this zone.

The Middle Littoral Zone

Below the barnacle zone in the middle littoral zone, the most conspicuous filter feeders are mussels. In favorable, surf-swept areas, these form dense beds that completely dominate. Mussels fasten themselves to rocks and to each other by strong strands, known as byssus threads. The byssus material is a viscous liquid that is secreted by a gland at the base of the mussel's foot. When the foot is extended, this liquid runs down a groove along the back side of the foot to the tip. When the tip of the foot is pressed close against a solid substrate and then withdrawn, a thin thread of byssus is drawn out. This quickly hardens to form a strong flexible thread, which is attached to the substrate at one end and to the mussel at the other.

The "mat" created by the mussels and their byssus threads forms a protected habitat for an assemblage of worms, crustaceans, small six-armed starfishes, small sea cucumbers, and other animals that otherwise could never survive in this turbulent zone. Along the Pacific, on exposed outer coasts subject to strong surf, the dominant mussel is the large Californian Mussel. Young Blue Mussels are also found among beds of very young sea mussels, but apparently cannot compete successfully here. They are the dominant mussel, however, in the quieter waters of bays and estuaries. Often associated with beds of large mussels—especially along their upper parts—are large clumps of the Leaf Barnacle. Close

Californian Mussel
Mytilus californianus
68

Blue Mussel
Mytilus edulis
69

Leaf Barnacle
Pollicipes polymerus
461, 465

inspection of a mussel bed may also reveal the presence of whelks—carnivorous gastropods of the genera *Thais* and *Purpurea;* sometimes mats of their bright yellow egg cases can be seen in moist protected spots. The lower border of the mussel bed often harbors predators—usually the abundant, large Ochre Sea Star, for one. Where predators are numerous enough to clear off patches of the mussels, other sessile animals or seaweeds have a chance to settle; thus the area's flora and fauna becomes more diverse, and the site takes on a patchy appearance.

Ochre Sea Star
Pisaster ochraceus
369

The most commonly seen crabs in the middle littoral zone and in lower parts of the upper littoral are the Striped Shore Crab of southern California and the Purple Shore Crab of the Pacific Northwest. Large Oregon Cancer Crabs may be found here too. Under rocks in channels or on coarse sediments, large numbers of flat crabs—the porcelain crabs of the genus *Petrolisthes*—are frequently found. Related to hermit crabs, the porcelain crabs differ from true crabs in that they have very long feelers or antennae and a different number of walking legs; moreover, the porcelain crabs are plankton feeders, whereas true crabs are predators and scavengers.

Striped Shore Crab
Pachygrapsus crassipes
331

Purple Shore Crab
Hemigrapsus nudus
326, 332

Oregon Cancer Crab
Cancer oregonensis
335

Mats of Aggregating Anemones may also be found in the middle littoral zone and in lower parts of the upper littoral zone. After growing to full size, the anemone reproduces by moving off in two directions at once and pulling itself in half. This process results in a mat, or clone of anemones that are all identical twins of the same sex. Anemones of different clones don't meet and mix. In fact, when the edge of one clone gets too close to the edge of another, the anemones fight each other; thus a small distance is maintained between adjacent clones. The larger, closely related Giant Green Anemone inhabits the lower parts of the middle littoral zone and the lower littoral zone.

Aggregating Anemone
Anthopleura elegantissima
439

Giant Green Anemone
Anthopleura xanthogrammica
440

Tide pools and channels in the middle littoral zone and adjacent parts of the zones above and below usually contain hermit crabs of the genus *Pagurus,* as well as small, large-headed fishes—sculpins, or tide-pool cottids—that often match the bright colors of the coralline algae and the sand in the pools. A fairly large snail called the Black Tegula is also prevalent in these areas, as are several species of limpets and, on exposed rock surfaces, the large Black Katy Chiton.

Black Tegula
Tegula funebralis
158

Black Katy Chiton
Katharina tunicata
184

Among the seaweeds common in the upper part of the middle littoral zone are Sea Lettuce and nori (*Porphyra*). In the more central parts of the zone, the gas-filled, bladderlike *Halosaccion* is frequently conspicuous. *Rhodomela* and *Odonthalia* may form dark heavy growths in the lower half of the middle littoral zone, where the Turkish Towel also occurs.

Sea Lettuce
Ulva lactuca
495

The Lower Littoral Zone

Turkish Towel
Gigartina exasperata
487

The boundary between the middle and lower littoral zones is not often apparent. In general, areas dominated by larger seaweeds are in the lower littoral zone. Here too are beds of Purple Sea Urchins, keyhole limpets (*Diodora* spp.), sea anemones such as *Epiactis* and *Tealia,* soft corals (*Alcyonaria*),

Red Sea Urchin
Strongylocentrotus franciscanus
435

Sunflower Star
Pycnopodia helianthoides
375

sea cucumbers (*Cucumaria, Stichopus, Eupentacta*), and occasional large Red Sea Urchins, solitary tunicates (*Styela*), and colonial tunicates such as *Amaurecium* and *Botrillus*. Larger invertebrates in this zone include the Giant Pacific Chiton, the Sunflower Star, and an occasional abalone or octopus, although the latter two are more characteristic of the sublittoral zone and deeper water. In southern California, the most common inshore octopuses are *Octopus bimaculoides* and *O. bimaculatus;* both are marked with a bright blue ring near the lateral base of the arm crown on each side—hence the popular name of two-spotted octopus, which is applied to both species. In central California, these are replaced by the Red Octopus, which also occurs offshore in southern California. The large, reddish-brown *Octopus dofleini* is the characteristic species of the Pacific Northwest and northward.

Bird Life Along Rocky Shores

The tremendous abundance of invertebrate life exposed by the rising and falling tides ensures a plentiful food supply for the many species of birds that frequent these areas. Many seabirds breed mainly on offshore islands or on steep cliffs facing the sea, where they are close to their food source—the sea—and also protected from most predators. Some birds, like the murres, puffins, and other members of the auk family, roost on the steepest cliffs facing the sea, forming colonies of many hundreds or even thousands.

An island or cliff can offer several types of nesting sites. Because seabirds have their own preference for nesting sites a distinctive parceling out of space occurs. The Pelagic Cormorant chooses narrow ledges and brackets on precipitous cliffs. Other kinds of cormorants choose steep slopes with rocky outcroppings.

Pelagic Cormorant
Phalacrocorax pelagicus
532

The colony structure is critical to the survival of seabirds. Although they are territorial when breeding, the territory is small and designed to protect the nest site only, thus permitting close spacing of breeding pairs. The size and density of bird colonies, as well as nest types and egg sizes, are extremely varied.

Murres are the most penguinlike of the auks. The female lays a single long pear-shaped egg on a narrow ledge. When half grown, the chick jumps off and flutters sometimes hundreds of feet down to the male parent in the water, who then feeds and cares for it until grown, while the female recoups.

Northern Fulmar
Fulmarus glacialis
600

Kittlitz's Murrelet
Brachyramphus brevirostris

Fulmars are dominant among competitors for large space. These large shearwaters simply prod murres out of the way and toss their eggs overboard. Seabirds are overwhelmingly colonial breeders, but a remarkable exception is the Kittlitz's Murrelet or "Eskimo Fog-bird." This solitary nester lays a single, protectively colored egg in the open near the summit of icy coastal mountains in Alaska and Siberia.

Many seabirds are migratory, possessing a keen sense of navigation and performing outstanding feats of migration. Some species make an annual voyage of several thousand miles across the equator.

Tufted Puffin
Fratercula cirrhata
540

Pigeon Guillemot
Cepphus columba
536

Black Oystercatcher
Haematopus bachmani
556

Fifty-six islands off Oregon shores have been collectively protected as Oregon Islands National Wildlife Refuge. These rocky outposts are usually frequented only by a few basking sea lions, gulls, and resting cormorants, but become a frenzy of activity in spring during the breeding season. Tufted Puffins nest in burrows of steep slopes at Haystack Rock off Cannon Beach, Right Rock off Yaquina Head, Three Arch Rock, Bandon Rocks, and Goat Island, all in Oregon. These birds are colorful and comical members of the auk family with flowing yellowish "eyebrows," bright orange, parrotlike bills, stubby bodies, and black plumage resembling coattails. Their flight is quite characteristic, the short heavy bodies being driven at high speed by their comparatively small, blunt wings. One of the most frequently seen alcids of these shores is the Pigeon Guillemot or "sea pigeon." Another resident bird of rocky coasts is the Black Oystercatcher. As these birds probe for limpets and mussels on exposed rocks, their shrill voices penetrate the noisy roar of the surf; their pink feet and red bills alone are seen, sometimes barely visible through the mist and fog.

Humans have always been a threat to seabird eggs and young, taking millions of eggs each year from nesting sites. Even today, large numbers of seabirds are being adversely affected as expanding fisheries encroach upon food resources and fishing boats are able to reach more islands. Oil and toxic chemicals spilled in coastal waters are also an increasing hazard to marine birds. The introduction of predators such as foxes, rats, and cats to many seabird islands has had drastic effects. The grazing of goats, pigs and rabbits has caused soil erosion and the destruction of nesting habitat. Even scientists, who try to be considerate, can disrupt breeding seabirds.

Alaska and the Far North

Untamed breakers of the Pacific Ocean crash against the granite cliffs of the exposed Alaskan outer coast. Alaska's glacial shorelines are brokenly timbered, rocky, sculptured by ice, and cluttered with icebergs. Seen from a ship, the mainland coast of Alaska and British Columbia is a continuous line of solid granite and volcanic mountains, with immense rivers and shimmering ice in the distance. Sandy beaches are few and far between. Sides of deep-water fjords rise to 8000 feet above sea level and extend fifty to seventy miles into the land.

The shoreline from southeastern Alaska to Puget Sound is jagged and deeply indented, and further extended by numerous islands. Off the southeast coast of Vancouver Island between Victoria and Nanaimo lie the twenty-six Gulf Islands, with numerous islets and reefs. Most of the coastline is rocky, plunging abruptly to the ocean. Wind and waves have sculptured the sandstone headlands of Malaspina Galleries on Gabriola Island into fantastic shapes.

The outer coast offers some of the best tide pools and diving opportunities. Lush and diverse faunas inhabit the luxuriant kelp forests and the zone of pink encrusting coralline algae

Sitka Crab
Cryptolithodes sitchensis

Green Sea Urchin
Strongylocentrotus droebachiensis
433

Mink
Mustela vison

Raccoon
Procyon lotor

just below the kelp. One may watch a Sunflower Star chasing an abalone across the rocks, the abalone twisting its shell back and forth in a desperate effort to dislodge the starfish's tube feet. Nearby a brightly colored sculpin may lie under a small ledge, in apparent harmony with a small octopus. Some peculiarly shaped crabs, including the Sitka Crab, whose leaflike shell covers its legs, or a beautiful box crab, might well escape your notice unless you knew what sorts of life to look for.

Where there is a limestone outcrop, as on the western side of Prince of Wales Island, rock-boring clams, urchins, peanut worms, sponges, and other animals may create complicated honeycombed condominiums for astonishing varieties and densities of animals.

An explorer of the northwest fjords may not see much of an intertidal fauna. In part this is because the steep walls of a fjord offer only limited intertidal habitats, but several other factors are also involved. Winter freezing and frequent exposure to freshwater limit what lives in the intertidal and shallow subtidal zones. Glacial silt may occur in a surface freshwater layer and prevent algae from receiving enough light. If a bay is stagnant, plankton may be too sparse to support large populations of filter feeders. In some bays, such as Saanich Inlet and Lake Nitinat on Vancouver Island, the deep waters behind the sill are so stagnant that all oxygen is gone and the water becomes a rather peculiar chemical soup. This occurs within easy snorkeling depth in Roosevelt Lagoon near Ketchikan, Alaska, and the curious visitor will see enormous populations of certain starfish, the Green Sea Urchin, and a few other species just above the anaerobic, or oxygenless, layer.

The intertidal zone of a fjord usually consists of a narrow rocky beach populated by rockweeds, barnacles, and mussels. Hermit crabs and true crabs live among the rocks and algae along with fishes such as pricklebacks, and sometimes remarkable numbers of clams. These are favored foods for starfish, as well as for crows, gulls, Minks, and Raccoons. Most of these predators do their hunting at low tide, but minks will sometimes plunge into the water and swim among the waving algae in search of crabs and other food.

THE ROCKY INTERTIDAL HABITAT: ANIMALS AND PLANTS

Seashells
Arctic Saxicave 54
Bifurcate Mussel 70
Black Abalone 83
Black Limpet 159
Black Musculus 75
Black Tegula 158
Blue Mussel 69
California Cumingia 46
California Frog Shell 109
California Nuttall's
Chiton 179
Californian Lucine 41
Californian Margin
Shell 125
Carinate Dove Shell 145
Carpenter's Cardita 31
Carpenter's Dwarf
Triton 103
Channeled Top Shell 153
Checkered Periwinkle 128
Chestnut Cowry 133
Clear Jewel Box 90
Common Northern Chink
Shell 146
Common Washington
Clam 49
Dall's Dwarf Turban 155
Dire Whelk 113
Dusky Tegula 149
Emarginate Dogwinkle 130
Eroded Periwinkle 137
False Pacific Jingle Shell 89
Festive Murex 98
File Limpet 165
Fingered Limpet 173
Flat-tipped Piddock 72
Frill-wing Murex 99
Frilled Dogwinkle 101
Giant Owl Limpet 172
Giant Pacific Bittium 121
Giant Pacific Chiton 180
Giant Rock Scallop 91
Great Keyhole Limpet 166
Green Abalone 82
Green Paper Bubble 134
Hartweg's Chiton 183
Hearty Rupellaria 55
Heath's Chiton 176
Hooded Puncturella 168
Ida's Miter 120
Japanese Abalone 79
Joseph's Coat Amphissa 116
Kelsey's Date Mussel 62

La Perouse's Kellia 42
Leafy Thorn Purpura 97
Lined Chiton 177
Lurid Dwarf Triton 105
Mask Limpet 171
Merten's Chiton 182
Norris Top Shell 141
Northern Horse Mussel 67
One-banded Chink
Shell 144
Onyx Slipper Shell 85
Oregon Triton 102
Pacific Half Slipper Shell 86
Pacific Orb Diplodon 25
Pacific Pink Scallop 95
Pacific Plate Limpet 170
Painted Spindle Shell 111
Pelta False Limpet 161
Pink Abalone 80
Poulson's Rock Shell 108
Red Abalone 84
Red Turban 157
Ringed Top Shell 151
Rough Keyhole Limpet 169
Rough Limpet 174
San Pedro Triphora 122
Scale-sided Piddock 73
Scaly Worm Shell 189
Seaweed Limpet 162
Sharp-keeled Lirularia 154
Shield Limpet 164
Sitka Periwinkle 143
Spiny Slipper Shell 87
Stearns' Mussel 71
Threaded Abalone 81
Tinted Wentletrap 106
Two-spotted Keyhole
Limpet 167
Unicorn 129
Unstable Limpet 163
Veiled Chiton 178
Volcano Limpet 175
Wavy Turban 150
Western Banded
Tegula 156
Western Ribbed Top
Shell 152
White-cap Limpet 160
White Northern Chiton 181
Wide-eared Scallop 93

Mammals
California Sea Lion 227
Guadalupe Fur Seal 226

BEACH HABITAT

By-the-wind Sailor
Velella velella
390

Sanderling
Calidris alba
570

For the barefoot beachcomber, a stroll along a Pacific Ocean beach—seemingly barren and inhospitable to life—can be a solitary experience of surf, sand, and wind. Remnants of life forms deposited onshore at the whim of the waves mark the crescent line of tidal surf. Windrows of the jellyfishlike By-the-wind-Sailor and ranks of seaweed tell of life in hospitable seas—yet these shifting sands seem to provide few congenial habitats for living organisms. In fact, however, a sandy or muddy beach conceals a surprisingly rich and peculiarly adapted community; it is just that most beach dwellers are not visible. The twinkling feet and probing bills of Sanderlings and sandpipers at the water's edge point to the abundance of unseen life forms. A world of clams, worms, and tiny animals seen nowhere else dominates the sands.

Sandy beaches on an exposed coast are areas of constant change and motion. Breakers pound ceaselessly, each wave lifting and moving quantities of sand. In the daily progression of tides, the beach may be subjected to sunlight, drying, rain, wind, and freezing. High waves tear subtidal plants and animals from their moorings and cast them up on the beach, pushing them to the highest part of the shore. High tides bring certain predators from the sea; low tides bring another set of predators from the land. Most of the specialized animals inhabiting this turbulent world are proficient burrowers; many of them are very small indeed.

Formation and Composition

A beach can be technically defined as noncohesive material affected by wave action along a body of water. There are many types of beaches, composed of particles of different sizes and subject to varying degrees of exposure to the surf. A beach may consist of sand, mud, shingle (or cobblestone), shells or shell fragments, or a mixture of these materials. Because of its nature, a beach is one of the least permanent of land forms. The nature of the materials that make up the beach, as well as the size, sorting, and quantity of these materials, determine whether the beach is a sand or shingle beach, or something in between. The relation of the shore to sea level and the resistance of the shore to erosion also contribute to the profile of a beach. Shingle or mixed beaches, for instance, occur on the protected shores along the Puget Sound and the Georgia Strait in Washington. In most bays, beach types overlap, providing a great variety of habitats; the plants and animals in such areas may be characteristic of rocky shores, mud flats, or sandy beaches.

Most sand beaches are composed largely of quartz and feldspar, hard materials derived either from the weathering of mountains—and delivered to the beaches by rivers—or from the erosion of sea cliffs. The size of sand particles on a beach usually fall within the range of 0.06–2 mm, but may be smaller or larger; the varying sizes of the particles, and of the spaces between the particles, provide possibilities for habitation by quite different life forms.

Sand is transported as a current, running parallel to the shore in the direction of the prevailing wave action. Along the Oregon coastline, for example, the sand is transported to the northern ends of the beaches in winter and to the southern ends in summer because of a seasonal reversal of wind and wave direction. The current of sand along a beach may be diverted by offshore canyons or by structures such as jetties; dams and irrigation projects on rivers may also divert the flow of small sand particles to the sea, leaving rocky or gravelly shorelines where extensive beaches once existed.

Waves are the most significant force operating on a beach, and waves, in turn, are dependent upon the winds that generate them. Severe wave action generally results in steeply sloping beaches of coarse sand, whereas gentle wave action or reduced wave height produces broad, flat areas of fine sand and mud. In winter, extreme tides and storms create large waves that carry most of the sand away, depositing it offshore as sandbars. The smaller waves of summer tend to wash the sand back and restore the beach to its former level.

Various processes determine the profile of a beach, including the nature and direction of waves, sediment transport, and tidal cycles, which alternately build up and erode the beach. A beach is usually seen to include the following zones:

1. The nearshore, or submerged portion, which extends seaward from the low-tide line.
2. The foreshore, or swash zone, which is the normal intertidal part of the beach.
3. The backshore, which is above the reach of most high tides; sloping slightly landward, the backshore includes the highest levels that are submerged by exceptionally high tides and storms.

The change in slope between the foreshore and backshore is called the berm crest. The berm, a nearly flat, terracelike area, is the seaward portion of the backshore. The area that extends from the foreshore to the place where the waves break is often called the surf zone.

Many interrelated factors affect the biological environment of a beach habitat. The size of sand grains on a beach and the total amount of space between the grains (porosity) are of great importance to the animals living in the sand. So is the water content of a beach, which depends partly on its porosity and partly on the tidal level.

The water table (the reservoir of water beneath the surface of the land) sinks faster and farther in coarse-grained beaches, because the average pore size between grains is greater and thus the water sinks through more easily and rapidly.

However, the water table tends to remain higher in fine sands, which, because they expose more surface area, have greater water-holding power, or capillarity. In addition, fine-sand beaches generally slope very gradually, so water tends neither to sink in nor to run off. When the interstices, or spaces between the grains retain water, the beach may seem solid yet yielding, a condition termed thixotropy. Our feet can easily make such wet sands sloppy and sticky. This thixotropic condition makes walking on the gooey mud flats of estuaries a strenuous and entertaining experience. When thixotropic beaches are a bit drier and harder, the sand whitens and feels firmer as we walk across it—a condition known as dilatancy. These thixotropic and dilatant properties are of great importance to burrowing animals. These creatures can dig into wet, soupy sand quickly, but have a difficult job penetrating dilatant deposits. Birds probably seek the softer sand next to the waves partly for the same reason; moreover, the wave action disturbs and reveals animals that have burrowed in the sand.

The rigors of life in shifting, wave-swept sands are great; consequently few species can live on beaches. Because sand is basically unstable—as many a would-be seashore homebuilder can attest—most animals must live within the beach rather than on it. Burrowing beneath the surface protects an animal from predation, wave impact, the risk of desiccation when the tide is out, and extremes of temperature. However, within its sandy burrow, the sand dweller faces the problems of finding food, an adequate oxygen supply, and a mate.

The animals of the beach rely largely on the following sources of food:

1. Plankton and detrital particles suspended in the water;
2. Organic molecules adsorbed to the surfaces of sand grains, together with bacteria, diatoms, protozoa, and other minute organisms living in the sand;
3. Seaweeds and the remains of animals washed up on the beach by waves during high tides and storms; and
4. Other inhabitants of the beach.

Specialized animals of various groups have evolved as filter feeders, substrate ingesters, scavengers, or predators. There is some overlap between scavengers and predators, as some of the predators will consume either living or dead animal matter.

Filter Feeders

Pacific Mole Crab
Emerita analoga
342

One of the most successful animals of the surf zone is the Pacific Mole Crab. This Mole Crab is a member of the ancient crustacean group called Anomura, which includes hermit crabs, porcelain crabs, and ghost shrimps. Mole crabs resemble neither shrimps, hermit crabs, nor true crabs; indeed, they are so adapted to life in the sand that one would hardly recognize them as crabs at all. The body of the Pacific Mole Crab is a smooth, oval shape and is covered by a hard carapace. This animal's flattened, streamlined shape and small, flat appendages serve efficiently for swimming and digging.

Like most animals that dominate marine environments, mole crabs feed on detritus and plankton. They move up and down with the tides, with each relocation burrowing backward into the sand, facing the sea. As each wave recedes, they extend their plumed antennae, capturing minute detritus and planktonic organisms. They then draw the antennae back through the mouth part, scraping off the food they have captured.

In summer, female Pacific Mole Crabs carry bright orange egg masses firmly attached to the undersides of their bodies. When it is time for the eggs to hatch, the females cease feeding and remain lower in the water. The young hatch as zoeae—strange-looking, spined, planktonic creatures that are carried great distances along the coasts by currents. They undergo several larval molts; when ready for the final molt that transforms them into adults, they seek out a sandy bottom near the shore.

Some bivalve mollusks have also adapted to living in the sandy open beaches between the tide lines or just below the low-tide level. Preeminent among the fast-digging, sand-dwelling clams is the Pacific Razor Clam, which is sought-after by gourmets during the lowest of spring tides. Sometimes, while cleaning a catch, the happy clam digger may discover a leechlike worm living within the mantle cavity of the Razor Clam. This highly specialized nemertean worm, called *Malacobdella,* is apparently harmless. It feeds upon microscopic crustacea that the clam draws in through its siphons.

Pacific Razor Clam
Siliqua patula
61

The large, heavy-shelled Pismo Clam lies just under the surface of the sand on the lowest intertidal and subtidal reaches on California beaches from Monterey Bay south. In some places, the shells of Pismo Clams become sites of attachment for colonies of the hydroid *Clytia bakeri;* the tufts of these animals are a give-away to clam diggers.

Pismo Clam
Tivela stultorum
43

Although the number of animal species on a sandy beach may be smaller than the quantity in the rocky intertidal zone, an individual species often attains immense numbers on a beach. Before regulations were imposed, clam diggers on one southern California beach took two million Pismo Clams (weighing an average of two pounds each) over a period of two and one half months; at least a million undersized individuals that had been dug up were left to die.

On some southern California beaches, countless thousands of small coquina clams, which measure about half an inch long, can sometimes be found in the surf zone. As waves wash these animals out of their burrows, they promptly dig in again, then extend their siphons to the water in order to feed, respire, and dispose of waste products. Like mole crabs, coquina clams move up and down the beach with the tides. They are not permanent residents of any particular beach; they may be present in vast numbers at one time, absent at another. Vast coquina communities—which are approximately five yards wide, up to two or three miles long, and contain as many as 20,000 individuals per square yard—have been observed on some beaches. Perhaps—like the sand they live in—communities of coquinas are moved along the shore with the longshore current of sand.

Nuttall's Cockle
Clinocardium nuttallii
33

Although it prefers quieter, muddy sands, the Basket or Nuttall's Cockle also occurs in clean sand. Because its siphon is very short, Nuttall's Cockle lives with the posterior end of its shell just below the surface of the substrate; it is also often found on the surface. A filter feeder like the Pismo Clam, Nuttall's Cockle is equipped with special papillae (nipplelike projections) on its siphons to exclude sand. Although they appear rather sedentary, cockles have a powerful, extensile foot, which they can use to push themselves away or flip over to get out of reach of predators.

Many edible clams may be found in the soft mud and sand under cobblestone beaches or in the sandy or muddy flats characteristic of relatively quiet, protected waters, such as these in the lower reaches of estuaries, in Puget Sound, or on the lee side of coastal islands such as Vancouver Island: The Common Pacific Littleneck, or Native Littleneck, the Japanese Littleneck, the Butternut, or Common Washington, Clam, and the Geoduck are all very delicious. Other tasty mollusks include the Blue Mussel and the Giant Pacific Oyster.

The Geoduck is the largest burrowing bivalve on American shores; it lives in a semipermanent burrow. To capture this prize, one must often dig down as much as one to two yards. Attempts to pull the clam out by its siphon breaks off the siphon, which is fatal to the clam. The Horse and Gaper clams live one to three feet down in a mixture of mud, sand, and gravel; they identify themselves by a large squirt of water as the siphon is retracted.

Common Pacific Littleneck
Prototbaca staminea
35

Japanese Littleneck
Tapes japonica
36

Common Washington Clam
Saxidomus nuttallii
49

Geoduck
Panopea generosa
57

Blue Mussel
Mytilus edulis
69

Giant Pacific Oyster
Crassostrea gigas
78

Horse Clam
Tresus capax

Pacific Gaper
Tresus nuttallii
56

Substrate Ingesters

Many animals, both terrestrial and marine, consume large quantities of sand, soil, or other such material. The digestive systems of these animals are equipped to make use of the minute organisms and organic matter that the substrate contains, while allowing the inorganic and nutritionally valueless remainder to pass through the system.

Open sandy beaches harbor fewer kinds of substrate ingesters than do the finer, richer, muddy sands of estuaries and other protected waters. Perhaps the most outstanding such creature is the blood worm (*Glycera* spp.). This animal occurs in vast numbers in well-circumscribed beds at intermediate tidal levels on beaches with medium to fine sand. A thriving bed of blood worms may contain more than 3000 animals per square foot. A mature blood worm is slightly more than an inch long. The hemoglobin in its blood accounts for its bright red color, from which it gets its common name. When the tide comes in, blood worms burrow down a few inches to avoid being washed out by the waves, then return to near the surface between the tides. At times the bed is marked by thousands of holes the size of a pin prick. These are caused as the worm passes close to the surface and sand grains tumble down into the burrow. The holes play a role in the aeration of the colony.

Scavengers and Predators

The remains of seaweeds and animals cast up on the beaches during high tides and storms are an abundant source of food for scavengers—opportunistic feeders of all sorts that have learned to make a living at the water's edge.

Among the most ubiquitous and successful exploiters of this food source are the sand fleas—also known as beach hoppers—which are amphipod crustaceans of the family Orchestiidae. One of the most easily recognized of these creatures along the Pacific Coast is the large California Beach Flea. It attains a body length of almost an inch, is somewhat flattened from side

California Beach Flea
Orchestoidea californiana
350

to side, and can hop about rather in the manner of a flea. The males are larger than the females and can also be distinguished by the enlarged, red feelers (their second antennae). Beach fleas (*Orchestoidea* spp.) seem to be evolving in a shift from sea to land. Unlike most amphipods, they no longer swim, breathe, or reproduce in the water; in fact they are poor swimmers and drown if submerged for too long. Yet they seem to require the salty dampness of the sea, and are thus bound to its margin. By the day they remain in burrows near the upper limits of the waves at high tide, or under piles of damp seaweed. When there is a falling tide during the evening or night, they come out by the thousands, searching the exposed intertidal sands and consuming all manner of organic remnants, thus cleaning the beach. When the tide returns, or at daybreak, they move back up the beach to a spot near the high-water line and excavate new burrows, in which they remain until the next ebb tide.

Various isopods (crustaceans similar to the related common garden sowbugs or pillbugs) also feed on dead animals and other beach debris. Harford's Greedy Isopod is a small, buglike creature that is found along beaches from British Columbia to Baja California. A horde of these swarming over the body of a dead fish can reduce it to a bare white skeleton in a surprisingly short time.

Harford's Greedy Isopod
Cirolana harfordi
351

Marine animals are not the only ones scavenging on the beach. Where windrows of seaweed are washed up, swarms of kelp flies (*Fucellia, Coelopa,* and other genera) are as numerous as the sand fleas. The maggots of these flies live in the decaying piles of seaweed, where the small, barrel-shaped, brown pupae can often be found.

Rove beetles—small, elongate beetles with short, truncated wing covers—are regularly found along the seashore as well, along with slow-moving darkling beetles and the more familiar, stout scarabs. On the lower beach—where the sand is wet and soft most of the time—a beautiful little snail called the Purple Dwarf Olive plows through the wet sand, scavenging for bits of animal matter and searching for small prey. The trail of this snail generally appears at the surface, but occasionally it is completely buried, creating a little dimple to mislead the clam digger. On the drier sands of the upper beach, the large-jawed and speedy tiger beetles (*Cicindela* spp.) are the most conspicuous of the indigenous predators. Others include predaceous running spiders, such as the wolf spiders and tarantulas.

Purple Dwarf Olive
Olivella biplicata
127

Predatory worms also live in these wet sands. These include the large nemerteans of the genus *Cerebratulus* and several species of polychaete clam worms (*Nereis*), blood worms (*Glycera*), and other annelids.

On relatively protected beaches, such as the lower reaches of large estuaries, the Lewis' Moon Shell can be found. After it has enveloped its prey with its large, fleshy foot and mantle, this predator uses its filelike radula to drill through the shells of clams, oysters, mussels, and other snails. It lays thousands of eggs; these, when cemented with mucus and pressed

Lewis' Moon Shell
Polinices lewisii
140

together with sand grains, form collarlike rings that often puzzle the beachcomber. During high tide, these egg cases crumble, releasing thousands of free-swimming larvae into the sea.

Preeminent among the larger scavengers are the sea gulls. These familiar birds patrol all types of shorelines and nearshore waters during the daytime, acting as both predators and scavengers. Some gulls have adapted to seashore life in an interesting manner: They break open the shells of clams, oysters, and mussels by dropping these animals onto a hard surface from a great height.

Long-billed shorebirds—such as sandpipers, godwits, and curlews—are also often seen probing the sand for prey—blood worms, beach hoppers, and other buried beach denizens.

Dunlin
Calidris alpina
578

Tight flocks of little Sanderlings and Dunlins—often in groups of hundreds—race up and down the beach, probing furiously at the lowest spot on the beach uncovered by the receding waves. They are searching for isopods, small beach shrimps, and small mole crabs. The patient observer may be lucky enough to spot a lone Curlew Sandpiper, foraging belly-deep in the water for food.

Curlew Sandpiper
Calidris ferruginea

Deer Mouse
Peromyscus maniculatus

Raccoon
Procyon lotor

By night, various terrestrial animals that live among the bunchgrasses or in the woods above the beach—such as Deer Mice, voles, shrews, skunks, and Raccoons—may venture out to prey on insects or to scavenge among the remains of animals cast up on the beach.

Redtail Surfperch
Asphistichus rhodoterus
272

During high tide, various fishes—surfperches (including Redtail, Shiner, and Walleye), Striped Bass, certain flatfishes, and others—move in over the lower intertidal zones. There they search out any hapless worms, isopods, mole crabs, amphipods, shrimps, clams, or other small animals that have been washed out of the sand. Larger crustaceans such as hermit crabs and true crabs may follow suit.

Shiner Perch
Cymatogaster aggregata
267

Walleye Surfperch
Hyperprosopon argenteum
273

Visitors from the Sea

A few truly marine animals visit the beaches to deposit their eggs or give birth to their young. On the Pacific beaches the most remarkable of these is the California Grunion.

Striped Bass
Morone saxatilis
278

California Grunion
Leuresthes tenuis
298

From San Francisco to southern California, from the end of March until the beginning of August, the waters come alive with these small, silvery fish. Every other week on the second night after the full moon (just after the high spring tides reach their highest point), each wave brings in thousands of these fish, each only about six to eight inches long. The females burrow rapidly, tail first, into the wet sand, until only their heads are exposed; then they begin to deposit their eggs. In the meantime, the males curl around the exposed heads of the females and deposit the milt, which runs down into the sand and fertilizes the eggs. The fish return to the sea on the next wave, and others of their kind are brought up to the beach. Since the eggs are laid just after the peak of the high tide, succeeding waves—which do not extend as far up the beach— only cover the eggs with more sand, rather than washing them out. The highest spring tides mark the beginning of the tides' descent; thus the tidal excursions that follow will be weaker, allowing the eggs to remain buried in the sand for two weeks, until the next high spring tide washes them out. At this time, the eggs promptly hatch, and the young are carried out into the surf. On more northerly beaches, various species of smelt spawn in a similar fashion, following the cycle of the tides.

The Washups

Visitors to a beach often find various kinds of animals, not part of the usual beach fauna, washed up on the sand. Jellyfish are familiar to just about everyone. The ones most frequently seen on Pacific beaches are probably the Moon Jellyfish and the Many-ribbed Hydromedusa. Often, all that is left of these creatures by the time they come within the surf zone are blobs of rather firm, completely transparent jelly. Other species, such as the large Purple Banded Jellyfish or the Lined Sea Nettle, may be found. The small and nearly spherical Sea Gooseberry, or "Cats' Eyes," is sometimes stranded on the beach in great numbers. This creature is a ctenophore, or comb jelly. Unlike true jellies, the comb jelly has tentacles that do not sting. In the sunlight, ctenophores refract light like a jewel; by night, they give off their own light by bioluminescence.

Moon Jellyfish
Aurelia aurita
384

Many-ribbed Hydromedusa
Aequorea aequorea
385

Purple Banded Jellyfish
Pelagia colorata

Lined Sea Nettle
Chrysaora melanaster

Sea Gooseberry
Pleurobrachia bachei
387

One spectacular creature that is frequently washed ashore is the By-the-wind Sailor. This gelatinous animal normally lives far out at sea, floating on the surface of tropical or subtropical waters of the central Pacific. Occasionally, however, strong storms or aberrant surface currents bring vast numbers of them to the shore, where they pile up in windrows for many miles. Each one is a colonial animal consisting of a horizontal platform, or float, from which polyps or tentacles dangle into the water. The animal gets its name from the bright blue, diagonal sail that stretches across the top of the float; it uses the sail to tack, in the way that a sailboat does. When By-the-wind Sailors decompose on the beach, all that is left of them is the transparent platform and sail; these show growth rings, which give them the appearance of a sliced onion.

Driftwood that has been floating for some time in the ocean is commonly riddled with the tubes of shipworms—bivalve mollusks of the genera *Teredo* and *Bankia*. The tubes of these animals are usually lined with calcium carbonate, a shelly material that the animals secrete. In addition, driftwood may also be found with clusters of Common Goose Barnacles attached to it, or with bushy clumps of colonial hydroids growing on its surface.

Common Goose Barnacle
Lepas anatifera
460

Mollusk shells, starfishes, sand dollars, and a wide variety of other invertebrates living offshore or in nearby rocky areas are sometimes also cast up on the beach, especially during storms or large ocean swells. The remains of vertebrate animals—such as fishes, rays, seabirds, or even sea lions—although less frequently found, are not rare along these shores. Beached whales are truly rare; the most remarkable instance on the American coast in recent times was the beaching of forty-one Sperm Whales on the Oregon shore in 1980.

Sperm Whale
Physeter Catodon
215

This survey of the animals of sandy beaches is by no means complete. Also living in this habitat are many small, shrimplike crustacea—among them, the opossum shrimps, or mysids (*Mysis* spp.), the females of which carry their young in brood pouches under their thoraxes. The grayish, nearly transparent body that is characteristic of these animals blends in with the sand and mud. Another group of small shrimp consists of the Crago shrimps, (*Crangon* spp.), which are often well camouflaged by their sandy, mottled color combination of gray, brown, and black. They swim in shallow water near the shore and follow the tides.

Many other animals are also adapted to the more protected sandy and muddy beaches—and many hours of discovery await the visitor to these coastal spots.

BEACH HABITAT: PLANTS AND ANIMALS

Seashells
Amethyst Gem Clam 27
Arctic Natica 142
Californian Cone 132
Californian Lucine 41
Common Northwest
Neptune 110
Common Washington
Clam 49
Common Western Spoon
Clam 40
Giant Western Nassa 115
Gould's Wedge Shell 30
Hemphill's Surf Clam 44
Pacific Razor Clam 61
Pacific White Venus 47
Pismo Clam 43
Punctate Pandora 88
Purple Dwarf Olive 127
Stimpson's Surf Clam 45
Transparent Razor Clam 64
Western Fat Dog
Whelk 114

Mammals
Harbor Porpoise 211
Northern Elephant Seal 224
Walrus 223

Fishes
California Grunion 298
Cutthroat Trout 284, 288
Pacific Herring 289
Redtail Surfperch 272
Striped Mullet 277
Walleye Surfperch 273
Yellowfin Croaker 242

Seashore Creatures
Armored Sea Star 363
By-the-wind Sailor 390
California Beach Flea 350
Common Goose
Barnacle 460
Harford's Greedy
Isopod 351
Pacific Mole Crab 342
Red Lineus 395
Spiny Mole Crab 347

Birds
American Crow 555
American Wigeon 522
Black-bellied Plover 579

Bonaparte's Gull 590
California Gull 595
Common Raven 554
Dunlin 578
Elegant Tern 584
Glaucous-winged Gull 594
Greater Yellowlegs 572
Heermann's Gull 591
Least Tern 587
Marbled Godwit 564
Mew Gull 598
Osprey 552
Pomarina Jaeger 551
Red Knot 566
Red-necked Phalarope 559
Red Phalarope 560
Ring Billed Gull 599
Sanderling 570
Semipalmated Plover 580
Snowy Plover 582
Wandering Tattler 576
Western Gull 596
Western Sandpiper 567
Whimbrel 563
Willet 573

Wildflowers
Beach Morning Glory 611
Beach Primrose 607
Beach Silvertop 609
California Thrift 618
Powdery Dudleya 610
Sea Rocket 612
Silky Beach Pea 617

SAND DUNE HABITAT

Compared with the sea and the land that border them, dunes seem relatively lifeless. Yet they contain much that interests the biologist, and they provide a unique landscape for a variety of recreational activities.

The wind, which helps to create ocean waves and currents, also has a role in shaping the dunes—the transitional world of shifting sands that border the beaches. Coastal sand dunes form where relatively low-lying land extends inland behind beaches that are subject to strong onshore winds. Where beaches are continually supplied with sand, great hills may form, sometimes extending as much as two or more miles inland.

The steep, rugged nature of much of the Pacific Coast prevents the establishment of continuous sand dunes; nonetheless the sand dunes in many West Coast areas are massive and complex. Extensive areas of sand dunes border the coasts of Oregon and Washington; in fact almost half of the Oregon coast—or 139 miles—is covered by dunes. These continue south to the southern tip of Baja California.

The largest portion of dune frontage extends from the southern third of Washington to Cape Blanco, Oregon, and is found in the low, narrow plains between high cliffs and promontories of erosion-resistant rock. A few widely separated dunes occur south of Cape Blanco in Oregon, and in California at Point St. George, Humboldt Bay, Point Arena, and Bodega Head. A wide expanse of dunes once extended south of the Golden Gate in San Francisco, but this area has been stabilized and developed. A large dune complex borders the shores around Monterey Bay; dunes also occur at Morro Bay near San Luis Obispo; and a massive series—with a combined frontage of twenty-three miles—extends just to the north and south of the Santa Maria River.

Dune Development and Types of Dunes

Sand dunes are formed by complex historical, physical, and biological processes. Sand from the ocean is carried to shore by the inward and upward surge of water that follows the breaking of waves, and the wind carries it farther inland. As the sand-castle builder, the hole digger, and the sand sculptor know, sand has distinctive properties. When mixed with just the right proportion of water, it behaves like a solid. But sand can also stream through the stem of an hourglass or cascade down the steep slopes of a sand dune.

This liquidlike property of sand contributes in a major way to the formation and movement of dunes. Another factor involves the flow of individual sand grains over the disturbed surface of a liquid mass of sand. Once the wind reaches at least eleven miles an hour, it picks up sand grains and arcs them forward, moving, sorting, and dropping them according to size and weight. When dropped, they bounce against other grains, as the wind continues the moving, bouncing flow. This process of sand movement is called *saltation* (from the Latin word for leaping). Through saltation, a dune can build up and move layer by layer.

The supply of sand, the topography of the shore, the climate, and the vegetation in an area together determine the location and features of sand dunes. Differences in environmental factors create different kinds of dune formations: foredunes, parallel ridges, precipitation ridges, transverse ridges, and deflation plains.

Sand dunes appear as a series of undulating ridges parallel to the shoreline, like waves on the sea. Those closest to the beach are usually the smallest; known as foredunes, they are less stable and of more recent origin than the secondary dunes farther inland. The hollows between the dunes are known as slacks or swales; when these swales intersect the water table, they are called deflation areas.

Foredunes are steep on the shore (or windward) side and slope more gradually on the protected lee side. They act as a barrier, preventing waves and high water from moving inland, and they also supply sand to replenish the areas closer to the sea. The wind transports sand inland, where it forms large dunes. Initiated by vegetation, the ridge is rapidly built with a large supply of sand, which is stabilized by a progression of plant types. As the shore extends seaward, the wind deposits sand along a new line of vegetation at the high-tide level, and less and less is carried inland to the older ridge. Over a long period of time, a series of these ridges develops; they are generally fifteen to forty feet high, although they may reach up to seventy-five feet.

European Beach Grass
Ammophila arenaria

At the turn of the century, European Beach Grass—also called Marram—was introduced into California to stabilize dune formation. At the time, the foredunes were ephemeral ridges of sand. The high, rather stable foredunes along the Oregon coast have developed mostly since the 1930s and are—like the California dunes—a product of the vigorous growth of European Beach Grass.

It is only lately that the unique character of foredunes has been widely appreciated; the deliberate attempt to stabilize them is now regarded as unfortunate. The effect of native plants on the foredunes was to initiate the parallel-ridge system, rather than to impede or control it, as the more aggressive European Beach Grass does. When plant cover takes over, dunes are no longer able to build and move.

Where there is no large foredune, or where there is an ample supply of sand behind the foredune, the wind continues to drive sand inland. If the sand encounters an area of vegetation, it begins to accumulate as a ridge in front of the vegetation barrier. This precipitation ridge, as it is known, becomes very steep on the lee side. After this side reaches an angle of about thirty-three degrees, a slip face is created; the sand tumbles down this face of the ridge and continues its forward movement until it encounters more vegetation—which is usually the edge of a maritime forest.

Eventually a foredune may become so high and steep that the wind cannot carry sand over it. At this point, the sand supply to the entire dune system is effectively cut off. The sand just inland of the foredune is blown away from the area; this exposes the water table and forms a wet area known as a deflation plain. The area is rapidly colonized by various plant forms that spread, change, and eventually create a stable, permanent forest. Large deflation plains occur in the extensive dune area at Coos Bay, Oregon.

The transverse-ridge pattern of dune development occurs only under certain conditions, which include an uninterrupted air flow in one direction, sufficient periods of dryness, sand that is deep enough to prevent the exposure of subsurface waters in the troughs between the ridges, a continuous supply of sand, and the absence of significant vegetation. The small crests of transverse ridges, which are usually about six feet high, are perpendicular to the northwesterly summer winds. Each winter these crests are partially obliterated, and each summer they are again brought to perfection. The profile of a transverse ridge is asymmetric, with a gentle slope (three to twelve degrees) to the windward side and a steep slip face on the leeward side. This profile is maintained as the ridge moves inland and is finally made permanent by progressive changes in vegetation. Distances between these ridges vary from 75 to 150 feet; crest length is also highly variable. This dune formation achieves its best development during the summer months on the broad expanses of sand from Florence, Oregon, south to Coos Bay.

One dune type unique to the Coos Bay dune system is the oblique ridge. Such dunes form a parallel series with their crests oriented obliquely to both the northwesterly and southwesterly winds. With its seasonal change of direction, the wind causes the slip face of the dunes to alternate as well, so that this slip face is maintained on the lee side.

From the beach, these spectacular dunes look like giant mounds that roll up to the Coast Range. They are much farther apart than transverse ridges, averaging 500 feet from crest to crest. They rise as high as 165 feet above their bases, which are often near the water table, and are long—up to 6000 feet.

Oblique ridges move slowly inland over a long period of time. They usually pour inland at an average rate of three to five feet per year, but may advance as fast as sixteen feet per year. They may divert streams, create or bury lakes, or cover forests in their path before reaching high terrain.

A parabola dune is formed by a "blowout," which is a break in the vegetation within a dune and the subsequent removal, by wind, of sand from that spot. The blowout may progress inland parallel to winds that come from one direction, and may widen from side to side, creating a curved shape similar to a parabolic curve. In some instances, the area between the arms of the curve loses so much of its sand to the wind that the water table is exposed, and the site thus becomes a deflation plain. Almost all of the dunes between Tillamook Head and Heceta Head in Oregon are parabola systems, as is the huge dune near Oso Flaco Lake in California. Well-developed parabola dunes also occur in Oregon at Sand Lake and between the Siltcoos and Umpqua rivers near Tahkenitch

European Sea Rocket
Cakile maritima

Yellow Sand Verbena
Abronia latifolia
605

Silver Beach Weed
Franseria chamissonis

American Dune Grass
Elymis mollus

Silky Beach Pea
Lathyrus littoralis
617

Beach Morning Glory
Calystegia soldanella
611

Seashore Bluegrass
Poa macrantha

Large-headed Sedge
Carex macrocephala

Camphor Dune Tansy
Tanacetum camphoratum

Seashore Lupine
Lupinus littoralis

Red Fescue
Festuca rubra

Creek, where they reach heights of more than 500 feet above sea level.

Plants and Animals

The sand-dune environment is an ever-changing, dynamic system, which includes dry, moving sands; wet, stabilized deflation areas; and many transitional areas. Although plants are arranged in groupings or communities that are more or less definite, these are by no means exact or inflexible. One community succeeds another, each one creating a suitable habitat for plants that will eventually succeed it.

Because coastal dunes are constantly bombarded with wind and salt spray, they provide a marginal living for the few plants that can tolerate this impoverished habitat. A walk from the foredunes to the mature dunes farther inland is a walk through time. The plants range in age and type from small, hardy annuals—pioneer species—to mature forests. Plants inhabiting sand dunes—particularly those nearest the sea—must be able to tolerate winds, occasional burial by sand, sand abrasion, salt spray, water deprivation, shifting soils, and salt soils. Initially, dune soils are nutritionally poor. The first nutrients are brought by salt spray, rain, and fog, as well as by seaweeds and other organic tidal litter. At first, these nutrients drain rapidly into the sand; however, as generations of pioneer plants are incorporated into the soil, its humus content is increased, as is the occurrence of minerals such as nitrogen and phosphorous. This creates a more favorable environment for other plants. Over time, soil conditions change radically; water leaches the calcium carbonate from shell fragments, which helps to improve the dunes' water-retention capacity and neutralize excess acidity. Increased plant growth provides shading, which lowers the surface temperatures and water evaporation. Roots bind the soil particles, thereby lessening erosion.

The most tolerant plants, the pioneers, are found in the dunes nearest the sea. One of the dune colonizers occurring closest to the water is European Sea Rocket, a fast-rooting succulent annual of the mustard family that was introduced from Europe. One of the most obvious dune plants is European Beach Grass. Introduced into California in 1896, this native of Europe has spread widely both by natural means and through its cultivation as a sand stabilizer. It spreads through a vigorous system of creeping underground stems and creates a very hummocky surface as mounds of sand accumulate around it. Conspicuous mounds are also formed by Yellow Sand Verbena and Silver Beach Weed. Other pioneers include American Dune Grass, Silky Beach Pea, and the photogenic Beach Morning Glory. A stable plant cover is developed by species such as Seashore Bluegrass and Large-headed Sedge, which can tolerate sand deposition and which have large seeds and spreading stems.

The growth of these pioneers alters the soil conditions to allow their replacement by plants such as Camphor Dune Tansy, Seashore Lupine, and Red Fescue. After the vegetation has

Evergreen Huckleberry
Vaccinium ovatum

Salal
Gualtheria shallon

Douglas-fir
Pseudotsuga menziesii

Sitka Spruce
Picea sitchensis

Western Hemlock
Tsuga heterophylla

Western Redcedar
Thuja plicata

Showy Scotch Broom
Cyticus scoparius

Spiny Gorse
Ulex europaeus

Ground Cone
Boschniakia hookeri

Common Ice Plant
Mesembryanthemum crystallinum
613

Black-tailed Deer
Odocoileus hemionus

White-footed Vole
Phenacomys albipes

Tundra Swan
Cygnus columbianus
530

Great Blue Heron
Ardea herodias
558

Beaver
Castor canadensis

River Otter
Lutra canadensis

Gray Whale
Eschrichtius robustus
193, 217

Osprey
Pandion haliaetus
552

Great Egret
Casmerodius albus

been well established, a community composed of various shrubs and tree seedlings begins to appear. In the Pacific Northwest, this community includes Evergreen Huckleberry, Salal, Shore Pine (a variety of Lodgepole Pine), and, in places protected from the wind, Douglas-fir, Sitka Spruce, Western Hemlock, and Western Redcedar. Showy Scotch Broom, another plant introduced from Europe for the purpose of sand stabilization, bedecks open dune habitats from Washington to California. In southern Oregon, the related Spiny Gorse—also introduced from Europe—has formed extensive, impenetrable thickets, to the nearly complete exclusion of other vegetation. Other interesting plants are the small Ground Cone, a parasite that lives on the roots of Salal. The beautiful Common Ice Plant has been introduced to the sandy slopes of central and southern California.

In dune areas, animal life is unexpectedly varied. Forest creatures such as Black-tailed Deer and the rare White-footed Vole look out on marshes where Tundra Swans overwinter, and Great Blue Herons fish with Beavers and River Otters. Not many yards away, mighty Gray Whales can be seen in their yearly migrations between Baja California and Alaska. In the bays and oceans are hundreds of species of fish and invertebrates, in addition to seals and sea lions. In the sky, eagles, Osprey, cormorants, and gulls can be spotted. The beautiful, white-garbed Great Egret can be seen along river banks, along with many other birds. The endangered Snowy Plover requires the driftwood tangles on sand spits near river mouths for its nesting grounds, while the Osprey prefers to rest on dead snags in forests buried by sand dunes. In and near these changing dunes, over twenty distinct microhabitats host more than 400 species of plants and animals.

Oregon Dunes

Some of the most extensive and spectacular dunes in the world occur between Heceta Head and Coos Bay, Oregon. These occupy a stretch of land that is over fifty miles long and extends up to two-and-a-half miles inland. In 1972, forty miles—32,186 acres, to be exact—of dunes, lakes, streams, and forest were set aside as the Oregon Dunes National Recreation Area.

These dunes began to evolve about a million years ago, but the materials and forces responsible date back almost sixty million years to the Eocene Epoch. Volcanic activity, which gradually built the Cascade Range, also left behind loose volcanic material. Later, granitic material eroded from the Klamath Mountains; carried by ocean currents, it was laid down alternately with volcanic sediment. About twenty million years ago, volcanic activity increased, causing uplifting that formed the Coast Ranges. At this time, these ancient dunes were covered by warm seas, which left their traces in fossil mollusks and sea lions.

The dunes continue to undergo cycles of submergence, rejuvenation, and stabilization. The coast of Oregon has a moist, mild climate, so vegetation has been an important factor in this cycle: It starts the dune-building process and also eventually buries dunes when either the wind dies or the sand supply runs out.

Foredunes, which now are a basic part of the dune scheme in Oregon, were not part of the original pattern. They are the direct result of the planting of European Beach Grass along the coast and the coastal estuaries south of the Oregon Dunes National Recreation Area. European Beach Grass has exhibited a marvelous ability to adapt to the harsh conditions of the beach. Unlike the natural pioneer species of the region, it grows very rapidly—fast enough to keep up with dune growth—and adjusts to sand burial.

Before the introduction of European Beach Grass, plant communities and sand alternately controlled this dune area. The percentage of dune area covered by vegetation has grown enormously, however, and is continuing to expand. It is estimated that, at the present growth rate, vegetation will cover the dunes almost completely within seventy-five or a hundred years.

There has been much discussion about whether natural rejuvenation is now possible, or whether human intervention is required—and desirable. Several restoration methods have been suggested; all of them involve destruction of both the European Beach Grass and the foredunes. Even if this restoration could be accomplished in environmentally sound ways, there is some question about whether there is an adequate supply of sand washing up on the beach to reestablish the dune pattern. Moreover, if defoliants are used to destroy the Beach Grass, they will also be fatal to indigenous flora and fauna. Satisfactory answers to these complex problems have by no means been found. Nonetheless, pressures from a concerned and appreciative public do assure that some attempt will be made to perpetuate the dunes for future generations to enjoy.

SAND DUNE HABITAT: PLANTS AND ANIMALS

Wildflowers
Beach Morning Glory 611
Beach Silvertop 609
Beach Strawberry 608
Common Ice Plant 613
Giant Coreopsis 602
Menzies' Wallflower 606
Narrow Goldenrod 603
Northern Dune Tansy 604
Sea Fig 615
Seaside Daisy 614
Silky Beach Pea 617
Tree Lupine 601
Yellow Sand Verbena 605

Birds
Great Blue Heron 558
Osprey 552
Tundra Swan 530

Mammal
Gray Whale 193, 217

PROTECTED MARINE ENVIRONMENTS:
BAYS AND ESTUARIES, SALT MARSHES, AND
WHARVES AND PILINGS

Marine environments that are protected from the full brunt of
ocean waves offer special kinds of habitats and support a
diverse flora and fauna. There are several different types of
protected habitats that occur along the Pacific Coast: bays and
estuaries, salt marshes, mud flats, and wharves and pilings.
Each provides the plants and animals that live there with
certain advantages and challenges.

Estuaries

Bodies of water that form at the mouths of rivers, where tidal
waters and fresh water meet and mix, are called estuaries.
Estuaries take many different forms: These include marine
embayments, bays, sounds, sloughs, lagoons, and inlets.
Deltas, mud flats, and salt marshes are all parts of estuaries.
These often mucky areas are among the earth's most
productive environments, providing an extremely rich and
important habitat for a great variety of life. The fluctuating
conditions caused by the interaction of salt water and fresh
water, however, also make this habitat an unstable and
demanding one. Plants and animals that live in estuaries must
be able to cope with these fluctuations; indeed they have
managed to do so through remarkable adaptations.

Estuaries occur all along the Pacific Coast. In California the
more important ones include Bodega Bay, Tomales Bay, San
Francisco Bay, Morro Bay, Newport Beach, and San Diego
Bay. San Francisco Bay is the only major ocean inlet between
Puget Sound and Baja California. Its tidewaters and wetlands
once covered nearly 700 square miles, but more than half of
this has been filled in.

On the border between Oregon and Washington, the mighty
Columbia River drains into the Pacific. This large embayment
is bounded by Cape Disappointment on the north and Fort
Stevens on the south. At Coos Bay, Oregon, there is another
large estuary.

Boundary Bay, which occurs on the border between British
Columbia and Washington, is a broad tidal flat of sand and
mud that dries out at low tide. South of the Fraser River delta
at Point Roberts, on the western side of the bay, is a low
shingle shelf known as Lily Point, where an enormous
sandstone cliff towers above a beach of mixed sand, mud, and
boulders. Low tides expose a cobblestone reef, and on the
other side of the bay, at White Rock, Eelgrass beds on
protected sand beach support a rich community of plants
and animals.

Farther south in Washington is Puget Sound, an enormous
glacially carved area the provides a variety of habitats ranging
from purely marine to estuarine, and grading into fresh water
in the upper reaches. The deep waters of the sound cover
former beaches of sand and gravel. This extensive area not only
contains mud flats, salt marshes, and protected bays of mixed
sand, mud, and cobblestone, but is also marked by sandy and
gravelly beaches, rocky reefs and headlands, islands, and
streams and rivers.

Several estuarine areas are found in Alaska. The Copper River

pierces the coastal mountain barrier and has created a large
delta east of Cordova, Alaska. Farther west, the Kenai
Peninsula separates two large inlets: Prince William Sound
and Cook Inlet. Prince William Sound has dozens of tributary
fjords and some active glaciers; the ruggedly beautiful fjords
and islands here are supremely serene, as they are well
protected from the fury of the North Pacific. Cook Inlet
contains elements not found in most of Alaska's other bays:
extensive lowland areas, large river inputs, active volcanoes,
tidal bores, and oil wells. Ketchemak Bay, near the mouth, is
widely considered one of Alaska's most productive fisheries.
In estuaries, the saline, nutrient-rich ocean waters that are
carried inland by the tides meet with the sediment-laden fresh
water; when this happens, chemical and physical interactions
take place that cause the particles carried by each to settle.
Particles are sorted according to size and density and spread
out over a wide area. This spreading eventually results in the
formation of broad sand or mud flats, through which the fresh
water flows in shallow, meandering channels at low tide; at
high tide, these flats are covered with shallow saline water. At
slack tide—when there is no horizontal motion of water either
way—the spreading of the water encourages deposition of the
smallest particles on the upper reaches of the flats.
Estuaries are among the most productive areas on earth,
supporting more plant and animal growth per unit of area
than even the best agricultural lands. In fact, the mean annual
production of an estuary is eight times as great as that of a
good corn field. Large marine-dominated estuaries are the
richest; estuaries dominated by rivers are usually not spread
out as well, nor do they trap nutrients as efficiently. Small
estuaries tend to fluctuate more in character with seasonal
changes in runoff and temperature; they are commonly less
fruitful than larger ones. The West Coast estuaries are
generally small in comparison with the larger estuaries in the
East. One of the West Coast's largest, the Columbia River
estuary, is river-dominated, as are most of the estuaries in
British Columbia and southern Alaska.
Until recently, the value of estuaries was not understood,
because much estuary plant growth consists of small to
microscopic algae that live in the water, and most of the
animals are either very small or are concealed in burrows
within the mud or the sand. The estuaries have been diked
and filled to create pastureland or cheap industrial sites, and
have even been used as refuse dumps. The destruction of
estuaries has occurred at an alarming rate: An estimated 215
million acres have already been lost to this habitat worldwide.
Estuaries serve not only as sources of food but also as homes for
many marine and terrestrial animals during at least part of
their lives. These inhabitants include the many saltwater
fishes, clams, oysters, crabs, shrimps, and lobsters that are
harvested commercially. In addition, estuaries are important as
natural flood-control devices, because they buffer the force of
storms and absorb runoff waters and organic wastes. Their
importance to shipping has long been appreciated.

Eelgrass
Zostera marina
508

The Flow of Energy

The energy that runs the complex community of plants and animals in an estuary comes ultimately from the sun, but by a route that is not immediately obvious. Estuaries support a luxuriant growth of algae, Eelgrass, and salt marsh plants. Some of this plant growth is directly consumed by animals, but even more of it contributes to the food web through the detritus cycle. Plants die back in the winter and decompose. Decomposition releases soluble substances into the water; the less soluble substances accumulate as small particles known collectively as detritus. Detrital particles drift in the water and accumulate as a fine, loose layer on the surface of the mud; as they drift, these particles become coated with organic molecules and bacteria. They can then serve as food for filter-feeding animals and substrate ingestors, which take in largely indigestible substances, digest what they can, and excrete the rest. Then the particles again become coated with organic material, and thus can serve as food once more.

The intense bacterial activity of the detritus cycle removes all free oxygen, creating a layer of black mud that is rich in iron sulfide. This mud gives off a characteristic rotten-egg smell, which is generated by the hydrogen sulfide gas trapped in the mud. At the surface of the mud, where free oxygen is present, the oxidation of iron compounds gives the mud a lighter color. Many plants and animals thrive in the oxygen-poor environment below by adjusting to or protecting themselves from periodic low water levels and rapid changes in salinity and temperature.

Eelgrass, a seed-producing marine plant, is tremendously prolific in estuaries. Its roots and stem serve to bind and stabilize the mud, and the plant provides food and habitat for many animals. The blades are grazed by a few animals, but they contribute to animal food cycles largely by supporting the growth of diatoms and small invertebrates that accumulate on them when they get old, and by providing detritus when they die back and disintegrate in late fall or early winter. A little later, we will take a closer look at an Eelgrass community.

The edges of estuarine mud flats are colonized by salt-tolerant plants called halophytes. These serve as extremely efficient sediment traps and produce much organic matter; nutrients brought in by both freshwater and ocean water are trapped in the estuary by these plants. These nutrients then spread over a broad area, promoting maximum utilization of the solar energy.

A few of the animal species common to estuaries—insect larvae, certain snails, oligochaete worms (relatives of earthworms), and perhaps some of the nematode worms— probably originated in fresh water; however, most have evolved from marine forms. Some survive by burying themselves in the mud. There they feed and respire while the tide is in; when the tide is out, they greatly reduce their metabolic rate and thus minimize their oxygen demand. Some animals, like clams, simply shut down by either withdrawing into holes or retreating with the tidal waters to different locations until the tide returns. The practice of burrowing into the mud enables most estuary animals to avoid drying out and to escape undue warming or chilling.

The water temperature in an estuary is influenced by fluctuations in air temperature to a much greater extent than is the case in the ocean. If the estuary is shallow, and the fresh and saline components are well mixed, temperature and salinity are usually the same from top to bottom, although temperatures in the shallow waters over mud flats may rise considerably in the summer. Oxygen and carbon dioxide levels in the water vary with photosynthesis, respiration, and decomposition of organic materials. Most animals can tolerate only a limited range of all the various conditions that exist in an estuary; thus each species selects that portion of an estuary where the normal changes in temperature, salinity, and the like fall within its range.

Types of Estuaries

The characteristics of any given estuary depend upon the geologic history of the region and the size and character of the river that flows through it. The factors that combine to influence an estuary's character include the following: seasonal fluctuations; the river's sediment load; the height of tides; the frequency, direction, and strength of storms; the amount of precipitation in the region; and the trend of the rock strata relative to the shoreline.

Different types of estuaries are created by different forces. In areas where the sea level has risen relative to the land, broad, flooded river mouths and embayments (partially enclosed estuarine waters) with numerous branches are formed. The salinity of the water changes gradually across an embayment as sea water at the mouth grades into fresh water at the upper end. But where the land has risen relative to sea level, rivers run more swiftly and produce narrow estuaries marked by abrupt changes in salinity. Where the relation between land and sea has been constant for a long time and the adjacent portion of the sea is shallow, the river deposits sediment, building an estuary and delta at its mouth. Deltas are ever-changing areas containing channels, marshes, or lakes.

Fjords, which occur along the coasts of Alaska and British Columbia, result when rising seawater fills deep, narrow glacial basins. Bar-built estuaries are formed where offshore sandbars rise above sea level and enclose shallow bodies of coastal water, which usually contain relatively little runoff from the land; the Coos Bay estuary in Oregon, for example, has been much extended by a sandspit. Fault-block estuaries, such as San Francisco Bay, are formed or controlled by the geologic structure: The upper reaches of this bay were formed by the drowning (or submergence) of the lower San Joaquin–Sacramento river system. During long periods of geologic stability, estuaries gradually broaden and flatten to produce broad, silted flats.

More important from a biological point of view are the patterns and variations of salinity within an estuary. The estuaries that occur along the Pacific Coast are classified according to the pattern of water circulation and flow; most are either river-dominated or marine-dominated, although there are some that do not belong to either category.

A river-dominated estuary is characterized by a large proportion of fresh water and relatively deep contours. The freshwater tends to flow out at the surface, while underneath a deep wedge of salt water is pushed landward considerable distances by the tide. Probably the classic example of a stratified river-dominated estuary is the Mississippi estuary. Here the freshwater flow is immense, while the tidal rise and fall is only about six inches. Because it is less dense, freshwater floats on top of the salt water, spreading out in a layer that becomes progressively thinner and broader toward the sea. A wedge of salt water slowly pushes up-stream along the bottom, extending about 150 miles from the river's mouth. In much of this stretch of the Mississippi estuary, it is possible to catch bottom-dwelling marine fishes while boating in water that, at the surface, is fresh enough to drink. The surface and borders of the estuary are essentially freshwater; bulrushes, whirligig beetles, water striders, and other freshwater flora and fauna characterize the landscape.

The Columbia River estuary is also river-dominated. Its form was affected by the rising of land and sea levels following the last ice age. Unlike many rivers, which spread out into large estuaries or deltas, the Columbia flows directly into the Pacific Ocean with virtually no change in width. The top layer of fresher water is detectable for many miles in the ocean; it is carried south in the summer and north in winter.

In marine-dominated estuaries, such as Coos Bay, Oregon, the input of freshwater is relatively small, and the rise and fall of the tide, considerable. Such estuaries tend to be broad and shallow, with comparatively small channels. Pushed by the tides, the denser, saltier marine water overrides the smaller amount of fresh water, then mixes with it as it sinks. Thus the water is more homogenous over the entire estuary; it exhibits little difference in salinity, temperature, or oxygen, although the salinity does decrease progressively with distance from the ocean. The margins of such estuaries are marine in character, because the water that flows out over the banks of the channels as the tides push in is primarily marine water. The edges are bordered by saltwater or brackish-water flora and fauna—such as *Ruppia*, salt-marsh plants, barnacles where there is a hard substrate they can attach to, and shipworms and Gribbles where pilings or stranded logs exist. At low tide, much of a marine-dominated estuary is drained, exposing extensive mud or sand flats.

Gribble
Limnoria lignorum

Many estuaries are neither river-dominated nor marine-dominated, but are more mixed or balanced. Small estuaries are subject to marked seasonal variation in runoff, and they thus support a less diversified plant and animal community. Most of the estuaries of central and southern California are highly seasonal with respect to the amount of fresh water that enters. A few may not even have enough flow in the dry

summer months to keep a channel to the sea open throughout
the dry season, and may form temporary saline ponds or
marshes behind a beach.

Estuarine mud flats are areas of mud or sandy mud that are
regularly exposed by the falling tides. As the flow of either
fresh water or marine water is slowed down upon entering the
estuary, the heavier sand and gravel particles are promptly
deposited in the channel, while the finer, lighter particles
remain in the water much longer. In river-dominated
estuaries, most of the fine particles are swept out to sea and
eventually deposited at the outer edges of the delta as mud
fans, which usually develop underwater. In marine-dominated
estuaries, the fine particles are carried over the flats by the
incoming marine water and finally deposited there at slack
tide. The falling tide generally has much less energy, at least
near the edges of the estuary, and does not resuspend most of
the particles; therefore the flats consist mostly of fine
sediments, whereas the upper and lower portions of the
channels—as well as portions of the flats near the mouth of
the estuary—tend to consist of sand or sandy mud. The
fineness of the sediments, their high water content, and the
influence of organic matter and bacteria tend to make the mud
flats of marine-dominated estuaries very soft and gooey.

Ecology

The lack of oxygen, the changes in salinity, and the lack of
sites for attachment in a mud flat all make for a rather
specialized fauna. Most of the animals are infauna—burrowing
worms, clams, and crustaceans—which live in the substrate,
especially in the soft, muddy bottom. Few animals live on the
surface of the mud flats all of the time, although some can
regularly be found there at certain times, such as when the
tide covers the flats. One of the most interesting animals
living in the highest parts of the mud flats in southern

California Fiddler
Uca crenulata
343

California is the rather scarce California Fiddler. This crab
digs a burrow at high tide, then plugs it so that it can retain
enough water for respiration while the tide is out. It feeds by
catching bits of drifting organic matter with its claws.

The channel of an estuary, its permanent link between the
ocean and the river or streams that feed it, serves as the
entrance and exit for a great number of marine species. Many
fish and larger invertebrates that live offshore as adults spend
much of their larval or juvenile life in the food-rich estuarine
environment, where they are also protected from some of the
predators that live in the more open coastal waters. Water is
present in the channel even at the lowest tides, so animals and
plants living there never have to cope with drying. However,
those that live in one place—such as Eelgrass, its epiphytes
(the plants and animals that are attached to it), and the
burrowing animals—may have to cope with rather drastic
changes of salinity as the tides move back and forth over them.
Planktonic organisms drift with the movements of the water.
These tiny plants and animals—especially phytoplankton
(mostly diatoms and dinoflagellates)—reproduce very rapidly

and serve as a base of the food web. Phytoplankton are the chief food of many filter feeders—including most clams, many tube worms, and barnacles—and are also consumed by most zooplankton and even a few species of fish. Some resident species of zooplankton reproduce in estuaries; these are much more prevalent in the upper reaches of an estuary than in nearby coastal waters. Zooplankton species that are abundant in the shallow coastal waters, however, are regularly swept into estuaries by incoming tides and thus are also especially numerous in the lower reaches of the estuary. A third, often prominent type of estuarine zooplankton consists of the larval or juvenile forms of the animals resident in the estuary, as well as those that make their homes in the shallow coastal waters.

Giant Western Nassa
Nassarius fossatus
115

Lewis' Moon Shell
Polinices lewisii
140

In some estuaries, great numbers of carnivorous snails, such as the Giant Western Nassa are abundant at the surface, and sometimes the large Lewis Moon Snail is present. The Giant Western Nassas, which have an acute sense of smell, are attracted by the odor of meat and will try to reach it if it is held above them. They deposit their eggs in tiny capsules on blades of Eelgrass; according to one patient observer, the process of laying each egg takes twelve-and-a-half minutes. A typical two-and-a-half-inch string of eggs contains forty-five capsules and takes nine hours to make.

California Bubble
Bulla gouldiana
135

Pacific Solitary Hydroid
Corymorpha palma

In southern estuaries, a large opisthobranch mollusk, the California Bubble, attains a length of about two inches. When this snail is crawling about in the mud, the mantle covers most of the shell. Another surface inhabitant of southern estuaries is the large Pacific Solitary Hydroid, which is well known in the Newport Beach and San Diego Bay area. When uncovered by a falling tide, this animal collapses onto the mud, where it is exposed to sun, wind, or rain until the tide rises again. Remarkably, this delicate-looking creature usually suffers no harm from being uncovered, unless it remains exposed for extremely long periods.

Mud Dwellers

Sea Pen
Stylatula elongata

The Sea Pen is also common in southern estuaries. These colonial coelenterates, relatives of sea anemones and jellyfishes, stick up from the mud like narrow, greenish feathers. When disturbed, Sea Pens retract their polyps and pull themselves down into the mud. In Puget Sound and the deeper subtidal waters of other estuaries, the large, plump, bright orange Gurney's Sea Pen occurs in beds, where it is preyed upon by various nudibranchs. Sea pens are bioluminescent: When they have adapted to the dark and are stimulated, they emit startling flashes of light. Gurney's Sea Pen, to name one, gives off a brilliant orange light when it is disturbed in the dark.

Gurney's Sea Pen
Ptilosarcus gurneyi
448

Buried Sea Anemone
Anthopleura artemisia

Ghost Shrimps
Callianassa spp.
344, 345

The Buried Sea Anemone may occur in estuaries in great numbers, as do ghost shrimps (*Callianassa* spp.). When the tide is in, ghost shrimps cause a water current to pass through their burrows, from which they extract plankton and detritus. Their digging and that of mud shrimps (*Upogebia* spp.) overturns and oxygenates the sediment in the mud flats. The

Blue Mud Shrimp
Upogebia pugettensis

Lug Worm
Arenicola pacifica
407

Innkeeper Worm
Urechis caupo
399

Arrow Goby
Clevelandia ios

California False Cerith
Batillaria attramentaria

Navanax
Navanax inermis
417

Hermissenda Nudibranch
Hermissenda crassicornis
428

California Brown Sea Hare
Aplysia californica
416

Purple Dwarf Olive
Olivella biplicata
127

Chestnut Cowry
Cypraea spadicea
133

Californian Cone
Conus californicus
132

Geoduck
Panopea generosa
57

Blue Mud Shrimp also feeds by filtering food from the water currents that it creates in its burrows. Mud shrimps are difficult to dig out, because the ground in which they live is so honeycombed with burrows that the water pours in almost as fast as the mud can be spaded out. Their U-shaped burrows are branched and have several enlarged places for turning around; they extend downward from the surface for about eighteen inches, horizontally for two to four feet, then up to the surface again. Each burrow is almost always inhabited by one male and one female. Mud shrimps use two pairs of legs for burrowing and as a basket for carrying mud; four other pairs function as paddles to keep the water circulating through the burrow while the mud basket serves as a strainer, catching the minute food particles in the water. The shrimp's tail, known as a telson, can be used to block water, or on occasion can be flipped to clean the burrow. The Blue Mud Shrimp will die if its body is not in contact on all sides with walls of its burrow. The abundant Pacific Lug Worm also makes J- or U-shaped burrows, through which water is circulated. Ghost shrimps and lugworms are especially abundant on mud flats that are somewhat sandy.

One of the more famous inhabitants of mud flats is the Innkeeper Worm, which spins a net in the opening of its burrow to retain suspended fine particles and periodically ingests the net and the food particles within it. The Innkeeper Worm and ghost shrimps are among those estuarine burrow-dwellers that are famous for their boarders—other animals that make use of their burrows. The small Arrow Goby fish uses the burrow of the Innkeeper as a refuge; as many as five Gobies have been found at one time in a single burrow. At least four species of animals are known to dwell within the tube of the Innkeeper as commensals, including two small species of pea crabs, *Scleroplax granulata* and *Peninixa franciscana;* one annelid worm, *Hesperone aventor;* and, in California, a species of shrimp, *Bateus longidactylus.*

A number of snails and sea slugs can be found on the lower reaches of mud flats. In California they include the California False Cerith and the Giant Western Nassa; in the southern part of the state, the large, reddish-brown, spotted Navanax is among the more impressive mollusks. The beautiful Hermissenda Nudibranch ranges throughout the Pacific Coast region. Along some California shores and estuaries, the large California Sea Hare, which grows up to sixteen inches long, is a familiar and spectacular animal. If sufficiently disturbed, it releases a secretion of sticky, deep purple dye and mucus. Sea hares are herbivorous and feed on various seaweeds.

The beautiful Purple Dwarf Olive can be found burrowing in sandy beaches on the coast and in the lower reaches of estuaries from British Columbia to the Baja. Tropical flora and fauna may also be found in the lower reaches of estuaries in southern California. Two such species are the Chestnut Cowrie and the California Cone.

Estuarine mud flats are most famous for their clams. The largest of these is the Geoduck, which is found from Alaska to

Pacific Gaper
Tresus nuttallii
56

Soft-shell Clam
Mya arenaria
59

Purple Shore Crab
Hemigrapsus nudus
326, 332

Yellow Shore Crab
Hemigrapsus oregonensis
329

Striped Shore Crab
Pachygrapsus crassipes
331

Pacific Terebellid Worm
Pista pacifica

Pacific Staghorn Sculpin
Leptocottus armatus

Shiner Perch
Cymatogaster aggregata
267

English Sole
Parophrys vetulus
308

Pacific Herring
Clupea harengus pallasi
289

Northern Anchovy
Engraulis mordax
295

Striped Bass
Morone saxatilis
278

Coho Salmon
Oncorhynchus kisutch

Chinook Salmon
Oncorhynchus tshawytscha
286

Cutthroat Trout
Salmo clarki
284, 288

Steelhead Trout
Salmo gairdneri

Baja California. This species lives in burrows that are often as deep as three feet; prior to the invention of the hydraulic pump, this clam was safe from harvesting. Another large clam, the Pacific Gaper, is one of the most sought-after clams in the sandy mud flats of Pacific Northwest estuaries. It occurs south as far as Baja California. As one approaches a Gaper Clam's burrow, the animal is often disturbed by the vibration and quickly retracts its large siphon, shooting out a jet of water a foot or so above the surface of the mud. The Soft-shell Clam is common near the upper margin of the intertidal zone from Alaska to Elkhorn Slough, just north of Monterey Bay in California.

Cockles, which have very short siphons and plump, heavily ribbed shells, are common close to the surface and can be collected with a rake. Numerous other clams—including the Bent-nose Macoma, the Baltic Macoma, the California Glass Mya, and species of piddocks that burrow in mud and shale—occur all along the coast in bays from Alaska to California. The·Purple Shore Crab and its close relative the Yellow Shore Crab are both abundant in mud flats in the Pacific Northwest. The Purple Shore Crab tends to occur in places where it can hide under rocks or pieces of wood, while the Yellow Shore Crab inhabits the edges of channels and salt marshes, where it burrows into the banks, emerging toward evening to feed. The Striped Shore Crab is found well above the high-tide line on rocky and hard-mud shores, especially in central and southern California.

Several predatory annelid worms inhabit estuaries; the largest is the *Neanthes brandti,* which can attain a length of about two feet and a width of about an inch. A most intersting deposit feeder is the large Pacific Terebellid Worm, whose hooded tubes, which are curiously bent over and have fingerlike extensions from the hood, extend almost two inches above the substrate; these tubes also extend down about a foot and a half into the substrate. This large worm is a spectacular sight: Constantly active, bright red respiratory gills appear as a mass of slender, branched tentacles at its anterior end; and many long, white feeding tentacles can be extended out for a considerable distance in all directions over the substrate, transporting selected detrital particles back to the worm's mouth.

Some fishes, such as the Pacific Staghorn Sculpin, the Shiner Perch, the Starry Flounder, and the Arrow Goby, are permanent residents of estuaries. Most of the fish in an estuary retreat to the channel as the tide ebbs; only during high tide do they move out over the mud flats and even into the lower parts of salt marshes to feed. Skates and rays root out clams, which they crush with their teeth. Sometimes a fish is found stranded on the mud, having been trapped there as the tide ebbed.

The commercially valuable fish that feed in estuaries include English Sole, Pacific Herring, Northern Anchovy, and Striped Bass. Coho Salmon, Chinook Salmon, Cutthroat Trout, Steelhead Trout (the migratory form of the Rainbow Trout),

American Shad
Alosa sapidissima
276

and Shad swim through estuaries on their way upstream to spawn. Their young often stay in the estuary for a time to feed and adjust to saltwater before migrating to the sea.

Eelgrass Communities

Eelgrass dominates many types of shallow channel bottoms, sand flats, and mud flats in bays, estuaries, and protected coastal places; it forms the basis for some of the most productive communities on earth. On most mud flats, Eelgrass occupies the shallow channels and lower parts of the flats, which are covered by water most of the time; it is generally separated from the pickleweed salt marsh or upper fringe of the flat by an area of more barren mud.

Eelgrass grows rapidly throughout the spring and summer, giving shelter to a great variety of crustaceans, fish, and other animals. As the blades become older, they also support heavy growths of diatoms, attached hydroids, and protozoans, along with the small worms and other animals that graze on this growth.

During late summer and early fall, Eelgrass plants flower and produce seed. The blades then die back and decompose, providing nutrients to a bloom of bacteria and small flagellates, as well as to other microorganisms, which in turn are consumed by larval bivalves and other animals that spawn in the warm temperatures of late summer.

One of the world's largest Eelgrass beds is in Izembek Lagoon, which lies near the tip of the Alaska Peninsula, facing the Bering Sea. This shallow lagoon contains an underwater meadow that stretches for miles, and thus provides a perfect setting for taking a close look at life in an Eelgrass bed.

An impressive renewal follows the melting of the winter ice. Plants emerge from rhizomes buried in the soft sediments and grow upward until they reach the surface of the lagoon, forming a nearly complete canopy by June. Few other communities have rates of photosynthesis as high as those at Izembek. As the Eelgrass blades age, they are colonized by algae, bryozoans, snails, minute mussels, amphipods, and other creatures. Fishes that are small enough to maneuver among the closely spaced plants feast on these epiphytic animals.

Helmet Crab
Telmessus chieragonus

The Helmet Crab abounds in the grass beds; the softer, sweeter portions of the plant near the basal meristem provide much of its food. This crab is preyed upon by gulls, which, at low tide on a calm day, may wade through the Eelgrass in search of a meal. When they find a Helmet Crab, they flip it over and devour its insides. One can sometimes see hundreds of crab carapaces floating away like tiny boats on the next rising tide.

River Otter
Lutra canadensis

Sea Otter
Enhydra lutris
234

Gray Whale
Eschrichtius robustus
193, 217

Bears, foxes, and River Otters sometimes hunt in the lagoon, and seals feed and give birth to pups on the sandbars. Sea Otters and Gray Whales occasionally drop in, apparently feeding on crabs and shrimp, respectively.

Ducks, shorebirds, gulls, terns, jaegers, and other birds nest around Izembek, but the air really becomes alive in August and September when the fall migrations start. Sandpipers are among the first to appear in large numbers. Terns fly above the Eelgrass, searching for small fish, including some that apparently bask on the Eelgrass blades floating on the waters surface. Some shorebirds feed on Eelgrass epiphytes or on the sand fleas that inhabit the windrows of Eelgrass detritus that line the shores. Others probe the mud for tiny clams. When frightened by an attacking falcon, huge flocks of sandpipers may rise up from the tide flats like enormous swarms of bees. Ducks and geese show up in large numbers in September, and the quiet lagoon is overtaken by a cacophony of bird sounds.

Northern Pintail
Anas acuta
527

Brant
Branta bernicla
528

Northern Pintails seem to prefer the Eelgrass seeds, while geese, especially the Brant, eat most of the plant. Eiders strip the epiphytic animals from the grass blades for food. According to each bird's internal timetable, they arrive, tank up for the long migration, and, as time goes on, grow more and more agitated. The noise level increases, and large flocks of waterfowl fly higher in the air. And then, riding the tailwinds of one of the great North Pacific storms at an altitude of perhaps 10,000 feet, they depart one night—some flying directly across the Gulf of Alaska—heading to Washington, Oregon, and California.

By this time, the bears are hibernating, and the foxes have their winter coats. If the winter is a severe one, large chunks of ice may drag across the shallow Eelgrass beds, gouging deep trenches in the soft mud. Heavy sea ice may compel the Sea Otters to attempt a crossing of the Alaska Peninsula, a forced march that many cannot survive. And the lagoon waits for the spring to begin life anew.

The steep-walled bays of the north—the fjords—offer a rather specialized habitat. The rocky sides of these bays do not always provide the same muddy home that estuarine creatures find farther south. Nonetheless, many of the fjords of the Northwest do have a mixture of fresh water and salt water— an environment congenial to a number of hardy species of plants and animals. Retreating glaciers left hundreds of fjords on the northwest coastline; most are long, deep, sinuous valleys with steep sides, which extend between the ocean and the coastal mountains. The debris excavated from the glaciers' paths piled up at their termini; this occurred, for example, in the Puget Sound region, which is covered by glacial debris. This debris, the raw material out of which beaches and sedimentary environments are created, also forms underwater dams, called sills, in most of the coastal fjords.

Bull Kelp
Nereocystis luetkeana
493

Black Abalone
Haliotis cracherodii
83

The sill of a fjord can support dense populations of filter-feeding invertebrates (tube worms, mussels, rock scallops, and others) as well as their predators. Lush beds of large Bull Kelp are also likely to be present. During the short periods of slack water during tidal changes, these locations can provide spectacular recreational dives. Some animals that normally occur on the outer coast—the Black Abalone, for example— can also be found on sills well within a fjord. A sill occurring within the intertidal zone can cause waterfalls to reverse as the water flows first one way, then the other, over the sill. A

Alaska Brown Bear
Ursus arctos middendorffi

Bald Eagle
Haliaeetus leucocephalus
553

Frilled Anemone
Metridium senile
444

Giant Pacific Octopus
Octopus dofleini
378

Beaver
Castor canadensis

Muskrat
Ondatra zibethicus

Raccoon
Procyon lotor

subtidal sill may produce frightening tidal currents for the unwary boater.

Near the head of a fjord, a stream has often deposited a small delta of sand and silt. Adult salmon may be splashing their way upstream to spawn, providing a magnet for Alaska Brown Bears and Bald Eagles.

Few of the rivers have managed to penetrate the towering mountain ranges paralleling the coast; as little as fifty miles inland, water is likely to drain off in some other direction. The mightiest of these northern rivers, the Yukon, begins less than twenty miles from the coast; nonetheless, it flows 1600 miles through northern Canada and Alaska before emptying into the Bering Sea.

Subtidal habitats within fjords can be quite interesting to observe. Scallops and crabs are abundant in some bays, and fishes plentiful in others. In still other fjords, fantastic gardens of pink and white Frilled Anemones can be found, growing up to several feet high. Swimming among such beauties must be something like heaven. Other curious animals include crinoids, large spider crabs, and the Giant Pacific Octopus. One may also encounter layers of jellyfish, usually where fresh water and salt water meet.

Salt Marshes

Coastal salt marshes, recognized by biologists as among the most productive habitats in the world, are part of the tidal marsh–estuarine ecosystem. This habitat supports halophytes —plants that are adapted to salty soils—and provides food and shelter to a wide range of birds and mammals. Each year thousands of resident and migratory birds use these coastal wetlands; the numerous mammals that occur here include Beaver, Muskrat, River Otters, Raccoon, and deer. Shellfish that live in the salt marsh habitat include clams, cockles, crabs, and commercial oysters.

Because the Pacific Coast rises rather abruptly from the ocean along much of its length, tidal salt marshes are more limited than on the Atlantic Coast, where the transition between land and sea is more often gradual. In the East, such marshes are often formed in combination with barrier beaches, whereas on the West Coast, they occur only in estuaries.

The Pacific Coast salt marshes generally begin above the mud flats, at about the mid point between high and low tides, where both an inundation of seawater and wave action prevent the establishment of terrestrial vegetation. Low marshes— those nearest the low-tide line—may be inundated by each high tide, whereas high marshes are usually covered with tidal water only a few times during the growing season.

Salt marshes provide a food-rich, protected habitat for many animals—both terrestrial and marine—and for the larval or juvenile stages of many fishes and invertebrates that live elsewhere as adults. Much of the plant material enters the food web as detritus, or recycled, dead plant material, instead of being consumed directly. Because different plants decompose at different rates, there is a constant source of food in a salt marsh—unlike the fluctuating seasonal supply provided by phytoplankton blooms in the open ocean. Furthermore, detrital particles are enriched by heavy growths of bacteria and other microorganisms on them and thus may be profitably recycled by animals.

The soft, muddy substrate of a salt marsh is easy to burrow into and therefore provides a perfect residence for burrowing detritus feeders. Burrowing filter feeders, which also inhabit the salt marsh, strain plankton and detrital particles from the water when the tide covers them. Although a salt marsh may be teeming with animal life, most of this is not evident to the casual observer, since many of the animals are small, and most spend their time burrowed in the substrate for protection from desiccation and predation.

Because halophytes can tolerate soils that are too saline for most plants, they compete successfully with other species and dominate the salt marsh environment. The salinity of the soil affects the growth and distribution of halophytes; most grow in soils that contain two to six percent salt.

Halophytes have evolved serveral means of coping with these highly saline conditions. One adaptation is the development of succulence, the ability to store fresh water within tissue. Also, like desert plants, many marine halophytes have thick, waxy leaves. The stems and leaves of many halophytes are glaucous (covered with fine waxy powder) or have a coating of soft hairs to aid in the external absorption and storage of water. In addition, also like desert plants, some plants here have decreased the surface area that is exposed in order to minimize evaporation. Thus other halophytes have round stems and small, round leaves. The succulence and smoothness of the leaves also enable the plants to better resist physical damage that can be inflicted by wind and tides.

In osmosis, substances always move from where they are more concentrated to where the concentration is less. Thus some plants in a salt marsh obtain fresh water by concentrating salts in root cells above the amount in the surrounding water, enabling an inflow of fresh water.

Cordgrass
Spartina foliosa

Cordgrass has salt glands under the surface of its leaves. The glands remove salt from the plant sap and deposit it on the outside surface; these deposits appear as white crystals of salt.

Sea Milkwort
Glaux maritima

Sea Milkwort accumulates salts in special glands, and excretes or removes excess salt by leaf abscission or through root excretion.

Spike Grass
Distichlis spicata

Pacific Silverweed
Potentilla pacifica

Various species of pickleweed (*Salicornia*) and Spike Grass dominate the low salt marsh zone. The high salt marsh zone supports Pacific Silverweed, as well as grasses (*Deschampsia*) and sedges (*Carex*), which cannot tolerate prolonged submersion in saltwater. The southern marshes (from northern California to Baja) harbor a large number of annuals that are found in more arid and temperate areas. Pickleweeds and Cordgrass are prominent; five other common species are known only within this range.

The vegetation undergoes a transition in nothern California. About a dozen plants are typical of the coastal marshes farther

Seaside Arrowgrass
Triglochin maritimum

Salt Rush
Juncus balticus

Tufted Hair Grass
Deschampsia sespitosa

Saltmarsh Bulrush
Scirpus robustus

Creeping Alkali Grass
Puccinelia phryganodes

Bear Sedge
Carex ursina

Jaumea
Jaumea carnosa

Dodder
Cuscuta salina

Brass Buttons
Cotula corenopifolia

Saltmarsh Sand Spurry
Spergularia marina

north, in Oregon and Washington. These include *Carex lyngbya,* a sedge, Seaside Arrowgrass, Salt Rush, Tufted Hair Grass, Spike Grass, Pacific Silverweed, and Saltmarsh Bulrush.

Another transition occurs between the marshes of Washington and Oregon and the Arctic marshes. Creeping Alkali Grass becomes dominant on the Alaskan marshes, but grades into Bear Sedge in southwestern areas of the state.

Several marsh species have a wide-ranging distribution, occurring from Point Barrow, Alaska, to Cabo San Lucas in Baja California. These species are Spikegrass, pickleweed, Jaumea, Dodder, Brass Buttons, Saltmarsh Sand Spurry, and Saltmarsh Bulrush. Dodder is a yellow, parasitic plant that grows as a long, thin, branching, weblike or threadlike formation in patches of pickleweeds.

The salt marsh not only serves as an important part of the food web and provides a habitat for a diverse community of life forms; it also moderates the effects of erosion and siltation, and acts as a flood control and a pollution buffer. Salt marshes can absorb runoff and can trap and degrade organic waste. When heavy runoff carrying sewage and septic-tank seepage enters an estuary, the salt marsh acts as a sponge. It slows the water and absorbs most of the waste material, allowing the water to enter the estuary gradually enough for the organic material to be decomposed and its nutrients used.

A recent study performed in Florida showed that a 1500-acre salt marsh can remove all of the nitrogen and one-fourth of the phosphorus from the domestic sewage produced by 62,000 people. However, each salt marsh has a certain limit, or carrying capacity, for sewage; if this capacity is exceeded, unaesthetic conditions and the eventual collapse of the marsh ecosystem result. A healthy salt marsh makes the water cleaner and more productive for estuarine organisms.

Wharves and Pilings

The web of life on a wharf is exceedingly complex. Although the wooden pilings of floating docks and wharves do not technically constitute a separate biological habitat, they nonetheless provide a very good place to observe a number of animals and plants that are normally found at lower levels of the intertidal zone. And such places also often harbor creatures —such as the infamous shipworms—that are seldom found in other environments.

Floating docks are usually built in protected places away from wave action. Where the water is fairly clear, attached animals and plants, as well as fishes, jellyfishes, and shrimps, may be readily observed swimming near the surface. Among the organisms that often live attached to floats are certain seaweeds, sponges, hydroids, sea anemones, tube-dwelling worms, barnacles, mussels, tunicates, sea urchins, sea cucumbers, and sea stars. As the seasons progress, or over the course of many years, a succession of life forms appears. With the help of a magnifying lens or a low-power microscope, the details of smaller animals and a host of microscopic forms can be seen. Some of these creatures live in tight associations with other animals, in either symbiotic or predatory relationships.

Sea Lettuce
Ulva lactuca
495

Sugar Wrack
Laminaria saccharina
494

Winged Kelp
Alaria spp.
489

Color Changer
Desmarestia lingulata

Californian Mussel
Mytilus californianus
68

Blue Mussel
Mytilus edulis
69

Bushy Wine-glass
Hydroids
Obelia spp.
482

Tiny Sea Spider
Halosoma viridintestinale

Giant Acorn Barnacle
Balanus nubilis
462, 466

Feathery Hydroid
Aglaophenia spp.
485, 486

Green Giant Anemone
Anthopleura xanthogrammica
440

Stearns' Sea Spider
Pycnogonum stearnsi
357

Stiff-footed Sea Cucumber
Eupentacta quinquesemita
424

False Pacific Jingle Shell
Pododesmus macrochisma
89

Kelp Crab
Pugettia producta

Algae
A number of species of seaweeds that usually occur in the lower intertidal or subtidal levels of the rocky intertidal habitat are also found on floats and piers. One of the most common green seaweeds is Sea Lettuce; the most conspicuous brown seaweed is Sugar Wrack. Other large brown seaweeds, such as Alaria, or Winged Kelp (*Alaria* spp.), and the Color Changer, are also found. The Color Changer contains sulfuric acid in its tissues and may bleach or dissolve organisms that come into contact with it—hence its common name. A beautiful red alga found around piers *Polyneura latissima* is characterized by an elaborate network of veins. Other finely branched, lacy red seaweeds, both delicate and beautiful, also occur here. And, in addition to the large seaweeds, many microscopic plants, or diatoms, are also present.

The types of animals and plants that live on the wharves and pilings along the Pacific Coast are determined by the degree of their exposure to wave action, extreme temperatures, oxygen, pollution, salinity, and nutrients. Zonation, although apparent, is not as striking as on the wharves and pilings on the Atlantic Coast. The highest zone occurring on exposed pilings often contains barnacles, a few California Mussels, sea anemones belonging to the genus *Anthopleura,* and a few rock crabs (*Pachygrapsus* spp.). On protected pilings, the Blue Mussel may replace the California Mussel.

Clusters of *Obelia* and *Clytia,* colonial hydroids, may be found in the upper and lower zones; the medusae, or free-swimming stages, of these animals are beautiful although minute. The Tiny Sea Spider feeds on the *Obelia* hydroids. This creature's green insides can be plainly seen through its transparent legs. Other colonial animals belonging to the phyla Entoprocta and Bryozoa may also be seen on pilings; some of these look like brown furry mats.

The Giant Acorn Barnacle, the largest barnacle on the West Coast, sometimes grows slightly below the highest zone of exposed pilings. The beautiful Feathery Hydroids and green sea anemones grow on empty barnacle shells. The most common sea spider is Stearns' Sea Spider, which is white to pale salmon in color; it can also be found on empty barnacle shells. Its larvae are somewhat parasitic, as they feed on the juices of hydroids and sea anemones.

In the lower zone of exposed pilings, starfish are plentiful. The white Stiff-footed Sea Cucumber and the False Pacific Jingle Shell also occur in this lower zone, along with the beautiful Frilled Anemone. The Kelp Crab, although fairly common here, is often overlooked, as it exactly matches the color of some of the large brown algae to which it clings. A Kelp Crab that has a leathery, sacklike protrusion on its abdomen is a rare find; this is the external, egg-bearing portion of a peculiar parasitic barnacle, *Heterosaccus californicus*. This barnacle is so modified for parasitic life that, were it not for its free-swimming larval stages, it would not be recognized as a barnacle at all, or perhaps even as an arthropod. Similar parasites of the same group are sometimes found on other crabs, including hermit crabs.

Thick-clawed Porcelain Crab
Pachycheles rudis
333

The Thick-clawed Porcelain Crab, which is found along the entire length of the Pacific Coast, resembles the porcelain crabs of rocky shores (members of the genus *Petrolisthes*), except that it has a larger, fatter abdomen and rough granulations on the upper surface of its big claws. The Thick-clawed Porcelain Crab seeks crevices and nooks for shelter, and is often at home in the discarded shells of barnacles.

Feather-duster worms are a spectacular part of the communities around wharfs and pilings. These annelid worms live in parchmentlike sandy tubes—which sometimes exceed a foot in length—and have large, bushy plumes of tentacles, in various shades of brown, yellow, purple, or red; which are used for respiration and plankton-feeding. Feather-duster worms often occur in masses with hydroids, sponges, and bryozoans that are attached to the bases of the tubes; other associates include nudibranchs, skeleton shrimps, and other tube worms.

Tubularian Hydroids
Tubularia crocea
481

California Stichopus
Parastichopus californicus
430

Club Tunicate
Styela clava

Sea Vase
Ciona intestinalis

Pacific Shipworm
Bankia setacea
187

Common Shipworm
Teredo navalis
188

In the extreme lower zone of protected pilings, enormous bushy clusters of Tubularian Hydroids may be found; this creature occurs in delicate shades of pink or red. Various kinds of crabs may be seen, along with several sea cucumber species; one of the largest in the Puget Sound area is the huge California Stichopus. Tunicates, or sea squirts, attach themselves to the pilings by means of a continuous "tunic," which covers the body. Two tunicates common to this habitat are the Club Tunicate and the Sea Vase, which has green siphons.

A few shipworms are present on the Pacific Coast. One species native to wharves and pilings of this area is the giant Pacific Shipworm, which is actually a clam. The larva drills a hole in the wood and grows, bores, or rasps its way through by rotating; in this way, it can follow the grain and avoid knots. A heavy attack of shipworms will reduce a new, untreated piling to the point of collapse in just six months. The Common Shipworm has become quite a pest on the West Coast. This creature rasps the wood with its shell. Its chief food is plankton, which it filters through its respiratory mechanism.

Other creatures pose a threat to the pilings as well. Gribbles, small crustaceans related to the common sow bugs and pill bugs familiar to gardeners, chew their way into wood exposed to marine water and apparently digest the cellulose. Concrete jackets used for protection in the Los Angeles harbor were penetrated by hordes of Flat-tipped Piddocks, another boring clam.

Flat-tipped Piddock
Penitella penita
72

Despite the rather limited nature of these manmade habitats, wharves and pilings nonetheless can be seen to support diverse communities of plants and animals. These environments have proven to be worthy of close observation.

PROTECTED MARINE ENVIRONMENTS: ANIMALS AND PLANTS

COASTAL WATERS: BEYOND THE INTERTIDAL ZONE

The coastal waters overlying the continental shelves are far richer in plant and animal life than is the open ocean beyond. Although comprising only about seven percent of the world's ocean area, they support more than ninety percent of the most productive fisheries. In such places, the sea floor also supports a rich bottom life, or benthos.

Waters that occur close to shore, along the open coast, or over shallow banks farther from shore are high-energy environments that are subject to active wave surge. This wave action sweeps away the fine sediments present, leaving sandy bottoms or exposed, rocky areas.

Life in the Kelp Beds

Along open coasts, water ranging from eighteen to ninety feet deep supports beds or forests of giant kelp, very large seaweeds belonging to the brown algae group. Large kelp beds moderate wave action significantly and help protect the beaches behind them from wave erosion. From central California southward, the kelp beds are mostly dominated by *Macrocystis*, while to the north, another kind of kelp, *Nereocystis*, becomes more important, although both occur over most of the range. These kelps are anchored to the rocky or sandy bottom by large, rootlike holdfasts. The long, often intertwined stipes, or stems, extend to the water's surface, where the fronds form a dense canopy. The canopy formed by *Macrocystis* consists of slender, ropy extensions of the stem; these bear small, leaflike blades all along their length, each of which has a gas bladder at its base. The long, hollow stem of the Bull Kelp ends in a single, inflated bulb or gas bladder, from the end of which numerous long, flat, straplike blades extend into the water. A third large seaweed, elk kelp (*Pelagophycus*), is sometimes found in southern California; it usually grows along the outer fringes of *Macrocystis* beds. When they are seen from a diver's point of view, kelp forests are extraordinarily impressive and beautiful. The giant columns of intertwined stipes rise from the dim depths like tree trunks or the columns of some great cathedral. The dense canopy filters out much of the light, but ever-changing shafts of sunshine penetrate the depths below. The whole system sways gently with the surging of waves passing through it, and numerous strangely shaped and colored fishes can be seen moving about.

The most extensive, spectacular, and best studied kelp beds occur along the coast of California. Some of these are several square miles in size and are harvested commercially for their alginates—gelatinous substances that are used extensively as thickeners and emulsion stabilizers in a wide variety of industries.

Kelp forests provide a variety of habitats for fishes, which are abundant and diverse in these waters. Only a few fish species found in and around kelp beds are exclusively kelp dwellers; many others are attracted to these areas by the abundant food. Of the more than 150 species of fishes known to live along the California coast, most can be found in kelp beds at one time or

Bull Kelp
Nereocystis luetkeana
493

California Scorpionfish
Scorpaena guttata
253

Lingcod
Ophiodon elongatus
247

Painted Greenling
Oxylebius pictus

Island Kelpfish
Alloclinus holderi

Giant Sea Bass
Stereolepis gigas
237

Rubberlip Seaperch
Rhacochilus toxotes
271

California Sheephead
Semicossyphus pulcher
257, 264

Kelp Bass
Paralabrax clathratus
238

Garibaldi
Hypsypops rubicundus
259, 260

Topsmelt
Atherinops affinis
294

Señorita
Oxyjulis californica
265

Blacksmith
Chromis punctipinnis

Halfmoon
Medialuna californiensis
275

Lacy-crust Bryozoan
Membranipora membranacea

California Spiral-tufted
Bryozoan
Bugula californica

Sea Otter
Enhydra lutris
234

another. Fifty to sixty species are common, but only fifteen to twenty are abundant and conspicuous enough to be regularly seen by divers. The composition of the fish community varies according to time and place, depending on such things as the season, the type of bottom, and the depth of the water. Fishes can be grouped according to their feeding habits. Some forage on the bottom between the holdfasts. California Morays, California Scorpionfish, several species of rockfish (*Sebastes* spp.), and Lingcod live on the bottom in almost continuous contact with the substrate, preying on other fish o sizable invertebrates. So do Painted Greenling, sculpins, and Island Kelpfish, which feed on smaller prey.

Several fishes spend most of their time cruising about above the substrate looking for choice food items, which they pick off of the stipes or canopy of the kelp. Among these are the Giant Sea Bass, which may attain a weight of 400 pounds. Several medium-sized, somewhat less impressive fish, also forage in this way, including the Pile Perch, Rubberlip Seaperch, California Sheephead, Kelp Bass, and the beautiful, bright golden Garibaldi.

Still other fishes—Topsmelt, Señorita, Blacksmith, and Halfmoon—take refuge in the kelp, feeding largely on plankton or other small organisms. Certain species browse the kelp forest from top to bottom, picking off small organisms wherever they can be found.

Invertebrates are also numerous in the kelp forests. Kelp holdfasts provide protection for a wide variety of sponges, worms, small arthropods, bryozoans, peanut worms, brittle stars, sea cucumbers, and others. Bryozoans—such as the Lacy-crust Bryozoan and the California Spiral-tufted Bryozoan —form colonies on the blades. Colorful nudibranchs may often be found among the fronds.

Sea urchins are active herbivores and thus can cause extensive damage to the kelp forests when they occur in large numbers. They chew off the stipes near the holdfast, and the detached kelp either drifts away or is washed up on nearby beaches. Normally, this phenomenon occurs in a rather extended cycle the sea urchins either die or migrate to other places after the kelp has been denuded, thus allowing the kelp bed to eventually reestablish itself. Off some southern California shores, where the waters are enriched by municipal sewage, the urchins are apparently able to survive by absorbing dissolved nutrients from the water. They then crop off new kelp starts as fast as they are formed and thereby prevent the reestablishment of the beds. This process has forced a kelp harvesting company in San Diego to take measures to control the sea urchins. Where Sea Otter populations have been reconstituted, as in the Monterey Bay area, the otters do a good job of keeping the sea urchins in check. Unfortunately the Sea Otters also feast upon abalones (*Haliotis* spp.)—a hab that brings them into conflict with abalone hunters.

Inshore Rocky Bottoms

Because kelps grow mostly on rocky substrates, nearshore

rocky bottoms support fish and invertebrate faunas similar to those of the kelp beds along the open coasts. Like the kelp forests farther out, these inshore areas contain diverse microhabitats, where small fish can hide and larger ones can forage. The myriads of plankton-feeding invertebrates in both of these habitats provide abundant and varied food for fish. Nearshore rocky areas are home to a large proportion of crevice- and cave-dwelling fishes, such as sculpins, blennies, gunnels, pricklebacks, and eels. The most conspicuous fishes, however, are those that roam over the substrate in schools or loose aggregations, looking for invertebrates. These are mostly surfperches, rockfishes, wrasses, porgies, and drums.

Most of the fish in these habitats, and most of the invertebrates as well, produce great numbers of pelagic or oceanic, larvae. This means that new areas can be rapidly colonized. An interesting example of this is found off southern California, where certain extended sewage-outfall pipes go beyond the rocky areas, across several miles of muddy bottom. These have formed spectacular, very narrow reefs, which harbor large populations of invertebrates and fishes that would otherwise be rare or absent in the area. Deliberately constructed concrete reefs, old automobile bodies, and sunken boats can also quickly increase the populations of such fish in muddy-bottomed bays or along sandy bottoms adjacent to open shoreline.

Offshore rocky bottoms that are deeper than about 165 feet are the most poorly known of all marine habitats because of the difficulties involved in sampling or studying them closely. Certain fishes that are considered rare may in fact be fairly abundant in such habitats. The fishes most frequently taken from such areas include various scorpion fish species, such as Pacific Ocean Perch and several rockfishes. Some of these move into the upper water levels at night to feed on the larger planktonic crustacea, which also move up at night to feed on the abundant smaller plankton in the upper layers of water. Here they are taken by commerical fishermen. In the Gulf of Alaska, the standing crop of Pacific Ocean Perch was once estimated at more than half a billion pounds. Between 1963 and 1968, commercial fishing reduced this stock by sixty percent.

Pacific Ocean Perch
Sebastes alutus

Soft Bottoms
On the continental shelf, most of the bottom is soft and rather monotonous; it is covered with sand, sandy mud, or silt, bits of broken shell, and other fine materials. Inshore areas are usually covered with coarse materials such as sand and shell fragments. This gives way to sandy or fine mud in basins and the deeper, offshore waters, but some of these areas are harder and more consolidated than others.

Where soft bottoms occur, the number of species of fishes and invertebrates drops off sharply. The species present are rather consistently correlated with bottom type and depth, probably because of specialized feeding habits.

Only about fifty species of fishes are found on soft bottoms, of

which fifteen to twenty are regularly caught. Two to five
species make up the bulk of the fish biomass. Many demersal
(bottom-dwelling) fishes occur in relatively narrow depth
ranges. However, those found at depths greater than 300 feet
tend to range out to sea over much greater ranges of depth
than do most of those living on the shelf proper.

The invertebrates found on sandy bottoms include sand
dollars, the burrowing Heart Urchin, fat ophiliid worms,
some clams and scallops, flatfishes (such as English Sole), and
sanddabs. Finer sediments support a greater variety of burrow
dwellers and substrate ingesters: worms, bivalves, sea
cucumbers, sea pens, basket stars, commercial shrimps, several
species of flatfishes, and small octopuses and squids.

Heart Urchin
Lovenia cordiformis
377

English Sole
Parophrys vetulus
308

Open Waters
In the deeper, open waters offshore, the upper part of the
water column is an enormous, nearly featureless realm. Since
this area lacks diversity of the habitats on the bottom, it is
inhabited by a limited number of species. Less than two
percent of all known species of fish occur here; most of them
are concentrated over the continental shelves, because these
waters are much richer in plankton and other organisms. In
spite of the paucity of species, several of the fishes pulled from
these waters are considered among the most valuable sport or
commercial fish, either because they occur in enormous
numbers or because they are especially desirable as food.

Among the most important commercial species are small
plankton-feeding fishes that occur in immense schools—such
as Pacific Herring, Northern Anchovy, and Pacific Sardine.
These are also very important food for certain larger predators.
Most pelagic fishes and squids have streamlined bodies that
permit continuous, rapid swimming. They are usually silvery
or white on the sides and bottom, and bluish or greenish
above; this coloration renders them less visible from any angle.
The majority of fishes and squids in open waters are predators.
Because they rely on vision, they are found in the upper 200
to 300 feet, where they can see their prey. Furthermore, most
of the creatures upon which they prey—plankton, and larger
fish and invertebrates feeding on the plankton—also live
farther up in the water column.

Pacific Herring
Clupea harengus pallasi
289

Northern Anchovy
Engraulis mordax
295

Pacific Sardine
Sardinops sagax

Predatory fishes feed largely on these small fishes, on the larger
crustacean plankton, and on squids. They are typically large
and have smooth, spindle-shaped bodies, deeply forked tails,
and large mouths with many sharp teeth. Some of the familiar
predators are sharks, tunas, mackerels, jacks, billfishes, and
salmons. The cooler, northern waters tend to be dominated by
the salmons and their relatives, while in the warmer ocean
waters, tunas and billfishes are foremost. These fishes move
north and south according to seasonal changes in surface water
temperatures; they perform extended east-west migrations as
well.

Salmons are particularly interesting. These important sport
and commercial fishes migrate extensively throughout the
North Pacific as adults, returning to freshwater rivers and

streams—often traveling far inland—to spawn. This habit of the salmons gives rise to a great variety of problems and controversies with respect to land and water uses that may affect their spawning streams—and even to international jurisdictional disputes.

Squids are also important—both as predators and as food for many fishes, marine birds, and mammals. The best-known squid along the West Coast is the Opalescent Squid. Large schools of this species are found in inshore shelf waters and around kelp beds.

Opalescent Squid
Loligo opalescens
381

Pelagic Birdlife

Birds that spend long periods at sea must develop special adaptations to meet their water needs, given the lack of fresh water. Like fish, they do this in two ways: by means of special salt-excreting mechanisms, and by increasing the concentration and thus reducing the quantity of their urine in order to conserve water. They can drink seawater; they excrete excess salt from enlarged nasal glands.

The birds that are most thoroughly adapted to marine life include members of the order Procellariiformes, which are sometimes called tube-nosed swimmers. These range from the huge, long-winged, web-footed Wandering Albatross of southern oceans, which has a wingspan of twelve feet, to the smallest storm-petrels, which are no longer than a songbird. These seabirds have a unique feature: Their nostrils are situated in raised tubes on the bill. It has been suggested that this probably channels air over the olfactory organs in the nasal membranes. Tube-noses have a sense of smell so acute that they can track fish and squid underwater.

Wandering Albatross
Diomedea exulans

Black-footed Albatross
Diomedea nigripes
548

The Black-footed Albatross may be seen flying over the waters off the Pacific Coast most often during summer and fall. Once thought to be the only member of this family that occurred in North America, it is smaller than its exotic cousin, the Wandering Albatross; but with a wingspan of seven feet, the Black-footed is still one of the largest birds in the Pacific.

Pink-footed Shearwater
Puffinus creatopus
546

The related shearwaters are smaller than albatrosses, but no less adept at foraging over the high seas. The Pink-footed Shearwater is fairly common over the outer continental shelf, sometimes occurring in flocks of fifty or more birds. Along with many other pelagic birds, the Pink-footed Shearwater follows fishing vessels in the hope of turning up a meal.

Least Storm-Petrel
Oceanodroma microsoma

One of the smallest birds of the open western waters is the Least Storm-Petrel, which only grows to about six inches. An irregular visitor to the waters off southern California, this dark little bird makes its home in the San Benitos Islands, which are west of Baja California in the Pacific.

Double-crested Cormorant
Phalacrocorax auritus
533

Brandt's Cormorant
Phalacrocorax penicillatus
534

Several species of cormorants occur offshore along the Pacific Coast. Double-crested Cormorants often fly high above the water; their long tails and long heads distinguish them, as does their flight posture—the long neck is held in a distinctly crooked position as the bird flies. Brandt's Cormorant is a fairly large, sturdy-looking bird. It can often be seen feeding in the nearshore waters along the Pacific, making shallow

Pelagic Cormorant
Phalacrocorax pelagicus
532

California Gull
Larus californicus
595

Thayer's Gull
Larus thayeri
592

Western Gull
Larus occidentalis
596

Black-legged Kittiwake
Rissa tridactyla
593

Red-legged Kittiwake
Rissa brevirostris

dives for fish. The Pelagic Cormorant is smaller and rather slender. At home in the cooler waters of the North Pacific, Pelagics are capable of making very deep dives for their food. In flight, this bird can be recognized by its slim profile and long, thin, straight neck.

In winter, the California Gull is one member of the family of gulls and terns that may be seen wheeling and diving over offshore waters. This gray-and-white winter visitor is smaller than Thayer's Gull, which also spends the winter on the Pacific Coast. The Western Gull is resident all year round; it breeds on offshore islands, and is the only widespread, dark-backed gull on the West Coast.

The Black-legged and Red-legged kittiwakes are more pelagic than many of the other gulls. Kittiwakes have a distinctive style of flight, gliding and banking more frequently than many of the larger gulls, and diving readily to the surface of the water for food.

Marine Mammals

No group of animals has inspired the imagination of human beings more than whales and dolphins. Indeed, there seems to be a mystical bond between us—a kinship of sorts that has been recognized in art, legend, and literature. Like us, these marine mammals are warm-blooded and fur-bearing; they nurse their young and are very intelligent. Yet marine mammals are remarkably adapted to an environment in which we are nearly helpless, and about which we know very little—despite all our ingenious technology.

The abundance of marine mammals off our Pacific shores reflects the vast food resources in the waters extending from the Aleutian Islands to the tip of Baja California and west to the Hawaiian Leeward Islands. In spring, the shallow bowl of the Arctic Ocean experiences a brief and explosive bloom of algae, making it one of the most productive areas in the world for phytoplankton. And because of the intensive nutrient mixing during sunlit months, the Bering Sea is the richest of all fisheries of its size. It has the largest clam beds and one of the largest salmon runs in the world.

As a result, numerous and diverse marine mammals inhabit this enormous region, and about one sixth of the thirty-eight species found here occur nowhere else in the world. They have adapted to a multitude of habitats, from frigid, icebound shores to warm subtropical shoals, and some migrate between the two.

Humpback Whale
Megaptera novaeangliae
198, 218

Gray Whale
Eschrichtius robustus
193, 217

Sperm Whale
Physeter catodon
215

Killer Whale
Orcinus orca
201, 209

In summer the great baleen whales sieve for crustaceans and small fishes in northern waters, traveling south in winter to breed and calve in more temperate waters. Similarly, the Humpback Whale calves in warm waters off Hawaii and Mexico, then travels north to Glacier Bay to feed on krill (planktonic crustaceans and larvae) and herring. The Gray Whale has the longest migration of all mammals, traveling from its summer feeding areas in the Arctic to lagoons off Mexico each year. The Sperm Whale, or "Cachalot," plumbs submarine canyons off California for giant squid. Killer

Minke Whale
Balaenoptera acutorostrata
194, 222

Blue Whale
Balaenoptera musculus
197, 219

White Whale
Delphinapterus leucas

Narwhal
Monodon monoceros

Whales ply the salmon-rich waters off British Columbia, and schools of dolphins and porpoises frolic from the Gulf of California to the Gulf of Alaska.

Whales, dolphins, and porpoises—the cetaceans—are divided into two large groups, the baleen whales, or Mysticetes, and the toothed whales, or Odontocetes. Baleen whales range in size from the Minke Whale, which grows to a length of thirty feet, to the Blue Whale, which, at one hundred feet, is the largest animal that has ever lived. Some of these reach speeds of forty miles per hour in short bursts.

Baleen whales feed by straining massive amounts of plankton and larvae from the water; the special baleen plates in their mouths act like a giant colander, retaining the tiny animals but allowing the sea water to be returned to the ocean.

The Gray Whale, which is probably the most familiar to West Coast whale-watchers, is the most primitive baleen whale; it has only 160 shore baleen plates on each side of its jaw, compared with 300 for most species in this group.

The toothed whales include the beaked and sperm whales and two species of arctic-oriented whales, the White Whale (or "Beluga"), and the Narwhal. Also included in this group are the Killer Whales, dolphins, and porpoises.

Cetaceans are well equipped to capture deep ocean prey. Members of the rorqual family can dive up to 1150 feet and remain submerged for up to fifty minutes, although they usually don't need to, given that the krill on which they feed is located in the upper layers of water.

Record dives are held by toothed whales. Sperm Whales in pursuit of giant squid have become entangled in cables on the ocean floor as deep as 3700 feet, and they are able to stay submerged as long as seventy-five minutes. This amazing diving ability is made possible by several changes in their breathing patterns. Although the lung capacity of whales, relative to their size, is only about half that of land animals, eighty to ninety percent of the air in the lungs is replaced in a rapid blow, compared with only ten to twenty percent in land animals. Modification of the capacity of blood and lungs to absorb and carry oxygen, combined with greatly increased myoglobin in the muscles, enables the whale to store much more oxygen. Also, a cetacean's muscles can function for a long time without oxygen. During a dive, the animal's heart rate decreases, and the blood bypasses nonessential organs. During deep dives, the small amount of air in the lungs is squeezed into special passages to prevent nitrogen from being absorbed into the blood.

Cetaceans are the only animals other than elephants that have larger brains than humans. This has sparked much speculation about their intelligence. In the deep offshore waters, where little light penetrates, hearing is the most important sense, and in cetaceans this too is well developed, aiding them in their search for food. Several species have demonstrated great capacity for learning and an uncanny ability to communicate. This ability is not well understood, and many aspects of the group's social life remain an intriguing mystery.

Ice floes, rocky islands, and isolated beaches of the Arctic and Pacific oceans serve as haul outs and breeding grounds for other marine mammals, the pinnipeds—which include seals, sea lions, and the Walrus. The Arctic Ocean provides various niches for a range of arctic seals. The Pribilof Islands of the Bering Sea are a breeding place for Northern Fur Seals, which gather yearly, forming the largest concentration of marine mammals. The Pacific Harbor Seal prefers sandy shores and inland waters of the Pacific between eastern Alaska and Oregon. Caves and cliffs along the Oregon coast furnish a protected habitat for the Steller Sea Lion. And San Miguel Island, off California, has one of the largest concentrations of pinniped species in the world.

The habitat of the Walrus consists of thousands of square miles of ice; at the water line, these massive brown animals slurp up clams from the bottom of cold northern seas. The Polar Bear also inhabits arctic ice packs.

The Sea Otter is king of the kelp forests from the Aleutians to California. Once common along the northern parts of the coast, Sea Otters were nearly exterminated by fur traders. Ironically, their return was hastened by the testing of large nuclear bombs on Amchitka Island in the Aleutians; the otters were then transplanted to safer regions farther south. Sea otters roll over and over in the water as part of their ceaseless preening behavior; lacking a blubber layer, these mammals depend on air bubbles trapped in their fur to keep them warm.

Following the North Pacific-California current south along the Pacific Coast and on out to sea, in the open ocean beyond the breakers are several forms of life most equipped to ride out the heavy seas. Bull Kelp anchored far offshore bobs in the waves, with sea birds resting atop it. The bull whip and giant kelps form beds that serve as refuge and home for hundreds of marine animals. Seals, sea lions, and an occasional Sea Otter may be seen bobbing along with the bulbs of the kelp. The grotesque Northern Elephant Seal, which—like the Sea Otter —is making a comeback after near extinction, is occasionally found as far north as Cape Arago, Oregon.

Appreciation of the behavioral and physiological characteristics of marine mammals had led to interest in their ancient origins, and the descent of sea mammals from their terrestrial ancestors has only partly been unraveled. The clearest fossil records date from the late Oligocene and early Miocene, twenty-five million years ago. Hundreds of different forms have been discovered at a site called Pyramid Hill in California's San Joaquin Valley. An otterlike pinniped represents a "missing link" between the terrestrial ancestors of bears and some of the eared sea lions. The discovery of these fossils also established the fact that, although seals and sea lions are superficially similar, they are not very closely related to each other.

Although sea mammals have managed to adapt remarkably to the many challenges of ocean living, their greatest challenge is that of human exploitation. The intense hunting of whaling days greatly depleted many populations of sea mammals: One species, the Steller Sea Cow, was brought to extinction only twenty-seven years after its discovery. Slow-moving and unafraid, this huge seaweed grazer provided meat for Russian hunters and for European and American whalers seeking furs and oil.

Bowhead Whale
Balaena mysticetus

Right Whale
Eubalaena glacialis
196, 216

Guadalupe Fur Seal
Arctocephalus townsendi
226

Bryde's Whale
Balaenoptera edeni

Marine mammals are now partially protected by domestic and international regulations; nonetheless, it will take many years to rebuild strong populations of the endangered Bowhead, Right, Blue, and Humpback whales, and the endangered Guadalupe Fur Seal. Sperm, Bryde's, and Minke whales are still hunted by the Soviets and Japanese, and Soviet catcher boats hunt Gray Whales to provide meat for Siberian villages. Many species are taken for scientific research.

Although public awareness and interest in marine mammals have promoted conservation efforts, there is still a great deal of conflict regarding their protection, and much remains to be done in their behalf.

COASTAL WATERS: ANIMALS

1 Coastline

Near Prince Rupert, British Columbia

Rocky Shores

2 Beach with Bullwhip Kelp

Pacific Rim National Park, Vancouver Island, British Columbia

Rocky Shores

3 Coastline

Queen Charlotte Islands, British Columbia

Rocky Shores

4 Forested island
Willapa Bay, Washington

Bays and Estuaries

5 Cordgrass and other marshland grasses
Northern Willapa Bay, Washington

Bays and Estuaries

6 Rialto Beach
Olympic National Park, Washington

Beaches

7 Arch Rock
Boardman State Park, Oregon

Rocky Shores

8 Seastacks
Cape Sebastian State Park, Oregon

Rocky Shores

9 Coastline
Cape Kiwanda, Oregon

Rocky Shores

10 Sandy Beach   Oregon Dunes National Recreation Area

Sand Dunes

11 Shore with   Oregon Dunes National Recreation Area
European Beach Grass

Sand Dunes

12 Hummocks formed   Near Cape Sebastian, Oregon
by Beach Grass

Sand Dunes

13 Endert's Beach   Redwood National Park, California

Beaches

14 Coastline   San Francisco area, California

Cliffs

15 Surfgrass and algae on rocks at low tide   Monterey Bay, California

Bays and Estuaries

16 Coast with Monterey Cypress

Monterey, California

Cliffs

17 Saltmarsh Dodder on Pickleweed

Point Reyes, California

Bays and Estuaries

18 Coastline

Carmel, California

Rocky Shores

19 Pinnacle Cove — Point Lobos State Reserve, California

Rocky Shores

20 Coastline — Point Lobos State Reserve, California

Rocky Shores

21 Stormy Seas — Big Sur, California

Rocky Shores

22 Coastline

Davenport, California

Cliffs

23 Salt Marsh

Morro Bay, California

Bays and Estuaries

24 Morro Rock

Morro Bay, California

Oceanic Island

HOW TO USE THE COLOR PLATES

The color plates on the following pages include seven major groups of animals and plants: seashells, mammals, fishes, seashore creatures, seaweeds and algae, birds, and wildflowers.

Table of Contents
For easy reference, a table of contents precedes the color plates. The table is divided into two sections. On the left, we list each major group of animals or plants. On the right, the major groups are usually subdivided into smaller groups, and each small group is illustrated by a symbol. For example, the large group of seashore creatures is divided into small groups made up of similar animals, such as crabs or octopuses and squids. Similarly, the large group of fishes is divided into small groups, such as eel-like fishes or flatfishes.

Captions for the Color Plates
The black bar above each color plate contains the following information: the plate number, the common and scientific names of the animal or plant, its dimensions, and the page number of the full species description. To the left of each color plate, the habitats where you are likely to encounter the species are always indicated in blue type. Additionally, you will find either an important fact, such as the phylum and class of a seashore creature (also in blue type), or a range map.
The chart on the facing page lists the dimensions given and the blue-type information or map provided for each major group of animals or plants.

CAPTION INFORMATION

Dimensions   Blue Type/Art

Seashells
Length, width, or height   Specific habitat

Mammals
Length of adult   Range map or
                                                range description

Fishes
Maximum length of adult   Specific habitat

Seashore Creatures
Length, width, or height   Phylum and class

Seaweeds and Algae
Height or length   Specific habitat

Birds
Length, usually of adult male, from   Range map
tip of bill to tail   showing breeding,
                                                winter, and/or
                                                permanent range

Wildflowers
Plant height and flower length or   Flowering time
width

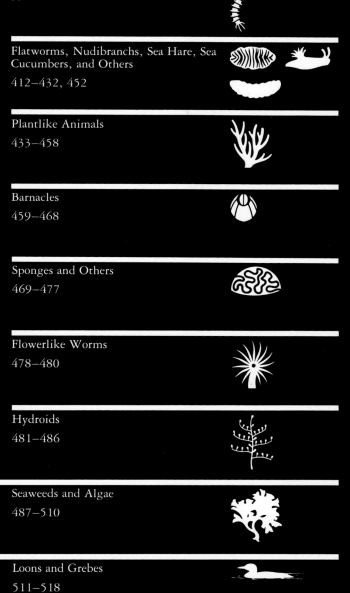

25 Pacific Orb Diplodon

Diplodonta orbella
p. 323

Length: ⅜–1⅜"

Rocky Shores

Habitat
Under rocks or in empty
bivalve shells

26 Common Pacific Egg Cockle

Laevicardium
substriatum
p. 323

Length: ¾–1⅜"

Bays and Estuaries

Habitat
In sand

27 Amethyst Gem Clam

Gemma gemma
p. 323

Length: ⅛"

Beaches; Bays and Estuaries

Habitat
On sand or mud flats

28 Californian Mactra

Mactra californica
p. 324

Length: 1⅛–1⅞″

Bays and Estuaries

Habitat
Buried in sand flats or in sandy mud

29 Carpenter's Tellin

Tellina carpenteri
p. 324

Length: ½–⅝″

Bays and Estuaries

Habitat
In sand or sandy mud

30 Gould's Wedge Shell

Donax gouldii
p. 325

Length: ⅝–⅞″

Beaches

Habitat
In sand

31 Carpenter's Cardita

Glans subquadrata
p. 325

Length: ¼–½″

Rocky Shores

Habitat
Attached to undersides of rocks

32 Giant Pacific Cockle

Trachycardium quadrigenarium
p. 326

Height: 2¼–5½″

Bays and Estuaries

Habitat
In firm, sandy mud

33 Nuttall's Cockle

Clinocardium nuttalli
p. 326

Length: 2–5½″

Bays and Estuaries

Habitat
In sand or mud

Glycymeris subobsoleta
p. 326

Length: ⅞–1½"

Offshore Waters

Habitat
In sand or gravel

Protothaca staminea
p. 327

Length: 1½–2⅜"

Bays and Estuaries

Habitat
In coarse, sandy mud

Tapes japonica
p. 327

Length: 1½–2½"

Bays and Estuaries

Habitat
In sandy mud

37 California Glass Mya
Cryptomya californica
p. 328
Length: ½–1⅛"

Bays and Estuaries

Habitat
In mud

38 Baltic Macoma
Macoma balthica
p. 328
Length: 1½"

Bays and Estuaries

Habitat
In mud or sandy mud

39 Salmon Tellin
Tellina nuculoides
p. 329
Length: ½–¾"

Bays and Estuaries

Habitat
In sand

40 Common Western Spoon Clam

Periploma planiusculum
p. 329

Length: 2½"

Beaches

Habitat
In sand

41 Californian Lucine

Epilucina californica
p. 330

Length: ¾–1½"

Rocky Shores, Beaches, and Offshore Waters

Habitat
In sand or gravelly rubble

42 La Perouse's Kellia

Kellia laperousi
p. 330

Length: ½–1⅛"

Rocky Shores; Wharves, Docks, and Pilings

Habitat
Among bivalves

43 Pismo Clam
Tivela stultorum
p. 330
Length: 2½–6¼"

Beaches

Habitat
In sand flats

44 Hemphill's Surf Clam
Spisula hemphilli
p. 331
Length: 2½–6"

Beaches

Habitat
In sand or sandy mud

45 Stimpson's Surf Clam
Spisula polynyma
p. 331
Length: 2¾–5½"

Beaches

Habitat
In sand, mud, or gravel

46 California Cumingia
Cumingia californica
p. 332
Length: ³⁄₄–1³⁄₈″

Rocky Shores
Habitat
In gravel and rock crevices

47 Pacific White Venus
Amiantis callosa
p. 332
Length: 2½–4½″

Beaches
Habitat
In sand

48 Common California Venus
Chione californiensis
p. 333
Length: 1½–3″

Bays and Estuaries; Offshore Waters
Habitat
In sand

49 Common Washington Clam
Saxidomus nuttalli
p. 333
Length: 2¾–4¾"

Rocky Shores and Beaches

Habitat
In sand

50 Bent-nose Macoma
Macoma nasuta
p. 334
Length: 1¼–3¼"

Bays and Estuaries

Habitat
In sandy mud

51 Pacific Grooved Macoma
Leporimetis obesa
p. 334
Length: 1⅝–3½"

Bays and Estuaries

Habitat
In sand or muddy sand

52 White Sand Macoma
Macoma secta
p. 334

Length: 2–4½″

Bays and Estuaries

Habitat
In sand or sandy mud

53 Rough Piddock
Zirfaea pilsbryi
p. 335

Length: 5¼″

Bays and Estuaries

Habitat
Thick mud, clay, or soft shale

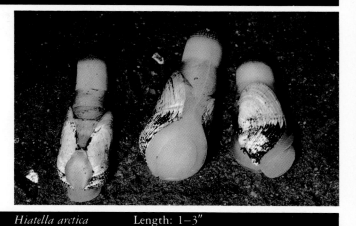

54 Arctic Saxicave
Hiatella arctica
p. 335

Length: 1–3″

Rocky Shores

Habitat
In crevices and old bore holes

55 Hearty Rupellaria

Rupellaria carditoides   Length: ¾–1¾"
p. 336

Rocky Shores

Habitat
In holes in soft rock

56 Pacific Gaper

Tresus nuttallii   Length: 5½–7½"
p. 336

Bays and Estuaries

Habitat
In sand and sandy mud

57 Geoduck

Panopea generosa   Length: 3½–9"
p. 337

Bays and Estuaries

Habitat
In sandy mud

Bays and Estuaries

Habitat
In heavy clay or soft shale

Bays and Estuaries

Habitat
In sand or mud

Bays and Estuaries

Habitat
In heavy mud, clay, and
peat

61 Pacific Razor Clam
Siliqua patula
p. 338

Length: 3–6¼"

Beaches

Habitat
In sand

62 Kelsey's Date Mussel
Lithophaga plumula kelseyi
p. 339

Length: 1–2⅜"

Rocky Shores and Offshore Waters

Habitat
In soft shale, thick mollusk shells, or coral

63 Rosy Jackknife Clam
Solen rosaceus
p. 339

Length: 1½–3"

Bays and Estuaries

Habitat
In sand

64 Transparent Razor Clam
Siliqua lucida
p. 340
Length: 1–1½"

Beaches

Habitat
In sand

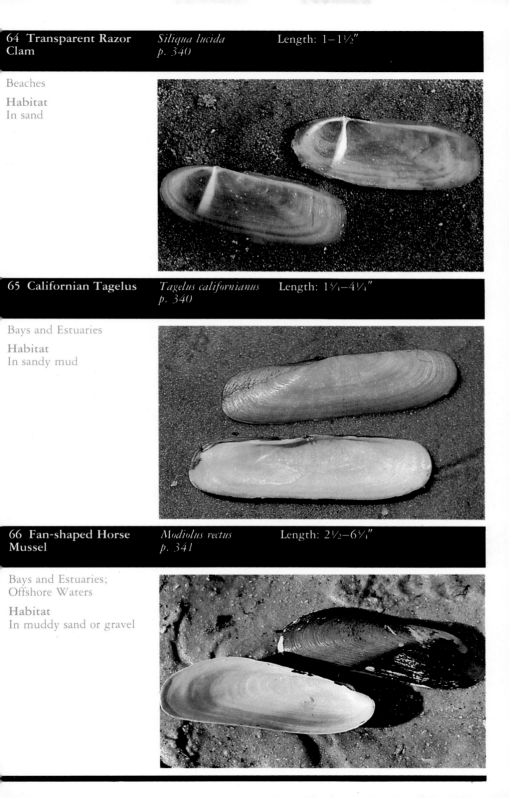

65 Californian Tagelus
Tagelus californianus
p. 340
Length: 1¾–4¼"

Bays and Estuaries

Habitat
In sandy mud

66 Fan-shaped Horse Mussel
Modiolus rectus
p. 341
Length: 2½–6¾"

Bays and Estuaries;
Offshore Waters

Habitat
In muddy sand or gravel

67 Northern Horse Mussel

Modiolus modiolus
p. 341

Length: 2–9″

Rocky Shores and Offshore Waters

Habitat
Among gravel and rocks

68 Californian Mussel

Mytilus californianus
p. 341

Length: 2–10″

Rocky Shores and Offshore Waters

Habitat
On rocks

69 Blue Mussel

Mytilus edulis
p. 342

Length: 1¼–4″

Rocky Shores; Bays and Estuaries; Wharves, Docks, and Pilings

Habitat
On rocks or wooden structures

70 Bifurcate Mussel
Septifer bifurcatus
p. 342
Length: ⅝–2″

Rocky Shores

Habitat
On undersides of rocks and in crevices

71 Stearns' Mussel
Hormomya adamsiana
p. 343
Length: ½–1″

Rocky Shores

Habitat
In crevices or under rocks

72 Flat-tipped Piddock
Penitella penita
p. 343
Length: 1¼–3″

Rocky Shores; Bays and Estuaries

Habitat
In clay and soft rock

73 Scale-sided Piddock
Parapholas californica
p. 344
Length: 3–5⅞"

Rocky Shores; Bays and
Estuaries

Habitat
In clay or shale or other
soft rock

74 Ribbed Horse Mussel
Ischadium demissum
p. 344
Length: 4"

Bays and Estuaries; Salt
Marshes

Habitat
On rocks

75 Black Musculus
Musculus niger
p. 345
Length: 1–2¼"

Rocky Shores; Bays and
Estuaries; Offshore Waters

Habitat
In muddy gravel

76 Ribbed Horse Mussel
Ischadium demissum Length: 4"
p. 344

Bays and Estuaries; Salt Marshes

Habitat
On rocks

77 Native Pacific Oyster
Ostrea lurida Length: 1½–3½"
p. 345

Bays and Estuaries

Habitat
On rocks and in mud flats and gravel bars

78 Giant Pacific Oyster
Cassostrea gigas Width: 2–12"
p. 346

Bays and Estuaries

Habitat
On rocks, soft mud, firm sand, or gravel

79 Japanese Abalone
Haliotis kamtschatkana
p. 346

Length: 4–6"

Rocky Shores

Habitat
Among rocks

80 Pink Abalone
Haliotis corrugata
p. 347

Length: 6–10"

Rocky Shores

Habitat
On rocks

81 Threaded Abalone
Haliotis assimilis
p. 347

Length: 4–6"

Rocky Shores

Habitat
On rocks

82 Green Abalone

Haliotis fulgens
p. 348

Length: 6–8″

Rocky Shores

Habitat
On rocks

83 Black Abalone

Haliotis cracherodii
p. 348

Length: 3–6″

Rocky Shores

Habitat
On rocks

84 Red Abalone

Haliotis rufescens
p. 348

Length: 8–12″

Rocky Shores

Habitat
On rocks

85 Onyx Slipper Shell   *Crepidula onyx*   Width: 1–2″
p. 349

Rocky Shores and Offshore
Waters

Habitat
On rocks, other shells, or
stacked on top of one
another

**86 Pacific Half-slipper
Shell**   *Crepipatella lingulata*   Width: ½–⅞″
p. 349

Rocky Shores and Offshore
Waters

Habitat
On rocks and living or
dead shells

87 Spiny Slipper Shell   *Crepidula aculeata*   Length: ½–1¼″
p. 350

Rocky Shores

Habitat
On rocks and other hard
objects

88 Punctate Pandora

Pandora punctata
p. 350

Length: 1–2⅞″

Beaches; Bays and Estuaries

Habitat
In sand and mud

89 False Pacific Jingle Shell

Pododesmus macrochisma
p. 351

Length: 1–4″

Rocky Shores; Wharves, Docks, and Pilings

Habitat
On rocks, pilings, and shells

90 Clear Jewel Box

Chama arcana
p. 351

Width: 1½–3½″

Rocky Shores; Wharves, Docks, and Pilings

Habitat
On rocks, pilings, or gravel

91 Giant Rock Scallop
Hinnites giganteus
p. 351
Width: 1½–9½"

Rocky Shores

Habitat
On rocks

92 Giant Pacific Scallop
Patinopecten caurinus
p. 352
Length: 4–11"

Offshore Waters

Habitat
In sand or gravel

93 Wide-eared Scallop
Leptopecten latiauratus
p. 352
Height: ¾–1⅜"

Rocky Shores and Offshore
Waters

Habitat
On rocks, rubble, kelp,
and hard objects

94 Pacific Calico Scallop
Argopecten circularis
p. 353

Length: 1½–3½″

Offshore Waters

Habitat
On sand and mud

95 Pacific Pink Scallop
Chlamys hastata hericius
p. 353

Height: 2–3¼″

Rocky Shores and Offshore Waters

Habitat
On rocks, sand, or mud

96 Iceland Scallop
Chlamys islandica
p. 353

Height: 1¾–4″

Offshore Waters

Habitat
On coarse sand or gravel

97 Leafy Thorn Purpura
Ceratostoma foliatum
p. 354
Height: 1¾–3⅜″

Rocky Shores and Offshore Waters

Habitat
On and among rocks

98 Festive Murex
Pteropurpura festiva
p. 354
Length: 1½–2¾″

Rocky Shores

Habitat
On mud or rocks

99 Frill-wing Murex
Pteropurpura macroptera
p. 355
Height: 1¾–2¾″

Rocky Shores and Offshore Waters

Habitat
On rocks and in crevices

100 Giant Forreria

Forreria belcheri
p. 355

Height: 2½–5¾"

Bays and Estuaries;
Offshore Waters

Habitat
On sand

101 Frilled Dogwinkle

Nucella lamellosa
p. 356

Height: 1–3¼"

Rocky Shores

Habitat
On rocks

102 Oregon Triton

Fusitriton oregonensis
p. 356

Height: 3–5"

Rocky Shores and Offshore
Waters

Habitat
On sand and rubble

103 Carpenter's Dwarf Triton
Ocenebra interfossa
p. 357
Height: ½–⅞"

Rocky Shores

Habitat
Among rocks

104 Atlantic Oyster Drill
Urosalpinx cinerea
p. 357
Height: ½–1¾"

Bays and Estuaries

Habitat
On and among rubble near oyster beds

105 Lurid Dwarf Triton
Ocenebra lurida
p. 357
Height: ½–1½"

Rocky Shores and Offshore Waters

Habitat
Among rocks and on rocky gravel

106 Tinted Wentletrap
Epitonium tinctum
p. 358
Height: ⅜–⅝″

Rocky Shores and Offshore Waters

Habitat
In sand near sea anemones

107 Greenland Wentletrap
Epitonium greenlandicum
p. 358
Length: 2″

Offshore Waters

Habitat
On rocks, sand, or mud

108 Poulson's Rock Shell
Roperia poulsoni
p. 359
Length: 2⅜″

Rocky Shores; Wharves, Docks, and Pilings

Habitat
On rocks and pilings

109 California Frog Shell

Bursa californica
p. 359

Height: 1½–5"

Rocky Shores and Offshore
Waters

Habitat
Among rocks

110 Common Northwest Neptune

Neptunea lyrata
p. 360

Height: 2½–6½"

Beaches; Bays and
Estuaries; Offshore Waters

Habitat
On sand or mud

111 Painted Spindle Shell

Fusinus lupteopictus
p. 360

Height: ½–1"

Rocky Shores

Habitat
On and under rocks and
under kelp

112 Western Lean Nassa   *Nassarius mendicus*   Height: ½–⅞"
p. 360

Bays and Estuaries;
Offshore Waters

Habitat
On sand or sandy mud

113 Dire Whelk   *Searlesia dira*   Height: 1–1⅞"
p. 361

Rocky Shores

Habitat
On rocks

114 Western Fat Dog Whelk   *Nassarius perpinguis*   Height: ¾–1"
p. 361

Beaches and Offshore
Waters

Habitat
On sand

115 Giant Western Nassa

Nassarius fossatus
p. 362

Height: 1¼–2"

Beaches and Offshore Waters

Habitat
On sand and mud

116 Joseph's Coat Amphissa

Amphissa versicolor
p. 362

Height: ⅜–¾"

Rocky Shores and Offshore Waters

Habitat
In rock rubble

117 Eastern Mud Whelk

Ilynassa obsoleta
p. 363

Height: ⅝–1¼"

Bays and Estuaries

Habitat
On mud flats

118 Western Mud Whelk

Nassarius tegula
p. 363

Height: ½–¾"

Bays and Estuaries

Habitat
On sand and mud

119 California Horn Shell

Cerithidea californica
p. 364

Height: 1–1¾"

Bays and Estuaries

Habitat
On mud flats

120 Ida's Miter

Mitra idae
p. 364

Height: 3¼"

Rocky Shores and Offshore Waters

Habitat
Among rocks and in kelp beds

121 Giant Pacific Bittium

Bittium eschrichtii
p. 365

Height: ⅜–¾"

Rocky Shores and Offshore Waters

Habitat
Under and among rocks

122 San Pedro Triphora

Triphora pedroana
p. 365

Height: ⅛–⅜"

Rocky Shores and Offshore Waters

Habitat
Among gravel

123 Carpenter's Turrid

Megasurcula carpenteriana
p. 365

Height: 1¾–3¾"

Offshore Waters

Habitat
On mud

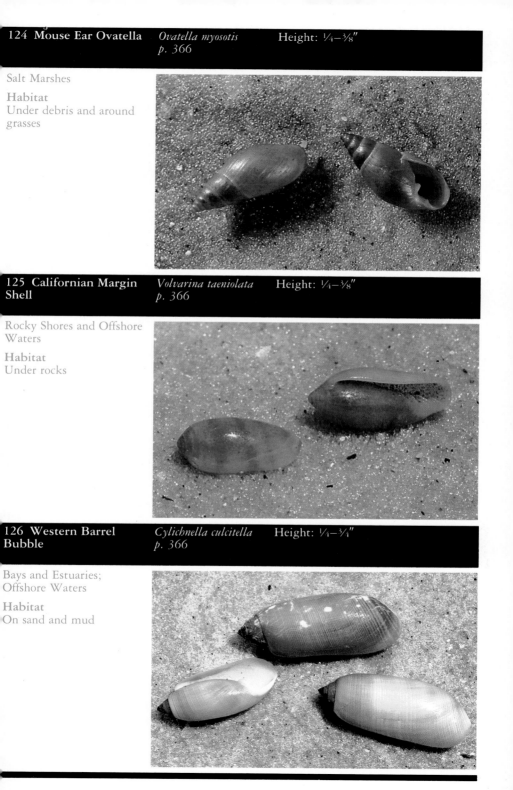

124 Mouse Ear Ovatella   *Ovatella myosotis*   Height: ¼–⅜″
                              p. 366

Salt Marshes

Habitat
Under debris and around
grasses

125 Californian Margin   *Volvarina taeniolata*   Height: ¼–⅜″
Shell   *p. 366*

Rocky Shores and Offshore
Waters

Habitat
Under rocks

126 Western Barrel   *Cylichnella culcitella*   Height: ¼–¾″
Bubble   *p. 366*

Bays and Estuaries;
Offshore Waters

Habitat
On sand and mud

127 Purple Dwarf Olive

Olivella biplicata
p. 367

Height: ½–1½"

Beaches; Bays and Estuaries

Habitat
On sand

128 Checkered Periwinkle

Littorina scutulata
p. 367

Height: ½"

Rocky Shores

Habitat
On rocks

129 Unicorns

Acanthina spp.
p. 368

Height: 1⅝"

Rocky Shores

Habitat
On rocks and pilings among mussels and barnacles

130 Emarginate Dogwinkle

Nucella emarginata   Height: ⅞–1⅛"
p. 368

Rocky Shores

Habitat
On rocks or in rocky crevices

131 Californian Melampus

Melampus olivaceus   Height: ⅛–⅝"
p. 369

Bays and Estuaries; Salt Marshes

Habitat
On mud flats

132 Californian Cone

Conus californicus   Height: ¾–1⅝"
p. 369

Gravelly Beaches and Offshore Waters

Habitat
In sand or gravel

133 Chestnut Cowry
Cypraea spadicea
p. 369
Length: 1–2½"

Rocky Shores and Offshore
Waters

Habitat
Under ledges or stones

134 Green Paper Bubble
Haminoea virescens
p. 370
Height: ½–¾"

Rocky Shores

Habitat
In rocky areas among
seaweeds

135 California Bubble
Bulla gouldiana
p. 370
Height: 1½–2½"

Bays and Estuaries;
Offshore Waters

Habitat
In mud and near eelgrass

136 Californian Banded Pheasant Shell
Tricolia compta
p. 371
Height: ³⁄₈″

Bays and Estuaries

Habitat
On eelgrass

137 Eroded Periwinkle
Littorina keenae
p. 371
Height: ¹⁄₂–³⁄₄″

Rocky Shores

Habitat
On rocks

138 Carpenter's Baby Bubble
Rictaxis punctocaelatus
p. 371
Height: ³⁄₈–⁵⁄₈″

Offshore Waters

Habitat
In sand

139 Recluz's Moon Shell
Neverita reclusiana
p. 372
Height: 1–2¾″

Bays and Estuaries

Habitat
On sand

140 Lewis' Moon Shell
Polinices lewisii
p. 372
Height: 2¼–5½″

Bays and Estuaries

Habitat
On sand

141 Norris Top Shell
Norrisia norrisi
p. 373
Width: 1¼–2¼″

Rocky Shores

Habitat
On kelp and other algae

142 Arctic Natica

Natica clausa
p. 373

Height: ⅝–2⅛"

Beaches

Habitat
On sand

143 Sitka Periwinkle

Littorina sitkana
p. 374

Height: ½–⅞"

Rocky Shores

Habitat
On rocks among seaweeds

144 One-banded Chink Shell

Lacuna unifasciata
p. 374

Height: ¼–⅜"

Rocky Shores; Bays and Estuaries

Habitat
Among eelgrass and seaweeds

145 Carinate Dove Shell   *Alia carinata*   Height: ¼–⅜"
p. 374

Rocky Shores; Bays and
Estuaries

Habitat
Among grasses and algae

146 Common Northern   *Lacuna vincta*   Height: ¼–⅝"
Chink Shell   *p. 375*

Rocky Shores

Habitat
Usually among seaweeds

147 Varicose Solarielle   *Solariella varicosa*   Height: ¼–½"
p. 375

Bays and Estuaries;
Offshore Waters

Habitat
In sand or mud

148 Puppet Margarite
Margarites pupillus
p. 376
Height: ⅜–½"

Bays and Estuaries;
Offshore Waters

Habitat
On sand, mud, or rubble

149 Dusky Tegula
Tegula pulligo
p. 376
Height: ¾–1⅝"

Rocky Shores

Habitat
Among and on kelp

150 Wavy Turban
Astraea undosa
p. 376
Width: 2–4¼"

Rocky Shores

Habitat
On rocks

151 Ringed Top Shell
Calliostoma annulatum Height: ⅝–1¼"
p. 377

Rocky Shores

Habitat
On kelp or rocks among
kelp

152 Western Ribbed Top Shell
Calliostoma ligatum Height: ¾–1"
p. 377

Rocky Shores

Habitat
Among algae and under
rocks

153 Channeled Top Shell
Calliostoma canalicatum
p. 378
Height: ⅝–1½"

Rocky Shores

Habitat
On kelp or rocks among
kelp

154 Sharp-keeled Lirularia

Lirularia acuticostata Height: ⅛–¼"
p. 378

Rocky Shores and Offshore Waters

Habitat
In coarse gravel

155 Dall's Dwarf Turban

Homalopoma luridum Width: ¼–⅜"
p. 378

Rocky Shores

Habitat
Under rocks

156 Western Banded Tegula

Tegula eiseni Height: ⅝–⅞"
p. 379

Rocky Shores

Habitat
On rocks and under kelp

157 Red Turban   *Astraea gibberosa*   Width: 1½–3″
p. 379

Rocky Shores

Habitat
On rocks

158 Black Tegula   *Tegula funebralis*   Height: ¾–1¾″
p. 380

Rocky Shores

Habitat
On rocks

159 Black Limpet   *Collisella asmi*   Length: ⅜–½″
p. 380

Rocky Shores

Habitat
On tegula shells

160 White-cap Limpet

Acmaea mitra
p. 381

Length: ¾–1¾"

Rocky Shores

Habitat
On rocks

161 Pelta False Limpet

Williamia peltoides
p. 381

Length: ¼–½"

Rocky Shores

Habitat
Under rocks

162 Seaweed Limpet

Notoacmaea insessa
p. 381

Length: ½–⅞"

Rocky Shores

Habitat
On kelp and other algae

163 Unstable Limpet
Collisella instabilis
p. 382
Length: ¾–1½"

Rocky Shores

Habitat
On kelp

164 Shield Limpet
Collisella pelta
p. 382
Length: 1–2⅛"

Rocky shores

Habitat
On rocks and kelp
holdfasts

165 File Limpet
Collisella limatula
p. 382
Length: 1–1¾"

Rocky Shores

Habitat
On rocks

166 Great Keyhole Limpet

Megathura crenulata
p. 383

Length: 3–4⅞"

Rocky Shores

Habitat
On rocks

167 Two-spotted Keyhole Limpet

Megatebennus bimaculatus
p. 383

Length: ½–⅞"

Rocky Shores

Habitat
Under stones and on kelp

168 Hooded Puncturella

Puncturella cucullata
p. 384

Length: ½–1⅛"

Rocky Shores

Habitat
Among and under rocks

169 Rough Keyhole Limpet

Diodora aspera
p. 384

Length: 1–2¾″

Rocky Shores

Habitat
On rocks

170 Pacific Plate Limpet

Notoacmaea scutum
p. 384

Length: 1–2⅜″

Rocky Shores

Habitat
On rocks

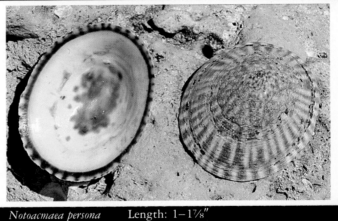

171 Mask Limpet

Notoacmaea persona
p. 385

Length: 1–1⅞″

Rocky Shores

Habitat
On sheltered rocks or in crevices

172 Giant Owl Limpet
Lottia gigantea
p. 385

Length: 1¾–4½"

Rocky Shores

Habitat
On rocks and cliffs

173 Fingered Limpet
Collisella digitalis
p. 386

Length: ¾–1⅜"

Rocky Shores

Habitat
On vertical rock surfaces

174 Rough Limpet
Collisella scabra
p. 386

Length: ¾–1⅜"

Rocky Shores

Habitat
On rocks

175 Volcano Limpet   *Fissurella volcano*   Length: 1–1⅝"
p. 387

Rocky Shores

Habitat
On or under rocks

176 Heath's Chiton   *Stenoplax heathiana*   Length: 1½–3"
p. 387

Rocky Shores

Habitat
Under stones in sand

177 Lined Chiton   *Tonicella lineata*   Length: 2"
p. 387

Rocky Shores

Habitat
On rocks covered with
coralline algae

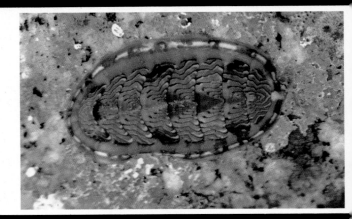

178 Veiled Chiton

Placiphorella velata
p. 388

Length: 2"

Rocky Shores

Habitat
In crevices and on undersides of rocks covered with coralline algae

179 California Nuttall's Chiton

Nuttallina californica
p. 388

Length: 2"

Rocky Shores

Habitat
On rocks, in crevices, or among barnacles and mussels

180 Giant Pacific Chiton

Cryptochiton stelleri
p. 388

Length: 5–13"

Rocky Shores

Habitat
Among rocks

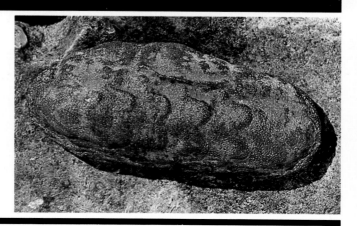

181 White Northern Chiton

Ischnochiton albus
p. 389

Length: ⅜–¾"

Rocky Shores

Habitat
On or under stones

182 Mertens' Chiton

Lepidozona mertensii
p. 389

Length: ½–1½"

Rocky Shores

Habitat
Under rocks

183 Hartweg's Chiton

Cyanoplax hartwegii
p. 390

Length: ¾–1¼"

Rocky Shores

Habitat
On or under rocks or under algae

184 Black Katy Chiton · *Katharina tunicata* · Length: 1½–3″
p. 390

Rocky Shores

Habitat
On rocks

185 Hairy Mopalia · *Mopalia ciliata* · Length: 1–2″
p. 391

Rocky Shores

Habitat
In sheltered crevices and on
and under rocks

186 Mossy Chiton · *Mopalia muscosa* · Length: 3⅝″
p. 391

Rocky Shores

Habitat
On rocks

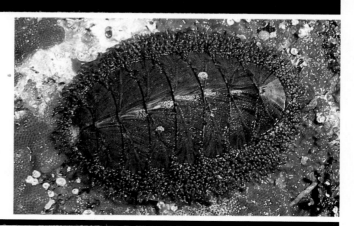

187 Pacific Shipworm
Bankia setacea
p. 391
Length: ½″

Bays and Estuaries;
Wharves, Docks, and
Pilings

Habitat
In wharf piles, wooden
ship hulls, and submerged
wood

188 Common Shipworm
Teredo navalis
p. 392
Length: ¼″

Wharves, Docks, and
Pilings

Habitat
In wharf piles, wooden
ship hulls, and submerged
wood

189 Scaly Worm Shell
Serpulorbis squamigerus
p. 392
Width: ¼–½″

Rocky Shores; Wharves,
Docks, and Pilings

Habitat
On pilings or rocks

190 Indian Money Tusk

Dentalium pretiosum
p. 393

Length: 1–2"

Bays and Estauries;
Offshore Waters

Habitat
In sand and mud

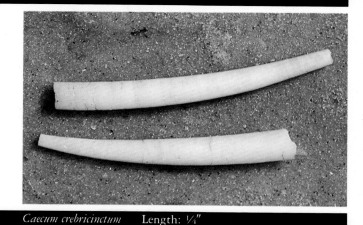

191 Many-ringed Caecum

Caecum crebricinctum
p. 393

Length: ¼"

Offshore Waters

Habitat
In gravel under seaweeds
and in sand

192 Six-sided Tusk

*Dentalium
neohexagonum*
p. 393

Length: 1–1¾"

Bays and Estuaries;
Offshore Waters

Habitat
On sandy mud

193 Gray Whale

Eschrichtius robustus
p. 395

Length: to 46'

Offshore Waters

Range
Bering and Chukchi seas to
Baja California.

194 Minke Whale

*Balaenoptera
acutorostrata*
p. 395

Length: to 33'

Bays and Estuaries;
Offshore Waters; Open
Ocean

Range
Bering and Chukchi seas to
equator.

195 Fin Whale

Balaenoptera physalus
p. 396

Length: to 79'

Offshore Waters and Open
Ocean

Range
Bering Sea to Cabo San
Lucas, Baja California.

196 Right Whale
Eubalaena glacialis
p. 396
Length: to 53'

Offshore Waters and Open Ocean

Range
Gulf of Alaska and southeastern Bering Sea to central Baja California.

197 Blue Whale
Balaenoptera musculus
p. 397
Length: to 98'

Open Ocean

Range
Southern Chukchi Sea to Panama. Aleutian Islands and Gulf of Alaska to central California in summer; Baja California to Panama in winter.

198 Humpback Whale
Megaptera novaeangliae
p. 397
Length: to 53'

Offshore Waters and Open Ocean

Range
Chukchi Sea to southern Mexico.

199 False Killer Whale
Pseudorca crassidens
p. 398

Length: to 19′ 6″

Bays and Estuaries;
Offshore Waters

Range
Aleutian Islands and Prince
William Sound, Alaska, to
Central America and
northern South America.

200 Risso's Dolphin
Grampus griseus
p. 398

Length: to 13′

Open Ocean

Range
Off Stuart Island, British
Columbia, to Mexico.

201 Killer Whale
Orcinus orca
p. 399

Length: to 31′

Offshore Waters and Open
Ocean

Range
Chukchi Sea to equator.

202 Dall's Porpoise

Phocoenoides dalli
p. 399

Length: to 7′

Open Ocean

Range
Bering and Okhotsk seas;
Pribilof Islands to Baja
California.

203 Common Dolphin

Delphinus delphis
p. 400

Length: to 8′6″

Offshore Waters

Range
Victoria, British
Columbia, to equator.

204 Bottlenosed Dolphin

Tursiops truncatus
p. 400

Length: to 12′

Bays and Estuaries;
Offshore Waters

Range
S. California to tropics.

205 Bottlenosed Dolphin

Tursiops truncatus
p. 400

Length: to 12'

Bays and Estuaries;
Offshore Waters

Range
S. California to tropics.

206 Common Dolphin

Delphinus delphis
p. 400

Length: to 8'6"

Offshore Waters

Range
Victoria, British
Columbia, to equator.

207 Striped Dolphin

Stenella coeruleoalba
p. 401

Length: to 9'

Open Ocean

Range
Bering Sea to northwestern
South America.

208 Pacific White-sided Dolphin *Lagenorhynchus obliquidens* Length: to 7′6″
p. 401

Offshore Waters

Range
Amchitka Island in Aleutians, throughout Gulf of Alaska to tip of Baja California.

209 Killer Whale *Orcinus orca* Length: to 31′ ⊗
p. 399

Offshore Waters and Open Ocean

Range
Chukchi Sea to equator.

210 Dall's Porpoise *Phocoenoides dalli* Length: to 7′
p. 399

Open Ocean

Range
Bering and Okhotsk seas; Pribilof Islands to Baja California.

211 Harbor Porpoise   *Phocoena phocoena*   Length: to 6'
p. 402

Beaches; Bays and Estuaries

Range
Gulf of Alaska and eastern
Aleutian chain to S.
California; uncommonly
from Chukchi and Beaufort
seas.

212 Risso's Dolphin   *Grampus griseus*   Length: to 13'
p. 398

Open Ocean

Range
Off Stuart Island, British
Columbia, to Mexico.

213 False Killer Whale   *Pseudorca crassidens*   Length: to 19'6"
p. 398

Bays and Estuaries;
Offshore Waters

Range
Aleutian Islands and Prince
William Sound, Alaska, to
Central America and
northern South America.

214 Short-finned Pilot Whale

Globicephala macrorhynchus
p. 402

Length: to 23'

Open Ocean

Range
Aleutian Islands, Alaska, to Guatemala.

215 Sperm Whale

Physeter catodon
p. 403

Length: to 69'

Open Ocean

Range
Bering Sea to equator.

216 Right Whale

Eubalaena glacialis
p. 396

Length: to 53'

Offshore Waters and Open Ocean

Range
Gulf of Alaska and southeastern Bering Sea to central Baja California.

217 Gray Whale
Eschrichtius robustus
p. 395
Length: to 46'

Offshore Waters

Range
Bering and Chukchi seas to
Baja California.

218 Humpback Whale
Megaptera novaeangliae
p. 397
Length: to 53'

Offshore Waters and Open
Ocean

Range
Chukchi Sea to southern
Mexico.

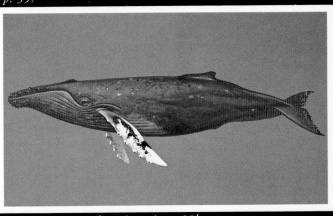

219 Blue Whale
Balaenoptera musculus
p. 397
Length: to 98'

Open Ocean

Range
Chukchi Sea to Panama.
Aleutian Islands and Gulf
of Alaska to central
California in summer; Baja
California to Panama in
winter.

220 Sei Whale

Balaenoptera borealis
p. 403

Length: to 62'

Offshore Waters

Range
Gulf of Alaska to vicinity
of Islas Revillagigedo, off
Baja California.

221 Fin Whale

Balaenoptera physalus
p. 396

Length: to 79'

Offshore Waters and Open
Ocean

Range
Bering Sea to Cabo San
Lucas, Baja California.

222 Minke Whale

Balaenoptera
acutorostrata
p. 395

Length: to 33'

Bays and Estuaries;
Offshore Waters; Open
Ocean

Range
Bering and Chukchi seas to
equator.

| 223 Walrus | *Odobenus rosmarus* p. 404 | Length: Pacific race over 8'2"–11'10" (males); over 7'6"–9'6" (females) |

Rocky Shores, Beaches, and Ice Floes

| 224 Northern Elephant Seal | *Mirounga angustirostris* p. 404 | Length: 14'9"–21'4" (males); 9'10"–11'6" (females) |

Rocky Shores and Beaches

| 225 Northern Fur Seal | *Callorhinus ursinus* p. 405 | Length: 6'3"–7'3" (males); 3'8"–4'8" (females) |

Open Ocean

226 Guadalupe Fur Seal *Arctocephalus townsendi* p. 406 Length: to 6'3" (males); to 4'6" (females)

Rocky Shores

227 California Sea Lion *Zalophus californianus* p. 406 Length: 6'6"–8'2" (males); 5'–6'6" (females)

Rocky Shores and Offshore Waters

228 Steller Sea Lion *Eumetopias jubatus* p. 407 Length: 8'10"–10'6" (males); 6'3"–7'3" (females)

Rocky Shores and Offshore Waters

229 Ribbon Seal
Phoca fasciata
p. 407
Length: to 6′ (males)

Ice Floes

230 Ringed Seal
Phoca hispida
p. 407
Length: 4′3″–5′3″ (males)

Rocky Shores

231 Pacific Harbor Seal
Phoca vitulina
p. 408
Length: 4′–5′7″

Bays and Estuaries

| 232 Northern Elephant Seal | *Mirounga angustirostris* p. 404 | Length: 14'9"–21'4" (males); 9'10"–11'6" (females) |

Rocky Shores and Beaches

| 233 Bearded Seal | *Erignathus barbatus* p. 408 | Length: 8–11' (males) |

Arctic Waters

| 234 Sea Otter | *Enhydra lutris* p. 409 | Length: 2½–6' |

Rocky Shores; Bays and Estuaries

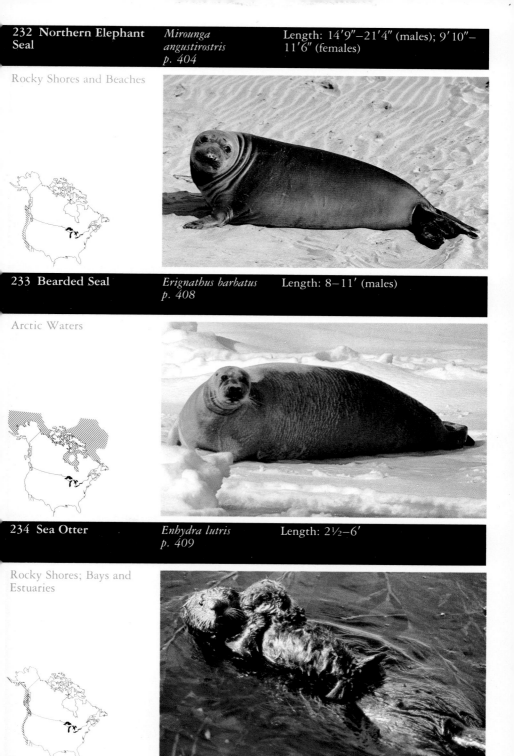

235 Brown Rockfish

Sebastes auriculatus
p. 411

Length: to 21½"

⊗

Rocky Shores and Offshore
Waters

Habitat
Shallow, low-profile reefs

236 Grunt Sculpin

*Rhamphocottus
richardsoni*
p. 411

Length: to 3¼"

Rocky Shores and Offshore
Waters

Habitat
Rocks and reefs in
intertidal zone and below
low tide level

237 Giant Sea Bass

Stereolepis gigas
p. 411

Length: to 7'5"

Rocky Shores

Habitat
Rocky areas and kelp beds

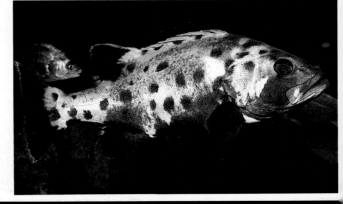

238 Kelp Bass

Paralabrax clathratus
p. 412

Length: to 28″

Rocky Shores around kelp
beds

Habitat
Reefs, wrecks, and kelp
beds

239 Blue Rockfish

Sebastes mystinus
p. 412

Length: to 30″ ⊗

Rocky Shores and Offshore
Waters

Habitat
Over rocky reefs and soft
bottoms

240 Kelp Rockfish

Sebastes atrovirens
p. 412

Length: to 17″ ⊗

Rocky Shores and Offshore
Waters

Habitat
Rocky reefs and kelp beds

241 Black Rockfish

Sebastes melanops
p. 413

Length: to 24"

⊗

Rocky Shores and Offshore
Waters

Habitat
Over rocks and soft
bottoms

242 Yellowfin Croaker

Umbrina roncador
p. 413

Length: to 18"

Beaches; Bays and Estuaries

Habitat
Over sand, in surf zone,
near rocks or kelp

243 Yellowtail Rockfish

Sebastes flavidus
p. 414

Length: to 26"

⊗

Rocky Shores and Offshore
Waters

Habitat
Over deep reefs and soft
bottoms

244 Widow Rockfish   *Sebastes entomelas*   Length: to 21"

p. 414

Rocky Shores and Offshore
Waters

Habitat
Low-profile reefs in sandy
or silty areas

245 Bocaccio   *Sebastes paucispinis*   Length: to 3'

p. 414   Juvenile

Rocky Shores and Offshore
Waters; juveniles in Bays
and Estuaries

Habitat
Over rocky reefs and soft
bottoms

246 Kelp Greenling   *Hexagrammos*   Length: to 21"

decagrammus   Female

p. 415

Rocky Shores; Bays and
Estuaries

Habitat
Shallow reefs

247 Lingcod

Ophiodon elongatus
p. 415

Length: to 5'

Bays and Estuaries;
Offshore Waters

Habitat
Over reefs and soft bottoms

248 China Rockfish

Sebastes nebulosus
p. 416

Length: to 17" ⊗

Rocky Shores and Offshore
Waters

Habitat
Rocky areas with caves and
crevices

249 Quillback Rockfish

Sebastes maliger
p. 416

Length: to 24" ⊗

Rocky Shores and Offshore
Waters

Habitat
Rocky reefs with caves and
crevices

250 Kelp Greenling

Hexagrammos decagrammus
p. 415

Length: to 21"

Rocky Shores; Bays and Estuaries

Habitat
Shallow reefs

251 Buffalo Sculpin

Enophrys bison
p. 416

Length: to 15"

Bays and Estuaries; Wharves, Docks, and Pilings

Habitat
Over shallow reefs and soft bottoms around piers and wrecks

252 Cabezon

Scorpaenichthys marmoratus
p. 417

Length: to 3'3"

Bays and Estuaries; Offshore Waters

Habitat
Rocks and reefs in intertidal zone

253 California Scorpionfish　*Scorpaena guttata*　Length: to 17″
p. 417

⊗

Offshore Waters

Habitat
Shallow reefs and kelp beds

254 Red Irish Lord　*Hemilepidotus hemilepidotus*　Length: to 20″
p. 418

Rocky Shores; Bays and
Estuaries; and Offshore
Waters

Habitat
Shallow, rocky reefs

255 Snubnose Sculpin　*Orthonopias triacis*　Length: to 4″
p. 418

Rocky Shores and Offshore
Waters

Habitat
Rocks between high and
low tide levels

256 Shortspine Thornyhead

Sebastolobus alascanus
p. 418

Length: to 30″

⊗

Offshore Waters

Habitat
Over deep, soft bottoms

257 California Sheephead

Semicossyphus pulcher
p. 419

Length: to 3′

Rocky Shores; Bays and Estuaries; and Offshore Waters

Habitat
Reefs and kelp beds

258 Spotted Ratfish

Hydrolagus colliei
p. 419

Length: to 3′2″

⊗

Offshore Waters

Habitat
Over soft bottoms

259 Garibaldi
Hypsypops rubicundus
p. 420
Length: to 14″
Juvenile

Bays and Estuaries;
Offshore Waters

Habitat
Reefs and kelp beds

260 Garibaldi
Hypsypops rubicundus
p. 420
Length: to 14″

Bays and Estuaries;
Offshore Waters

Habitat
Reefs and kelp beds

261 Rainbow Seaperch
Hypsurus caryi
p. 420
Length: to 12″

Bays and Estuaries;
Wharves, Docks, and
Pilings; and Offshore
Waters

Habitat
Reefs, piers, and kelp beds;
bays and outer coast

262 Yelloweye Rockfish *Sebastes ruberrimus* Length: to 3'
p. 420

Rocky Shores and Offshore
Waters

Habitat
Reefs and caves

263 Vermilion Rockfish *Sebastes miniatus* Length: to 36"
p. 421

Rocky Shores and Offshore
Waters

Habitat
Over rocky reefs and soft
bottoms

**264 California
Sheephead** *Semicossyphus pulcher* Length: to 3'
p. 419 Juvenile

Rocky Shores; Bays and
Estuaries; and Offshore
Waters

Habitat
Reefs and kelp beds

265 Señorita

Oxyjulis californica
p. 421

Length: to 10"

Rocky Shores; Bays and
Estuaries

Habitat
Reefs and kelp beds

266 Giant Kelpfish

Heterostichus rostratus
p. 422

Length: to 24"

Rocky Shores; Bays and
Estuaries; and Offshore
Waters; Kelp Beds

Habitat
Rocky areas with eelgrass,
leafy red algae, jointed
coralline algae, or kelp
beds

267 Shiner Perch

Cymatogaster aggregata
p. 422

Length: to 8"

Bays and Estuaries;
Wharves, Docks, and
Pilings

Habitat
In bays around piers; on
outer coast, and near reefs
and kelp beds

268 Kelp Perch

Brachyistius frenatus
p. 422

Length: to 8½"

Bays and Estuaries; Kelp
Beds

Habitat
In kelp beds among fronds

269 Striped Seaperch

Embiotoca lateralis
p. 423

Length: to 15"

Rocky Shores; Bays and
Estuaries; and Wharves,
Docks, and Pilings

Habitat
Reefs, piers, and kelp beds;
in bays and offshore areas

270 Opaleye

Girella nigricans
p. 423

Length: to 26"

Rocky Shores; Offshore
Waters around kelp beds

Habitat
Shallow reefs and kelp beds

271 Rubberlip Seaperch

Rhacochilus toxotes
p. 423

Length: to 18"

Rocky Shores; Bays and
Estuaries; and Wharves,
Docks, and Pilings

Habitat
Reefs, piers, and kelp beds

272 Redtail Surfperch

*Amphistichus
rhodoterus*
p. 424

Length: to 16"

Beaches and Offshore
Waters

Habitat
Steeply sloping sandy
beaches and other sandy
areas

273 Walleye Surfperch

*Hyperprosopon
argenteum*
p. 424

Length: to 12"

Beaches; Wharves; Docks,
and Pilings

Habitat
In surf, over sand, and
around piers, reefs, and
kelp beds

274 Bermuda Chub   *Kyphosus sectatrix*   Length: to 20"
p. 425

Reefs and Kelp Beds

Habitat
Near shore on coral reefs
and over rocks

275 Halfmoon   *Medialuna californiensis*   Length: to 19"
p. 425

Rocky Shores and Offshore
Waters around kelp beds

Habitat
Reefs and kelp beds

276 American Shad   *Alosa sapidissima*   Length: to 30"
p. 425

Bays and Estuaries

Habitat
Bays, estuaries, and fresh
water

277 Striped Mullet

Mugil cephalus
p. 426

Length: to 18″

Beaches; Bays and Estuaries

Habitat
Coasts, estuaries, and fresh
water

278 Striped Bass

Morone saxatilis
p. 426

Length: to 6′

Bays and Estuaries

Habitat
Inshore over various
bottoms

279 Bonefish

Albula vulpes
p. 427

Length: to 3′

Bays and Estuaries;
Offshore Waters

Habitat
Shallow waters over soft
bottoms

280 Ocean Whitefish *Caulolatilus princeps* Length: to 3'4"
p. 427

Offshore Waters

Habitat
Over soft bottoms and reefs

281 Yellowtail *Seriola lalandei* Length: to 5'
p.. 427

Offshore Waters and
around kelp beds

Habitat
Near surface around reefs,
islands, and kelp beds

282 Yellowfin Tuna *Thunnus albacares* Length: to 6'
p. 428

Open Ocean

Habitat
On surface and at mid-
depths in open seas

283 Sockeye Salmon

Oncorhynchus nerka
p. 428

Length: to 33"

Bays and Estuaries

Habitat
Surface waters of open
ocean and freshwater
streams, rivers, and lakes

284 Cutthroat Trout

Salmo clarki
p. 429

Length: to 30"

Beaches; Bays and
Estuaries; Offshore Waters

Habitat
Inshore marine and
estuarine waters and coastal
streams

285 Sablefish

Anoplopoma fimbria
p. 429

Length: to 3'4"

Offshore Waters

Habitat
Over soft bottoms in deep
water

286 Chinook Salmon   *Oncorhynchus*   Length: to 4′10″
                              tshawytscha   Female
                              p. 430

Bays and Estuaries;
Offshore Waters

Habitat
Ocean near surface and at
mid-depths

287 Striped Mullet   *Mugil cephalus*   Length: to 18″
                              p. 426

Beaches; Bays and Estuaries

Habitat
Coasts, estuaries, and fresh
water

288 Cutthroat Trout   *Salmo clarki*   Length: to 30″
                              p. 429

Beaches; Bays and
Estuaries; Offshore Waters

Habitat
Inshore marine and
estuarine waters and coastal
streams

289 Pacific Herring

Clupea harengus pallasi
p. 430

Length: to 18″

Beaches; Bays and
Estuaries; Offshore Waters

Habitat
Inshore waters

290 Pacific Hake

Merluccius productus
p. 430

Length: to 3′

Deep Offshore Waters

Habitat
Surface to bottom of open
sea

291 Chub Mackerel

Scomber japonicus
p. 431

Length: to 25″

Offshore Waters

Habitat
Mostly warm coastal waters
over continental shelf

292 Pacific Tomcod

Microgadus proximus
p. 431

Length: to 12″

Bays and Estuaries;
Wharves, Docks, and
Pilings; Offshore Waters

Habitat
Over soft bottoms, and
around piers and jetties in
bays

293 Jack Mackerel

Trachurus symmetricus
p. 432

Length: to 32″

Rocky Shores; Offshore
Waters near kelp beds

Habitat
Offshore on surface and at
midwater; around reefs and
kelp beds

294 Topsmelt

Atherinops affinis
p. 432

Length: to 14½″

Bays and Estuaries; Kelp
Beds

Habitat
Surface waters near shore,
in bays, and around kelp
beds

295 Northern Anchovy
Engraulis mordax
p. 432
Length: to 9"

Bays and Estuaries;
Offshore Waters

Habitat
Coastal surface waters

296 Bay Pipefish
Syngnathus leptorhynchus
p. 433
Length: to 14"

Bays and Estuaries

Habitat
Eelgrass beds in bays

297 Pacific Lamprey
Lampetra tridentata
p. 433
Length: to 30"

Bays and Estuaries;
Offshore Waters

Habitat
Close to shore; large inland streams

298 California Grunion
Leuresthes tenuis
p. 433

Length: to 7½"
Female

Offshore Waters and
Beaches

Habitat
Off sandy beaches

299 Plainfin
Midshipman
Porichthys notatus
p. 434

Length: to 15"

Bays and Estuaries

Habitat
Over sand and mud

300 Blackeye Goby
Coryphopterus nicholsi
p. 434

Length: to 6"

Bays and Estuaries;
Offshore Waters

Habitat
Over sand and mud near
reefs, in bays and off coast

301 Spotted Cusk-Eel

Chilara taylori
p. 435

Length: to 14¼"

Bays and Estuaries;
Offshore Waters

Habitat
Over and in soft bottoms

302 Penpoint Gunnel

Apodichthys flavidus
p. 435

Length: to 18"

Rocky Shores; Bays and
Estuaries

Habitat
Intertidal areas near rocks
and shallow eelgrass beds

303 Wolf-Eel

Anarrhichthys ocellatus
p. 435

Length: to 6'8"

⊗

Rocky Shores and Offshore
Waters

Habitat
Reefs and wrecks with
large crevices

304 California Moray
Gymnothorax mordax
p. 436
Length: to 5'

Rocky Shores

Habitat
Shallow, rocky reefs with
crevices and caves

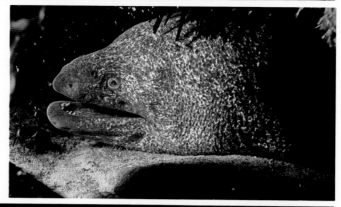

305 Pacific Halibut
Hippoglossus stenolepis
p. 436
Length: to 8'9"

Offshore Waters

Habitat
Over soft bottoms

306 Pacific Sanddab
Citharichthys sordidus
p. 436
Length: to 16"

Bays and Estuaries;
Offshore Waters

Habitat
Over soft bottoms

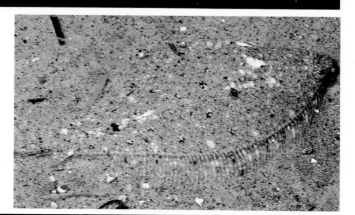

307 Starry Flounder

Platichthys stellatus
p. 437

Length: to 3′

Bays and Estuaries;
Offshore Waters

Habitat
In bays and estuaries, and
off open coast

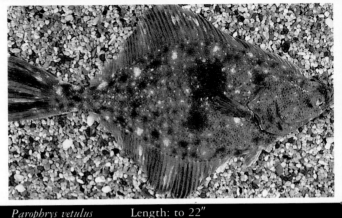

308 English Sole

Parophrys vetulus
p. 437

Length: to 22″

Bays and Estuaries;
Offshore Waters

Habitat
Over soft bottoms

309 C-O Sole

Pleuronichthys coenosus
p. 438

Length: to 14″

Offshore Waters

Habitat
Over soft bottoms and
rocks

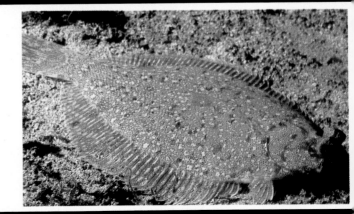

310 Rock Sole   *Lepidopsetta bilineata*   Length: to 24"
p. 438

Offshore Waters

Habitat
Over rocks and soft
bottoms

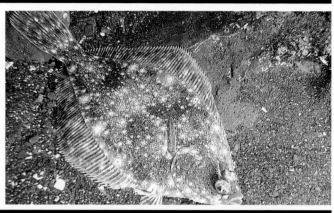

311 Diamond Turbot   *Hypsopsetta guttulata*   Length: to 18"
p. 438

Bays and Estuaries

Habitat
Over soft bottoms

312 California Halibut   *Paralichthys*   Length: to 5'
californicus
p. 439

Bays and Estuaries;
Offshore Waters

Habitat
Over soft bottoms

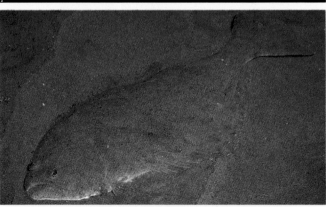

313 Bat Ray

Myliobatis californica
p. 439

Length: to 6′ ⊗

Bays and Estuaries;
Offshore Waters

Habitat
Shallow, sandy areas in
bays and on coast

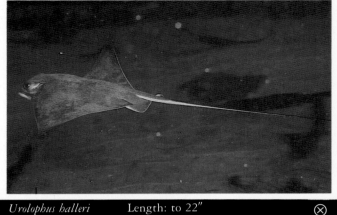

314 Round Stingray

Urolophus halleri
p. 439

Length: to 22″ ⊗

Bays and Estuaries;
Offshore Waters

Habitat
Over sand or mud in
shallow bays and off coast

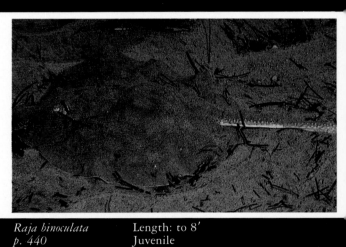

315 Big Skate

Raja binoculata
p. 440

Length: to 8′
Juvenile

Bays and Estuaries;
Offshore Waters

Habitat
Over soft bottoms

316 Thornback *Platyrhinoidis* Length: to 3'
 triseriata
 p. 440

Bays and Estuaries;
Offshore Waters

Habitat
Over sand and mud

317 Pacific Electric *Torpedo californica* Length: to 4'6" ⊗
Ray *p. 440*

Bays and Estuaries;
Offshore Waters

Habitat
Over mud and sand in
shallow waters, and in kelp
beds

318 Pacific Angel Shark *Squatina californica* Length: to 5'
 p. 441

Offshore Waters and Reefs

Habitat
On sand and mud bottoms

319 Leopard Shark

Triakis semifasciata
p. 441

Length: to 6'6"

Bays and Estuaries;
Offshore Waters

Habitat
Over sand and mud in
shallow bays, and inshore
waters

320 White Shark

Carcharodon carcharias
p. 441

Length: to 21'

⊗

Offshore Waters

Habitat
Coastal surface waters

321 Ocean Sunfish

Mola mola
p. 442

Length: to 13'

Offshore Waters

Habitat
Surface of open seas

322 Blue Shark

Prionace glauca
p. 442

Length: to 12'7"

Bays and Estuaries;
Offshore Waters

Habitat
In shallow coastal waters
over sand or mud, and far
out at sea

323 Spiny Dogfish

Squalus acanthias
p. 443

Length: to 5'

Offshore Waters

Habitat
In temperate and
subtropical waters over soft
bottoms

324 White Sturgeon

Acipenser
transmontanus
p. 443

Length: to 12'6"

Bays and Estuaries

Habitat
Over soft bottoms in ocean;
in deep pools of large rivers

325 Commensal Crabs
Pinnotheres spp.
p. 445
Width: ⅝″

Bays and Estuaries

Phylum Arthropoda, Class
Crustacea

326 Purple Shore Crab
Hemigrapsus nudus
p. 445
Width: 2¼″

Rocky Shores; Bays and
Estuaries

Phylum Arthropoda, Class
Crustacea

327 Black-clawed
Mud Crab
Lophopanopeus bellus
p. 445
Width: 1⅜″

Bays and Estuaries

Phylum Arthropoda, Class
Crustacea

328 Flat Porcelain Crab   *Petrolisthes cinctipes*   Length: 1"
p. 446

Rocky Shores

Phylum Arthropoda, Class
Crustacea

329 Yellow Shore Crab   *Hemigrapsus*   Width: 1⅜"
oregonensis
p. 446

Bays and Estuaries;
Salt Marshes

Phylum Arthropoda, Class
Crustacea

330 Dungeness Crab   *Cancer magister*   Width: 9¼"
p. 446

Bays and Estuaries;
Offshore Waters

Phylum Arthropoda, Class
Crustacea

331 Striped Shore Crab
Pachygrapsus crassipes
p. 447
Width: 1⅞"

Rocky Shores

Phylum Arthropoda, Class
Crustacea

332 Purple Shore Crab
Hemigrapsus nudus
p. 445
Width: 2¼"

Rocky Shores; Bays and
Estuaries

Phylum Arthropoda, Class
Crustacea

333 Thick-clawed
Porcelain Crab
Pachycheles rudis
p. 447
Length: ¾"

Rocky Shores; Wharves,
Docks, and Pilings

Phylum Arthropoda, Class
Crustacea

334 Shield-backed Kelp Crab *Pugettia producta* Length: 4¾"
p. 447

Rocky Shores and Offshore Waters

Phylum Arthropoda, Class Crustacea

335 Oregon Cancer Crab *Cancer oregonensis* Width: 1⅞"
p. 448

Rocky Shores; Wharves, Docks, and Pilings; Offshore Waters

Phylum Arthropoda, Class Crustacea

336 Red Crab *Cancer productus* Width: 6¼"
p. 448

Rocky Shores and Offshore Waters

Phylum Arthropoda, Class Crustacea

337 Turtle Crab   *Crypotolithodes*   Width: 2¾″
sitchensis
p. 449

Rocky Shores

Phylum Arthropoda, Class
Crustacea

338 Pacific Rock Crab   *Cancer antennarius*   Width: 4⅝″
p. 449

Rocky Shores; Bays and
Estuaries; and Offshore
Waters

Phylum Arthropoda, Class
Crustacea

339 Blue-handed Hermit   *Pagurus samuelis*   Length: ¾″
Crab   *p. 449*

Rocky Shores

Phylum Arthropoda, Class
Crustacea

340 Sharp-nosed Crab　　*Scyra acutifrons*　　Length: 1¾"
　　　　　　　　　　　　　　p. 450

Rocky Shores; Wharves,
Docks, and Pilings

Phylum Arthropoda, Class
Crustacea

341 Masking Crab　　*Loxorhynchus crispatus*　　Length: 4"
　　　　　　　　　　　　p. 450

Rocky Shores; Wharves,
Docks, and Pilings

Phylum Arthropoda, Class
Crustacea

342 Pacific Mole Crab　　*Emerita analoga*　　Length: 1⅜"
　　　　　　　　　　　　　p. 450

Beaches

Phylum Arthropoda, Class
Crustacea

343 California Fiddler Crab

Uca crenulata
p. 451

Width: ¾"

Bays and Estuaries

Phylum Arthropoda, Class Crustacea

344 Beach Ghost Shrimp

Callianassa affinis
p. 451

Length: 2⅝"

Bays and Estuaries

Phylum Arthropoda, Class Crustacea

345 Bay Ghost Shrimp

Callianassa californiensis
p. 452

Length: 4⅝"

Bays and Estuaries

Phylum Arthropoda, Class Crustacea

346 California Rock Lobster

Panulirus interruptus
p. 452

Length: 16"

Rocky Shores and Offshore
Waters

Phylum Arthropoda, Class
Crustacea

347 Spiny Mole Crab

*Blepharipoda
occidentalis*
p. 452

Length: 2⅜"

Beaches

Phylum Arthropoda, Class
Crustacea

348 Coon-stripe Shrimp

Pandalus danae
p. 453

Length: 5¾"

Bays and Estuaries;
Offshore Waters

Phylum Arthropoda, Class
Crustacea

| 349 Mottled Tube-maker | *Jassa falcata* p. 453 | Length: 3/8" |

| 350 California Beach Flea | *Orchestoidea californiana* p. 454 | Length: 1 1/8" |

| 351 Harford's Greedy Isopod | *Cirolana harfordi* p. 454 | Length: 3/4" |

352 Western Sea Roach
Ligia occidentalis
p. 454
Length: 1"

Rocky Shores; Bays and
Estuaries

Phylum Arthropoda, Class
Crustacea

353 Western Sea Roach
Ligia occidentalis
p. 454
Length: 1"

Rocky Shores; Bays and
Estuaries

Phylum Arthropoda, Class
Crustacea

354 Vosnesensky's Isopod
Idotea wosnesenskii
p. 455
Length: 1⅜"

Rocky Shores

Phylum Arthropoda, Class
Crustacea

355 Smooth Skeleton Shrimp

Caprella laeviuscula
p. 455

Length: 2″

Rocky Shores; Bays and Estuaries; and Wharves, Docks, and Pilings

Phylum Arthropoda, Class Crustacea

356 Clawed Sea Spider

Phoxichilidium femoratum
p. 456

Length: ⅛″

Rocky Shores

Phylum Arthropoda, Class Pycnogonida

357 Stearns' Sea Spider

Pycnogonum stearnsi
p. 456

Length: ½″

Rocky Shores; Wharves, Docks, and Pilings

Phylum Arthropoda, Class Pycnogonida

358 Burrowing Brittle Star

Amphiodia occidentalis
p. 456

Width: 13¾"

Rocky Shores; Bays and Estuaries

Phylum Echinodermata, Class Stelleroidea, Subclass Ophiuroidea

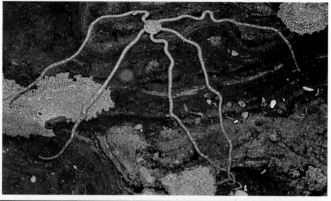

359 Dwarf Brittle Star

Axiognathus squamatus
p. 457

Width: 2¼"

Rocky Shores

Phylum Echinodermata, Class Stelleroidea, Subclass Ophiuroidea

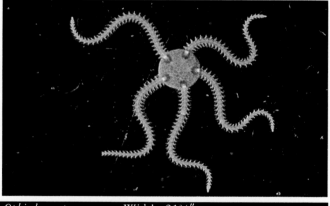

360 Panama Brittle Star

Ophioderma panamense
p. 457

Width: 21¾"

Rocky Shores and Offshore Waters

Phylum Echinodermata, Class Stelleroidea, Subclass Ophiuroidea

361 Esmark's Brittle Star
Ophioplocus esmarki
p. 458
Width: 8¾"

Rocky Shores and Offshore
Waters

Phylum Echinodermata,
Class Stelleroidea, Subclass
Ophiuroidea

362 Daisy Brittle Star
Ophiopholis aculeata
p. 458
Width: 8"

Rocky Shores and Offshore
Waters

Phylum Echinodermata,
Class Stelleroidea, Subclass
Ophiuroidea

363 Armored Sea Star
Astropecten armatus
p. 458
Width: 12"

Beaches; Bays and Estuaries

Phylum Echinodermata,
Class Stelleroidea, Subclass
Asteroidea

364 Spiny Brittle Star

Ophiothrix spiculata
p. 459

Width: 12¾″

Rocky Shores and Offshore Waters

Phylum Echinodermata, Class Stelleroidea, Subclass Ophiuroidea

365 Pacific Comet Star

Linckia columbiae
p. 459

Width: 7¼″

Rocky Shores

Phylum Echinodermata, Class Stelleroidea, Subclass Asteroidea

366 Pacific Henricia

Henricia leviuscula
p. 459

Width: 7¼″

Rocky Shores and Offshore Waters

Phylum Echinodermata, Class Stelleroidea, Subclass Asteroidea

367 Broad Six-rayed Sea Star

Leptasterias hexactis
p. 460

Width: 4"

Rocky Shores

Phylum Echinodermata,
Class Stelleroidea, Subclass
Asteroidea

368 Troschel's Sea Star

Evasterias troschelii
p. 460

Width: 16"

Rocky Shores

Phylum Echinodermata,
Class Stelleroidea, Subclass
Asteroidea

369 Ochre Sea Star

Pisaster ochraceus
p. 460

Width: 20"

Rocky Shores

Phylum Echinodermata,
Class Stelleroidea, Subclass
Asteroidea

370 Giant Sea Star

Pisaster giganteus
p. 461

Width: 24"

Rocky Shores; Bays and
Estuaries; Wharves, Docks,
and Pilings

Phylum Echinodermata,
Class Stelleroidea, Subclass
Asteroidea

371 Bat Star

Patiria miniata
p. 461

Width: 8"

Rocky Shores

Phylum Echinodermata,
Class Stelleroidea, Subclass
Asteroidea

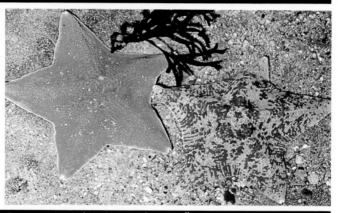

372 Leather Star

Dermasterias imbricata
p. 461

Width: 9½"

Rocky Shores; Bays and
Estuaries; Offshore Waters

Phylum Echinodermata,
Class Stelleroidea, Subclass
Asteroidea

373 Spiny Sun Star

Crossaster papposus
p. 462

Width: 14"

Rocky Shores and Offshore
Waters

Phylum Echinodermata,
Class Stelleroidea, Subclass
Asteroidea

374 Dawson's Sun Star

Solaster dawsoni
p. 462

Width: 20"

Offshore Waters

Phylum Echinodermata,
Class Stelleroidea, Subclass
Asteroidea

375 Sunflower Star

*Pycnopodia
helianthoides*
p. 462

Width: 52"

Rocky Shores and Offshore
Waters

Phylum Echinodermata,
Class Stelleroidea, Subclass
Asteroidea

376 Eccentric Sand Dollar

Dendraster excentricus
p. 463

Width: 3″

Bays and Estuaries;
Offshore Waters

Phylum Echinodermata,
Class Echinoidea

377 Heart Urchin

Lovenia cordiformis
p. 463

Length: 3″

Bays and Estuaries;
Offshore Waters

Phylum Echinodermata,
Class Echinoidea

378 Giant Pacific Octopus

Octopus dofleini
p. 463

Length: 16′

Rocky Shores and Offshore
Waters

Phylum Mollusca, Class
Cephalopoda

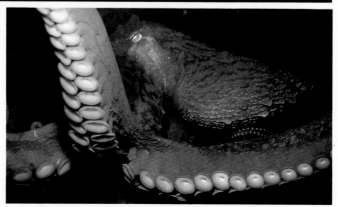

379 Two-spotted **Octopus**

Octopus bimaculatus *p. 464*

Length: 30″

Rocky Shores and Offshore Waters

Phylum Mollusca, Class Cephalopoda

380 Two-spotted **Octopus**

Octopus bimaculatus *p. 464*

Length: 30″

Rocky Shores and Offshore Waters

Phylum Mollusca, Class Cephalopoda

381 Opalescent Squid

Loligo opalescens *p. 464*

Length: 7⅝″

Offshore Waters and Open Ocean

Phylum Mollusca, Class Cephalopoda

382 Beroë's Comb Jelly
Beroe cucumis
p. 465
Height: 4½"

Bays and Estuaries;
Offshore Waters

Phylum Ctenophora

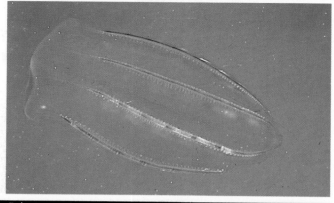

383 Purple Jellyfish
Pelagia noctiluca
p. 465
Width: 4"
⊗

Offshore Waters; Bays and
Estuaries

Phylum Cnidaria, Class
Scyphozoa

384 Moon Jellyfish
Aurelia aurita
p. 466
Width: 16"
⊗

Bays and Estuaries;
Offshore Waters

Phylum Cnidaria, Class
Scyphozoa

385 Many-ribbed   *Aequorea aequorea*   Width: 7"
Hydromedusa   *p. 466*

Bays and Estuaries;
Offshore Waters

Phylum Cnidaria, Class
Hydrozoa

386 Penicillate Jellyfish   *Polyorchis penicillatus*   Height: 1⅝"
    p. 466

Bays and Estuaries;
Offshore Waters

Phylum Cnidaria, Class
Hydrozoa

387 Sea Gooseberry   *Pleurobrachia bachei*   Height: 1⅛"
    p. 467

Offshore Waters

Phylum Ctenophora

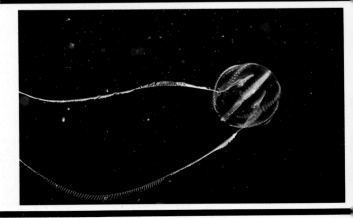

388 Angled Hydromedusa   *Gonionemus vertens*   Width: ¾"
p. 467

Bays and Estuaries

Phylum Cnidaria, Class Hydrozoa

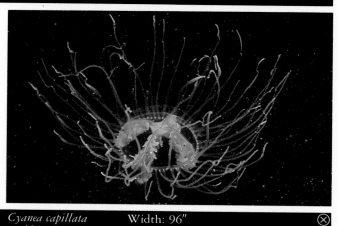

389 Lion's Mane   *Cyanea capillata*   Width: 96"   ⊗
p. 467

Offshore Waters

Phylum Cnidaria, Class Scyphozoa

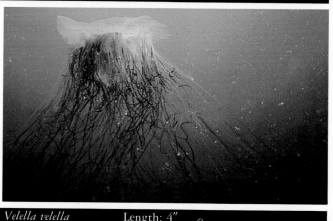

390 By-the-wind Sailor   *Velella velella*   Length: 4"
p. 468

Rocky Shores, Beaches, and Open Ocean

Phylum Cnidaria, Class Hydrozoa

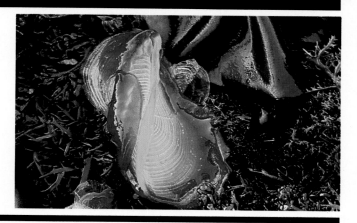

391 Bat Star Worm *Ophiodromus pugettensis* Length: 1½"
p. 468

Bays and Estuaries;
Offshore Waters

Phylum Annelida, Class
Polychaeta, Subclass
Errantia

**392 Polydora Mud
Worm** *Polydora ligni* Length: 1"
p. 469

Bays and Estuaries

Phylum Annelida, Class
Polychaeta, Subclass
Sedentaria

**393 Sinistral Spiral
Tube Worm** *Spirorbis borealis* Length: ⅛"
p. 469

Rocky Shores; Bays and
Estuaries

Phylum Annelida, Class
Polychaeta, Subclass
Sedentaria

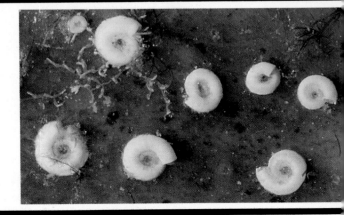

394 Common White Synapta

Leptosynapta inhaerens
p. 470

Length: 6"

Offshore Waters

Phylum Echinodermata,
Class Holothuroidea

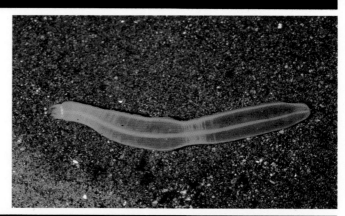

395 Red Lineus

Lineus ruber
p. 470

Length: 8"

Rocky Shores and Beaches

Phylum Rhynchocoela,
Class Anopla

396 Red Tube Worm

Serpula vermicularis
p. 470

Length: 4"

Rocky Shores; Bays and
Estuaries; and Wharves,
Docks, and Pilings

Phylum Annelida, Class
Polychaeta, Subclass
Sedentaria

397 Tailed Priapulid Worm   *Priapulus caudatus*   Length: 3¼"
Worm   p. 471

Bays and Estuaries

Phylum Aschelminthes

398 Agassiz's Peanut Worm   *Phascolosoma agassizii*   Length: 4¾"
Worm   p. 471

Rocky Shores and Bays
and Estuaries

Phylum Sipuncula

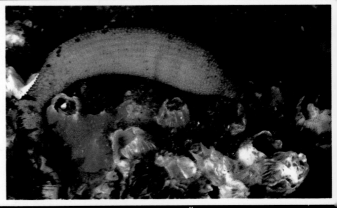

399 Innkeeper Worm   *Urechis caupo*   Length: 7¼"
p. 472

Bays and Estuaries

Phylum Echiura

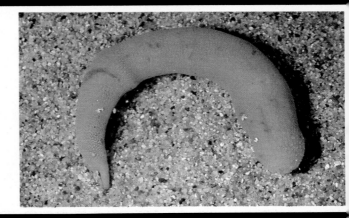

400 Eyed Fringed Worm *Cirratulus cirratus*   Length: 4¾"
p. 472

Rocky Shores

Phylum Annelida, Class
Polychaeta, Subclass
Sedentaria

**401 Chevron
Amphiporus** *Amphiporus angulatus* Length: 6"
p. 472

Rocky Shores and Offshore
Waters

Phylum Rhynchocoela,
Class Enopla

**402 Chevron
Amphiporus** *Amphiporus angulatus* Length: 6"
p. 472

Rocky Shores and Offshore
Waters

Phylum Rhynchocoela,
Class Enopla

403 Opal Worm   *Arabella iricolor*   Length: 24"
p. 473

Bays and Estuaries

Phylum Annelida, Class
Polychaeta, Subclass
Errantia

404 Two-gilled Blood   *Glycera dibranchiata*   Length: 15⅛"
Worm   *p. 473*

Beaches; Bays and Estuaries

Phylum Annelida, Class
Polychaeta, Subclass
Errantia

405 Clam Worm   *Nereis virens*   Length: 36"
p. 474

Rocky Shores; Bays and
Estuaries; Offshore Waters

Phylum Annelida, Class
Polychaeta, Subclass
Errantia

406 Six-lined Nemertean   *Tubulanus sexlineatus*   Length: 8"
p. 474

Rocky Shores; Wharves,
Docks, and Pilings

Phylum Rhynchocoela,
Class Anopla

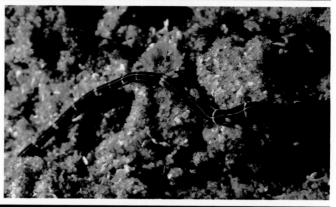

407 Lug Worm   *Arenicola cristata*   Length: 12"
p. 475

Bays and Estuaries

Phylum Annelida, Class
Polychaeta, Subclass
Sedentaria

408 Leafy Paddle Worm   *Phyllodoce* spp.   Length: 18"
p. 475

Rocky Shores and Offshore
Waters

Phylum Annelida, Class
Polychaeta, Subclass
Errantia

409 Eighteen-scaled Worm   *Halosydna brevisetosa*   Length: 4⅜″
p. 475

Rocky Shores; Bays and Estuaries

Phylum Annelida, Class Polychaeta, Subclass Errantia

410 Fifteen-scaled Worm   *Harmothoe imbricata*   Length: 2½″
p. 476

Rocky Shores; Bays and Estuaries

Phylum Annelida, Class Polychaeta, Subclass Errantia

411 Twelve-scaled Worm   *Lepidonotus squamatus*   Length: 2″
p. 476

Rocky Shores and Offshore Waters

Phylum Annelida, Class Polychaeta, Subclass Errantia

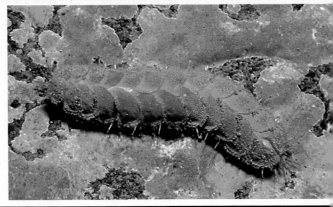

412 Tapered Flatworm *Notoplana acticola* Length: 2⅜″
p. 477

Rocky Shores

Phylum Platyhelminthes,
Order Polycladida

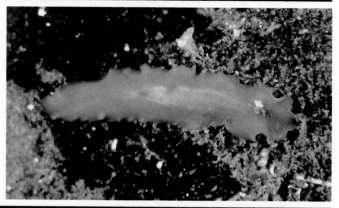

413 Oval Flatworm *Alloioplana californica* Length: 1½″
p. 477

Rocky Shores

Phylum Platyhelminthes,
Order Polycladida

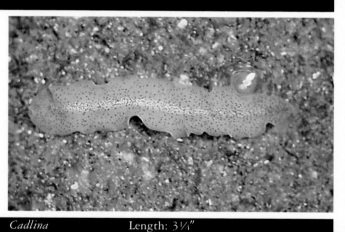

**414 Yellow-edged
Cadlina** *Cadlina
luteomarginata*
p. 477
Length: 3¼″

Rocky Shores

Phylum Mollusca, Class
Gastropoda, Subclass
Opisthobranchia

415 Blue-and-gold Nudibranch

Hypselodoris californiensis
p. 478

Length: 2⅝″

Rocky Shores

Phylum Mollusca, Class Gastropoda, Subclass Opisthobranchia

416 California Brown Sea Hare

Aplysia californica
p. 478

Length: 16″

Rocky Shores; Bays and Estuaries

Phylum Mollusca, Class Gastropoda, Subclass Opisthobranchia

417 Navanax

Navanax inermis
p. 478

Length: 8″

Bays and Estuaries

Phylum Mollusca, Class Gastropoda, Subclass Opisthobranchia

418 Red Sponge Nudibranch

Rostanga pulchra
p. 479

Length: 1¼"

Rocky Shores

Phylum Mollusca, Class
Gastropoda, Subclass
Opisthobranchia

419 Salted Doris

Doriopsilla
albopunctata
p. 479

Length: 2¾"

Rocky Shores

Phylum Mollusca, Class
Gastropoda, Subclass
Opisthobranchia

420 Rough-mantled Doris

Onchidoris bilamellata
p. 479

Length: 1"

Rocky Shores

Phylum Mollusca, Class
Gastropoda, Subclass
Opisthobranchia

421 Monterey Doris
Archidoris montereyensis
p. 480
Length: 2″

Rocky Shores

Phylum Mollusca, Class
Gastropoda, Subclass
Opisthobranchia

422 Sea Lemon
Anisodoris nobilis
p. 480
Length: 10″

Rocky Shores

Phylum Mollusca, Class
Gastropoda, Subclass
Opisthobranchia

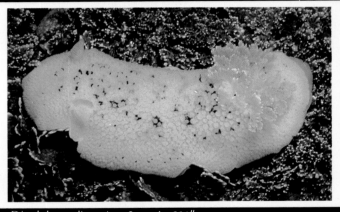

423 Ring-spotted Doris
Diaulula sandiegensis
p. 481
Length: 3⅝″

Rocky Shores

Phylum Mollusca, Class
Gastropoda, Subclass
Opisthobranchia

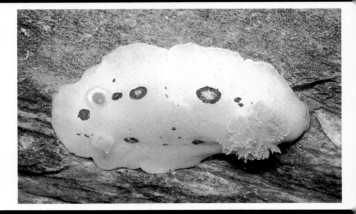

424 Stiff-footed Sea Cucumber

Eupentacta quinquesemita
p. 481

Length: 4"

Rocky Shores

Phylum Echinodermata,
Class Holothuroidea

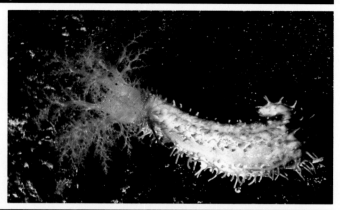

425 Dwarf Sea Cucumber

Lissothuria nutriens
p. 481

Length: ¾"

Rocky Shores and Offshore
Waters

Phylum Echinodermata,
Class Holothuroidea

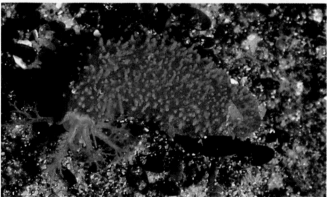

426 Red Sea Cucumber

Cucumaria miniata
p. 482

Length: 10"

Rocky Shores

Phylum Echinodermata,
Class Holothuroidea

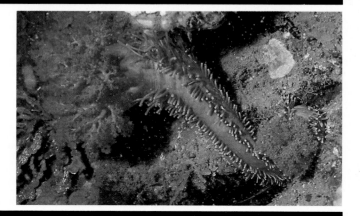

427 Bushy-backed Sea Slug   *Dendronotus frondosus*   Length: 4⅛"
p. 482

Rocky Shores; Bays and Estuaries; Wharves, Docks, and Pilings

Phylum Mollusca, Class Gastropoda, Subclass Opisthobranchia

428 Hermissenda Nudibranch   *Hermissenda crassicornis*   Length: 3¼"
p. 482

Rocky Shores; Bays and Estuaries; Wharves, Docks, and Pilings

Phylum Mollusca, Class Gastropoda, Subclass Opisthobranchia

429 Sea Clown Nudibranch   *Triopha catalinae*   Length: 6"
p. 483

Rocky Shores and Offshore Waters

Phylum Mollusca, Class Gastropoda, Subclass Opisthobranchia

430 California Stichopus

Parastichopus californicus
p. 483

Length: 16"

Rocky Shores; Wharves, Docks, and Pilings; Offshore Waters

Phylum Echinodermata, Class Holothuroidea

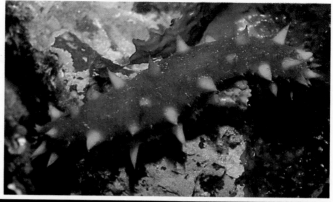

431 Elegant Eolid

Flabellinopsis iodinea
p. 484

Length: 3⅝"

Bays and Estuaries; Wharves, Docks and Pilings; Offshore Waters

Phylum Mollusca, Class Gastropoda, Subclass Opisthobranchia

432 Hopkins' Rose

Hopkinsia rosacea
p. 484

Length: 1¼"

Rocky Shores

Phylum Mollusca, Class Gastropoda, Subclass Opisthobranchia

433 Green Sea Urchin *Strongylocentrotus* Width: 3¼"
droebachiensis
p. 484

Rocky Shores

Phylum Echinodermata,
Class Echinoidea

434 Purple Sea Urchin *Strongylocentrotus* Width: 4"
purpuratus
p. 485

Rocky Shores

Phylum Echinodermata,
Class Echinoidea

435 Red Sea Urchin *Strongylocentrotus* Width: 5"
franciscanus
p. 485

Rocky Shores and Offshore
Waters

Phylum Echinodermata,
Class Echinoidea

436 Northern Red Anemone

Tealia crassicornis
p. 485

Width: 5"

Rocky Shores

Phylum Cnidaria, Class Anthozoa, Order Actiniaria

437 Club-tipped Anemone

Corynactis californica
p. 486

Width: 1¼"

Rocky Shores; Bays and Estuaries; Wharves, Docks, and Pilings

Phylum Cnidaria, Class Anthozoa, Order Corallimorpharia

438 Proliferating Anemone

Epiactis prolifera
p. 486

Width: 2"

Rocky Shores

Phylum Cnidaria, Class Anthozoa, Order Actiniaria

439 Aggregating Anemone

Anthopleura elegantissima
p. 486

Height: 20″

Rocky Shores

Phylum Cnidaria, Class Anthozoa, Order Actiniaria

440 Giant Green Anemone

Anthopleura xanthogrammica
p. 487

Height: 12″

Rocky Shores

Phylum Cnidaria, Class Anthozoa, Order Actiniaria

441 Proliferating Anemone

Epiactis prolifera
p. 486

Width: 2″

Rocky Shores

Phylum Cnidaria, Class Anthozoa, Order Actiniaria

442 Orange Cup Coral   *Balanophyllia elegans*   Height: ⅜″
p. 487

Rocky Shores

Phylum Cnidaria, Class
Anthozoa, Order
Scleractinia

443 Orange Cup Coral   *Balanophyllia elegans*   Height: ⅜″
p. 487

Rocky Shores

Phylum Cnidaria, Class
Anthozoa, Order
Scleractinia

444 Frilled Anemone   *Metridium senile*   Height: 18″
p. 488

Bays and Estuaries;
Wharves, Docks, and
Pilings; Offshore Waters

Phylum Cnidaria, Class
Anthozoa, Order Actiniaria

445 Ghost Anemone   *Diadumene leucolena*   Height: 1½"
p. 488

Bays and Estuaries

Phylum Cnidaria, Class
Anthozoa, Order Actiniaria

446 Red Soft Coral   *Gersemia rubiformis*   Height: 6"
p. 488

Rocky Shores

Phylum Cnidaria, Class
Anthozoa, Subclass
Octocorallia

447 Trumpet Stalked   *Haliclystus* spp.   Height: 1"
Jellyfish   *p. 489*

Seaweeds and Surf Grass

Phylum Cnidaria, Class
Scyphozoa

448 Gurney's Sea Pen *Ptilosarcus gurneyi* Height: 18″
p. 489

Bays and Estuaries;
Offshore Waters

Phylum Cnidaria, Class
Anthozoa, Subclass
Octocorallia

449 Monterey Stalked Tunicate *Styela montereyensis* Height: 10″
p. 489

Rocky Shores

Phylum Chordata, Class
Ascidiacea

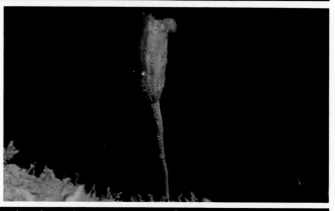

450 Club Hydroid *Clava leptostyla* Width: 1″
p. 490

Bays and Estuaries;
Wharves, Docks, and
Pilings

Phylum Cnidaria, Class
Hydrozoa

451 Red Soft Coral   *Gersemia rubiformis*   Height: 6"
p. 488

Rocky Shores

Phylum Cnidaria, Class
Anthozoa, Subclass
Octocorallia

**452 Slipper Sea
Cucumber**   *Psolus chitonoides*   Length: 4¾"
p. 490

Rocky Shores; Bays and
Estuaries; Offshore Waters

Phylum Echinodermata,
Class Holothuroidea

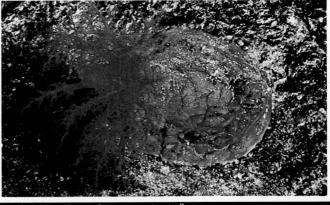

**453 Giant Feather
Duster**   *Eudistylia polymorpha*   Length: 10"
p. 490

Rocky Shores; Bays and
Estuaries; Wharves, Docks,
and Pilings

Phylum Annelida, Class
Polychaeta, Subclass
Sedentaria

454 Giant Feather Duster

Eudistylia polymorpha
p. 490

Length: 10″

Rocky Shores; Bays and Estuaries; and Wharves, Docks, and Pilings

Phylum Annelida, Class Polychaeta, Subclass Sedentaria

455 Banded Feather Duster

Sabella crassicornis
p. 491

Length: 2″

Rocky Shores; Bays and Estuaries; Wharves, Docks, and Pilings

Phylum Annelida, Class Polychaeta, Subclass Sedentaria

456 Giant Feather Duster

Eudistylia polymorpha
p. 490

Length: 10″

Rocky Shores; Bays and Estuaries; Wharves, Docks, and Pilings

Phylum Annelida, Class Polychaeta, Subclass Sedentaria

457 Red Tube Worm   *Serpula vermicularis*   Length: 4"
p. 491

Rocky Shores; Bays and
Estuaries; Wharves, Docks,
and Pilings

Phylum Annelida, Class
Polychaeta, Subclass
Sedentaria

458 Red Tube Worm   *Serpula vermicularis*   Length: 4"
p. 491

Rocky Shores; Bays and
Estuaries; Wharves, Docks,
and Pilings

Phylum Annelida, Class
Polychaeta, Subclass
Sedentaria

**459 Red-striped Acorn
Barnacle**   *Megabalanus
californicus*   Width: 2⅜"
p. 492

Rocky Shores

Phylum Arthropoda, Class
Crustacea

460 Common Goose Barnacle

Lepas anatifera
p. 492

Length: 6"

Beaches; and Offshore Waters

Phylum Arthropoda, Class Crustacea

461 Leaf Barnacle

Pollicipes polymerus
p. 492

Length: 3¼"

Rocky Shores

Phylum Arthropoda, Class Crustacea

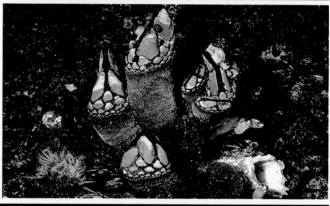

462 Giant Acorn Barnacle

Balanus nubilis
p. 493

Width: 4⅜"

Rocky Shores

Phylum Arthropoda, Class Crustacea

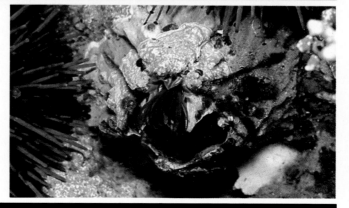

463 Volcano Barnacle   *Tetraclita rubescens*   Height: 2″
p. 493

Rocky Shores

Phylum Arthropoda, Class
Crustacea

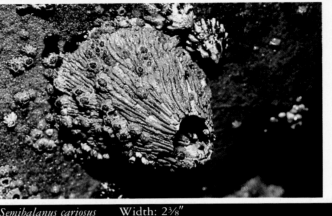

464 Thatched Barnacle   *Semibalanus cariosus*   Width: 2⅜″
p. 493

Rocky Shores

Phylum Arthropoda, Class
Crustacea

465 Leaf Barnacle   *Pollicipes polymerus*   Length: 3¼″
p. 492

Rocky Shores

Phylum Arthropoda, Class
Crustacea

466 Giant Acorn Barnacle

Balanus nubilis
p. 493

Width: 4⅜"

Rocky Shores

Phylum Arthropoda, Class
Crustacea

467 Little Striped Barnacle

Balanus amphitrite
p. 494

Height: ¾"

Rocky Shores; Bays and
Estuaries; Wharves, Docks,
and Pilings

Phylum Arthropoda, Class
Crustacea

468 Bay Barnacle

Balanus improvisus
p. 494

Width: ½"

Bays and Estuaries

Phylum Arthropoda, Class
Crustacea

469 Crumb of Bread Sponge

Halichondria panicea
p. 494

Width: over 12"

Rocky Shores; Wharves, Docks, and Pilings

Phylum Porifera, Class Demospongiae

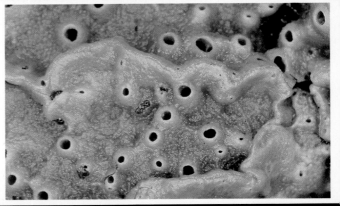

470 Boring Sponge

Cliona celata
p. 495

Width: ⅛"

Rocky Shores

Phylum Porifera, Class Demospongiae

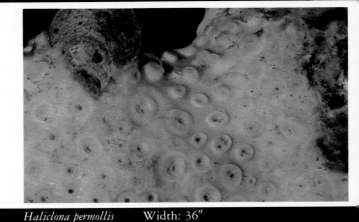

471 Purple Sponge

Haliclona permollis
p. 495

Width: 36"

Rocky Shores; Wharves, Docks, and Pilings

Phylum Porifera, Class Demospongiae

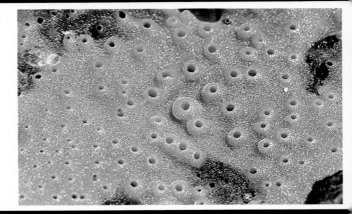

472 Purple Stylasterine   *Allopora porphyra*   Width: 6″
p. 496

Rocky Shores

Phylum Cnidaria, Class
Hydrozoa

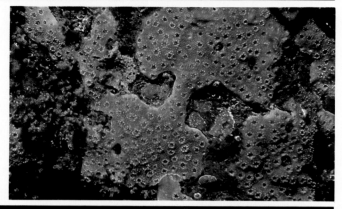

473 Velvety Red Sponge   *Ophlitaspongia pennata* Width: 36″
p. 496

Rocky Shores

Phylum Porifera, Class
Demospongiae

**474 Taylor's Colonial
Tunicate**   *Metandrocarpa taylori* Width: 8″
p. 496

Rocky Shores

Phylum Chordata, Class
Ascidiacea

475 Heath's Sponge   *Leucandra heathi*   Height: 4⅜"
p. 497

Rocky Shores; Wharves,
Docks, and Pilings

Phylum Porifera, Class
Calcispongiae

476 Red Beard Sponge   *Microciona prolifera*   Width: 8"
p. 497

Bays and Estuaries;
Wharves, Docks, and
Pilings

Phylum Porifera, Class
Demospongiae

477 Smooth Red Sponge   *Plocamia karykina*   Width: 10"
p. 497

Rocky Shores

Phylum Porifera, Class
Demospongiae

478 Luxurious Fringed Worm   *Cirriformia luxuriosa*   Length: 6"
p. 498

Rocky Shores; Bays and Estuaries

Phylum Annelida, Class Polychaeta, Subclass Sedentaria

479 Curly Terebellid Worm   *Thelepus crispus*   Length: 11¼"
p. 498

Rocky Shores; Bays and Estuaries

Phylum Annelida, Class Polychaeta, Subclass Sedentaria

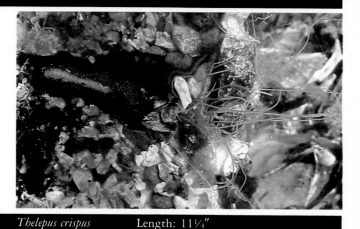

480 Curly Terebellid Worm   *Thelepus crispus*   Length: 11¼"
p. 498

Rocky Shores; Bays and Estuaries

Phylum Annelida, Class Polychaeta, Subclass Sedentaria

481 Tubularian Hydroid *Tubularia crocea* Width: 12"
p. 498

Bays and Estuaries

Phylum Cnidaria, Class
Hydrozoa

**482 Bushy Wine-glass
Hydroid** *Obelia* spp. Height: 8"
p. 499

Rocky Shores and Offshore
Waters

Phylum Cnidaria, Class
Hydrozoa

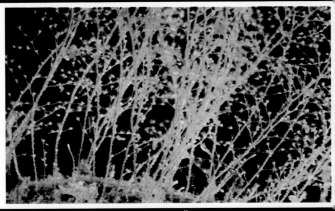

**483 Fern Garland
Hydroid** *Abietinaria* spp. Height: 12"
p. 499

Rocky Shores and Offshore
Waters

Phylum Cnidaria, Class
Hydrozoa

484 Halecium Hydroid
Halecium halecinum
p. 500
Height: 3″

Rocky Shores

Phylum Cnidaria, Class
Hydrozoa

485 Feathery Hydroid
Aglaophenia spp.
p. 500
Height: 24″

Rocky Shores; Wharves,
Docks, and Pilings

Phylum Cnidaria, Class
Hydrozoa

486 Feathery Hydroid
Aglaophenia spp.
p. 500
Height: 24″

Rocky Shores; Wharves,
Docks, and Pilings

Phylum Cnidaria, Class
Hydrozoa

487 Turkish Towel

Gigartina exasperata
p. 502

Length: 12–20″

Rocky Intertidal

Habitat
On rocks in lower
intertidal and subtidal
zones

488 Iridescent Seaweed

Iridaea cordata
p. 502

Blade length: 1–3′

Rocky Intertidal

Habitat
Lower rocky intertidal and
upper subtidal zones

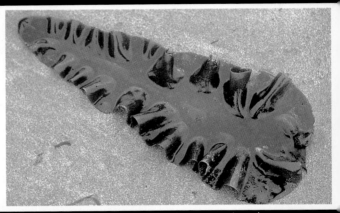

489 Winged Kelp

Alaria spp.
p. 502

Main blade length: 6–10′

Rocky Intertidal

Habitat
Lower intertidal zone on
moderate to exposed shores

490 Giant Perennial Kelp

Macrocystis spp.
p. 502

Blade length: 10–15"

Rocky Intertidal

Habitat
Subtidal zone, in areas exposed to open sea

491 Giant Perennial Kelp

Macrocystis spp.
p. 502

Blade length: 10–15"

Rocky Intertidal

Habitat
Subtidal zone, in areas exposed to open sea

492 Feather Boa

Egregia menziesii
p. 503

Blade length: to 30'

Rocky Intertidal

Habitat
On rocks in lower intertidal and subtidal zones

493 Bull Kelp

Nereocystis luetkeana
p. 503

Length: 10–100′

Rocky Intertidal

Habitat
Upper subtidal zone

494 Sugar Wrack

Laminaria saccharina
p. 504

Blade length: 2′ or longer

Rocky Intertidal

Habitat
On rocks, wharfs, or shells
in the intertidal and
subtidal zones

495 Sea Lettuce

Ulva lactuca
p. 504

Length: 4–20″

Rocky Intertidal;
Bays and Estuaries

Habitat
On rocks; epiphytic on
other algae in upper and
intertidal zones; often
floating on mud flats

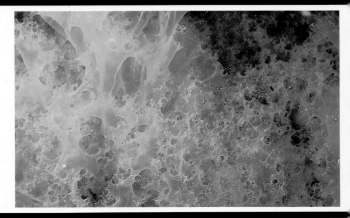

496 Sea Palm

Postelsia palmaeformis Height: to 20"
p. 505

Rocky Intertidal

Habitat
Exposed portions of outer
coast, often with mussels
and barnacles

497 Sea Staghorn

Codium fragile Length: to 16"
p. 505

Rocky Intertidal

Habitat
Middle to lower intertidal
zone and subtidal regions
of rocky shores

498 Sea Sack

Halosaccion Length: 6"
glandiforme
p. 505

Rocky Intertidal

Habitat
On rocks in mid-intertidal
zone, in sheltered and
exposed areas

499 Rockweed   *Fucus distichus*   Length: 4–20″
                    p. 506

Rocky Intertidal

Habitat
On rocks in mid-intertidal
zone

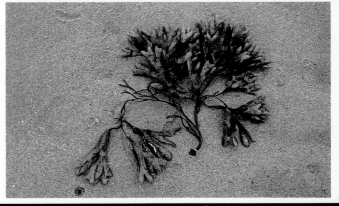

500 Little Rockweed   *Pelvetiopsis limitata*   Length: 2½–6″
                          p. 506

Rocky Intertidal

Habitat
Very high in rocky
intertidal zone on exposed
coasts

501 Fir Needle   *Analipus japonicus*   Length: 2–10″
                     p. 506

Rocky Intertidal

Habitat
On rocks in mid-intertidal
zone

502 Nail Brush

Endocladia muricata
p. 507

Height: 2–4″

Rocky Intertidal

Habitat
On rocky shores in high
intertidal zone

503 Black Pine

Rhodomela larix
p. 507

Strand length: to 12″

Rocky Intertidal

Habitat
On rocks in the mid- to
lower intertidal zone

504 Tar Spot

Ralfsia pacifica
p. 507

Crust diameter: 1–4″

Rocky Intertidal

Habitat
On rocks and solid
substrates high in the
intertidal zone

505 Coralline Algae *Corallina* spp. Height: 2–4"
p. 508

Rocky Intertidal

Habitat
In tide pools in lower
intertidal and upper
subtidal zones

506 Coralline Algae *Corallina* spp. Height: 2–4"
p. 508

Rocky Intertidal

Habitat
In tide pools in lower
intertidal and upper
subtidal zones

507 Encrusting Coral *Lithothamnium* Minute
pacificum
p. 508

Rocky Intertidal

Habitat
On rocks in tide pools in
lower intertidal and
subtidal zones

508 Eelgrass   *Zostera marina*   Blade length: to 4′
p. 508

Bays and Estuaries

Habitat
In quiet protected bays
with muddy bottoms

509 Surf Grass   *Phyllospadix* spp.   Blade length: to 6′
p. 509

Rocky Intertidal

Habitat
On exposed rocky shores

510 Enteromorpha   *Enteromorpha* spp.   Length: to 8″
Green Algae   *p. 509*

Rocky Intertidal

Habitat
Attached to rocks in upper
intertidal zone, in tidal
pools or freshwater seepage

511 Arctic Loon
Gavia arctica
p. 512
Length: 23–29"

Bays and Estuaries;
Offshore Waters

512 Red-throated Loon
Gavia stellata
p. 512
Length: 24–27"

Bays and Estuaries;
Offshore Waters

513 Red-necked Grebe
Podiceps grisegena
p. 513
Length: 18–22"

Bays and Estuaries;
Offshore Waters

514 Western Grebe

Aechmophorus occidentalis
p. 513

Length: 22–29"

Bays and Estuaries;
Offshore Waters

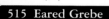

515 Eared Grebe

Podiceps nigricollis
p. 514

Length: 12–14"

Bays and Estuaries;
Offshore Waters

516 Horned Grebe

Podiceps auritus
p. 514

Length: 12–15¼"

Bays and Estuaries;
Offshore Waters

517 Common Loon   *Gavia immer*   Length: 28–36"
p. 515

Bays and Estuaries

518 Pied-billed Grebe   *Podilymbus podiceps*   Length: 12–15"
p. 515

Bays and Estuaries

519 White-winged Scoter   *Melanitta fusca*   Length: 19–23½"
p. 516

Bays and Estuaries;
Offshore Waters

520 Black Scoter *Melanitta nigra* Length: 17–20½"
p. 516

Bays and Estuaries;
Offshore Waters

521 Surf Scoter *Melanitta perspicillata* Length: 17–21"
p. 517

Bays and Estuaries;
Offshore Waters

522 American Wigeon *Anas americana* Length: 18–23"
p. 517

Beaches; Bays and Estuaries

523 Greater Scaup
Aythya marila
p. 518
Length: 15½–20″

Offshore Waters

524 Bufflehead
Bucephala albeola
p. 518
Length: 13–15½″

Bays and Estuaries;
Offshore Waters

525 Harlequin Duck
Histrionicus histrionicus
p. 519
Length: 14½–21″

Rocky Shores and Offshore
Waters

526 Oldsquaw

Clangula hyemalis
p. 519

Length: 19–22½"

Rocky Shores; Bays and
Estuaries

527 Northern Pintail

Anas acuta
p. 520

Length: 25–29" (males); 20½–
22½" (females)

Bays and Estuaries; Salt
Marshes

528 Brant

Branta bernicla
p. 521

Length: 23–26"

Bays and Estuaries

529 Emperor Goose
Chen canagica
p. 521
Length: 26–28"

Bays and Estuaries; Salt
Marshes

530 Tundra Swan
Cygnus columbianus
p. 522
Length: 47–58"

Salt Marshes

531 Brown Pelican
Pelecanus occidentalis
p. 522
Length: 45–54"

Rocky Shores; Bays and
Estuaries; Offshore Waters

Rocky Shores; Bays and
Estuaries; Offshore Waters

Rocky Shores and Offshore
Waters

Rocky Shores and Offshore
Waters

535 Common Murre
Uria aalge
p. 524
Length: 16–17"

Open Ocean

536 Pigeon Guillemot
Cepphus columba
p. 525
Length: 12–14"

Rocky Shores and Offshore
Waters

537 Xantus' Murrelet
*Synthliboramphus
hypoleucus*
p. 525
Length: 9½–10½"

Open Ocean and Oceanic
Islands

538 Ancient Murrelet
Synthliboramphus antiquus
p. 525
Length: 9½–10½"

Open Ocean and Oceanic Islands

539 Horned Puffin
Fratercula corniculata
p. 526
Length: 14½"

Offshore Waters and Open Ocean

540 Tufted Puffin
Fratercula cirrhata
p. 526
Length: 14½–15½"

Offshore Waters, Open Ocean, and Cliffs

541 Rhinoceros Auklet   *Cerorhinca monocerata*   Length: 14½–15½"
p. 527

Offshore Waters and Open
Ocean

542 Cassin's Auklet   *Ptychoramphus
aleuticus*
p. 527   Length: 8–9"

Open Ocean

543 Leach's Storm-Petrel *Oceanodroma leucorhoa* Length: 7½–9"
p. 528

Open Ocean

**544 Short-tailed
Shearwater** *Puffinus tenuirostris*
p. 529 Length: 13–14"

Open Ocean

545 Sooty Shearwater *Puffinus griseus*
p. 529 Length: 16–18"

Open Ocean

**546 Pink-footed
Shearwater** *Puffinus creatopus*
p. 530 Length: 20"

Open Ocean

547 Buller's Shearwater
Puffinus bulleri
p. 530
Length: 16½–18″

Open Ocean

Range
After nesting season ranges
in Northern Pacific,
especially from Monterey
Bay in central California
north to Washington and
British Columbia

548 Black-footed
Albatross
Diomedea nigripes
p. 531
Length: 28–36″

Open Ocean

Range
Along the entire Pacific
Coast of North America

549 Great Skua
Catharacta skua
p. 531
Length: 20–22″

Open Ocean

Range
Bipolar. Visitors from
Antarctica occur on Pacific
Coast

550 Parasitic Jaeger
Stercorarius parasiticus Length: 16–21"
p. 531

Open Ocean

551 Pomarine Jaeger
Stercorarius pomarinus Length: 20–23"
p. 532

Beaches; Bays and
Estuaries; Offshore Waters;
Open Ocean

552 Osprey
Pandion haliaetus Length: 21–24½"
p. 533

Beaches; Bays and Estuaries

553 Bald Eagle

Haliaeetus leucocephalus
p. 533

Length: 30–43"

Bays and Estuaries; River Mouths

554 Common Raven

Corvus corax
p. 534

Length: 21½–27"

Beaches

555 American Crow

Corvus brachyrhynchos
p. 534

Length: 17–21"

Beaches; Bays and Estuaries

556 Black Oystercatcher *Haematopus bachmani* Length: 17–17½"
p. 535

Rocky Shores

557 Belted Kingfisher *Ceryle alcyon* Length: 11–14½"
p. 535

Bays and Estuaries

558 Great Blue Heron *Ardea herodias* Length: 42–52"
p. 535

Rocky Shores; Bays and Estuaries

559 Red-necked Phalarope

Phalaropus lobatus
p. 536

Length: 6½–8"

Beaches; Bays and Estuaries; Offshore Waters

560 Red Phalarope

Phalaropus fulicaria
p. 536

Length: 7½–9"

Beaches; Offshore Waters, and Open Ocean

561 Virginia Rail

Rallus limicola
p. 537

Length: 8½–10½"

Salt Marshes

562 Clapper Rail

Rallus longirostris
p. 537

Length: 14–16½"

Salt Marshes

563 Whimbrel

Numenius phaeopus
p. 538

Length: 15–18¾"

Rocky Shores, Beaches,
and Salt Marshes

564 Marbled Godwit

Limosa fedoa
p. 538

Length: 16–20"

Beaches and Salt Marshes

565 Short-billed Dowitcher
Limnodromus griseus
p. 539
Length: 10½–12″

Bays and Estuaries

566 Red Knot
Calidris canutus
p. 539
Length: 10–11″

Beaches

567 Western Sandpiper
Calidris mauri
p. 540
Length: 6–7″

Beaches and Salt Marshes

568 Least Sandpiper   *Calidris minutilla*   Length: 5–6½"
p. 540

Bays and Estuaries

569 Rock Sandpiper   *Calidris ptilocnemis*   Length: 8–9"
p. 541

Rocky Shores

570 Sanderling   *Calidris alba*   Length: 7–8¾"
p. 541

Beaches

571 Lesser Yellowlegs

Tringa flavipes
p. 542

Length: 9½–11"

Rocky Shores and Salt
Marshes

572 Greater Yellowlegs

Tringa melanoleuca
p. 542

Length: 12½–15"

Rocky Shores, Beaches,
and Salt Marshes

573 Willet

Catoptrophorus
semipalmatus
p. 543

Length: 14–17"

Beaches and Salt Marshes

574 Spotted Sandpiper *Actitis macularia* Length: 7½–8″
p. 543

Bays and Estuaries; Salt
Marshes

575 Surfbird *Aphriza virgata* Length: 10″
p. 544

Rocky Shores and Offshore
Waters

576 Wandering Tattler *Heteroscelus incanus* Length: 11″
p. 544

Rocky Shores and Beaches

577 Black Turnstone

Arenaria melanocephala
p. 545

Length: 9"

Rocky Shores, Salt Marshes, and Offshore Waters

578 Dunlin

Calidris alpina
p. 545

Length: 8–9"

Beaches

579 Black-bellied Plover

Pluvialis squatarola
p. 546

Length: 10½–13½"

Beaches and Salt Marshes

580 Semipalmated Plover

Charadrius semipalmatus
p. 546

Length: 6½–8″

Beaches; Bays and Estuaries

581 Killdeer

Charadrius vociferus
p. 547

Length: 9–11″

Coastal Fields

582 Snowy Plover

Charadrius alexandrinus
p. 547

Length: 6–7″

Beaches; Bays and Estuaries

583 Forster's Tern
Sterna forsteri
p. 547

Length: 14–16¼"

Bays and Estuaries

584 Elegant Tern
Sterna elegans
p. 548

Length: 16–17"

Beaches; Bays and Estuaries

585 Common Tern
Sterna hirundo
p. 548

Length: 13–16"

Bays and Estuaries

586 Caspian Tern   *Sterna caspia*   Length: 19–23"
                                   p. 549

Bays and Estuaries;
Offshore Waters

587 Least Tern   *Sterna antillarum*   Length: 8½–9½"
                              p. 549

Beaches; Bays and Estuaries

588 Forster's Tern   *Sterna forsteri*   Length: 14–16¼"
                                 p. 547

Bays and Estuaries

589 Sabine's Gull   *Xema sabini*   Length: 13–14″
                         p. 550

Offshore Waters and Open
Ocean

590 Bonaparte's Gull   *Larus philadelphia*   Length: 12–14″
                            p. 550

Rocky Shores; Beaches;
Bays and Estuaries

591 Heermann's Gull   *Larus heermanni*   Length: 18–21″
                           p. 551

Beaches and Offshore
Waters

592 Thayer's Gull

Larus thayeri
p. 551

Length: 22½–25″

Offshore Waters

593 Black-legged Kittiwake

Rissa tridactyla
p. 552

Length: 16–18″

Open Ocean

594 Glaucous-winged Gull

Larus glaucescens
p. 552

Length: 24–27″

Rocky Shores; Beaches;
Wharves, Docks, and
Pilings; Open Ocean

Beaches; Bays and Estuaries

Rocky Shores; Beaches;
Wharves, Docks, and
Pilings; Open Ocean

Offshore Waters

598 Mew Gull
Larus canus
p. 555
Length: 16–18"

Beaches and Offshore
Waters

599 Ring-billed Gull
Larus delawarensis
p. 555
Length: 18–21"

Beaches

600 Northern Fulmar
Fulmarus glacialis
p. 556
Length: 17–20"

Open Ocean

601 Tree Lupine
Lupinus arboreus
p. 558

Plant height: 2–9'
Flower length: over ½"

Coastal areas near dunes

Flowers
March–June

602 Giant Coreopsis
Coreopsis gigantea
p. 558

Plant height: 1–10'
Flower width: to 3"

Bluffs near dunes

Flowers
March–May

603 Narrow Goldenrod
Solidago spathulata
p. 559

Plant height: 2–32"
Flower length: about ¼"

Coastal areas near dunes

Flowers
June–September

604 Northern Dune Tansy   *Tanacetum douglasii*   Plant height: 8–24″
                                  p. 559   Flower width: about ½″

Dunes

Flowers
June–September

605 Yellow Sand Verbena   *Abronia latifolia*   Flower width: 1–2″
                                 p. 560   Creeper

Dunes

Flowers
May–August

606 Menzies' Wallflower   *Erysimum menziesii* ·   Plant height: 1–8″
                                 p. 560   Flower width: ½–¾″

Dunes

Flowers
March–May

607 Beach Primrose *Oenothera* — Flower width: ½–1¼"
cheiranthifolia — Creeper
p. 560

Beaches

Flowers
April–August

608 Beach Strawberry *Fragaria chiloensis* — Flower width: about ¾"
p. 561 — Creeper

Bluffs near dunes

Flowers
March–August

609 Beach Silvertop *Glehnia leiocarpa* — Plant height: 2½"
p. 561 — Flower width: 3–4"

Beaches and Dunes

Flowers
May–July

610 Powdery Dudleya

Dudleya farinosa
p. 562

Plant height: 4–14"
Flower width: about ⅜"

Beaches and nearby bluffs

Flowers
May–September

611 Beach Morning Glory

Calystegia soldanella
p. 562

Flower width: 1½–2½"
Creeper

Beaches

Flowers
April–September

612 Sea Rocket

Cakile edentula
p. 563

Plant height: 6–20"
Flower width: ¼"

Beaches

Flowers
July–September

613 Common Ice Plant *Mesembryanthemum*   Flower width: 1″
crystallinum   Creeper
p. 563

Dunes

Flowers
March–October

614 Seaside Daisy *Erigeron glaucous*   Height: 4–16″
p. 564   Flower width: 1½–2½″

Dunes and coastal fields
and hills

Flowers
April–August

615 Sea Fig *Mesembryanthemum*   Flower width: 1½–2½″
chilense   Creeper
p. 564

Dunes

Flowers
April–September

| 616 Salt-Marsh Club-flower | *Cordylanthus maritimus* p. 565 | Plant height: 8–16" Flower length: ¾" |

Salt marshes

Flowers
May–September

| 617 Silky Beach Pea | *Lathyrus littoralis* p. 565 | Plant height: 8–24" Flower length: ¾" |

Dunes and Beaches

Flowers
April–June

| 618 California Thrift | *Armeria maritima* p. 566 | Plant height: 2–16" Flower width: ¾–1" |

Beaches

Flowers
March–August

SEASHELLS

As every beachcomber knows, a visit to the seashore offers the pleasure of collecting the shells that have been washed ashore by the tides. On the Pacific Coast, a wide variety of shells are found, from the large Gaper clams to the tiny, delicate Amethyst Gem Clam and Purple Dwarf Olive. This section describes some of the most typical and interesting shells that can be found along North America's western shores.

Pacific Orb Diplodon
Diplodonta orbella
25

3/8–13/8″ (1–3.5 cm) long. Almost circular, strongly inflated; umbones central, pointing forward; ligament strong, external. Exterior whitish, often covered with a thin, brownish or yellowish periostracum; with irregular, concentric growth wrinkles and fine, concentric, threadlike growth lines. Interior white; left valve with a strong, split central tooth under umbo and a long oblique tooth under ligament shelf; right valve with a small, triangular tooth under umbo and an oblique, elongately triangular tooth under front part of ligament shelf.

Habitat
Under rocks or in empty bivalve shells, intertidally to water 120′ (37 m) deep.

Range
Alaska to Gulf of California.

Comments
This species is either covered with cemented sand grains or enclosed in a feltlike, very irregular nest of plant remains bound together with mucus. Nests often have long extensions that may help to anchor them.

Common Pacific Egg Cockle
Laevicardium substriatum
26

3/4–13/8″ (1.9–3.5 cm) long. Small, broadly ovate, slightly oblique, inflated, thin-shelled; umbones prominent; elongate, pointed, smoothish areas present on upper part of front and back ends. Exterior yellowish gray, with narrow, interrupted radiating rays of reddish brown; color rays between very obscure, pale radiating ridges; obscure growth lines present. Interior whitish, stained and spotted with reddish brown and yellow; hind margin smooth, with reddish-purple edge, lower margin finely scalloped; hinge arched, with 2 central teeth in each valve; side teeth narrow, flattened.

Habitat
In sand, from near low-tide line to water 150′ (46 m) deep.

Range
Mugu Bay, California, to S. Baja California.

Comments
A common species in bays and estuaries, this is also called the Little Egg Cockle.

Amethyst Gem Clam
Gemma gemma
27

1/8″ (3 mm) long. Very small, broadly oval to almost circular or triangular, inflated; umbones near center; lunule obscure. Exterior yellowish or grayish white, usually tinged with pale purple, or purplish with pale margin; shiny, with fine growth lines or wrinkles. Interior suffused with purple; pallial sinus narrow, pointing upward; side teeth obscure; margin finely and obscurely toothed.

Habitat
On sand or mud flats above low-tide level; also subtidally to water 330′ (100 m) deep.

Range
Puget Sound to San Diego, California; Nova Scotia to Florida, Texas, and the Bahamas.

Comments
This tiny species, introduced to the Pacific Coast in the late 19th century, is also known as the Gem Venus Clam or the Gem Shell. The sexes are separate and the fertilized eggs develop within the mantle folds of the female. From there— about 200 young are released per female—they escape as burrowing young ready to burrow in the mud or sand. The life span of this clam seems to be not more than 2 years.

California Mactra
Mactra californica
28

1⅛–1⅞″ (2.8–4.8 cm) long. Small, oval, thin-shelled; umbones near middle; ligament very small; a broad, low, flattened ridge runs from umbones to narrow, squared-off hind end. Exterior white, with grayish-brown, fibrous periostracum; smooth except for fine concentric growth lines and fine, low concentric wrinkles below umbones. Interior white; flat side teeth close to central teeth, 2 in right valve, 1 in left.

Habitat
Buried in sand flats or in sandy mud, in bays and offshore, intertidally to water 70′ (21 m) deep.

Range
Puget Sound to Costa Rica.

Comments
Also called the California Surf Clam, this is the most commonly found mactra in California and is locally gathered for clam chowder.

Carpenter's Tellin
Tellina carpenteri
29

½–⅝″ (13–16 mm) long. Ovate, almost oblong, thin-shelled; hind margin concave just below umbones; umbones a little behind middle. Exterior grayish white, usually flushed with pink and with opaque white spots; with fine concentric grooves; especially near lower margin and front end, becoming fine, erect ridges at hind end. Interior whitish, flushed with pink; right valve with 2 central teeth and 1 long front side tooth; left valve with 1 central tooth and 1 weak hind side tooth.

Habitat
In sand or sandy mud, at low-tide line in bays to water 600′ (183 m) deep.

Range
S. Alaska to Panama.

Comments
In tellinids the siphons are separate. The inhalent siphon is used like a vacuum cleaner to suck up minute detrital particles, microscopic animals, and diatoms from the surface of

the substrate. The species honors Philip P. Carpenter (1819–
1877), British conchologist, the first to seriously study the
mollusks of our Pacific Coast.

Gould's Wedge Shell
Donax gouldii
30

⅝–⅞" (16–22 mm) long. Triangular, wedge-shaped,
inflated, thick-shelled; hind end flattened; hind margin gently
convex. Exterior yellowish white, or suffused or rayed with
pale brown, often with concentric bands or lines of bluish
purple; with shallow, obscure radial grooves. Interior whitish,
usually suffused with purplish or brownish blue; margin
strongly toothed and grooved, especially hind part.

Habitat
In sand, on surf-washed beaches.

Range
Monterey, California, to S. Baja California.

Comments
On the Pacific Coast this species is also known as the Bean
Clam. If waves disturb the upper sand layer, it digs more
deeply into the sand. Frequently a colonial hydroid (*Clytra
bakeri*) lives on its valves. A related species, the California
Donax or Wedge Clam (*D. californicus*), found from Santa
Barbara, California, to southern Baja California, is about the
same size, but is more elongate and lacks the colored bands
and rays.

Carpenter's Cardita
Glans subquadrata
31

¼–½" (6–13 mm) long. Small, oblong, inflated, thick-
shelled; upper and lower margins almost parallel, front end
somewhat narrowed, rounded; umbones near front end.
Exterior yellowish white, covered with a thin, yellowish
periostracum; with strong, rounded, irregularly knobby radial
ribs spotted with reddish brown. Interior white, spotted with
brown near hind end of upper margin; lower and side margins
strongly scalloped; hinge has 1 strong, triangular central tooth
in right valve, 2 narrow central teeth at right angles in left
valve; 2 side teeth in each valve.

Habitat
Attached to undersides of rocks, from near low-tide line to
water 300' (91 m) deep.

Range
British Columbia to N. Baja California.

Comments
This common species is attached by its byssus to wharf
pilings. Sometimes it is listed as *G. carpenteri* or *G. minuscula*.
The eggs and young are brooded in the mantle cavity until the
young have well-formed shells. They are often found clinging
to the parent's shell.

Giant Pacific Cockle
Trachycardium
quadrigenarium
32

2¼–5½" (5.7–14 cm) high. Large, obliquely and broadly oval, strongly inflated; umbones large; ligament strong. Exterior grayish white, covered with a thin, brownish periostracum; with many narrow, slightly flattened ribs; ribs on hind three-quarters of shell have small, pointed, triangular spines on hind side; ribs on front quarter have spines on front side. Interior white; margin strongly grooved and scalloped.

Habitat
In firm, sandy mud, in bays and quiet waters 35–450' (10.7–137 m) deep.

Range
Monterey Bay, California, to S. Baja California.

Comments
On the Pacific Coast this species is often called the Spiny Cockle, and is used locally for food. Although it is large it can use its strong foot to leap out of the sand. Young shells are usually more transversely oval.

Nuttall's Cockle
Clinocardium nuttalli
33

2–5½" (5.1–14 cm) long. Large, broadly ovate to almost circular, moderately inflated; umbones curved forward, in front of middle; ligament long. Exterior grayish, covered with a light brown to yellowish-brown, thin but tough periostracum, with occasional dark concentric bands; numerous flattened ribs present, with transversely elongated beads that are absent on narrower ribs at hind end. Interior dull yellowish white; margin strongly scalloped.

Habitat
In sand or mud, intertidally to water 180' (55 m) deep.

Range
Bering Sea to San Diego, California.

Comments
This large cockle is also known on the Pacific Coast as the Basket Cockle or Heart Cockle; it was once called *C. corbis*. It is commercially fished in Puget Sound and British Columbia and sold in markets and restaurants. Older shells become higher and more oblique. Alternating broad and narrow growth bands reflect the tidal cycle. The broad bands are formed during period of high spring tides, when the animals are covered and can feed for longer periods, and the narrow bands are formed during neap tides, when they are exposed more of the time. The related Fucan Cockle (*C. fucanum*) is smaller, somewhat less inflated, and with ribs that are narrower, angled, and fewer in number. It occurs from Sitka, Alaska, to Monterey, California.

West Coast Bittersweet
Glycymeris subobsoleta
34

⅛–1½" (2.2–3.8 cm) long. Almost round, usually longer than high, moderately compressed, with hind end slightly angled; top margin angled by small umbones that are close, separated by narrow, pointed, sunken ligament area. Exterior white, chalky, sometimes with small, brown zigzag markings, and covered with a brown, feltlike periostracum, which is often worn and usually found only along margin; broad, low, flattened ribs with narrow interspaces present, ribs usually worn. Interior white, flushed wth yellow in center, often grayish brown near finely toothed margin; hinge line curved, broad, with many small teeth; small middle teeth absent in large specimens.

Habitat
In sand or gravel, from low-tide line to water 300' (91 m) deep.

Range
Alaska to S. California.

Comments
This species appears to be most abundant between southern British Columbia and Oregon.

Common Pacific Littleneck
Protothaca staminea
35

1½–2⅜" (3.8–7 cm) long. Broadly and ovately oblong, moderately inflated, thick-shelled; hind end broad; umbones near front end; lunule obscure. Exterior yellowish white or brownish, sometimes with large, brownish splotches or zigzag markings and spots; with many axial riblets that are broadest on hind slope; on front half, riblets are beaded by concentric ridges, which are crowded near margin; on hind half, riblets are crossed by irregular growth lines. Interior white; pallial sinus deep, narrow, pointed; side teeth absent; margin finely toothed.

Habitat
In coarse, sandy mud, in bays or on open coast near rocks and rubble, in lower half of intertidal zone.

Range
Aleutian Islands, Alaska, to S. Baja California.

Comments
This species is much sought after by both commercial and sport fishermen as a delicacy. In southern British Columbia this clam grows to legal size, 1¼" (3 cm) long, in 3 years, while in Alaska it takes 8 years. Hybrids between this species and others seem to occur. The species name is a Latin adjective meaning "full of threads," and refers to the fine, crowded riblets. The related Toughsided Littleneck (*P. laciniata*), sometimes listed as a subspecies or variety of the Common Pacific Littleneck, is larger, reaching 3½" (8.9 cm) in length; it is thicker, with stronger, fluted concentric ridges, and occurs from Monterey Bay, California, to northern Baja California.

Japanese Littleneck
Tapes japonica
36

1½–2½" (3.8–6.4 cm) long. Ovately oblong, inflated, thick-shelled; lunule shallow, bordered by incised line. Exterior grayish or brownish white, often with brown and whitish radial spots; concentric ridges present, strongest at front end, and crossed by radial riblets that are narrower and stronger at hind end. Interior mostly whitish, with hind end and elongate, rounded pallial sinus purplish; front and lower margins sometimes also purplish; side teeth absent.

Habitat
In sandy mud in bays, just below the surface intertidally.

Range
Puget Sound to San Francisco Bay, California.

Comments
This species has been listed as *T. philippinarum* and is also known as the Manila Clam. In about 1935, it was accidentally introduced into Puget Sound with seed oysters imported from Japan. It spread rapidly and is now commercially fished in British Columbia and Washington.

California Glass Mya
Cryptomya californica
37

½–1⅛" (1.3–2.8 cm) long. Broadly elliptical, compressed, thin-shelled; front end broadly rounded; hind end obliquely flattened and angled at lower end; right valve larger and slightly more convex than left valve; umbones near center. Exterior white; with fine concentric growth lines and obscure radial grooves on hind end, especially conspicuous near lower margin and on thin, brown periostracum, which is fibrous at hind margin. Interior white; pallial sinus very shallow to absent; large ligament shelf in left valve.

Habitat
Burrowing in mud from mid-tide level to just below low-tide line.

Range
S. Alaska to northern Peru.

Comments
This species is always associated with burrowing shrimps of the genera *Callianassa* and *Upogebia,* and with the echiuroid worm *Urechis.* It burrows near the shrimp and worm species so that its short siphons can enter their neighboring burrows. It obtains its food from the water circulating there. This enables it to live deeper in the mud and to be better protected from predators.

Baltic Macoma
Macoma balthica
38

¾–1½" (1.9–3.8 cm) long. Rounded, thin, moderately flattened. Chalky white, with ragged, dark brown periostracum, usually worn off upper part of valves. Valves equal; umbones prominent, central. Surface with fine concentric lines. Separate tubular siphons extending more than 10 times length of valves.

Habitat
In mud or sandy mud in quiet bays and brackish estuaries; well above low-tide line and below in shallow water.

Range
On both coasts: Bering Sea to central California; Arctic to Georgia.

Comments
Their remarkably long siphons enable macomas to live nearly 12" (30 cm) below the surface of the bottom. At low tide one can sometimes see their whitish siphons in quiet tide pools, actively waving like worms. *M. balthica* is a principal winter food of the black duck (*Anas rubripes*).

Salmon Tellin
Tellina nuculoides
39

½–¾" (13–19 mm) long. Broadly ovate, somewhat flattened, moderately thick-shelled; both ends rounded; umbones behind middle. Exterior smooth, whitish, often stained with pink; with 10–15 irregularly spaced, dark grayish-purple or reddish-brown concentric growth lines. Interior whitish, usually suffused with pinkish orange; muscle scars and pallial line prominent; right valve with 2 central teeth, strong front and hind side teeth; left valve with 1 central tooth.

Habitat
In sand, from low-tide line to 200' (61 m).

Range
Aleutian Islands, Alaska, to San Pedro, California.

Comments
This species was once called *T. salmonea* because its interior is frequently salmon-colored. The species name was given because the outline of the shell resembles that of many species in the genus *Nucula*.

Common Western Spoon Clam
Periploma planiusculum
40

1½–2½" (3.8–6.4 cm) long. Moderately large, broadly ovate; right valve considerably more convex than flattened left valve; front end twisted; umbones about one-third shell length from hind end. Exterior white; periostracum thin, yellowish brown, wrinkled and grainy on hind end and near margin; smoothish, with concentric growth ridges and wrinkles. Interior white, pearly; oblong ligament shelf directed obliquely toward front end, with buttress forming an oblique rounded ridge ending at upper end of short, slightly pointed pallial sinus. Foot slender; siphons long. No byssus.

Habitat
In sand just below low-tide line.

Range
Point Conception, California, to northern Peru.

Comments
Shells, even those with living animals, are cast up on beaches after storms. The species name is derived from the Latin adjective *planus* ("flat"), referring to the flattened left valve.

Californian Lucine
Epilucina californica
41

¾–1½" (1.9–3.8 cm) long. Almost circular to broadly ovate; umbones near middle of upper margin; lunule spearhead-shaped and entirely in right valve, fitting closely into recessed area in left valve; ligament cleft deep, elongate, near surface. Exterior dull white; with many fine, rounded or somewhat flattened concentric ridges separated by narrow grooves and crossed by fine, obscure, hairlike lines. Interior white; hinge with 2 central teeth under umbones, small front tooth in right valve fused to base of projecting lunule; 1 strong side tooth in right valve, 2 in left valve; margin thickened, faintly wrinkled, edge smooth.

Habitat
In sand or gravelly rubble, from below low-tide line to water 240' (73 m) deep.

Range
Crescent City, California, to central Baja California.

Comments
Although this species is sometimes placed in the genus *Codakia,* it differs in having an external ligament, strong hind side teeth, and no radial sculpture.

La Perouse's Kellia
Kellia laperousi
42

½–1⅛" (1.3–2.8 cm) long. Relatively large, transversely and broadly elliptical, inflated; umbones nearly central. Exterior whitish, covered with a thin, yellowish periostracum; smooth near upper margin except for fine, concentric growth lines; concentric ridges stronger toward lower margin. Interior whitish; in right valve 1 knoblike central tooth under umbo, and 2 long hind side teeth; in left valve 2 central teeth under umbo, not joined at top, and 1 long hind side tooth; margin smooth.

Habitat
Among bivalves, from near low-tide line to water 210' (64 m) deep.

Range
Bering Sea to Gulf of California.

Comments
One of the largest members of the family, it is commonly found nestling among bivalves on pilings and in mussel and jewel box beds. When the animal moves about it often extends the fleshy mantle tissue out over the shell. The species name honors the leader of a French expedition to the Pacific in the 18th century.

Pismo Clam
Tivela stultorum
43

2½–6¼" (6.4–15.9 cm) long. Large, elongately triangular, somewhat flattened, thick-shelled; umbones large, near center; a rounded angle runs from umbones to lower end of bluntly rounded hind end; front end evenly rounded. Exterior whitish, often with irregularly arranged, pale reddish-brown rays, hind slope often darker; thin, grayish-yellow, shiny periostracum gives shell a grayish-tan color; smooth except for growth wrinkles. Interior whitish or cream-colored; pallial sinus small, pointed; hinge strong; front side tooth in both valves and hind central tooth in left valve large.

Habitat
In sand flats, intertidally to water 80' (24 m) deep.

Range
Central California to S. Baja California.

Comments
Once extensively dug for in California, the population gradually declined, and now there is a minimum length limit of 5" (12.7 cm) and a catch limit of 15 clams a day per person; no commercial digging is allowed. Some of the biggest are estimated to be 45–50 years old.

Hemphill's Surf Clam
Spisula hemphilli
44

2½–6" (6.4–15.2 cm) long. Large, oval, moderately thick-shelled; front part of upper margin concave, hind part convex; umbones near middle, bent forward. Exterior yellowish white, with thin, brown periostracum, which is fibrous and wrinkled near hind end, forming concentric ridges; smooth except for fine growth lines; a strong, angled ridge runs from umbones to lower end of hind margin, with a lower, narrow ridge present on each side of strong ridge; minor ridges enclose area where periostracum is wrinkled. Interior dull white, shiny around smooth margin.

Habitat
In sand or sandy mud, from just below low-tide line to water 150' (46 m) deep.

Range
Santa Barbara, California, to N. Baja California.

Comments
This fairly common and delicious species is also known as Hemphill's Dish Clam. The species name honors Henry Hemphill (1830–1914), who was a well-known California conchologist.

Stimpson's Surf Clam
Spisula polynyma
45

2¾–5½" (7–14 cm) long. Large, oval to almost triangular, moderately flattened, thick-shelled; umbones near middle, pointed, curved forward; ligament short. Exterior whitish, with a thin, pale to dark brown, fibrous periostracum, with fine threadlike ridges and wrinkles at hind end behind obscure line that runs from umbones to lower end of hind margin; smooth except for strong growth lines. Interior white; large, squared-off pallial sinus near hind muscle scar; hinge with 1 smooth side tooth in left valve, 2 in right valve.

Habitat
In sand, mud, or gravel, from low-tide line to water 350' (107 m) deep.

Range
On both coasts: Arctic to Puget Sound, and to Rhode Island.

Comments
The genus name is probably based on the Latin adjective *spissus* ("thick"), which may refer to the thickness of the larger specimens. The species name is probably based on 2 Greek words, *poly* ("many") and *nema* ("thread"), referring to the crowded growth lines on the surface. These clams are very sensitive to fine sediments and silts in the water.

California Cumingia
Cumingia californica
46

¾–1⅜" (1.9–3.5 cm) long. Broadly ovate; hind end narrowed, pointed; front end broadly rounded; umbones near center; lunule moderately long; external ligament narrow, short. Exterior dull grayish white; with sharp, irregular concentric ridges and fine, obscure radial grooves. Interior white; internal ligament broadly triangular; central teeth small; side teeth strong.

Habitat
In gravel and rock crevices, intertidally to water 150′ (46 m) deep.

Range
Mendocino County, California, to S. Baja California.

Comments
This shell nestles in rock crevices and therefore often becomes somewhat misshapen in growth. The animal's siphons are 2–3 times as long as the shell. The genus name honors Hugh Cuming (1791–1865), well-known English collector.

Pacific White Venus
Amiantis callosa
47

2½–4½" (6.4–11.4 cm) long. Large, oval, thick-shelled; hind end slightly angled; umbones between center and rounded front end; ligament strong. Exterior white, with a very thin, transparent, grayish or yellowish periostracum; strong, regular, occasionally branching concentric ridges present. Interior white; ligament shelf with fine wrinkled surface; pallial sinus small, sharply pointed; each valve has long hind central tooth.

Habitat
In sand, from below low-tide line to water 25′ (7.6 m) deep.

Range
Santa Barbara, California, to S. Baja California.

Comments
Also known in California as the Sea Cockle, the flesh of this species is delicious. However, it is only moderately common and therefore rarely sought.

Common Californian Venus
Chione californiensis
48

1½–3" (3.8–7.6 cm) long. Almost circular, flattened toward lower margin, thick-shelled; hind end often slightly squared off; umbones pointed, curved forward; lunule large; escutcheon bordered by angled ridges. Exterior yellowish white, sometimes tinged with brown in front; with low, broad radial ribs crossed by strong, distant, erect, sometimes flattened, slightly wavy concentric ridges; sculpture reduced on hind slope. Interior white, usually with purple splotch at front end; hinge and central teeth strong; front side teeth absent, hind ones obscure; lower and front margins finely grooved or toothed.

Habitat
In sand, on flats in bays near low-tide level, and offshore in water 60–150' (18–46 m) deep.

Range
Santa Barbara, California, to Panama.

Comments
In Greek mythology, Chione was the daughter of Boreas, the north wind. This species is delicious, but is not as abundant as the related Frilled Californian Venus, or Wavy Chione (*C. undatella*), which is fished commercially in southern California. Found from Santa Barbara, California, to Peru, it is the same size, but has more numerous and finer concentric ridges; it is also more vividly marked with brown.

Common Washington Clam
Saxidomus nuttalli
49

2¾–4¾" (7–12.1 cm) long. Large, oblongly ovate, moderately inflated, thick-shelled, gaping at hind end; front end evenly rounded, hind end sometimes somewhat flattened; umbones large; lunule absent; ligament strong. Exterior grayish yellow to brownish, often with rust-brown splotches; finely and strongly concentrically ridged, the ridges irregular and crowded at front end, erect and platelike at hind end. Interior white, stained with purple along hind margin; pallial sinus deep, narrow.

Habitat
Deeply buried in sand in bays or off rocky coasts, from near low-tide line to water 150' (50 m) deep.

Range
Central California to N. Baja California.

Comments
Also known as the Butter Clam. Very young clams are smoothish and may have brown radial streaks near the upper margin. The related Smooth Washington Clam (*S. gigantea*), which is also called the Butter Clam, is 2¾–4" (7–10.2 cm) long. It is found from Alaska to Monterey, California, and is somewhat higher, whiter, and smoother. Both of these clams are prized as food. The Smooth Washington Clam is the most important commercially in British Columbia.

Bent-nose Macoma
Macoma nasuta
50

1¼–3¼″ (3.2–8.3 cm) long. Broadly ovate, moderately thick-shelled; hind end narrowed, twisted; front end rounded; umbones central; right valve with low, broad ridge running from umbo to lower hind end, widening toward hind end. Exterior yellowish white or grayish white; periostracum grayish brown, fibrous; smoothish, with irregular growth lines or wrinkles. Interior white; pallial sinus large, reaching front muscle scar in left valve; 2 central teeth in right valve, 1 in left valve.

Habitat
In sandy mud, intertidally in bays to water 152′ (46 m) deep off open coast.

Range
Kodiak Island, Alaska, to S. Baja California.

Comments
A moderately large, rather common shell. The Latin species name means "large-nosed" and refers to the narrowed hind end. The related Stained Macoma (*M. inquinata*), ranging from the Aleutian Islands, Alaska, to Santa Barbara, California, is smaller and not as high; its hind end is not as sharply pointed.

Pacific Grooved Macoma
Leporimetis obesa
51

1⅝–3½″ (4.1–8.9 cm) long. Large, broadly oblong, almost ovate, moderately inflated, thick-shelled; both ends rounded; umbones large, central; deeply set ligament in front part of narrow cleft; hind end made wavy by broad ridge in right valve that runs from umbo to hind end, and by corresponding furrow in left valve. Exterior grayish white to pale brownish white; with fine, irregular, concentric growth lines especially prominent on hind end. Interior white, with yellowish spot in center; 2 central teeth in each valve; a deeply set ligament pit present next to hind central tooth.

Habitat
In sand or muddy sand, intertidally in bays to water 152′ (46 m) deep offshore.

Range
Point Conception, California, to S. Baja California.

Comments
This species is sometimes placed in the genus *Psammotreta*. A related species is the Atlantic Grooved Macoma (*L. intastriata*), found from South Carolina to the West Indies. It is a thinner, pure white shell with sharper, fine concentric ridges, especially near the margin.

White Sand Macoma
Macoma secta
52

2–4½″ (5.1–11.4 cm) long. Large, broadly ovate, slightly compressed, moderately thin-shelled; left valve usually noticeably flatter than right valve; wavy hind margin raised and pinched together, with notch between it and slightly sunken ligament; umbones in middle; in right valve a low ridge runs from umbo to hind end. Exterior pale yellowish white to white; periostracum thin, pale yellowish; smooth except for fine, concentric growth lines. Interior white; with ridge running diagonally for short distance from end of ligament shelf, with deep, irregular groove above ridge.

Habitat
In sand and sandy mud, intertidally in bays to water 33–152′ (10–46 m) deep offshore.

Range
Vancouver Island, British Columbia, to central Baja California.

Comments
This common, large macoma is delicious, but the gut is usually filled with sand when taken. The animal will void this material if soaked for a time in clean sea water. The species name is a Latin adjective meaning "cut" and refers to the sharp notch behind the ligament.

Rough Piddock
Zirfaea pilsbryi
53

5¼″ (13.3 cm) long. Hind end long with relatively straight margin. Shell whitish to grayish white, with brown periostracum. Hind surface smooth except for concentric growth lines; front end surface rough, with coarse concentric ridges bearing short spines. Gape wide; valves strong, with groove from umbo to lower margin.

Habitat
Thick mud, clay, and soft shale; low intertidal and subtidal zones in estuaries, lagoons, and bays.

Range
Alaska to Baja California.

Comments
The Rough Piddock is known to burrow more than 18″ (46 cm) into sandstone, shale, and clay. It grows to a larger size than its East Coast relative, the Great Piddock (*Z. crispata*).

Arctic Saxicave
Hiatella arctica
54

1–3″ (2.5–7.6 cm) long. Irregularly oblong to broadly ovate, thick-shelled; hind end gaping, broader than front end, often squared off; an angle runs from umbones to lower hind end, often with a second weaker umbonal ridge above; umbones in front of center; ligament short, stout. Young shells often with fine scales or spines on ridges. Exterior chalky white; periostracum thin, pale to dark brown, often rubbed off; rough, irregular growth lines or wrinkles present. Interior gray or grayish white; hinge with narrow ligament platform behind umbones. Siphons red-tipped.

Habitat
Nestling in crevices and old bore holes, from near low-tide line to water 600′ (183 m) deep.

Range
On both coasts: Arctic seas to Panama, and to the West
Indies.

Comments
Because of its nestling habit, this species becomes very
irregular in shape. Those shells that lack the spiny radial ribs
even in the young stage and that nearly always bore into soft
rock are often called *H. striata*.

Hearty Rupellaria
Rupellaria carditoides
55

¾–1¾" (1.9–4.4 cm) long. Moderately large, almost circular
to elongately ovate, outline usually irregular, inflated, thick-
shelled; umbones large, near front end; ligament short,
strong, in cleft. Exterior chalky white; with strong, irregular
growth lines and fine radial threads that fork along rounded
ridge running from umbones to lower hind end; threads
generally somewhat worn. Interior white; each valve with 2
central teeth; pallial sinus moderately deep, rounded.

Habitat
Nestling in holes in soft rock, from low-tide line to water
240' (75–80 m) deep.

Range
Vancouver Island, British Columbia, to S. Baja California.

Comments
This species is sometimes placed in the genus *Petricola*. It does
not actively bore into rock, but nestles in a pre-existing hole,
which it may enlarge slightly by moving its valves against the
walls of the hole. The shell's varying and irregular outline is
caused by its nestling habit.

Pacific Gaper
Tresus nuttallii
56

5½–7½" (14–19 cm) long. Large, oblongly oval, moderately
thin-shelled, inflated; umbones large, a third shell length
from front end; ligament narrow, external, on both sides of
umbones; hind end broad, rounded, with large gap for
siphons. Exterior yellowish white, with brown periostracum,
fibrous near margin and readily flaking off; smooth except for
irregular growth lines. Interior white; central teeth weak,
small side teeth near central teeth; pallial sinus large, deep.

Habitat
In sand and sandy mud, from low-tide line to water 100'
(30 m) deep.

Range
Puget Sound to central Baja California.

Comments
Commonly known on the Pacific Coast as the Gaper, this
species lives about 1–3' (0.3–0.9 m) under the surface in
sand; the long siphons are united for most of their length and
reach to just below the surface. As the siphons are withdrawn,
water squirts several feet into the air. This delicious clam is

dug for extensively, though not commercially, in northern California and Oregon. The related Alaskan Gaper or Horse Clam (*T. capax*), found from Alaska to Monterey, California, is about the same size, but more broadly oval, more inflated, and with its lower margin more deeply rounded.

Geoduck
Panopea generosa
57

3½–9" (8.9–22.9 cm) long. Large, oblong, moderately thick-shelled; rounded front end and squared-off hind end have rounded corners; valves gape everywhere except at umbones; umbones in front of middle, projecting above upper margin; ligament short, stout. Exterior grayish white to yellowish white, with a thin, yellowish-brown periostracum; with strong, irregular concentric growth wrinkles and, in young shells, fine, microscopic radial sculpture. Interior whitish; pallial sinus small, rounded; each valve has 1 small tooth under umbo and a strong ligament platform.

Habitat
In sandy mud in bays, intertidally to water 50' (15 m) deep.

Range
S. Alaska to central Baja California.

Comments
This species has long, united siphons that reach the surface when the clams lie 4 or more feet deep in their burrows. The siphons cannot be retracted into the shell; they may constitute half the weight of the animal, which can weigh 8 pounds or more. The exposed fleshy parts are covered with a tough, reddish-brown skin. This clam lives to about 16 years. The Geoduck is supposedly one of the finest eating clams on the West Coast, but it is relatively scarce and difficult to dig out. In recent years, however, divers with hydraulic clam diggers have taken great numbers in Puget Sound.

Chubby Mya
Platyodon cancellatus
58

1¾–3" (4.4–7.6 cm) long. Oblong, inflated, thick-shelled; hind end somewhat narrowed, squared off, widely gaping; umbones large, about a third shell length from hind end; umbo in right valve projects over margin of left valve; umbone tips worn. Exterior chalky white; periostracum thin, pale yellowish brown in young shells, darker and fibrous in old shells, and usually present only on hind end; strong, crowded concentric ridges present, made minutely wavy by obscure radial riblets. Interior white; pallial sinus deep, rounded; moderately large ligament shelf in left valve.

Habitat
Boring into heavy clay or soft shale, intertidally.

Range
British Columbia to San Diego, California.

Comments
This species is also known as the Checked Borer or the Checked Soft-shell Clam. It burrows deeply into soft rock and

uses its long, united siphons to take in water and food and
expel wastes. The genus name is made up of 2 Greek words,
platys ("broad" or "flat") and *odos* ("tooth"), referring to the
flat, toothlike shelf in the left valve.

Soft-shell Clam
Mya arenaria
59

1–5½" (2.5–14 cm) long. Ovate, moderately thin-shelled;
front end rounded; hind end narrowed, rounded; umbones
near center. Exterior grayish white, chalky, with a thin, light
brown periostracum; irregular concentric growth lines and
ridges present. Interior white; pallial sinus deep, squared off;
internal ligament in left valve on large, horizontally projecting
shelf with sharp, raised edges; right valve with ligament in
oval pit deep under umbo.

Habitat
In sand and mud, intertidally to water 240' (73 m) deep.

Range
On both coasts: Alaska to central California, and Labrador to
North Carolina.

Comments
In England this species is known as the Sand-gaper, and
northeastern American Indians called it the Manninose. It has
long been important as a food source. In about 1865 or 1870,
it was introduced into California, and has gradually spread
north, reaching Alaska about 1959. This clam can withstand
anaerobic conditions for several days.

False Angel Wing
Petricola pholadiformis
60

1½–2¼" (3.8–5.7 cm) long. Elongate, cylindrical, thin-
shelled; front end inflated, becoming gradually flatter toward
hind end; umbones a fifth shell length from front end;
ligament short, external. Exterior white; front end with low,
scaly riblets; riblets finer and without scales on rest of shell.
Interior white; ribs in front end visible as grooves; pallial sinus
deep, narrow.

Habitat
In heavy mud, clay, and peat, in lower part of intertidal zone.

Range
On both coasts: introduced into California and Washington;
Gulf of St. Lawrence to Texas.

Comments
This species is sometimes found boring into waterlogged
wood. As its common name suggests, the shell closely
resembles members of the angel wing family.

Pacific Razor Clam
Siliqua patula
61

3–6¼" (7.6–17 cm) long. Large, elongately oblong,
compressed, moderately thin-shelled; front end rounded, hind
end slightly squared off; umbones about one-quarter shell
length from front end; ligament strong, in elongate, pointed
cleft. Exterior grayish white, sometimes stained with brown;

periostracum thin, brown to olive-green, tough, usually with dark concentric lines; smooth except for fine growth lines. Interior whitish, faintly flushed with pale purple; with a low, flat, gradually widening white ridge from below hinge area toward margin, slanting toward front end; 1 thin central tooth and 1 moderately long, thin hind side tooth in right valve; 2 thin central teeth and 2 long hind side teeth in left valve.

Habitat
In sand on open beaches intertidally, especially near low-tide line.

Range
Eastern Aleutian Islands, Alaska, to Pismo Beach, California.

Comments
Known as the Northern Razor Clam on the Pacific Coast, this delicious species is dug commercially from Oregon to Alaska; only shells more than 4½" (11.4 cm) long may be taken. A closely related species, Dall's Razor Clam (*S. alta*), is found from south-central Alaska to the Bering Sea and Siberia. It is higher and more broadly oblong, with the hind end more strongly squared; the internal white ridge is higher, narrower, and straighter.

Kelsey's Date Mussel
Lithophaga plumula kelseyi
62

1–2⅜" (2.5–6 cm) long. Elongately cylindrical, with front two-thirds of shell inflated, hind end compressed; upper margin slightly angled in middle, lower margin gently convex, hind end narrowly and bluntly squared; umbones behind broadly rounded front end. Exterior brown, glossy; smooth except for irregular growth ridges, with 2 shallow furrows running from umbones to hind end on either side of a broad, low ridge; covered with a thin layer of grainy lime, layer thicker and strongly and irregularly wrinkled on ridge, and ending in a limy, wedgelike extension beyond end of valves. Interior grayish purple; margin smooth.

Habitat
In soft shale, thick mollusk shells, and coral, from low-tide level to water 150' (46 m) deep.

Range
Mendocino County, California, to San Diego, California.

Comments
The typical Feathered Date Mussel (*L. plumula*), ranging from the Gulf of California to Peru, is somewhat smaller, and, unlike Kelsey's Date Mussel, the thick, limy incrustation of the ridge near the hind end has featherlike wrinkles that diverge from a central ridge.

Rosy Jackknife Clam
Solen rosaceus
63

1½–3" (3.8–7.6 cm) long. Elongately oblong; front end straight and inclined forward, hind end rounded, slightly narrowed; upper and lower margins straight, parallel; ligament narrow, moderately long. Exterior whitish, often tinged with pink; periostracum thin, shiny, grayish green; smooth except for fine growth wrinkles. Interior whitish, flushed with pink; 1 central tooth in each valve.

Habitat
In sand in bays at low-tide line.

Range
Humboldt Bay, California, to central Mexico.

Comments
Like all members of the genus *Solen,* this clam lives in a permanent vertical burrow; it moves up and down by opening and closing the valves, which grip the sides of the burrow.

Transparent Razor Clam
Siliqua lucida
64

1–1½" (2.5–4.5 cm) long. Elongately oblong, compressed, thin-shelled, gaping at both ends; upper margin almost straight, lower margin convex; umbones small, one-quarter shell length from front end; ligament small, in narrow cleft. Exterior whitish, translucent; pale purplish near front end, with 3 broadening rays of interrupted purplish splotches on hind three-quarters of shell. Interior whitish; with strong, opaque, white, vertical ridge below umbones; left valve with 2 strong central teeth; right valve with 2 narrow central teeth at right angles.

Habitat
In sand, from low-tide line to water 150' (46 m) deep.

Range
Central California to N. Baja California.

Comments
This thin species is characterized by its pale purplish rays of splotches. The Latin species name means "light" or "bright," referring to the shining, translucent shell. It is preyed upon by the starry flounder (*Platichthys stellatus*).

Californian Tagelus
Tagelus californianus
65

1¾–4¼" (4.4–10.8 cm) long. Elongately oblong, narrow, moderately thin-shelled; umbones near center; a pronounced groove runs from umbones to middle of hind end, with hind margins above it somewhat pressed together. Exterior whitish or yellowish, often with irregular, incised, reddish-brown vertical lines in central area; with thin, yellowish periostracum, thicker, darker, and fibrous on hind end; smooth except for growth lines. Interior white; ligament shelf moderately short.

Habitat
In sandy mud on flats in bays intertidally.

Range
N. California to Panama.

Comments
This species is also known as the California Jackknife Clam on

the Pacific Coast. It digs deep burrows, down to 20″ (50.8 cm), although it usually stays about 4″ (10.2 cm) below the surface; 2 holes reveal the presence of its 2 siphons. When disturbed it moves rapidly down to the end of its burrow. In southern California it is used as fish bait.

Fan-shaped Horse Mussel
Modiolus rectus
66

2½–6¾″ (6.4–17.1 cm) long. Large, narrowly oblong, moderately thin-shelled, evenly inflated; lower margin straight or slightly concave, upper margin straight, oblique, roundly angled at hind end; umbones large, a sixth shell length behind rounded, compressed front end. Exterior whitish or pale bluish white, covered with periostracum that is yellowish brown on hind two-thirds, darker brown on front third, and with irregular, darker, fringed projections on hind part. Interior whitish; margin smooth.

Habitat
In muddy sand or gravel, intertidally to water 150′ (46 m) deep.

Range
Vancouver Island, British Columbia, to Gulf of California.

Comments
This species, also called the Straight Horse Mussel, usually builds a "nest" of sand or mud particles and byssal threads to help anchor it to the sand or mud.

Northern Horse Mussel
Modiolus modiolus
67

2–9″ (5.1–22.9 cm) long. Large, oval, inflated, moderately heavy; middle of upper margin bluntly angled, lower margin straight or very slightly concave; rounded umbones just behind narrowed front end. Exterior pale purplish gray, covered with a pale to dark brown, hairy periostracum; smooth except for irregular, concentric growth ridges. Interior grayish white; margin smooth.

Habitat
Among gravel and rocks, from just below low-tide line to water 600′ (183 m) deep.

Range
On both coasts: Arctic to Monterey, California, and to New Jersey.

Comments
The periostracum easily flakes off dry adult shells, and in young shells it is drawn out into triangular, pointed projections. This large mussel is frequently used as fish bait, and in some parts of Europe as food. Living up to 20 years or more, it can survive subzero temperatures for several days.

Californian Mussel
Mytilus californianus
68

2–10″ (5.1–25.4 cm) long. Elongately fan-shaped or triangular, inflated, moderately thick-shelled, with hind end rounded; lower margin straight, with a narrow gap between valves for byssus; umbones small, pointed, bent downward. Exterior purplish gray, covered with smooth, dark brown periostracum; sculptured with numerous irregular, flattened radiating ribs, interspaces darker. Interior grayish to grayish white, with hind end bluish black; ligament narrow, on a chalky shelf that is pitted below; 2 strong, small teeth near umbones.

Habitat
On rocks, intertidally to water 150′ (46 m) deep.

Range
Alaska to central Mexico.

Comments
This species dominates mussel beds in exposed rocky situations all along the Pacific Coast of North America. It grows to a larger size than any other mussel. Large, elongated shells occur on rocky, exposed coasts, while smaller, broader shells live in more sheltered bays. Although this species is said to be one of the richest in vitamins, it is eaten only locally and more commonly used as fish bait.

Blue Mussel
Mytilus edulis
69

1¼–4″ (3.2–10.2 cm) long. Elongately fan-shaped, thin-shelled, with hind end rounded; middle of top margin bluntly angled, lower margin straight; umbones at pointed front end. Exterior purplish gray, covered with a tough, thin, smooth, dark brownish to bluish-black periostracum. Interior bluish white, with margin and oval muscle scar near hind end bluish gray to bluish black; ligament long, narrow, under front half of upper margin on a narrow, chalky shelf that is pitted below; 4–7 small teeth at front end.

Habitat
Attached to rocks and wooden structures near low-tide line.

Range
On both coasts: Alaska to S. Baja California, and Arctic to South Carolina; also South America.

Comments
This is among the most common and widespread marine bivalves. It has been widely used as food for centuries, especially in Europe, where it is raised commercially. On the Pacific Coast *M. edulis* is found more in protected waters or slightly deeper in the intertidal zone than *M. californianus*, the larger, hardier Californian Mussel. It is fastened less firmly to the rock and moves to the edge of mixed mussel beds. Because it is more sensitive to wave shock and is the preferred prey of some of the carnivorous whelks, it usually does not get well established along the open, unprotected coast.

Bifurcate Mussel
Septifer bifurcatus
70

⅝–2″ (1.6–5.1 cm) long. Elongately fan-shaped, inflated, upper margin angled in center, hind end broadly rounded; bottom margin straight; umbones at pointed front end.

Exterior yellowish white, covered with a blackish-brown periostracum; broad, low, branching radiating ribs present, roughened by irregular growth lines and ridges. Interior silvery white, often with pale purplish splotches near hind end; with broad, triangular shelf across pointed end and broad, elongate ligament shelf along most of upper margin; 6–7 small teeth present behind ligament shelf; front half of lower margin with fine teeth, hind end broadly toothed.

Habitat
Attached to undersides of rocks and in crevices, at low-tide line.

Range
Crescent City, California, to S. Baja California.

Comments
In Northern California this mussel is usually lower in the intertidal zone under rocks, while in southern California it is most plentiful in the middle zones in crevices or among other mussels. The valves of this abundant species, also called the Branch-ribbed Mussel, are frequently roughened and ridged because the mussels grow in crowded colonies and crevices. Young shells are less inflated than adults.

Stearns' Mussel
Hormomya adamsiana
71

½–1" (13–25 mm) long. Small, elongately triangular, upper half inflated, bottom side flattened; lower margin slightly concave below a rounded angle running from umbo to hind end; upper margin convex, moderately angled in middle; umbones at pointed front end. Exterior grayish white, covered with a periostracum that is dark brown on upper half, yellowish brown on lower half; with strong, roughened radial ribs that branch, those near flattened lower margin finer and more numerous. Interior lustrous bluish gray to purplish brown; ligament strong, on a deeply placed shelf; 9–12 small teeth behind ligament, 2–3 behind umbones; hind margin scalloped.

Habitat
In crevices or under rocks, intertidally to just below low-tide level.

Range
Central California to Gulf of California.

Comments
This variable species lives in clusters. It is also called Adams' Mussel.

Flat-tipped Piddock
Penitella penita
72

1¼–3" (3.2–7.6 cm) long. Moderately large, elongately ovate; front part inflated, divided by oblique groove from elongated, somewhat flattened hind part; umbones one-quarter shell length from front end; front gap in lower margin closed over in adults by shelly extensions that extend up over front end and curve over reflected upper margin in front of umbones; 1 triangular accessory plate present just behind umbones. Exterior whitish; periostracum brownish; front part with fine, crowded ridges, scaly where they cross radial ridges; hind part with low concentric wrinkles, a fibrous periostracum, and a leathery extension at end of each valve that curls outward when dry. Interior white; with a narrow oblique ridge and a small, slender projection under umbones.

Habitat
In clay and soft rock, from low-tide line to water 72' (22 m) deep.

Range
Alaska to central Baja California.

Comments
This is the most common piddock on the California coast. The shape and length of the shell vary considerably, depending on the hardness of the rock into which the animal bores. It contributes significantly to the biological erosion of coastal shale along the northern West Coast. In some areas erosion is further accelerated by people breaking off the exposed rock to gather piddocks.

Scale-sided Piddock
Parapholas californica
73

3–5⅞" (7.6–14.9 cm) long. Large, elongately ovate, moderately thick-shelled; front end inflated, divided by oblique furrow from elongate hind end; an oblique, curving, angled ridge runs from upper margin to lower part of rounded hind end; 2 grooved accessory plates on upper margin, a narrow, elongate plate covering gap at lower hind margin, lower front gap closed by calcareous extensions. Exterior grayish white; front part with crowded, wavy, scaly concentric ridges, hind part with strong, brownish periostracum forming thick, horny, overlapping plates. Interior white; a broad, triangular, spoon-shaped projection present under umbones.

Habitat
In clay or shale and other soft rock, from low-tide level to water 30' (9 m) deep.

Range
Bodega Bay, California, to central Baja California.

Comments
This large boring species is conspicuous because of the thick periostracal plates at its hind end. It usually forms a thick shelly tube at the opening of its burrow that fits over the end of the shell. Though these bivalves burrow only about 12" (30 cm) into the rock, where abundant they are an important factor in rock erosion.

Ribbed Horse Mussel
Ischadium demissum
74, 76

4" (102 mm) long. Oblong-oval, narrow and round at front end, long and wide toward rear; lower margin indented. Yellowish brown to brownish black, glossy. Soft tissues lemon-yellow. Many strong radiating ribs. Umbones behind front end; gape for byssal tuft, 2 slitlike siphons with frilled edges.

Habitat
In salt marshes and brackish, muddy estuaries; between high- and low-tide line.

Range
Introduced into San Francisco Bay, Newport Bay, and Los Angeles Harbor; Gulf of St. Lawrence to Florida and Texas.

Comments
The Ribbed Horse Mussel is a particularly rugged species, able to tolerate water temperatures up to 133°F (56.1°C) and salinities twice that of normal sea water.

Black Musculus
Musculus niger
75

1–2¼" (2.5–5.7 cm) long. Oval, thin-shelled, compressed; upper margin gently curved, lower margin almost straight, with a long, narrow byssal gap; umbones near rounded front end. Exterior covered with a persistent, dark brown to blackish-brown periostracum; with many fine, low, crowded, beaded radial riblets becoming obscure toward center. Interior whitish or bluish gray; a series of minute teeth present below umbones; finely scalloped at margins.

Habitat
In muddy gravel, in water 6–350' (1.8–107 m) deep.

Range
On both coasts: Arctic to Puget Sound, and to Long Island Sound.

Comments
This northern species, also called the Black Mussel and the Little Black Mussel, is a burrowing mollusk. The adult often uses its byssal threads to form a cocoon around its shell, rather than as a means of attachment. It moves through and over gravel and mud using its long foot. The Discord Mussel (*M. discors*), same range, is smaller, slightly more inflated, paler in color, and has radial riblets only on the front end; there is a fine, curving, shallow groove running from the umbones to the hind end of the bottom margin.

Native Pacific Oyster
Ostrea lurida
77

1½–3½" (3.8–8.9 cm) long. Irregular, usually broadly oval, somewhat narrowed at upper end; right valve generally flatter than left valve. Exterior grayish white or purplish brown, occasionally rayed; irregularly wrinkled or concentrically scaly, sometimes with a few broad, angled ridges that result in an irregularly scalloped margin. Interior grayish white, usually tinged with green; right valve has fine teeth on each side of large, triangular ligament; left valve has corresponding pits.

Habitat
On rocks near low-tide line and in beds on mud flats and gravel bars in estuaries and bays.

Range
S. Alaska to S. Baja California.

Comments
Known also as the Olympia Oyster or California Oyster, this is
the common native oyster on the Pacific Coast and has long
been harvested commercially. Many people claim that its
flavor is far superior to that of any other oyster. Its importance
has now been overshadowed by the Giant Pacific Oyster. *Ostrea
lurida* reverses sex fairly regularly. Pollution, siltation,
dredging, and filling have eliminated this species from several
areas where it was formerly abundant.

Giant Pacific Oyster
Crassostrea gigas
78

2–12″ (5.1–30.5 cm) long. Large, irregular, broadly ovate to
narrowly elongate, narrowed at upper end. Exterior grayish
white, sometimes with purplish-brown spots; strongly ridged
and fluted at growth lines; margin wavy or angularly
scalloped. Interior white, with oval muscle scar near hind
margin, scar white or tinged with purplish brown; ligament
large; margin smooth.

Habitat
On rocks, soft mud, firm sand, or gravel, intertidally.

Range
S. Alaska to N. California.

Comments
This species is also known as the Japanese Oyster or Miyagi
Oyster. It is now the principal commercial oyster on our
northwestern coast. Beginning in 1922, "seed," or larval,
oysters were brought over every year from Japan, but
established colonies in British Columbia and Washington
can usually supply them now, and larval oysters are only
occasionally imported. If not harvested, these oysters may live
more than 20 years. They are more efficient and more selective
feeders than the native oyster (*O. lurida*) and can be grown in
waters too silty or otherwise unsuitable for the latter.

Japanese Abalone
Haliotis kamtschatkana
79

4–6″ (10–15 cm) long. Thin, varying from elongately oval
with a fairly high spire and a rough, irregular surface to
broadly oval and flattened with a smoother surface. Exterior
mottled greenish and brown; 3–6 open holes with raised
edges. Interior iridescent white, with no obvious muscle scar.

Habitat
Among rocks, in shallow water at low tide in the northern
part of its range and in deeper water farther south, especially
at depths of 35–50′ (10–15 m).

Range
Sitka, Alaska, to Point Conception, California.

Comments
The range of this species includes northern Japan and Siberia.

Because this shell is small and thin, it is not used commercially, although the flesh is delicious. It may be one of the mollusks preyed upon by the sea otter. In an action that ranks it with the few tool-using animals, the otter brings its prey and a stone to the surface and, while swimming on its back, breaks the shell open by beating it against the stone on its chest.

Pink Abalone
Haliotis corrugata
80

6–10″ (15–25 cm) long. Broadly oval to almost circular, high. Exterior pale greenish to pinkish brown, with interrupted spiral cords crossed by regular, slanting, wavy ridges; 2–4 open holes with raised edges; area below row of holes strongly knobby with axial ridges and a strong spiral ridge. Interior brightly iridescent, pinkish and greenish, with a large muscle scar, a scalloped edge, and a greenish to reddish margin.

Habitat
On rocks, intertidally to water 180′ (55 m) deep; most common in depths of 20–80′ (6–24 m).

Range
Monterey, California, to central Baja California.

Comments
This species feeds mainly on giant kelp, but also on other seaweeds. Very sedentary, it lives in relatively quiet waters and does not thrive at temperatures below 14°C. It is of considerable commercial importance and is the principal abalone taken in southern California; the legal minimum size limit is 6″ (15 cm). Until they reach 3–4″ (7.6–10.2 cm) in length, the young of this species remain under rocks and in crevices. The body of the animal and its long, slender tentacles are black.

Threaded Abalone
Haliotis assimilis
81

4–6″ (10–15 cm) long. Oval, high. Exterior greenish or reddish, mottled with red or blue-green, with spiral cords of varying strength, sometimes bearing white spots, crossed occasionally by low, wavelike ridges; 4–6 open holes with raised, tubelike edges. Interior pearly white with some pinkish and green iridescence; no muscle scar.

Habitat
On rocks in water 10–120′ (3–40 m) deep.

Range
Point Conception, California, to central Baja California.

Comments
This relatively uncommon species is rarely taken by divers. The animal is yellowish white mottled with brown and has short, brownish-yellow tentacles. It is sometimes listed as a subspecies of *H. kamtschatkana*.

Green Abalone
Haliotis fulgens
82

6–8″ (15–20 cm) long. Broadly oval, low. Exterior greenish to reddish brown, strongly and irregularly grooved; 5–7 small, circular open holes. Interior pearly, with bright bluish and greenish iridescence, and with a large, well-marked muscle scar.

Habitat
On rocks, in water 10–25″ (3–10 m) deep.

Range
Point Conception, California, to central Baja California.

Comments
The Green Abalone spawns from early summer to early fall, a female shedding up to 3.5 million eggs each year. Individuals may live up to 20 years. The chief predator of this abalone is the octopus, but moray eels living nearby may afford some protection. This species was once the principal basis for commercial abalone fishing in southern California, carried on mainly by the Japanese. Severe exploitation radically reduced the population, and now it forms only a minor part of the industrial catch and is not much in demand. The Latin species name, *fulgens* ("shining"), refers to the bright, iridescent interior.

Black Abalone
Haliotis cracherodii
83

3–6″ (7–15 cm) long, occasionally larger. Broadly oval, deeply cupped. Exterior bluish or greenish black, occasionally lighter at apex; smooth, sometimes with indistinct undulations; 5–8 open holes flush with surface. Interior pearly white, with greenish or pinkish iridescent flecks and a narrow dark border around the edge.

Habitat
On rocks, intertidally to water 20′ (6 m) deep. Prefers more surf than most abalones.

Range
Coos Bay, Oregon, to Baja California.

Comments
Although this is the most common abalone on the Pacific Coast, it has little commercial value because of its relatively small size and dark flesh. Spawning occurs from late spring through the summer. Growth is slowest in winter and is inhibited where there is much pollution or little algal growth. Specimens without holes are occasionally found. A subspecies (*H. c. californiensis*) from Guadalupe Island, off Baja California, has 12–16 small holes.

Red Abalone
Haliotis rufescens
84

8–12″ (20–30 cm) long. Largest abalone in North America. Broadly oval, flattened. Exterior reddish, with several broad, wavelike ridges crossed by fine, spiral threads; 3–4 open oval holes with slightly raised edges. Interior has pinkish, pale blue, or pale greenish iridescence, a large muscle scar in center, and a narrow reddish margin.

Habitat
On rocks, intertidally to water over 540' (164 m) deep; most abundant in depths of 20–40' (6–12 m).

Range
Oregon to central Baja California; most abundant in California between Monterey and San Luis Obispo Bay.

Comments
Red abalones attain sexual maturity at about 6 years of age, spawning between February and April. Large abalones may be 15–20 or more years old. The shell is prized for its beautiful red color and bright iridescence. This abalone is the most important commercially and is the species usually served in restaurants. Successful reestablishment and protection of sea otters along the California coast have brought complaints from abalone fishermen that the otters take too many.

Onyx Slipper Shell
Crepidula onyx
85

1–2" (2.5–7 cm) long. Thick, low to somewhat arched, with apex bent to 1 side and projecting slightly over rear edge; base ovate. Exterior brownish, covered when fresh by a pale brown periostracum; smooth or with concentric lines. Interior chestnut-brown to pale brown, glossy; shelf white, bearing a sinuous edge.

Habitat
On rocks, other shells, or stacked on top of each other, in shallow water in bays and lagoons; also on open coast from low-tide level to water 300' (91 m) deep.

Range
Monterey, California, to Peru.

Comments
The species name of this abundant shell stems from the shiny chestnut-brown color of its interior. Described by G. B. Sowerby in 1824, it was among the first *Crepidula* species found in Pacific waters. When stacked on top of each other, the smaller animals at the top are males and the larger ones at the bottom are females. Most of the young first mature as males and later change sex, becoming females.

Pacific Half-slipper Shell
Crepipatella lingulata
86

½–⅞" (13–22 mm) wide. Conical, low, with apex near edge; base almost round. Exterior whitish, often mottled with pale brown, irregularly wrinkled. Interior glossy, with pale brown and white mottling; shelf roughly triangular, attached on 1 side with a shallow indentation on far edge, and on shorter side with a convex edge.

Habitat
On rocks and living or dead shells, in shallow depths to water 300' (91 m) deep.

Range
N. Alaska to central Baja California.

Comments
The surface of this abundant mollusk is often covered with marine growth. The species name is based on the Latin word *lingula* ("little tongue"), referring to the small decklike shelf.

Spiny Slipper Shell
Crepidula aculeata
87

½–1¼" (1.3–3.2 cm) long. Moderately low, thin, with spiral apex near rear edge but not projecting; base broadly ovate. Exterior whitish, usually strongly mottled with reddish brown, with curved, radiating spiny ridges, whitish when fresh. Interior mottled whitish and brown; shelf white, with a sinuous edge and radial fold.

Habitat
On rocks and other hard objects in shallow water.

Range
On both coasts: central California to Chile; North Carolina to Florida, Texas, and the West Indies.

Comments
This species is common in the Atlantic and rarer in California. It is often found on other shells and on mangrove roots. Unlike most slipper shells, its early whorls are strongly spiralled, as is the sculpture on the body whorl. The gill and mantle cavity of the snail are modified for plankton feeding.

Punctate Pandora
Pandora punctata
88

1–2⅞" (2.5–7.3 cm) long. Moderately large, broadly crescent-shaped, compressed; upper margin concave, lower margin convex; front end broadly rounded, hind end narrowed and curved upward; flattened right valve somewhat smaller than slightly convex left valve. Exterior white; left valve with upper margin flattened, shelflike, with strong, sharp angle running from umbo to angulately cut-off hind end, where angle becomes a flattened ridge; right valve with narrower shelflike upper margin and 2 faint, curving grooves below; surface of both valves smooth except for concentric growth lines and, on right valve, fine, irregular, zigzag radial scratches. Interior dull pearly white; with fine, scattered pits; 2 long, diverging teeth in right valve, 1 long tooth in left valve. Siphons short, united except at ends.

Habitat
In sand and mud, from just below low-tide line to water 120' (37 m) deep.

Range
Vancouver Island, British Columbia, to Gulf of California.

Comments
This species is easily distinguished by its relatively large size, its curved, flattened upper margin, and its pitted interior.

False Pacific Jingle Shell
Pododesmus macrochisma
89

1–4″ (2.5–10.2 cm) long. Large, irregularly circular to broadly ovate, moderately thick-shelled; right valve thick or thin, with byssal hole closed at upper margin. Exterior grayish white, sometimes tinged with green; with ribs usually scalloped or wrinkled by irregular growth lines. Interior greenish, with irregular white splotches; smoothish or grooved at lower margin; left valve has 1 large and 1 small muscle scar; on left valve ligamental depression elongate, slightly curved.

Habitat
On rocks, pilings, and shells, from low-tide line to water 200′ (61 m) deep.

Range
Alaska to Baja California.

Comments
Sometimes this shell is called the Pearly Monia or the Abalone Jingle. The green color inside the upper valve is due to minute algae living within the shell. Two subspecies have been recognized; typical *P. m. macrochisma*, ranging from Alaska to Monterey, California, which has stronger sculpture, with both valves thick; and *P. m. cepio*, from Monterey to Baja California, with finer ribbing and a thinner shell.

Clear Jewel Box
Chama arcana
90

1½–3½″ (3.8–8.9 cm) long. Almost circular, with left valve attached and cupped, right valve slightly convex. Exterior translucent or waxy white, right valve often tinged with pink or orange near umbo; with many leafy, scaly, concentric ridges bearing numerous longer, irregular, leafy projections. Interior opaque white; margin translucent white, irregular.

Habitat
On rocks, pilings, or gravel, from near low-tide line to water 260′ (79 m) deep.

Range
Oregon to central Baja California.

Comments
This species has usually been listed erroneously as *C. pellucida*, which is a distinct species found in Peru and Chile. In the southern part of its range, the Clear Jewel Box occurs only below low-tide level, and is found in deeper water than farther north. Off southern California these shells sometimes aggregate on siltstone reefs.

Giant Rock Scallop
Hinnites giganteus
91

1½–9½″ (3.8–24.1 cm) high. Irregularly circular to broadly ovate, thick-shelled, attached by right valve; in young shells front ears twice as long as hind ears, irregular in adults; byssal notch strong, triangular, often obscure in young shells. Exterior grayish or reddish brown, with many crowded, scaly riblets. Interior white, tinged with dark purple on and below hinge; smooth; with large, circular muscle scar in middle; ligament in a narrow, pointed groove in thickened hinge area.

Habitat
On rocks, from low-tide line to water 150' (46 m) deep.

Range
British Columbia to central Baja California.

Comments
This species is also known as the Purple-hinged Rock Scallop and often listed as *H. multirugosus*. They are delicious, and have been depleted in some areas. Young shells live free, actively swimming, but then attach themselves to rocks. Once attached, they grow slowly and take 25 years or more to reach full size. The mantle edge is bright orange. Sexually mature specimens spawn in April in central California.

Giant Pacific Scallop
Patinopecten caurinus
92

4–11" (10.2–28 cm) long. Largest living scallop. Large, almost circular, thin-shelled, somewhat flattened; ears equal. Exterior of right valve whitish; with about 24 broad, flattened ribs; ears with growth lines; byssal notch deep. Exterior of left valve reddish or pinkish gray; with about 17 rounded ribs crossed by fine, threadlike concentric ridges; ears with very fine growth lines. Interior whitish, often with reddish margin.

Habitat
In sand or gravel, in water 60–300' (18–91 m) deep.

Range
Central Alaska to N. California.

Comments
This species is also known on the Pacific Coast as the Weathervane Scallop. Commercial fishermen trawling for bottom-feeding fish sometimes bring up large numbers.

Wide-eared Scallop
Leptopecten latiauratus
93

¾–1⅜" (1.9–3.5 cm) high. Almost circular, oblique, thin-shelled, translucent; elongately triangular hind ears longer than front ears; right front ear oblong, with 5 scaly ribs, deep triangular byssal notch below, and 7–8 small teeth along lower margin; left front ear triangular. Exterior orange or yellowish brown to dark brown, with numerous narrow, white, festooned or zigzag lines, white lines usually absent on orange shells; with 12–14 low, rounded ribs present. Interior pale orange or brown, often with a broad, darker edge at broadly wavy lower margin.

Habitat
Attached to rocks, rubble, kelp, and hard objects, from low-tide line to water 150' (46 m) deep.

Range
Point Reyes, California, to Gulf of California.

Comments
Also called the Broad-eared Scallop, this species usually attaches itself by a byssus to wooden pilings, floating barges, and other hard objects.

Pacific Calico Scallop
Argopecten circularis
94

1½–3½" (3.8–8.9 cm) long. Almost circular, slightly longer than high, with hind end long and slightly compressed; ears equal; byssal notch small, triangular. Exterior yellowish white or orange, usually strongly splotched with purplish red, or dark reddish brown; with 20–22 broad, flattened ribs, and very fine, crowded, erect concentric threads in interspaces. Interior whitish, stained with brown; ears with strong grooved ridges; margin strongly scalloped.

Habitat
On sand and mud, in water 10–150' (3–46 m) deep.

Range
Santa Barbara, California, to Peru.

Comments
Although this scallop is not fished commercially, it is eaten locally. Shells from the northern part of the range are less convex, less inflated, and less brightly colored, and have been called Speckled Scallops (*A. aequisulcatus*). They gradually intergrade with shells from the south, and both should probably be considered forms of a single species.

Pacific Pink Scallop
Chlamys hastata hericius
95

2–3¼" (5.1–8.3 cm) high. Almost circular; front ears slightly more than twice length of hind ears; byssal notch deep, squarish, with small teeth on lower margin. Exterior white, yellowish, orange, or purple, often rayed with paler colors or with concentric purplish rings, right valve often paler than left valve; with 18–22 large, rounded ribs, and many fine, scaly ribs on and between larger ribs; lower margin finely toothed. Interior whitish or tinged with pale purplish, margin often darker; furrowed.

Habitat
On rocks, sand, or mud, from low-tide line to water 500' (152 m) deep.

Range
S. Alaska to Santa Barbara, California.

Comments
This species is usually covered by or encased in the sponges *Myxilla incrustans* and *Mycale adhaerans*. In this mutually beneficial relationship, the sponge camouflages the scallop, and the scallop's hard, scaly surface may ward off the sponge's predators. The related Pacific Spear Scallop (*C. h. hastata*) ranges from Monterey, California, to San Diego. It is slightly smaller and more colorful; the main ribs are narrower, fewer, and more strongly spiny.

Iceland Scallop
Chlamys islandica
96

1¾–4" (4.4–10.2 cm) high. Broadly ovate, moderately compressed; front ears 2–3 times longer than hind ears, right front ear with sharply angled byssal notch, left front ear with shallow notch. Exterior whitish, dull reddish gray, orange, or purplish red, often streaked radially or with concentric bands;

with many low, rounded riblets often scaly; very fine, scaly sculpture between ribs. Interior white or tinged with orange or reddish purple; furrowed; margin finely scalloped.

Habitat
On coarse sand or gravel, in water 6–1000' (1.8–305 m) deep.

Range
On both coasts: Alaska to Puget Sound, and Arctic to S. Massachusetts.

Comments
This species is often covered with marine growth. In Greenland and Iceland it is used for food. A commercial fishery has been attempted in Norway.

Leafy Thorn Purpura
Ceratostoma foliatum
97

1¾–3⅜" (4.4–8.6 cm) high. Ovate, large, with an elevated, conical spire; yellowish to light brown, sometimes with a pale spiral band, or white with brown bands, or pure white. Each whorl has 3 large, thin, leafy, wavy, flanges, which are finely and closely ridged on front side; between flanges several strong spiral cords present that may be knobby where they cross an obscure rib; larger cords make whorls angled. Aperture ovate. Inner and outer lips margined and freestanding; outer lip toothed, with strong spine near base. Canal expanded, closed, and turned up and twisted at end.

Habitat
On and among rocks, intertidally and just below low-tide line to water 10' (3 m) deep; also in depths to 200' (61 m), especially in the southern part of its range.

Range
Alaska to San Pedro, California.

Comments
This shell is also called the Foliated Thorn Purpura or the Leafy Hornmouth. The size and color vary in different locations: those in the Puget Sound area and northward are darker and larger, while those in southern Oregon and California are smaller and white; in cental Oregon there are white shells banded with brown. This species feeds on scallops, clams, and other bivalves, and also on barnacles. Spawning has been observed in late February and March. Eggs are laid in yellow cases, each containing from 30–80 eggs. Several females often deposit their egg capsules together.

Festive Murex
Pteropurpura festiva
98

1½–2¾" (3.8–7 cm) high. Elongately ovate; yellowish or pale brown. Whorls convex, smooth, with fine, shallow, reddish-brown spiral grooves; each whorl has 3 low flanges that are curved backward and finely and densely frilled on front; 1 prominent knob between every 2 flanges. Aperture oval, with a flange extending to end of closed canal. Outer lip finely scalloped, with 5–7 teeth inside.

Habitat
On mud or rocks in bays or on mud flats; smaller shells on rocks along outer coast at low-tide line.

Range
Santa Barbara, California, to Baja California.

Comments
This species is often abundant on mud flats, where it has been observed spawning. It is sometimes listed in a distinct subgenus, *Shaskyus,* because of its backward-curled growth lines and supposed radular differences.

Frill-wing Murex
Pteropurpura macroptera
99

1¾–2¾" (4.4–7 cm) high. Elongately ovate; brown. Whorls convex, each with 3 broad, winglike flanges, usually strongly fluted, and with a wavy margin; fine, crowded, wavy ridges on front, and wider, spreading ridges on back; between flanges whorls have several broad, low, darker brown spiral ridges, sometimes with wide, white spiral bands, and occasionally a strong knob. Aperture oval, with raised margin, highest and slightly wavy at outer lip. Canal closed, long, curved.

Habitat
On rocks and in crevices, intertidally and at low-tide line to water 60′ (18 m) deep.

Range
Monterey Bay, California, to N. Baja California.

Comments
This species has also been placed in the genera *Murex* and *Pterynotus.* The related Three-wing Murex (*P. trialata*) is found from Catalina Island, California, to central Baja California. It is slightly larger, with the whorls more shouldered and the flanges not as wide or as fluted.

Giant Forreria
Forreria belcheri
100

2½–5¾" (6.4–14.6 cm) high. Large; yellowish brown, occasionally with indistinct darker spiral bands. Spire moderately elevated, with strongly angled whorls bearing large, hollow, triangular spines. Body whorl broad, strongly angled below shoulder, with large, hollow spines at angle; spines continue as sharp or rounded riblike ridges over top half of body whorl; bottom half with spiral groove ending in a triangular spine on outer lip. Aperture broadly oval, white within. Canal moderately long, open.

Habitat
On sand, near low-tide line in bays and lagoons, and in water 60–100′ (18–30 m) deep.

Range
Point Mugu, California, to central Baja California.

Comments
This large species is often found close to oyster and mussel beds and may feed on these bivalves. The species name honors

Sir Edward Belcher (1799–1877), captain of the British naval vessel on whose cruise this species was found.

Frilled Dogwinkle
Nucella lamellosa
101

1–3¼" (2.5–8.3 cm) high. Ovate to elongate, spire broadly to elongately conical; white to light brown, sometimes banded. Spire whorls have 2 smooth spiral cords, sometimes worn and obscure, crossed by fine axial ridges, which usually become strong, erect frills forming hollow spines on spiral cords; some specimens practically smooth, without axial frills. Body whorl with more numerous spiral cords and spines. Columellar callus broad, white. Aperture ovate, yellowish within. Outer lip broadly flared, white, with 3 rounded teeth. Canal moderately long, narrowly open, curved.

Habitat
On rocks, especially in crevices or sheltered places, intertidally to just below low-tide line.

Range
The Bering Straits, Alaska, to central California.

Comments
This common dogwinkle, sometimes listed as *Thais lamellosa*, is extremely variable and can be almost smooth or strongly sculptured with frills and spines. It drills holes in the shells of barnacles, mussels, and other prey. In the Pacific Northwest this is one of the most important whelks, playing an important role in limiting the lower boundary of the acorn barnacle zone and the upper spread of mussels.

Oregon Triton
Fusitriton oregonensis
102

3–5" (7.6–12.7 cm) high. Elongate, with a high spire; whitish, covered by a thick, grayish-brown periostracum, with axial ridges and spiral rows of bristles. Whorls strongly convex, with slender axial ribs crossed by paired spiral cords. Aperture broadly oval, with a strong, knoblike tooth on parietal wall near upper end, and a moderately long, slightly curved canal at base. Inner and outer lips smooth, pure white. Operculum horny, oval, dark brown.

Habitat
On sand and rubble, from low-tide line to water 400' (122 m) deep.

Range
Bering Sea to San Diego, California.

Comments
Although nothing is known of its feeding habits, this triton, like other members of its family, probably preys on mollusks. A female was observed in Alaska, just below the low-tide line laying egg capsules in a spirally arranged mass on stones. She covered them with a mucous coating and then crawled back into deeper water without brooding them.

Carpenter's Dwarf Triton
Ocenebra interfossa
103

½–⅞″ (13–22 mm) high. Ovate, elongate, with spire less than half shell length; gray or yellowish. Whorls shouldered and flattened below suture, with about 10 distant axial ribs crossed by strong spiral cords of alternating widths, often resulting in strongly latticed sculpture; intersections somewhat knobby; fine, thin axial threads make spiral cords and interspaces scaly. Parietal and columellar callus with a raised margin. Aperture oval. Outer lip slightly flaring, internally grooved. Canal broad, open or almost closed.

Habitat
In somewhat sheltered places among rocks, intertidally to water 20′ (6 m) deep.

Range
Alaska to N. Baja California.

Comments
This carnivorous species is also known as the Sculptured Rock Shell. The species name, based on 2 Latin words, *inter* ("between") and *fossa* ("ditch"), refers to the deep channels between the strong spiral cords. A smaller, more strongly latticed form is found from Washington to Baja California; it is sometimes separated as a distinct species called the Clathrate Dwarf Triton (*O. atropurpurea*).

Atlantic Oyster Drill
Urosalpinx cinerea
104

½–1¾″ (1.3–4.4 cm) high. Oval, with elevated spire about half shell length; grayish or yellowish white, often with brown spiral bands. Whorls convex, with about 12 low, rounded axial ribs crossed by numerous spiral cords; finer scaly spiral threads between ribs. Aperture elongately ovate, white, yellowish or brownish within. Outer lip sometimes thickened within, with 2–6 small teeth inside. Canal open, relatively broad.

Habitat
On and among rubble near oyster beds, intertidally to water 25′ (76 m) deep.

Range
On both coasts: Washington to central California, and Nova Scotia to NE. Florida.

Comments
This species was introduced at the same time as oysters into both California and England about 100 years ago. It is probably the greatest predator of the common Eastern Oyster, although it also feeds on other bivalves, some gastropods, and even crabs. Using its radula, it drills a hole in the prey's shell, then inserts its proboscis to feed.

Lurid Dwarf Triton
Ocenebra lurida
105

½–1½″ (1.3–3.8 cm) high. Elongately ovate, with spire about a third to a half shell length; whitish, yellowish, or brown, occasionally banded. Whorls convex, with 6–10 low ribs, sometimes obscure, crossed by strong spiral cords usually made beaded or scaly by fine axial ridges; grooves between cords also frequently marked by scaly axial threads. Base slightly constricted. Aperture ovate. Outer lip thick, with a wavy margin and 6–7 teeth within. Canal short.

Habitat
Among rocks and on rocky gravel, from low-tide line to water 180' (55 m) deep.

Range
Sitka, Alaska, to N. Baja California.

Comments
This species is common at low-tide level north of Point Conception, California; farther south it is found in deeper water. It seems to prefer barnacles to mussels and has also been observed to rasp Gumboot Chitons (*Cryptochiton stelleri*). This is a highly variable species, not only in form but in the strength of the axial ribs, and has been divided into several subspecies. It is also known as the Lurid Rock Shell.

Tinted Wentletrap
Epitonium tinctum
106

⅜–⅝" (10–16 mm) high. Slender, elevated; white, with a brown band below suture. Whorls smooth, convex, separated by deep suture, and crossed by 10–12 strong, thin ribs, which are often angled on shoulder below suture. Aperture broadly oval, with a somewhat thickened lip.

Habitat
In sand near sea anemones, intertidally to 150' (46 m) deep.

Range
Vancouver, British Columbia, to Baja California.

Comments
This species lives in sand among colonies of the small sea anemone *Anthopleura elegantissima,* on which it feeds. It is also found with the larger green anemone *Anthopleura xanthogrammica.* Its sand-encrusted egg capsules are connected by a slender thread. The species name is a Latin adjective meaning "tinted" or "painted" and refers to the color band below the suture. A related species, the Money Wentletrap (*E. indianorum*), is larger, more slender, and does not have a subsutural color band or angled, spiny ribs. It is found below the low-tide line from Alaska to Vancouver Island, and in deeper water south to Monterey, California.

Greenland Wentletrap
Epitonium greenlandicum
107

2" (51 mm) long. Tall, conical. Dull yellowish white. 11–12 convex whorls separated by deep sutures; whorl with 12 stout, flat, vertical ribs, all vertically aligned, and 8–9 rounded spiral cords. Aperture circular; lips thick; no umbilicus. Operculum brown, horny.

Habitat
On rock, sand, or mud bottoms; in water 60–567' (18–173 m) deep.

Range
Alaska to British Columbia; Arctic to Long Island.
Comments
This showy wentletrap is one of the largest in the North Atlantic, and is covered with prominent spiral sculpture.

Poulson's Rock Shell
Roperia poulsoni
108

2⅜" (60 mm) long, 1⅛" (28 mm) wide. Spindle-shaped. Whitish, with many narrow, brown spiral stripes. Periostracum thin, brownish. Spire tall, apex sharp; 5–6 whorls, each with 8–9 bumpy ribs crossed by fine spiral lines and 4–5 large cords, the latter making the bumps on the ribs. Aperture oval, long, white inside; outer lip thick, with 7–8 teeth; siphonal canal moderately long, nearly closed.

Habitat
On rocks and pilings; in tide pools; near low-tide line and below in shallow water.
Range
S. California to Baja California.

Comments
This snail, which feeds on barnacles, mussels, and other bivalves and snails by rasping out the soft parts is, in turn, eaten by the Pacific Rock Crab.

California Frog Shell
Bursa californica
109

1½–5" (3.8–12.7 cm) high. Broadly oval, large, with a conical spire; yellowish white to pale brown, sometimes with brown spiral lines. Whorls strongly angled with 2 flanges on opposite sides, and with 2–3 strong, pointed knobs between flanges; surface sculptured with many irregular spiral threads. Body whorl has a row of small knobs. Parietal wall and broad columellar area covered by a white ridged or toothed callus. Aperture ovate, white. Outer lip flaring and expanded, toothed within with V-shaped canal at top and longer, slanting canal at base. Columella and outer lip often edged with gray.

Habitat
Among rocks in shallow water, or on sand in water to 300' (91 m) deep.
Range
Monterey Bay, California, to Baja California.

Comments
This large, stout shell is apparently a scavenger, as it is frequently found in crab and lobster traps. The young live in sandy gravel between rocks in shallow water, but the adults inhabit deeper water. The shell is very common in Baja California, and until recently it was sold for food in southern California. Some of the flattened, oval species in this genus resemble leather purses—hence the generic name, which is Latin for "purse."

Common Northwest Neptune
Neptunea lyrata
110

2½–6½" (6.4–16.5 cm) high. Large, heavy-shelled, with an acutely conical spire, a broad body whorl, and a drawn-out, open, backward-curved canal; yellowish to pale reddish brown, often with darker spiral ridges. Whorls have strong spiral cords, 2–3 on spire whorls and 7–8 or more on body whorl; axial ribs often on last 2–3 whorls, forming knobs on top cord; ribs occasionally sharp, erect, flangelike. Columella white, strongly twisted, with margined callus. Aperture broadly ovate, smooth and white within. Outer lip strongly convex, flaring at margin. Operculum oval, rather large.

Habitat
On sand or mud, from low-tide line to water 300' (91 m) deep in northern part of its range, and to 5000' (1524 m) farther south.

Range
Arctic to central California.

Comments
This species is also known as the Ridged Whelk. The oval, flattened egg capsules are fastened by a short stalk to stones or dead shells and grouped together in a dome-shaped mass of 15–40 capsules. Like all northern whelks, the young hatch in the crawling stage.

Painted Spindle Shell
Fusinus luteopictus
111

½–1" (13–25 mm) high. Spindle-shaped, small, with spire about half shell length; reddish brown, with a whitish or yellowish-white spiral band in middle of whorls, or with center of axial ribs whitish; base and canal pale. Spire whorls convex, each with 9–10 strong axial ribs crossed by 2 strong spiral cords, forming elongate beads on ribs, making them somewhat angled. Body whorl with lower, less angled ribs. Base has numerous spiral cords below ribs. Columella smooth, slightly convex. Aperture oval, with a white spiral callus at top. Outer lip ridged within and slightly flaring. Canal slightly twisted, moderately long.

Habitat
On and under rocks and under kelp at low-tide line, and offshore to water about 130' (40 m) deep.

Range
Monterey Bay, California, to N. Baja California.

Comments
This little species is often covered with the small spiral shells of a serpulid marine worm (*Spirorbis*). The genus name is derived from the Latin word for spindle, *fusus*. The species name is formed from 2 Latin words, *luteus* ("yellow") and *pictus* ("painted"), and refers to the yellowish band on the shell.

Western Lean Nassa
Nassarius mendicus
112

½–⅞" (13–22 mm) high. Narrowly ovate, slender, with an elongately conical spire half to two-thirds shell length; yellowish to brown, usually with white spiral bands. Whorls convex, with strong axial ribs crossed by flattened spiral cords, often forming beads on ribs; on last 2 whorls, ribs sometimes fewer, broader, and occasionally angled. Aperture ovate, pointed at upper end. Outer lip ridged within, lower two-thirds sometimes slightly flaring. Siphonal ridge strong. Parietal and columellar callus margined.

Habitat
On sand or sandy mud, from near low-tide line to water 200′ (75 m) deep.

Range
Kodiak Island, Alaska, to central Baja California.

Comments
Unlike most western dog whelks, which usually live buried in sand, this species often crawls about on the surface. It often scavenges bait in shrimp traps or on setlines. In the southern part of their range the shells commonly have fewer but stronger, wavelike axial ribs and are occasionally listed as a distinct subspecies, Cooper's Dog Whelk (*N. m. cooperi*).

Dire Whelk
Searlesia dira
113

1–1⅞″ (2.5–4.8 cm) high. Elongate, moderately thick-shelled, with spire about half shell length; grayish to yellowish brown, with pale spiral grooves, especially in worn shells. Spire whorls convex; early whorls have strong, rounded axial ribs crossed by strong spiral cords; later whorls have obscure axial ribs and flattened spiral cords so that evenly convex body whorl appears regularly grooved and without axial ribs. Aperture elongately ovate, brownish or grayish brown within. Outer lip edge finely toothed, with whitish spiral ridges within. Canal moderately long.

Habitat
On wave-washed rocks intertidally.

Range
Alaska to N. California. Abundant in Pacific Northwest, less so in California.

Comments
This common species is basically a scavenger, but does occasionally prey on living animals. It cannot drill through the shells of prey animals but must extend its long proboscis into soft parts. It feeds mainly on mollusks, but will also eat crabs, barnacles, worms, and fish. The genus name commemorates the eminent British paleontologist Searles V. Wood (1798–1880). The Latin species name means "fearful" or "ominous," and probably refers to the gloomy gray color of the shell.

Western Fat Dog Whelk
Nassarius perpinguis
114

¾–1″ (19–25 mm) high. Elongately ovate, stout, with an elevated spire slightly more than half shell length; yellowish white, occasionally with reddish-brown bands below suture and in middle of whorls. Spire whorls evenly convex, separate by an indented suture, with about 5 narrow spiral cords, beaded where they cross weaker axial riblets, resulting in an evenly latticed sculpture. Body whorl also latticed, with a strong furrow at base above prominent siphonal ridge. Aperture broadly ovate. Outer lip ridged within. Inner lip curved, with fine ridges and beads. Canal short, twisted.

Habitat
On sand, from low-tide line to water 250' (76 m) deep.

Range
Central California to central Baja California.

Comments
This species, sometimes called the Western Fat Nassa, is often abundant at low-tide level in bays and lagoons, but is also common in deeper water.

Giant Western Nassa
Nassarius fossatus
115

1¼–2" (3.2–5.1 cm) high. Ovate, pointed, relatively large, with an acute, conical spire more than half shell length; yellowish gray to pale reddish brown or orange-brown. Spire whorls convex, with about 5 spiral cords beaded where they cross narrow, low, rounded axial ribs. Aperture ovate, pointed and narrowly notched at top. Outer lip finely toothed at margin and ridged within. Canal short and wide. Siphonal ridge strong, partly covered by columellar callus, with a prominent channel between it and base of body whorl. Parietal and columellar callus shiny, orange to grayish white, irregularly ridged.

Habitat
On sand and mud, from near low-tide mark to water 60' (18 m) deep.

Range
Vancouver Island, British Columbia, to central Baja California.

Comments
This species, also known as the Channeled Dog Whelk or Channeled Nassa, is the largest Pacific Coast dog whelk and among the most abundant. In some specimens the axial ribs decrease in number in the first and second whorls and become stronger, somewhat slanted, and slightly angled and beaded at the periphery, especially on the body whorl. The animal is basically a scavenger, moving actively about in search of food, but has been observed feeding on small clams, using its long proboscis, which can extend more than an inch.

Joseph's Coat Amphissa
Amphissa versicolor
116

⅜–¾" (10–19 mm) high. Ovate to elongately ovate; yellowish or pinkish white, with reddish-brown spots or splotches, which may be arranged spirally or in a zigzag axial pattern; occasionally brown with a few white spots. Whorls gently to strongly convex, separated by a deep suture, and with strong, slanting axial ribs crossed by spiral cords. No ribs on base of body whorl, which is sculptured with spiral cords. Columella has a well-defined, margined callus. Aperture elongately ovate. Outer lip with spiral ridges within.

Habitat
In rock rubble, from near low-tide line to water 150' (46 m) deep.

Range
Vancouver, British Columbia, to N. Baja California.

Comments
The Latin species name, which means "of various colors," and the common name attest to the color variation found in this species; the axial ribs also vary in strength. The related Columbian Amphissa (*A. columbiana*), found from Alaska to southern California, is larger, ¾–1⅛" (1.9–2.8 cm) high, with finer, more numerous axial ribs and many more spiral threads.

Eastern Mud Whelk
Ilynassa obsoleta
117

⅝–1¼" (1.6–3.2 cm) high. Ovate, thick-shelled, with spire about half shell length; light brown, reddish brown, or dark brown. Whorls convex, with moderately deep suture, usually eroded apex, and crowded, low, slanting axial ribs crossed by low, flat spiral cords. Body whorl with obscure axial ribs. Columella curved, with a projecting spiral ridge at base. Aperture oval. Outer lip with spiral ridges within. Canal broad, short. Parietal wall callused, often reddish brown.

Habitat
On mud flats, especially near low-tide line.

Range
On both coasts: introduced on the Pacific Coast from Vancouver Island, British Columbia, to central California; Gulf of St. Lawrence, Canada, to NE. Florida.

Comments
This abundant species is also called the Eastern Mud Nassa, the Mud Dog Whelk, the Mud Basket Shell, and the Common Mud Snail, and is often listed in the genus *Nassarius*. The shell is usually eroded. The animal prefers to feed on microscopic plant life, but will also eat dead animal matter and has been seen feeding on living marine worms. The egg capsules are erect, vase-shaped, and somewhat flattened; they are covered with ridges arranged in a zigzag pattern. The young emerge as free-swimming larvae.

Western Mud Whelk
Nassarius tegula
118

½–¾" (13–19 mm) high. Broadly ovate, thick-shelled, with spire about half shell length: brownish gray to brownish, usually with a reddish-brown spiral line or row of spots on knobbed part of ribs. Whorls have strong, low axial ribs crossed by spiral cords, forming elongated knobs; on last third of body whorl, axial ribs disappear. Base has spiral threads or fine spiral grooves. Columella has a spiral ridge at base.

Aperture oval, broad. Outer lip thick, with a strong ridge outside and 5–8 teeth inside, upper tooth double. Canal slightly twisted. Parietal callus broad, shiny, ridged at upper end, and thickened at outer margin and over basal ridge.

Habitat
On sand and mud in bays at low-tide line.

Range
San Francisco Bay, California, to Baja California.

Comments
Also known as the Western Mud Nassa and the Covered-lip Nassa, this shell is abundant on the mud flats of bays in southern California. It attacks bubble shells and scavenges dead animal material.

California Horn Shell
Cerithidea californica
119

1–1¾" (2.5–4.4 cm) high. Tall-spired; moderately large, heavy; brown, with several white spiral bands. Whorls well rounded, with many strong, rounded axial ribs crossed by weak spiral threads, and with several broad, yellowish axial ridges. Aperture round, with a broad, expanded outer lip.

Habitat
Intertidal mud flats in quiet bays and estuaries.

Range
Bolinas Bay, California, to central Baja California.

Comments
Like other members of genus *Cerithidea,* large numbers of these shells may be encountered on exposed mud flats. The snails feed on fine organic detritus and plankton, and parasitize fishes and marine birds.

Ida's Miter
Mitra idae
120

3¼" (83 mm) high. Long, spindle-shaped. Shell dark brown under thick, black periostracum. Apex sharp, spire tall, 7–8 whorls; body whorl one-half total length; surface with fine lines crossed by fine longitudinal ribs. Aperture long, narrow, inner lip with 3 spiral ridges. Head and foot white.

Habitat
Among rocks, in tide pools, and in kelp beds; from low-tide line to moderately deep water.

Range
N. California to Baja California.

Comments
Ida's Miter is uncommon in tide pools, but fairly common in kelp beds. The striking contrast of its black shell and white body makes it easy to identify.

Giant Pacific Bittium
Bittium eschrichtii
121

⅜–¾" (10–19 mm) high. Acutely elongate; grayish or reddish brown. Whorls slightly convex, with flattened, smooth spiral cords separated by squared grooves half as wide as cords. Aperture ovate, with a slight, shallow canal at base.

Habitat
Under and among rocks, intertidally to water 180' (55 m) deep.

Range
Alaska to Baja California.

Comments
This species is relatively large for the genus *Bittium*. It is abundant under rocks, where it feeds on algal detritus. A southern subspecies, the Monterey Bittium (*B. e. montereyense*), is the same size; it is usually shinier and whitish with brown spots, and is found on algae at low-tide level, and in water to 60' (18 m) deep.

San Pedro Triphora
Triphora pedroana
122

⅛–⅜" (3–10 mm) high. Small, elongate, sinistral; yellowish brown, beads paler. Whorls slightly convex, bearing 2 spiral rows of beads and a weak central row of beads, which gradually increases in strength to make 3 nearly equal-sized beaded cords on body whorl. Body whorl also has beaded basal cord. Aperture ovate, with an almost closed canal at base.

Habitat
Among gravel, at or below low-tide line to water 150' (46 m) deep.

Range
Monterey, California, to N. Baja California.

Comments
This is the most commonly encountered sinistral snail in southern California.

Carpenter's Turrid
Megasurcula carpenteriana
123

1¾–3¾" (4.4–9.5 cm) high. Moderately large, heavy, spindle-shaped, with narrowly conical spire about half shell length; pale yellowish brown to dark brown, usually with reddish-brown spiral lines. Spire whorls concave, with a low, rounded angle at periphery, and with fine, crowded, beaded or roughened spiral threads crossed by prominent growth lines; on body whorl, growth lines form broad, S-shaped curves. Body whorl has a rounded or knobbed angle at periphery and a narrowed base. Aperture elongately oblong. Outer lip thin, minutely toothed, with reddish-brown spots inside, and with a broad, shallow notch above, convexly curved below. Canal moderately long. Operculum heavy, elongately ovate.

Habitat
On mud, in water 30–300' (9–91 m) deep.

Range
Central California to central Baja California.

Comments
The species name honors Philip P. Carpenter (1819–1877), eminent British malacologist.

Mouse Ear Ovatella
Ovatella myosotis
124

¼–⅜″ (6–10 mm) high. Narrowly ovate to elongate, with elongately conical spire less than half shell length; dark brown to purplish brown. Apex slightly tilted. Spire whorls almost flat-sided; all whorls with a low, broad ridge just below well-defined suture, smooth except for irregular wrinkles toward top. Columella with a large, erect, platelike ridge above, and a slightly smaller, oblique ridge at base. Aperture narrowly ovate, pointed above, rounded below. Outer lip thin, with slightly reflected white margin, sometimes with tooth within. Parietal wall has a low ridge.

Habitat
Under debris and around grasses, on edges of salt marshes and bays above high-tide mark.

Range
On both coasts: British Columbia to central California, and Nova Scotia to the West Indies.

Comments
This species is also known as the Mouse Ear Marsh Snail. Like most other members of its family, it feeds on minute particles of plant life, using its radula to scrape them from the surface. This air-breathing snail lives in semiterrestrial situations.

Californian Margin Shell
Volvarina taeniolata
125

¼–⅜″ (6–10 mm) high. Elongate, oblong to almost cylindrical, small, glossy, with short spire and a conical, rounded apex. Body whorl cylindrical, smooth, glossy; yellowish orange, usually with broad, whitish spiral bands. Aperture narrow, broader at base. Outer lip thickened, sinuous, flaring out near base. Lower part of columella and base white, with 4 strongly oblique spiral ridges.

Habitat
Under rocks, from low-tide level to water 150′ (46 m) deep.

Range
Point Conception, California, to Ecuador.

Comments
This species is common underneath rocks at very low tide.

Western Barrel Bubble
Cylichnella culcitella
126

¼–¾″ (6–19 mm) high. Oblong, cylindrical, with a flat or elevated spire and a large, cylindrical body whorl; yellowish brown, with reddish-brown spiral threads. Nuclear whorl tilted, white, smooth. Later whorls with broad, shallow channel with strong cord at edge. Body whorl has elevated cord above a narrow, deep channel, and an evenly convex shoulder, gently convex on left side but straight or slightly concave on outer-lip side; body whorl covered with fine, microscopic, wavy spiral threads that are more crowded near top. Aperture narrow, broader below. Outer lip thin, continuous with cord around spire, rounded base, and thickened, convex columellar callus, which has a low to strong ascending ridge at upper end.

Habitat
On sand and mud, from low-tide line to water 150' (46 m) deep.

Range
Kodiak Island, Alaska, to central Baja California.

Comments
This bubble feeds on other gastropods. The shells that occur from Alaska to Monterey, California, have a lower, flattened spire, and a weaker columellar ridge. Formerly *Tornatina*.

Purple Dwarf Olive
Olivella biplicata
127

½–1½" (1.3–3.8 cm) high. Broadly ovate, relatively large, stout, smooth, with a convexly to sharply conical spire; brownish gray to almost white, with a fine, dark line below suture, and a brown or orange line at upper margin of purplish siphonal band. Spire whorls almost straight-sided; suture very narrowly channeled. Body whorl convex, broad. Aperture elongately triangular. Outer lip thin, flaring at base, often slightly purplish within, with a brown margin. Parietal callus thick, reaching from top of aperture to base. Columellar fold strong, twisted, with 2–4 ridges.

Habitat
On sand, from low-tide line to water 150' (46 m) deep.

Range
Vancouver Island, British Columbia, to Baja California.

Comments
Young and immature shells are often strongly tinged with purple. Mating and spawning occur throughout the year. The female lays dome-shaped capsules on empty bivalves or other hard objects. From these the young emerge as free-swimming larvae, although they can swim only short distances in the water close to the bottom. Most of these animals are buried in sand during the day but emerge at night, remaining active on the surface and burrowing again before dawn.

Checkered Periwinkle
Littorina scutulata
128

½" (13 mm) high. Moderately conical. Brownish to nearly black, with lighter spots in irregularly checkered pattern; edge of lip with whitish spots against brown interior. 5 whorls, surface smooth, shiny. Columella narrow. Operculum horny, brownish.

Habitat
On rocky shores; between high- and low-tide lines.

Range
Alaska to Baja California.

Comments
This periwinkle tolerates exposure less well than the Eroded Periwinkle (*L. keenae*), which shares the same habitat. At low tide it hides in crevices and among algal holdfasts.

Unicorns
Acanthina spp.
129

1–1⅝″ (25–41 mm) high. Spindle-shaped. Blue-gray, with rows of small, dark dots, or checkered black and white. 5–6 whorls with slight shoulder, and spiral cords or threads, shallow suture. Outer lip with sharp spine, siphonal canal short. Operculum oval, horny, brownish.

Habitat
On rocks and pilings, among mussels and barnacles, in protected places; between high- and low-tide lines.

Range
Puget Sound to Baja California.

Comments
Among the various species of unicorns are the Angled Unicorn (*A. spirata*), which measures 1⅝″ (41 mm) long and 1″ (25 mm) wide, has a ridged shoulder, and is pale blue-gray with rows of dots, and the Checkered Unicorn (*A. paucilirata*), a southern species that is smaller than *A. spirata*, but is distinguished by its pattern of large, black and white checks; it ranges from southern California to Baja California. These snails drill through the shells of barnacles and mussels to get at the soft tissue of their prey.

Emarginate Dogwinkle
Nucella emarginata
130

⅞–1⅛″ (2.2–2.8 cm) high. Ovate, typically with large body whorl and short, broadly conical spire, occasionally with a taller spire; yellowish to dark brown, sometimes banded. Whorls convex; with irregular, prominent spiral ribs, sometimes knobby and usually alternating with weaker ribs. Columella curved, flattened, sometimes white. Aperture large, oval, yellowish to brownish within. Outer lip slightly flaring, margin wavy. Canal short, narrow.

Habitat
On rocks or in rocky crevices, near beds of mussels, intertidally.

Range
Alaska to N. Baja California.

Comments
An abundant and variable species in relative size of body whorl and spire, and in sculpture; in some localities the spiral cords are strongly knobby. This whelk may be important in determining the species composition of mussel beds on exposed, often rocky coastline. Because it prefers to prey on young *Mytilus edulis*, it leaves the older mussel beds as pure or nearly pure stands of *Mytilus californianus*. It also preys on barnacles.

Californian Melampus
Melampus olivaceus
131

⅜–⅝" (10–16 mm) high. Broadly top-shaped, with a low, conical spire and a large body whorl; brown, with narrow, white spiral bands on body whorl; covered with a brownish periostracum. Smooth, occasionally with faint, crowded axial ridges. Body whorl with rounded shoulder, narrowing toward base. Columella has a slanting ridge. Aperture narrow above, broad and rounded below. Outer lip thin, dark brown within, with a white callus bearing numerous spiral ridges farther within. Parietal wall has several teeth.

Habitat
On mud flats in salt marshes, near high-tide line.

Range
California to Gulf of California.

Comments
Known in California as the Salt Marsh Snail and as the Olive Ear Snail. It is generally found at the high-tide drift line.

Californian Cone
Conus californicus
132

¾–1⅛" (1.9–4.1 cm) high. Spire low, broadly conical, convex; yellowish brown, with an obscure, whitish band at angle, covered with a thin, brown periostracum that may be axially and finely fibrous. Early spire whorls have a low, angled shoulder; later whorls flattened, with a few obscure spiral grooves. Body whorl has a rounded shoulder, and is smooth except for obscure spiral threads that become strong toward base on lower third. Aperture narrow above, wide below, with a shallow notch at upper end. Outer lip thin, whitish within.

Habitat
In sand or gravel near rubble, from low-tide line to water 100' (20 m) deep.

Range
San Francisco, California, to S. Baja California.

Comments
This species preys on a greater variety of animals than does any other known cone shell. Its preferred foods are living gastropods, which it captures by spearing them with a modified radular tooth, paralyzing them with poison, and swallowing the prey whole.

Chestnut Cowry
Cypraea spadicea
133

1–2½" (2.5–6.4 cm) long. Ovate, narrowed at 1 end, with an evenly rounded back; smooth, shiny; back pale pinkish white, with a large, irregular spot of light chestnut-brown or grayish brown in middle, surrounded by a narrow, irregular, dark reddish-brown margin; base pure white. Both lips have numerous small teeth.

Habitat
Under ledges or stones, just below low-tide line to water 120' (36.6 m) deep; mostly at 25–40' (7.6–12.2 m).

Range
Monterey, California, to central Baja California. Rare north to Point Conception.

Comments
This is the only cowry in Californian waters; it is rarely found north of Santa Barbara. The animal's mantle is bright orange, with dark reddish-orange, wartlike knobs; the foot is white.

Green Paper Bubble
Haminoea virescens
134

½–¾" (13–19 mm) high. Broadly ovate, thin-shelled, fragile; yellowish green. Spire sunken, with a minute perforation. Body whorl narrowed at top, with crowded, fine, curved axial growth ridges, and crowded, microscopic grooves. Aperture very large, constituting more than two-thirds of body whorl. Outer lip thin; upper part high and arched forward, lower part wide and expanded. Parietal wall has thin callus. Columellar wall thickened, narrow, strongly concave, turned backward over base.

Habitat
In rocky areas among seaweeds and in bays, near low-tide line.

Range
Puget Sound to Gulf of California.

Comments
The related Gould's Paper Bubble (*H. vesicula*), ranging from Alaska to the Gulf of California, is ¾" (19 mm) high and has a more barrel-shaped body whorl, which is about equal to the aperture in size. Its outer lip is not as highly arched, and the shell is brown or yellowish.

California Bubble
Bulla gouldiana
135

1½–2½" (3.8–6.4 cm) high. Largest bubble shell in the world. Broadly ovate, large, thin-shelled; grayish, with small, dark spots edged on right with white; covered with a thin, brown periostracum. Spire has a narrow depression with smooth or grooved walls. Body whorl smooth except for fine axial growth ridges and crowded, microscopic spiral threads. Aperture wide, rounded below. Outer lip thin, arched well above top of whorl. Parietal wall covered with a thin glaze. Columellar wall white, thickly folded, turned backward over base of shell, continuous with outer lip.

Habitat
In mud and near eelgrass, from low-tide line to water 150' (46 m) deep.

Range
Santa Barbara, California, to Gulf of California.

Comments
This species, also called the Cloudy Bubble Snail, is conspicuous because of its size and its inflated form and thin shell. Spawning occurs in summer. Long, tangled yellow egg stripes are laid on eelgrass or on mud.

**Californian Banded
Pheasant Shell**
Tricolia compta
136

¼–⅜" (6–10 mm) high. High-spired; grayish white to
greenish brown, with irregular white or brownish axial streaks
or spots, and numerous fine, brownish, slightly slanting spiral
lines. Whorls smooth, gently convex. Umbilicus narrow,
chinklike.

Habitat
On eelgrass in shallow water.

Range
Santa Barbara, California, to N. Baja California.

Comments
This abundant species is often washed ashore. The specific
name is a Latin adjective meaning "adorned" or "polished,"
describing the smooth, patterned shell.

Eroded Periwinkle
Littorina keenae
137

½–¾" (13–19 mm) high, almost as wide. Broadly ovate,
narrow, body whorl longer than spire; brownish gray, with
irregular, scattered whitish spots. Whorls convex, eroded.
Eroded area present next to whitish columella, which is
expanded where it joins lip. Aperture dark brown, with a
white spiral band at bottom.

Habitat
On rocks along shoreline above high-tide line.

Range
Puget Sound to Baja California.

Comments
The Eroded Periwinkle, also known as *L. planaxis*, usually
feeds on microscopic algae and diatoms, but its radula can also
scrape pieces off larger seaweeds. These snails are adapted to
both aerial and underwater respiration and can even tolerate
several days in fresh water, thus representing a sort of halfway
point in the evolutionary emergence of marine forms directly
to the land.

Carpenter's Baby Bubble
Rictaxis punctocaelatus
138

⅜–⅝" (10–16 mm) high. Evenly elliptical, with a spire
about a third shell length; whitish, with a broad, grayish-
brown band on lower part of spire whorls and 2 bands on body
whorl. Nuclear whorl smooth, rounded, tilted. Spire whorls
convex, with deeply incised suture; whorls have crowded,
flattened spiral cords, grooves between with oval pits,
rendering edges of cords wavy. On lower body whorl, grooves
wider and fine axial riblets that separate pits more noticeable.
Columella strongly twisted, with lower end bordering left side
of aperture; a strong ascending ridge present at upper end.
Aperture elongately ovate, pointed above, rounded below.

Habitat
In sand, from low-tide line to water 150' (46 m) deep.

Range
Alaska to central Baja California.

Comments
Also called the Striped Barrel Shell, the species name is from 2
Latin words, *punctum* ("a little hole") and *caelatus* ("carved in
relief"), and refers to the rows of hollowed pits. The genus
name is formed with the Latin words *rictus* ("open mouth")
and *axis* ("pole" or "axis"), referring to the exposed, twisted
columella. The animal deposits eggs in a gelatinous sac that is
attached to the substrate by a slender thread. A similar species
is Rehder's Baby Bubble (*Acteon candens*), which ranges from
North Carolina to Cuba, and is larger, more solid, and glossy.

Recluz's Moon Shell
Neverita reclusiana
139

1–2¾" (2.5–7 cm) high, only slightly less wide. Broadly
round, large, heavy, smooth; pale brown to grayish brown,
with a dark band below suture or occasionally brown stains,
and with a paler base. Spire moderately high, conical. Base
rounded. Umbilicus broad and partially or almost entirely
covered by a white or pale brownish grooved extension of thick
callus covering parietal wall.

Habitat
On sand in lagoons and bays, in shallow depths to water 150'
(46 m) deep.

Range
Santa Barbara, California, to the Gulf of California.

Comments
There is considerable variation in the height of the spire and
the size of the umbilical callus, which has led some experts to
separate the high specimens into a distinct subspecies. There
are, however, too many intergrades to warrant such a
distinction. Like that of the Atlantic Shark Eye, the umbilical
callus may be whitish to brownish, a difference that may be
connected in both species to the abundance and kind of food
that is available.

Lewis' Moon Shell
Polinices lewisii
140

2¼–5½" (5.7–14 cm) high. Largest living moon shell.
Almost round, large, thick; yellowish white to pale brown,
base usually paler; fresh shells covered with a thin, brown
periostracum that is frequently rubbed off. Whorls flattened
below suture, making them appear shouldered. Body whorl
occasionally has a shallow constriction below shoulder.
Umbilicus narrow, deep, partially covered by an extension of
columellar and parietal callus, which is yellowish white
stained with brown. Aperture pointed above, ovate, almost
semicircular. Operculum horny.

Habitat
On sand in bays, intertidally to water 600' (183 m) deep.

Range
Vancouver Island, British Columbia, to N. Baja California.

Comments
During locomotion, when fully expanded, the animal's foot is

very large. It preys chiefly on clams. After settling the very young are at first herbivorous, subsisting on diatoms and sea lettuce, and only later become carnivorous. The common and scientific names of this species honor Meriwether Lewis, who with William Clark explored the route to the Pacific in 1804–1806, and who brought back specimens of this shell.

Norris Top Shell
Norrisia norrisi
141

1¼–2¼" (3.2–5.7 cm) wide. Dome-shaped, thick, smooth, flattened; chestnut-brown, darker near umbilicus. Body whorl large, bluntly angled at periphery. Umbilicus deep, tinged with green at edge near columella. Aperture round. Operculum with many turns and a central beginning; edge of turns with thin, flat, horny, platelike projections, inner ones curling over when dry.

Habitat
On kelp and other algae near low-tide level.

Range
Point Conception, California, to central Baja California.

Comments
This abundant species has bright red soft parts. It feeds on several species of the larger brown algae. On kelp beds it migrates vertically, moving lower on the plants during the day, and coming up near the top at dusk. The young shells have 2 strong spiral cords on the body whorl. Both genus and species names honor Thomas Norris (died 1852), whose private collection of shells was one of the largest in England.

Arctic Natica
Natica clausa
142

⅝–2⅜" (1.6–6 cm) high, about as wide. Almost round; whitish, usually covered by a thin, tough, resistant, brown periostracum. Whorls convex, smooth, occasionally with very fine, wavy spiral grooves. Body whorl evenly rounded. Base convex. Umbilicus completely covered by a calcareous, white, semicircular callus. Operculum calcareous, slightly concave, smooth.

Habitat
On sand, intertidally in the northern part of its range, in water to 2800' (854 m) deep in south.

Range
On both coasts: Alaska to San Diego, California; Greenland to North Carolina.

Comments
This very common species, which is found in all cold waters around the North Pole, is an important food source for bottom-feeding fish. The large, carnivorous snails drill holes in the shells of other mollusks. They are closely related to the moon snails (*Polinices*). The Latin adjective *clausa* means "closed" and refers to the umbilicus, which is completely covered by the white callus.

Sitka Periwinkle
Littorina sitkana
143

½–⅞" (13–22 mm) high, almost as wide. Almost round, thick, body whorl as tall as spire; dark gray to reddish brown, often with a few white spiral bands. Whorls usually marked by strong spiral threads, but sometimes smooth. Columella white, flattened, almost shelflike. Aperture usually brownish.

Habitat
On rocks among seaweeds along low-tide line.

Range
N. Alaska to S. Oregon.

Comments
Both the sculpture and the color of this shell vary greatly. The first shell described was from Sitka, Alaska; hence its name. Like the Northern Yellow Periwinkle, it lays its eggs in gelatinous masses on rocks and algae. Since adults are easily dislodged and the egg masses easily dried out, it is most abundant where protected from waves and sunshine.

One-banded Chink Shell
Lacuna unifasciata
144

¼–⅜" (6–10 mm) high. Moderately elongate, small; yellowish brown. Whorls gently convex, appearing smooth but with minute and obscure grooves. Body whorl angled at periphery, where it is marked by a fine reddish-brown line. Umbilical furrow narrow and long. Columella and umbilicus white.

Habitat
Among eelgrass and seaweeds at low-tide level; under kelp in water 1–5′ (0.3–1.5 m) deep.

Range
Monterey, California, to Baja California.

Comments
The One-banded Chink Shell is very abundant on shore as well as in offshore kelp beds. It also lives on the blades and among the roots of eelgrass. It is sometimes called the One-banded Lacuna. The generic name is a Latin word meaning "ditch" or "crevice" and refers to the umbilical chink or furrow. A related species is the Carinate Chink Shell (*L. carinata*), found from Alaska to Monterey. It is larger, with a large, broad aperture and a wide, white umbilical furrow, which is strongly margined.

Carinate Dove Shell
Alia carinata
145

¼–⅜" (6–10 mm) high. Elongate, small, with an elevated, pointed spire; pale brown, with spiral bands of reddish-brown and white spots, sometimes with white band on body whorl; reddish-brown spots may be axially aligned; fresh shells covered with a moderately thin, brown, often rough periostracum. Whorls almost flat-sided to gently convex, smooth except for a few fine spiral grooves at base. Body whorl strongly to weakly angled at shoulder, angle strongest at aperture. Aperture elongate to almost rectangular, pinkish white to whitish within. Outer lip dark chestnut-brown inside and usually outside, slightly flaring at margin, strongly angled near upper end, with strong, elongate teeth within. Columella and most of parietal wall chestnut-brown.

Habitat
Among grasses and algae, from low-tide line to water 15′ (4.6 m) deep.

Range
S. Alaska to S. Baja California.

Comments
Known also as *Nitidella carinata, Columbella carinata,* and *Mitrella carinata,* or the Keeled Dove Shell, this species is often found on the giant kelp *Macrocystis.* It seems to feed on small organisms on the surface of the kelp rather than on the kelp itself. A small amphipod crustacean, *Pleustes,* lives with this species and mimics its size, shape, and color.

Common Northern Chink Shell
Lacuna vincta
146

¼–⅝″ (6–16 mm) high. Long, ovate, moderately thin; light brown, often with several narrow brown bands, spire occasionally with a reddish or purplish tip. Whorls smooth, rounded. Umbilicus narrow, bordered by a strong, angled ridge. Columella and umbilical furrow white. Aperture ovate, with a shallow depression between columella and inner lip. Outer lip thin.

Habitat
Generally among seaweeds, from low-tide level to shallow water.

Range
On both coasts: Arctic waters to N. California, and to Rhode Island.

Comments
This abundant species is also known as the Common Northern Lacuna. The female lays eggs in jellylike masses on seaweed fronds. The small, doughnut-shaped egg masses appear as bright bluish-green rings. The species name is a Latin word meaning "bound about" or "wound about" and refers to the color bands found on many specimens.

Varicose Solarielle
Solariella varicosa
147

¼–½″ (6–13 mm) high, slightly broader. Broadly conical; gray-brown or yellowish to white; surface often eroded. Whorls convex, slightly shouldered below suture, with low, rounded diagonal ribs and fine spiral threads that may be absent in large specimens or restricted to base and lower half of whorls. Body whorl sometimes bluntly angled at base, where low cord may be present. Umbilicus deep, narrow, funnel-shaped, surrounded by a double spiral cord. Aperture round.

Habitat
In sand or mud, in water 15–350′ (4.6–107 m) deep.

Range
On both coasts: Alaska to S. California, and Labrador to Maine.

Comments
The Alaskan specimens tend to be larger than those found on the Atlantic Coast, but they are not commonly encountered in shallow depths and must be dredged.

Puppet Margarite
Margarites pupillus
148

⅜–½" (10–13 mm) high, equally or slightly less wide. Sharply conical; whitish to yellowish gray. Whorls convex with strong, irregularly spaced spiral cords, crossed by very fine, slanting axial threads. Body whorl with strong cord at base, which is sculptured with fine spiral threads. Umbilicus very narrow. Aperture almost round.

Habitat
On sand, mud, or rubble; intertidally in northern part of its range; in water to 300' (91 m) deep farther south.

Range
Bering Sea to S. California.

Comments
This species is more common in the northern part of its range, where it is found in the littoral zone. Farther south it seeks cooler, deeper water. It is preyed upon by the Dire Whelk (*Searlesia dira*) and by the nudibranch *Dirona albolineata*.

Dusky Tegula
Tegula pulligo
149

¾–1⅝" (1.9–4.1 cm) high, slightly wider. Sharply conical; grayish, usually with light yellowish spots below suture and on body whorl. Whorls smooth, flattened. Body whorl strongly angled. Base flattened, yellowish. Umbilicus deep, round, moderately wide; umbilical area white. Aperture transversely oval.

Habitat
Among and on larger kelp low in the intertidal or subtidal areas; juveniles found on rocks.

Range
Alaska to Santa Barbara, California.

Comments
This species somewhat resembles the Brown Tegula, but has a deep, round umbilicus and a thin columella. The animal's foot is black with a blotched purplish or reddish-brown border; the mantle folds near the head are pinkish bordered with yellow. Also called the Northern Brown Turban.

Wavy Turban
Astraea undosa
150

2–4¼" (5.1–10.8 cm) wide, almost as high. Conical, large; light brown, covered by a thick, fibrous periostracum. Whorls coarsely sculptured with wavy, slanted, knobby axial ridges and with a strong, wavy, pinched-out cord at periphery. Base marked by a few spiral ridges; umbilical area white, ridged. Operculum oval, shelly, thick, pointed, with 3–4 strong, prickly ridges running from pointed edge.

Habitat
In rocky areas, from low-tide level to water 60' (18 m) deep.

Range
Point Conception, California, to central Baja California.

Comments
The Wavy Turban moves into shallower, warmer water when it reproduces. It is abundant in shallow water in southern California. The larger specimens are found in deeper water, especially among kelp.

Ringed Top Shell
Calliostoma annulatum
151

⅝–1¼" (1.6–3.2 cm) high, slightly narrower. Sharply conical, thin; yellow, with a pale purplish or mauve band at angled periphery and around umbilical area; beads regularly spotted with orange, tip often pinkish. Whorls flat, with numerous spiral rows of strongly beaded cords. Body whorl sharply angled. Base flattened, with many weakly beaded cords. Umbilicus absent. Aperture ovate to almost round.

Habitat
On kelp or rocks among kelp, intertidally in northern part of its range, and in water to 100' (30 m) deep farther south.

Range
S. Alaska to N. Baja California.

Comments
Also known as the Purple-ringed Top Shell, this omnivorous species is more common in the north, where it is often found on the blades of kelp, feeding on hydroids, bryozoans, or the kelp itself. On the sea floor it is both a predator and scavenger, taking detritus, copepods, anemones, or dead fish. When attacking live prey it sometimes rears up on the hind part of its foot, expands its lips and lunges at the prey. The foot of the animal is bright orange.

Western Ribbed Top Shell
Calliostoma ligatum
152

¾–1" (19–25 mm) high, slightly narrower. Conical, thick; dark yellow to brownish yellow, with occasional dark spots below the suture and periphery. Whorls convex, with light spiral cords. Body whorl bluntly angled. Base flat. Umbilicus absent. Aperture almost round.

Habitat
Among algae and under rocks intertidally.

Range
Alaska to central California.

Comments
This very common shell is also known as the Blue Top Shell because of the pearly bluish color revealed when the outer

shelly layer is worn away. *C. ligatum* flees from sea stars but, that failing, covers itself with mucus, which aids somewhat against capture. This species was once known as *C. costatum* and hence is also sometimes called the Costate Top Shell.

Channeled Top Shell
Calliostoma canaliculatum
153

⅝–1½" (1.6–3.8 cm) high and wide. Sharply conical; whitish yellow. Whorls flat or slightly convex, bearing numerous strong spiral cords, which may be beaded; grooves between spiral cords dark. Body whorl strongly angled. Base almost flat, without umbilicus, but indented in umbilical area. Aperture angularly ovate.

Habitat
On kelp or rocks among kelp, from near low-tide level to shallower water.

Range
S. Alaska to N. Baja California.

Comments
This common species lives in shallow water in the north, often on kelp blades. In the south it is smaller and lives in slightly deeper water. It is omnivorous, eating kelp, bryozoa, and hydroids growing on the kelp, and scavenging dead animals.

Sharp-keeled Lirularia
Lirularia acuticostata
154

⅛–¼" (3–6 mm) high, almost as wide or slightly wider. Conical; whitish or pale gray, with axial streaks of reddish brown, broadest at suture. Whorls convex, with 3 or more strong, narrow spiral cords, often bearing reddish-brown spots; many fine axial threads between cords. Body whorl angled above convex base, which bears numerous smaller cords. Umbilicus large and deep. Aperture round.

Habitat
In coarse gravel, often among kelp, below low-tide level.

Range
Sitka, Alaska, to N. Baja California.

Comments
This small species varies considerably in its relative height and the number of spiral cords. The species name is composed of 2 Latin words, *acuta* ("sharp") and *costata* ("ribbed"), and refers to the strong, narrow spiral cords.

Dall's Dwarf Turban
Homalopoma luridum
155

¼–⅜" (6–10 mm) high and wide. Almost round, small, thick; color variable, brown or greenish gray, reddish or white, sometimes whitish spotted with red. Whorls convex, with strong, smoothish spiral cords. Columella with a knob at base. Aperture round, white. Outer lip often with a narrow, pale margin. Operculum small, calcareous, smooth.

Habitat
Under rocks, from low-tide level to shallow water.

Range
Sitka, Alaska, to N. Baja California.

Comments
The shells of this small snail are important as homes for hermit crabs. Shells found in southern California are generally smaller than those found farther north. Some scientists have erroneously placed the northern shells, which usually have more striking reddish or purplish-red colors when worn, in a different species, Carpenter's Dwarf Turban (*H. carpenteri*). The related Berry Dwarf Turban (*H. baculum*) ranges from Puget Sound to Baja California. It is slightly smaller and lower and appears smoother, but has broad, low spiral cords, which make the whorls appear to be spirally grooved. It is purplish red.

Western Banded Tegula
Tegula eiseni
156

⅝–⅞″ (16–22 mm) high, about as wide. Broadly conical with a domed spire; brownish, occasionally with slanting axial white streaks. Whorls rounded, with numerous knobby spiral cords marked with alternating dark and white spots; whole surface with very fine spiral threads. Base flattened, with crowded, less knobby spiral cords; white, smooth area around deep, wide umbilicus. Aperture rounded.

Habitat
On rocks intertidally and under kelp below low-tide mark.

Range
Monterey, California, to Baja California.

Comments
The generic name *Tegula* is Latin, meaning "little tile," given because the typical species in the genus bears finely beaded sculpture resembling closely fitted roof tiles. The species name honors Gustav Eisen, a collector who worked in Baja California. It is sometimes called *T. mendella* and was previously known as *T. ligulata*.

Red Turban
Astraea gibberosa
157

1½–3″ (3.8–7.6 cm) wide, three-quarters as high. Conical, moderately low, thick; reddish or yellowish brown, covered by a coarse brown periostracum. Whorls sculptured with slanting axial ribs, crossed in lower half by incised spiral lines that render the ribs knobby. Body whorl with a strong cord bearing low, toothlike projections above flattened base. Base with numerous spiral cords, and depressed umbilical area, with curved groove. Aperture transversely ovate. Operculum thick, elongately oval, pointed at 1 end, with inner side smooth, flattened, greenish; outer side convex, white.

Habitat
On rocks, in shallow depths to water about 200′ (60–70 m) deep.

Range
British Columbia to Magdalena Bay, Baja California.

Comments
This species is characterized by its thick, oval, smooth operculum. In the northern part of its range it occurs in shallow water, but farther south it lives in depths of 50' (15 m) or more.

Black Tegula
Tegula funebralis
158

¾–1¾" (1.9–4.4 cm) high. Variable, from low and dome-shaped to conically elevated; purplish black. Whorls slightly convex, smoothish except for several weak spiral cords below suture, with upper cord scaly. Base rounded; white area around low, closed umbilicus. Aperture round, pearly white inside, with 2 small knobs at base of columella.

Habitat
On rocks intertidally.

Range
Vancouver, British Columbia, to central Baja California.

Comments
This is also known as the Black Turban. All *Tegula* snails are abundant and have stout, thick shells. The Black Tegula animal is almost completely black and prefers to feed on fleshy algae. During low tide it often groups in large numbers in crevices, moving higher on the rocks at night during high tides. It is most abundant in open situations not heavily covered with algae; exposed to the air much of the time, it may be partially adapted to life out of the water. Larger specimens may be 20 to 30 years old. Empty shells are usually inhabited by hermit crabs. The Black Limpet is found on the shells of this species and on the Speckled Tegula, feeding on microscopic algae that grow on the shells. The related Brown Tegula, or Brown Turban (*T. brunnea*), same size, is found from Oregon to the Santa Barbara Islands. It is similar but pale brown with a brownish-white base; it generally has a small protuberance at the base of the columella. The foot of the animal has an orange or red-brown border, and the folds near its head are bordered in yellow.

Black Limpet
Collisella asmi
159

⅜–½" (10–13 mm) long. Small, strongly elevated, with apex toward front end, and rear slope markedly convex; base broadly oval. Along base, sides concave so that the shell rests on both ends. Exterior smooth, dark brown to blackish, usually eroded. Interior brown or purplish brown to bluish gray with a brown margin.

Habitat
On tegula snails in the intertidal zone.

Range
British Columbia to Baja California.

Comments
This species is found only on Black and Speckled tegulas, where it feeds on the microscopic algae that grow on them. It

can easily move from one tegula shell to another when the
tegulas occur in groups. It does not establish itself on empty
shells and prefers those with the mollusk still inside.

White-cap Limpet
Acmaea mitra
160

¾–1¾" (1.9–4.4 cm) long. Thick, highly elevated, with a
nearly central apex; base broadly oval to round. Exterior and
interior smooth and white.

Habitat
On rocks below low-tide mark.

Range
Alaska to Baja California.

Comments
This species feeds on patches of small mosslike red algae and
on the encrusting coralline alga with which it is commonly
associated. It spawns in winter when the water temperature is
low. The shell often has a pinkish, knobby coating of coralline
algae. It is most abundant in colder waters, but is frequently
washed up on shore. The genus name is based on the Greek
word *akme* ("point"), and the species name is the Latin word
meaning "cap." The related Corded White Limpet (*A.
funiculata*) has the same range, but is smaller, less elevated,
and has fine, uneven riblets on the surface.

Pelta False Limpet
Williamia peltoides
161

¼–½" (6–13 mm) long. Elevated, with elevated apex
pointing backward, a third from hind end; base broadly oval
to almost circular. Exterior smooth, straw-yellow; covered
with thin periostracum that is radially striped with pinkish
and greenish yellow; in fresh specimens periostracum extends
beyond shell margin. Interior yellowish white, with wide gap
in oval muscle scar; no noticeable siphonal furrow.

Habitat
Under rocks, intertidally to water 150' (46 m) deep.

Range
N. California to southern Mexico.

Comments
This species lives in greater depths than other members of its
family. The generic name honors William H. Dall (1845–
1927), outstanding American malacologist.

Seaweed Limpet
Notoacmaea insessa
162

½–⅞" (13–22 mm) long. High, with apex toward front end;
base elliptical. Exterior shiny, brown, smooth except for fine
striations. Interior brown.

Habitat
On stalks and holdfasts of kelp and other algae attached to
rocks at low-tide mark.

Range
S. Alaska to Baja California.

Comments
This limpet lives and feeds directly on the Feather Boa Kelp (genus *Egregia*), often scarring and otherwise damaging it considerably. The shell's elliptical basal outline is related to its habitat on the straplike kelp stems.

Unstable Limpet
Collisella instabilis
163

¾–1½" (1.9–3.8 cm) long. Moderately elevated, resting on long, convex sides; base narrow, elliptical. Exterior smooth, brown to yellowish brown. Interior whitish with a dark margin.

Habitat
On kelp at or below low-tide level.

Range
Alaska to San Diego, California.

Comments
This species lives on the holdfasts and stems of large kelp, especially *Laminaria*. The limpet partly surrounds the kelp and clasps it by the sides with its foot. As the shell develops, it becomes long and thin, with its sides extended downward because of the position of the foot and mantle. The species name is a Latin adjective meaning "unsteady," and refers to the fact that the shell rocks when resting on its sides.

Shield Limpet
Collisella pelta
164

1–2⅛" (2.5–5.4 cm) long. Heavy, moderately elevated, with apex toward front end, and sides slightly convex; base broadly elliptical to oval. Exterior grayish with irregular white, radial stripes, often forming a netlike pattern; smooth or with irregular, fine radial riblets, occasionally heavy. Interior pale bluish white with a dark brown central spot and a border of alternating dark and light spots.

Habitat
On rocks and kelp holdfasts intertidally.

Range
Alaska to Baja California.

Comments
Shield Limpets are often abundant on large smooth boulders in the lower intertidal zone. The largest Shield Limpets are found in the northern part of the range. Those that live on kelp holdfasts are very dark with obscure ribbing. This species feeds on various red and brown algae when the tide is in. It spawns throughout most of the year but is less active in summer off the coast of California. The Latin species name *pelta* ("small shield") refers to the shell's shape.

File Limpet
Collisella limatula
165

1–1¾" (2.5–4.4 cm) long. Low, with apex toward front end; base broadly oval. Exterior greenish brown or sometimes yellowish, darker shells occasionally mottled with white, with many fine, crowded, scaly or beaded riblets. Interior bluish white to white, usually with an irregular brown spot and a dark edge at margin.

Habitat
On rocks above high-tide level.

Range
Puget Sound to Baja California.

Comments
The name of this very common shell comes from its fine, filelike riblets. This shell and others in genus *Collisella* were previously classified in genus *Acmaea,* but their radular characteristics differ significantly and justified grouping them in a separate genus. The File Limpet feeds mostly on microscopic and encrusting algae. Spawning has been observed at most times of the year.

Great Keyhole Limpet
Megathura crenulata
166

3–4⅞″ (7.6–13 cm) long. Largest known keyhole limpet. Low, with a large oval hole toward the front; base elongately oval. Exterior yellowish or pinkish gray, with regular, fine radial ribs rendered beaded by concentric grooves. Interior white, with finely toothed margin.

Habitat
On rocks, from low-tide line to shallow depths; common on breakwaters.

Range
Monterey Bay, California, to central Baja California.

Comments
The opening of this keyhole limpet is distinctively large. The animal has a black or grayish mantle, which is larger than the shell, covering it entirely; it also has a massive yellow foot. It eats both seaweeds and colonial tunicates.

Two-spotted Keyhole Limpet
Megatebennus bimaculatus
167

½–⅞″ (13–22 mm) long. Low, with a large, broadly elongate hole near the middle; base broadly to elongately oval. Ends raised. Exterior yellowish brown, with dark grayish rays, and with low ribs roughened by concentric ridges. Interior white with thickened margin.

Habitat
Under stones and on kelp at or just below low-tide level.

Range
S. Alaska to Baja California.

Comments
The animal is much larger than the shell. The fleshy parts are variously colored, and the extended mantle edge covers part of the shell. This species has been observed to feed on compound tunicates and sponges, but may also feed on phytoplankton. The generic name is derived from the Greek words *megas* ("large") and *tebenna* ("robe") and refers to the mantle.

Hooded Puncturella
Puncturella cucullata
168

½–1⅛″ (1.3–2.8 cm) long. Highly elevated, with a small apex slightly hooked toward front, and a small, long slit behind apex; base broadly elliptical. Exterior dull gray, with 15–23 narrow principal ribs and several finer ribs between; strong ribs give finely notched margin an angled appearance. Interior white, with a convex shelf between slit and apex.

Habitat
Among and under rocks, at low-tide level and in water 120–450′ (35–140 m) deep off California.

Range
Alaska to La Paz, Baja California.

Comments
The similar Helmet Puncturella (*P. galeata*), ⅜–⅞″ (10–22 mm) long, has finer, more numerous ribs, a smooth margin, and a reinforced inner shelf at the slit; it is found from the Aleutian Islands to southern California in water 60–450′ (18–140 m) deep.

Rough Keyhole Limpet
Diodora aspera
169

1–2¾″ (2.5–7 cm) long. Moderately elevated, with a broad, oval hole slightly in front of middle; base broadly oval. Exterior grayish white to yellow with numerous irregular purplish-gray to brownish rays, and many rough radial ribs crossed by fine concentric threads.

Habitat
On rocks at low-tide line.

Range
Alaska to Baja California.

Comments
This species is preyed upon by various sea stars. It defends itself by extending the foot, elevating the shell, and enveloping the foot and shell with extended folds of mantle tissue, giving the sea star no firm place to attach its tube feet. Also, the commensal polychaete worm *Arctonoe vittata* commonly found with this limpet often bites the tube feet of an attacking sea star. In the southern part of its range, the shell is often dredged in shallow water and sometimes found on kelp stems. The species name, from the Latin *aspera* ("rough"), refers to the rough sculpture of the shell.

Pacific Plate Limpet
Notoacmaea scutum
170

1–2⅜″ (2.5–6 cm) long. Large, low, with a nearly central apex; base broadly elliptical to almost round. Exterior greenish to brownish gray with pale, irregular radial stripes or radially arranged spots, and with fine radial riblets that may become eroded. Interior bluish white with a brown spot of varying intensity, and with a broad, dark margin, usually with pale spots.

Habitat
On rocks intertidally.

Range
Alaska to Baja California.

Comments
This species moves up and down the rocks in rhythm with the tide and is most active at night. It flees predatory sea stars, which it can detect at a distance by chemical receptors along the mantle edge. Several authors have considered this species to be a Pacific Coast subspecies of the Atlantic Plate Limpet, but recent anatomical studies indicate that it is a distinct species. The species name *scutum* is a Latin word meaning "shield," referring to the shell's resemblance to a small oval shield.

Mask Limpet
Notoacmaea persona
171

1–1⅞" (2.5–4.8 cm) long. Moderately elevated, with apex in front of middle; base oval to almost elliptical. Exterior bluish or brownish gray, generally finely speckled with white, and smoothish or with fine vertical riblets, which may be eroded. Interior white to bluish with an irregular brown spot; margin either uniformly dark brown or spotted with white.

Habitat
On sheltered rocks or in crevices intertidally.

Range
Alaska to Monterey, California.

Comments
This is one of the most abundant limpets from California northward. It is most active at night during ebb tide, when it creeps about feeding on algae. The species name is Latin for "mask," and probably refers to a fancied resemblance of the internal brown spot to a mask.

Giant Owl Limpet
Lottia gigantea
172

1¾–4½" (4.4–10.8 cm) long. Largest limpet in North America. Low, with apex very close to front end; base broadly oval to elliptical. Exterior brownish with white spots generally in a roughly radial or netted pattern, especially near margin, and irregularly roughened. Interior with a bluish or darker area and a wide brown margin.

Habitat
On rocks and cliffs in high middle and upper littoral zones.

Range
N. Washington to central Baja California.

Comments
This is the only species in genus *Lottia*. It differs from other limpet genera in our waters in possessing a ring of small gill filaments under the mantle. Each *Lottia* tends to occupy a feeding territory that it keeps free of other animals by rasping off very small ones, such as barnacle larvae, and pushing larger ones off. The shell of the Giant Owl Limpet is frequently polished and sold as jewelry or souvenirs, and is commonly found in Indian food middens. The white spots are sometimes

obscure in large specimens and more obvious in small. The common name stems from the owl-like outline of the interior scar.

Fingered Limpet
Collisella digitalis
173

¾–1⅜" (1.9–3.5 cm) long. Moderately elevated, with pointed apex close to front, and long, convex rear slope; base oval. Exterior dark greenish gray to reddish brown with irregular white streaks or spots, and with coarse radiating ribs. Interior bluish white with a large, central, dark brown patch and a wavy border that may be dark brown interrupted by white, or white or bluish white with brown spots.

Habitat
On vertical rock surfaces in the intertidal zone where there is wave action.

Range
Alaska to Baja California.

Comments
This limpet, one of the most common on the Pacific Coast, occurs high in the intertidal zone, where it is exposed much of the time. It is found among barnacles, periwinkles, and algae, feeding upon the latter. The position of the apex and the strength of the sculpture on its shell can vary considerably. The Latin species name means "fingered," and probably refers to the strong ribs, which resemble fingers pressed together.

Rough Limpet
Collisella scabra
174

¾–1⅜" (1.9–3.5 cm) long. Heavy, moderately elevated, with apex toward front end; base broadly oval. Exterior pale grayish to greenish white, with paler, strong, rough ribs that project at the edge, giving margin a saw-toothed edge. Interior whitish, often with an irregular brown spot in center and with dark spots at the margin between rib ends.

Habitat
On rocks in upper part of intertidal zone and in places in spray zone.

Range
S. Oregon to Baja California.

Comments
This abundant species is distinguished by its rough ribs and saw-toothed edge. It is often found where *Collisella digitalis* occurs, though usually on more gently sloping surfaces. For more than 100 years, until 1945, it was confused with the related Test's Limpet (*C. conus*), which is smaller, ⅜–¾" (10–19 mm) long, with narrower, more distant ribs. Its margin is not strongly toothed, although the ribs still project, and the interior has a dark brown spot in the center. Test's Limpet ranges from Point Conception, California, to Baja California. In both species the sides of the foot are black with small white spots.

Volcano Limpet
Fissurella volcano
175

1–1⅝" (2.5–4.1 cm) long. Moderately elevated, with an elongate hole near middle; base oval. Exterior grayish white tinged with green, with reddish or purplish radial rays sometimes broken into lines; with many low, round radial ribs, which are often obscure. Interior white or greenish, with a pink line around the hole and a spotted border at margin.

Habitat
On or under rocks between tide levels.

Range
Crescent City, California, to Baja California.

Comments
This species is preyed upon by sea stars, which it can detect at a short distance, responding by fleeing. The reddish or purple streaks on the slopes of this shell resemble the streaks of lava flowing down from a crater. A color form, *F. v. crucifera*, has 4 white rays.

Heath's Chiton
Stenoplax heathiana
176

1½–3" (3.8–7.6 cm) long. Elongate; mottled greenish gray and white. Valves sharply arched; sculptured with longitudinal, branching ridges in middle, roughened or beaded ridges in side areas, and diamond-shaped pits near edge. Girdle mottled alternately dark and light greenish gray, with very small, flattened, minutely striated scales.

Habitat
Under stones in sand, intertidally to just below low-tide level.

Range
Mendocino County, California, to N. Baja California.

Comments
This species is very sensitive to light and hides under rocks during the day, coming out at night to feed on algae. The eggs are laid in May and June in the form of jellylike strings, which become caught in seaweed. In about a week the young escape to swim about for only an hour before settling on the bottom. It is sometimes confused with *Stenoplax magdalenensis* or *Ischnochiton magdalenensis,* a more southern species found in Baja California and the Gulf of California. That species is 2–4" (5.1–10.2 cm) long and has wavy ridges in the middle; the head valve and lower tail valve are strongly concave.

Lined Chiton
Tonicella lineata
177

2" (51 mm) long. Oval to oblong. Mottled reddish brown, with oblique zigzag lines of different color combinations, including light and dark red, light and dark blue, white, brown, or black; girdle greenish or yellowish, sometimes banded. Valves low, smooth, rounded; girdle smooth, leathery.

Habitat
On rocks covered with coralline algae; from low-tide line to water 180' (55 m) deep.

Range
Alaska to S. California.

Comments
The color and disruptive line-pattern of this striking chiton make it hard to confuse with any other species and provide it with excellent camouflage in the dense growths of coralline algae on which it feeds.

Veiled Chiton
Placiphorella velata
178

2" (51 mm) long. Oval, flattened. Broad, beige to tan girdle expanded in front as a head flap with green and red undersurface, narrow at rear, with scattered hairlike scales. Veil of fleshy tentacles on head. Valves short, wide, reddish or brownish, with white, tan, or greenish spots and streaks.

Habitat
In crevices and on undersides of rocks covered with coralline algae; from low-tide line to water 50' (15 m) deep.

Range
Alaska to Baja California.

Comments
The Veiled Chiton is the only chiton in American waters that, in addition to scraping food off rocks with its radula, also captures active animal prey. Small crustaceans and worms are usually swallowed whole, larger ones shredded by the radula and then consumed.

California Nuttall's Chiton
Nuttallina californica
179

2" (51 mm) long. Elongate, oval. Girdle mostly brown, with some white areas; wide, mossy, with short, rigid spines. Valves brown, olive, or dark gray, granulated on sides, with smooth central ridge. Inside surface bluish, sole of foot orange-yellow. 9 gills on either side of foot.

Habitat
On rocks in strong surf, in crevices, or among barnacles and mussels; from high-tide line to midtidal zone.

Range
Puget Sound to S. California. Not common north of Coos Bay, Oregon.

Comments
This chiton feeds mostly on red and green algae, and its shells are commonly overgrown by these algae, which erode some of the dark surface.

Giant Pacific Chiton
Cryptochiton stelleri
180

5–13" (12–33 cm) long. Largest chiton in the world. Long, oval, flattened; white. Valves butterfly-shaped; completely covered by girdle. Girdle reddish brown or pale brown, tough, leathery, made grainy by minute, blunt, red spines.

Habitat
Among rocks, near low-tide level to water 60' (18 m) deep.

Range
Alaska to Channel Islands, California.

Comments
This species is also known as the Gumboot Chiton. Unlike most chitons, *Cryptochiton* does not cling tightly to rock surfaces and is often found completely detached. When handled, it rolls slowly into a ball, armadillo-fashion, for protection. It is a slow-moving animal and feeds mainly on algae with thin fronds, such as sea lettuce. It keeps its surface free of organisms by secreting a mucus that swells on contact with water, preventing them from settling on its spines.

White Northern Chiton
Ischnochiton albus
181

⅜–¾" (10–19 mm) long. Small, long, elliptical; yellowish white or pale orange to light brown. Intermediate valves and upper part of tail valve sharply arched; lower part of tail valve straight or slightly concave; side areas slightly raised. Surface appears smooth, but is finely and obscurely grainy; obscure concentric grooves bluntly angled in intermediate valves at edge of side areas. Girdle has densely packed, elongate scales.

Habitat
On the under stones, intertidally to water 250' (76 m) deep. Prefers cold water.

Range
On both coasts: Arctic to S. California, and to Massachusetts.

Comments
The genus name is formed by adding the Greek adjective *ischnos* ("narrow") to the word *chiton;* the species name is a Latin adjective meaning "white."

Mertens' Chiton
Lepidozona mertensii
182

½–1½" (1.3–3.8 cm) long. Oblong, elliptical; pinkish or reddish brown, sometimes with darker or paler splotches. Valves sharply arched, strongly sculptured. Central areas of intermediate valves have radiating, narrow, sharp ridges with smooth interspaces; middle areas have narrow longitudinal ridges with short, broad radial riblets between; side areas with radiating rows of small, separated beads; end valves also with radial sculpture. Girdle with alternating splotches of pinkish red and yellowish white, clothed with crowded, smooth scales.

Habitat
Under rocks, intertidally to water 300' (91 m) deep. Abundant offshore in northern part of range.

Range
S. Alaska to N. Baja California.

Comments
Mertens' Chiton spawns in February in California. The egg cases released by the female have ridgelike projections with wavy edges. The species name honors Carl H. Mertens (1796–

1830), a German physician-naturalist. The genus name is derived from 2 Greek words, *lepis* ("scale") and *zona* ("girdle"), and refers to the scaly girdle. This species is sometimes confused with *Lepidozona cooperi,* but *L. cooperi* is never reddish and its girdle has subtler sculpturing and smaller scales.

Hartweg's Chiton
Cyanoplax hartwegii
183

¾–1¼" (1.9–3.2 cm) long. Oval, flattened; grayish green, irregularly mottled with blackish brown; interior of valves bright blue. Valves bluntly angled in center, with low diagonal ridge along edge of side areas. Valves finely and densely beaded in central area; side areas irregularly beaded and wrinkled. Girdle narrow, grayish brown, with very minute beads.

Habitat
On and under rocks or under algae intertidally.

Range
Monterey, California, to central Baja California.

Comments
This small southern chiton occurs higher in the intertidal zone than most chitons. It is most often found in the upper part of the middle littoral zone, especially where the rocks are covered with the small brown seaweed *Pelvetia.* It does not cling as tightly as most chitons and seeks protection from heavy surge under seaweed and in crevices. Its diet consists of *Pelvetia,* as well as some red and green algae. It is nomadic and is active chiefly at night when tide is low. Living so high in the intertidal zone, it has to withstand greater, more abrupt fluctuations in temperature, salinity, and moisture than do most chitons.

Black Katy Chiton
Katharina tunicata
184

1½–3" (4–8 cm) long. Long, ovate; uneroded valves grayish brown. Crowded, fine beads arranged in diagonal and radiating lines on side areas. Girdle wide, black or brown, naked, leathery, covering more than half of valves, and encroaching deeply between valves.

Habitat
On rocks, intertidally to just below low-tide line.

Range
Alaska to Monterey, California, occasionally further south.

Comments
This is one of the chitons that is not especially sensitive to light and is found on exposed rocks, often among seaweeds, where it feeds on diatoms and other algae. Its exposed mantle surface is thickly coated with a species of minute microscopic diatoms not found elsewhere in the surrounding environment. The females lay greenish eggs in the summertime. The living animal's foot is reddish to salmon-colored. The genus name honors Lady Katharine Douglas, who in 1815 sent the first specimens to England.

Hairy Mopalia
Mopalia ciliata
185

1–2″ (2.5–5 cm) long. Oval; grayish green or brownish, often mottled, and frequently with whitish splotches in center. Valves bluntly angled; beaded diagonal rib separates middle from side areas. Middle area with narrow longitudinal ridges, finer in center, with diagonal beads between ridges so that sculpture appears trellised; side areas with curved rows of beads; head valve with 10 radiating rows of beads. Girdle leathery, notched at rear, with many flat, brown bristles.

Habitat
In sheltered crevices and on and under rocks intertidally.

Range
Aleutian Islands, Alaska, to Baja California.

Comments
This species is common on exposed rocks and feeds not only at night but on foggy and cloudy days. It eats both plant and animal material, including bryozoans, sponges, hydroids, diatoms, and algae. After emerging from egg envelopes, larvae are free-swimming about a week before metamorphosis.

Mossy Chiton
Mopalia muscosa
186

3⅝″ (92 mm) long. Oval to oblong, flat. Girdle covered by stiff mossy hairs, dull brown, dark olive, or gray, wide, with slight notch at rear. Valves same color as girdle or paler, with flattened ridge down midline and fine, beaded longitudinal ridges in middle; crosswise-beaded ridges sometimes eroded on side. Valves often overgrown by algae or worm tubes. Inside surface bluish green to lilac.

Habitat
On rocks protected from heavy wave action, and in tide pools; between high- and low-tide lines.

Range
Alaska to Baja California.

Comments
The Mossy Chiton tolerates a wide variety of environmental conditions, including the reduced salinities of inland estuaries. The Hooked-bristled Chiton (*M. lignosa*) is somewhat smaller, 2¾″ (70 mm) long and 1⅞″ (48 mm) wide, variously combines blue, gray, green, brown, cream-color, and sometimes orange on its valves and girdle, and has a deep notch at the rear of the girdle.

Pacific Shipworm
Bankia setacea
187

Shell ½″ (13 mm) long; entire animal 39″ (1 m) long. Shell short, arc-shaped. White. Valves with sharp teeth at front end, umbones rounded, gapes wide, meeting each other at lower end. Mantle greatly extended, narrow, wormlike; separate siphons and 2 featherlike appendages at rear end; foot suckerlike.

Habitat
In wharf piles, wooden boat and ship hulls, and submerged

but not buried wood; from low-tide line to water 230' (70 m) deep.

Range
Alaska to Baja California.

Comments
Shipworm larvae, almost too small to be seen with the naked eye, settle on submerged wood, and bore in by scraping with their larval valves. Even though a piece of wood may be riddled with shipworms, the burrows do not intersect one another. This tunneling can utterly destroy any wooden structure in the sea.

Common Shipworm
Teredo navalis
188

Shell ¼" (6 mm) long; entire animal more than 12" (30 cm) long. Shell short, arc-shaped. White. Valves sharp and bladelike at front end; wide gape at each end, meeting at lower end; umbones flattened. Mantle greatly extended, narrow, wormlike; separate siphons and 2 paddlelike appendages at rear end; foot suckerlike.

Habitat
In wharf piles, wooden boat and ship hulls, and submerged but not buried wood; near low-tide line and below.

Range
Introduced into California; Newfoundland to Florida and Texas.

Comments
This shipworm was the bane of navies and merchant fleets from ancient times until the advent of metal-hulled vessels. Many a ship, structurally weakened by burrowing shipworms, has broken apart during a storm at sea. This species caused great damage in San Francisco Bay in the 1920s.

Scaly Worm Shell
Serpulorbis squamigerus
189

¼–½" (6–13 mm) wide. Growing in large, twisted masses; grayish white. Tube circular, with many longitudinal, finely roughened or scaly ridges, except for generally erect, fragile last part, which is smooth except for growth lines. No operculum.

Habitat
On pilings or rocks below low-tide line.

Range
Monterey Bay, California, to central Baja California.

Comments
Like other members of its family, this common shell feeds by entrapping food particles in the mucous threads and "nets" seen at the aperture of living specimens. The long, twisted tubes are anchored firmly to the substrate. In the northern part of their range they commonly occur singly or in small clusters, while in southern California they are often found in large aggregations.

Indian Money Tusk
Dentalium pretiosum
190

1–2″ (2.5–5.1 cm) long. Stout, moderately curved; white, often with yellowish rings. Smooth. Apex often partly eroded, with a deep slit on convex side.

Habitat
In sand and mud, in water 6–500′ (1.8–152 m) deep.

Range
Alaska to S. California.

Comments
This shell belongs to the Class Scaphopoda. Members of its genus are commonly called tooth shells. The species name is a Latin adjective meaning "valuable" or "precious," and was bestowed because Indians, particularly the Nootka of Vancouver Island, British Columbia, and elsewhere on the Northwest Coast and interior valued these shells greatly, using them as currency and for decoration.

Many-ringed Caecum
Caecum crebricinctum
191

¼″ (6 mm) long. Tubular, narrow, elongate, gradually increasing in diameter, with numerous fine, crowded, flattened rings; brownish to white, sometimes with dark brown splotches. Strong plug at 1 end, with a prominent, slanted, conical projection.

Habitat
In gravel under seaweeds below low-tide level, and in sand in water to 240′ (73 m) deep.

Range
Alaska to Baja California.

Comments
The width of this shell can vary, and the plug's projection may be considerably worn down. Like almost all caecums, it feeds on 1-celled animals living on the surfaces of sand grains and small pebbles. It is sometimes called the Many-named Caecum.

Six-sided Tusk
Dentalium neohexagonum
192

1–1¾″ (2.5–4.4 cm) long. Slender, gently curved; white, with scattered translucent-gray circular bands. Surface has circular growth lines and 6 strong, rounded longitudinal ribs, which become rounded angles or disappear near round aperture. Apex lacks slit.

Habitat
On sandy mud, in water 30–600′ (9–183 m) deep.

Range
Monterey, California, to Baja California.

Comments
Necklaces strung from these shells have been found in old Indian graves in southern California.

MAMMALS

Few animals have inspired as much legend and inquiry as the mammals of the seas—the whales, dolphins, seals, and related creatures. Their ease and agility in a world of water is a source of fascination, and their intelligence and ability to communicate have long intrigued observers. This section describes some of the most frequently seen marine mammals of the Pacific shores, from the mighty Blue Whale to the playful Sea Otter.

Gray Whale
Eschrichtius robustus
193, 217

To 46' (14 m). Viewed from above, body tapered at both ends; mottled gray, may appear uniformly slate-blue or white from surface. Baleen plates short, yellowish to white with yellowish-white bristles. Head narrowly triangular, sloping steeply downward from paired blowholes; long mouth line curving upward slightly; 2–5 deep lengthwise throat grooves. Back has low hump two-thirds of way from snout tip to flukes, followed by serrated ridge. No grooves on underside.

Habitat
Generally coastal waters. Migrate close to shore, calve in shallow southern lagoons.

Range
From Bering and Chukchi seas to Baja California.

Comments
Gray Whales can be seen along the Pacific Coast in late fall as they migrate to their winter calving and breeding grounds in bays of Baja California, and throughout the spring as they return to summer feeding in the Arctic. Early whalers called the Gray Whale the Devilfish because females strongly defend their calves against enemies, including Killer Whales (*Orcinus orca*), sharks, and people. Gray Whales leave a cloud behind them as they move. Their spout is not distinctive. These whales were believed near extinction early in the 20th century, but full protection since 1946 has allowed them to increase their numbers significantly, although they are still considered to be endangered. Habitat change in their breeding grounds is now their chief threat.

Minke Whale
Balaenoptera acutorostrata
194, 222

To 33' (10.1 m). Spindle-shaped, tapering toward rear; dark gray to black above, belly and underside of flippers white, crescent-shaped marks sometimes present on upper side in front of flippers, diagonal white band on flippers. Baleen plates yellowish white toward front, sometimes dark toward rear. Rostrum flat, narrow, pointed, triangular, with single median ridge along top; paired blowholes on top of head. Dorsal fin tall, crescent-shaped. Grooves along throat and chest end slightly before navel.

Habitat
Open seas, but mainly over continental shelf; sometimes in bays, inlets, and estuaries.

Range
In Pacific from Bering and Chukchi seas to equator. In Atlantic from pack ice to Lesser Antilles.

Comments
The Minke Whale is the smallest baleen whale in North American waters. Individuals often approach vessels and may be seen breaching, that is, leaping up through the water's surface. The forward position of the Minke Whale's dorsal fin, visible when the animal breaches, helps to distinguish this species from Sei and Blue whales.

Fin Whale
Balaenoptera physalus
195, 221

To 79' (24.1 m). Spindle-shaped, tapering toward rear; blue-black above, undersides white. Grayish-white chevron behind head, apex on midline of back, arms extending backward. Right lower lip, including mouth cavity, yellowish white, right upper lip occasionally also white, left lips dark. Right front baleen plates white, remainder striped with alternate yellowish white and bluish gray to grayish white. Snout V-shaped with single median ridge along top; top of head flat, with paired V-shaped blowholes. Dorsal fin steeply angled, placed far back. Back distinctly ridged behind dorsal fin. Grooves on throat and chest extend at least to navel.

Habitat
Inshore and offshore.

Range
Widely distributed. In Pacific from Bering Sea to Cabo San Lucas, Baja California. In Atlantic from Arctic Circle to Greater Antilles, including Gulf of Mexico.

Comments
The Fin Whale is also called the Razorback Whale because of the ridges between the dorsal fin and the tail. The crescent-shaped dorsal fin, an obvious characteristic, is easily seen at sea. The Fin Whale sometimes leaps clear of the surface, yet is also a deeper diver than some of the other baleen whales. Fin Whales feed in polar waters in the summer, and breed in temperate latitudes in the winter; they travel in pods of 2–5 whales. After the decline of the Blue Whale catch, Fin Whales were the principal species taken, and populations declined drastically. They are now protected except for one stock in the North Atlantic.

Right Whale
Eubalaena glacialis
196, 216

To 53' (16.2 m). Large, rotund; brown to almost black, mottled overall, with some white on chin and belly, baleen plates dark brownish to dark gray or black, may appear pale yellowish gray further offshore. Jaw highly arched, curves upward along side of head; bumps on head light yellowish, largest bump, or "bonnet," in front of large, paired blowholes. No dorsal fin or ridge. Flukes broad, tips pointed, greatly concave toward deep notch, dark below. Blow characteristic, V-shaped.

Habitat
Often near shore in shallow water; sometimes in large bays.

Range
In Pacific from Gulf of Alaska and southeastern Bering Sea to central Baja California. In Atlantic from Iceland to E. Florida, occasionally into Gulf of Mexico, rarely to West Indies.

Comments
This species was named the Right Whale by early whalers who considered it to be the "right" or "correct" whale to take, since it swims slowly, is easy to approach and kill, and does not sink when dead. Once killed, the Right Whale yielded an

abundance of valuable oil and baleen to be used for corset stays and other decorative or utilitarian objects. As an endangered species once depleted almost to extinction, these whales are now fully protected and more are being seen.

Blue Whale
Balaenoptera musculus
197, 219

To 98' (29.9 m). Spindle-shaped, tapering toward rear; light bluish gray above mottled with gray or grayish white, belly sometimes yellowish, baleen plates black. Rostrum broad, flat, nearly U-shaped, with single median ridge along top; paired blowholes on top of head. Dorsal fin extremely small, nearly triangular to crescent-shaped, far back on tail stock. Grooves on underside extend to or past navel. Blow high, oval.

Habitat
Usually open seas, but sometimes in shallow inshore waters.

Range
In Pacific from southern Chukchi Sea to Panama. In summer from Aleutian Islands and Gulf of Alaska to central California; in winter from Baja California to Panama. In Atlantic from Arctic Circle to Panama, including Gulf of Mexico.

Comments
The yellowish coloring on the belly of this species is due to diatoms accumulated in colder water, inspiring the alternate name Sulphur Bottom Whale. Of similar species, only the Blue Whale consistently lifts its flukes slightly above the surface when diving, a habit whalers term "fluking up." This animal is most likely to be seen off the Oregon coast from late May to June, and from August to October. The Blue Whale is probably the largest animal known, even larger than the dinosaurs. It has been estimated to reach a weight of about 196 tons (178,000 kg). At one time this animal was near extinction; protection has enabled its numbers to increase.

Humpback Whale
Megaptera novaeangliae
198, 218

To 53' (16.2 m). Robust, narrowing rapidly to tail; mostly black, belly sometimes white, flippers and underside of flukes nearly all white, baleen plates black with black or olive-black bristles. Top of head and lower jaw with string of fleshy knobs or protuberances randomly distributed; paired blowholes on top of head; distinctive, rounded projection on tip of lower jaw. Flippers very long, front edges scalloped. Dorsal fin small, variably shaped, placed on small hump slightly more than two-thirds of way back from head. Flukes notched, concave, rear edges scalloped. Blow wide, balloon-shaped.

Habitat
Along coast; usually on continental shelf or island banks; sometimes in open seas.

Range
Migratory. In Pacific from Chukchi Sea to southern Mexico. In Atlantic from northern Iceland and western Greenland south to West Indies, including Gulf of Mexico.

Comments
The median rostral ridges are not as obvious in the Humpback Whale as in other members of the family. Humpback Whales migrate seasonally, spending summer in high-latitude feeding grounds of the North Pacific and winter in low latitudes and warmer seas, where breeding occurs. They feed on krill and small schooling fishes, and are known to concentrate the food by forming a bubble curtain, created by releasing air bubbles while swimming in a circle beneath the water surface. Humpback Whales often "sing," vocalizing a long series of repeated phrases; the vocal patterns are apparently specific to separate populations of whales but may vary from year to year. Humpbacks sometimes leap clear of the water and may be seen slapping their flukes or a flipper on the surface.

False Killer Whale
Pseudorca crassidens
199, 213

To 19′6″ (5.9 m). Long, slender; black, often with faint gray blaze on belly between flippers; scars sometimes present. Head narrow, gently tapered from blowhole forward; rounded bump, or melon, on forehead somewhat overhangs long lower jaw; teeth large, strong. Dorsal fin tall, crescent-shaped, just behind middle of back. Flippers very long, with broad hump near middle of front edge.

Habitat
Tropical and warm temperate seas; strandings in sandy bays and estuaries.

Range
In Pacific from Aleutian Islands and Prince William Sound, Alaska, to Central America and northern South America. In Atlantic from Maryland to Venezuela, including eastern and northwestern Gulf of Mexico.

Comments
False Killer Whales have been known to steal fishes from both commercial and sport fishing lines. They often approach ships and frequently jump clear of the water despite their relatively large size. These animals feed and travel in groups of up to several hundred individuals.

Risso's Dolphin
Grampus griseus
200, 212

To 13′ (4 m). Robust toward front, tapers rapidly to narrow tail; dark gray at birth, darkening to almost black when young, with distinctive grayish-white regions on belly; numerous scars; color lightens overall, particularly on head, with increasing age; dorsal fin, flippers, and flukes usually remain dark. Head bulbous, V-shaped crease on front pointing downwards, dividing melon, or bump, into 2 parts; no distinct beak. Dorsal fin tall, distinctly crescent-shaped, at middle of back.

Habitat
Near surface of open temperate and tropical seas, most often seaward from outer edge of continental shelf; possibly coastal waters where shelf edge is close to shore.

Range
In Pacific from off Stuart Island, British Columbia, to Mexico. In Atlantic from E. Newfoundland to Lesser Antilles, including northern and eastern Gulf of Mexico.

Comments
These animals sometimes occur in herds of several hundred, but are more common in groups of a dozen or less. They sometimes ride bow waves.

Killer Whale ⊗
Orcinus orca
201, 209

To 31' (9.4 m). Males more robust than females; black with white, tan, or yellow region on undersides from lower jaw to anus extending onto sides behind dorsal fin; oval, white patch just above and behind eye; usually light gray saddle behind dorsal fin; undersides of flukes usually white. Head broad, rounded; mouth large; teeth large, pointed; no pronounced beak. Flippers large, paddle-shaped, rounded. Dorsal fin tall, distinctly crescent-shaped in females and juveniles, taller and erect in adult males, sometimes appears to bend forward.

Habitat
Upper layers of cooler coastal seas; occasionally large rivers and tropical seas.

Range
In Pacific from Chukchi Sea to equator. In Atlantic from pack ice to Lesser Antilles, including northern, eastern, and western Gulf of Mexico.

Comments
Killer Whales are often ferocious in their feeding habits. On occasion groups of these animals attack baleen whales, pinnipeds such as seals, and small Odontocetes. They are also known to feed on fishes, squids, sea turtles, and sea birds. They have been known to attack and mortally wound baleen whales, and then leave without eating them. While there are no reliable records of unprovoked attacks on humans, people should be extremely cautious of these animals.

Dall's Porpoise
Phocoenoides dalli
202, 210

To 7' (2.1 m). Extremely robust; head and flukes small. Shiny black overall, sides with large, conspicuous, oval white patch, sometimes with faint dark spots beginning well below dorsal fin and meeting at midriff; some individuals entirely black; dorsal fin usually white above, black below. Wide variation in pigmentation. Forehead slopes steeply to short, poorly defined beak; mouth small, narrow. Dorsal fin triangular, base long. Tail has pronounced keel above and below.

Habitat
Often well offshore and beyond outer edge of continental shelf, but also in deeper inshore waters.

Range
Bering and Okhotsk seas; Pribilof Islands to Baja California.

Comments
Dall's Porpoises are the most common porpoises in southeastern Alaska and British Columbia, and are usually seen in small herds of 20 or less. They are extremely fast swimmers, sometimes moving through the water so rapidly that they throw up a plume of water like the "rooster tail" of a racing hydroplane. They may ride bow waves. Its known predators include the Killer Whale and sharks. Many are harpooned intentionally by Japanese fishermen in the northern Pacific; some are killed by drifting into salmon nets.

Common Dolphin
Delphinus delphis
203, 206

To 8'6" (2.6 m). Spindle-shaped, slender, not robust; back black or brownish black, coloration and markings variable; chest and belly cream to white. Sides distinctly marked with hourglass or crisscross pattern of tan or yellowish tan. Beak well defined, moderately long, often dark with white tip. 1 or more dark stripes from center of lower jaw to flipper. Dorsal fin nearly triangular to distinctly crescent-shaped, usually black with lighter grayish region of varying size near middle, tip pointed.

Habitat
Offshore over outer continental shelf; rarely inshore.

Range
Worldwide. In Pacific from Victoria, British Columbia, to equator. In Atlantic from Newfoundland and Nova Scotia to northern South America.

Comments
These animals often travel in huge herds of more than a thousand. They frequently leap clear of the water and ride bow waves of vessels for a long time. They do not thrive in captivity.

Bottlenosed Dolphin
Tursiops truncatus
204, 205

To 12' (3.7 m). Robust; back usually dark gray, sides lighter gray, shading to pink or white on belly; individuals vary from albino to nearly black; distinct dark cape often on head and back; old females may have spots on belly. Beak well defined but relatively short; transverse groove between forehead and snout. Dorsal fin near center of back, prominent, broad-based, crescent-shaped, tip pointed.

Habitat
Inshore waters including estuaries, shallow bays, waterways, and freshwater rivers; sometimes to edge of continental shelf.

Range
In Pacific from S. California to tropics. In Atlantic from Nova Scotia to Venezuela, including Gulf of Mexico.

Comments
These dolphins feed on a wide variety of fishes, squids, shrimps, and crabs, and often follow trawlers and other fishing boats to feed on the unwanted fish that are thrown overboard

and on organisms stirred up by the nets. They are particularly adept at locating prey using echolocation, that is, projecting a sound beam and listening to the echo. They ride the bow waves of boats and even surf waves. There are many records of wild Bottlenosed Dolphins voluntarily approaching humans closely enough to be touched.

Striped Dolphin
Stenella coeruleoalba
207

To 9' (2.7 m). Moderately robust; top of head and back dark gray to bluish gray, sides lighter gray, throat and belly white. Black stripes on lower half of each side, single or double stripe from eye to flipper, another from eye to anus, usually with short branch on underside ending above and somewhat behind flipper. Beak black, long, sharply defined; black patch around each eye connected to beak. Dark cape on back. Distinctive light blaze usually extends up and back from light side into cape toward dorsal fin. Dorsal fin dark, crescent-shaped.

Habitat
Warmer temperate and tropical waters off edge of continental shelf; warm fingers of water in northern areas.

Range
In Pacific from Bering Sea to northwestern South America. In Atlantic from Halifax, Nova Scotia, to Lesser Antilles, including Gulf of Mexico.

Comments
These animals, which often occur in large herds of several hundred individuals, may ride bow waves and jump clear of the water. They feed at mid-depths on fishes, squids, and crustaceans. They often associate with schools of tunas in the eastern Pacific, and many Striped Dolphins are killed by accident when caught with the tunas in purse seines. Successful efforts are being made to reduce these losses.

Pacific White-sided Dolphin
Lagenorhynchus obliquidens
208

To 7' 6" (2.3 m). Spindle-shaped, cylindrical; head tapers continuously and smoothly to abbreviated dark beak. Back black, belly white, white or light gray stripe on both sides begins at forehead, curves over head, continues past dorsal fin, widening and curving toward anus, forming prominent light gray patch on flank. Narrow, dark stripe between corner of mouth and flipper, continuous with dark lips. Light gray zone on both sides from forehead to dorsal fin. Flippers gray with dark line from axil extending to dark area on flank. Dorsal fin tall, strongly crescent-shaped, base near middle of back, dark on forward third, remainder light gray. Flukes dark.

Habitat
Offshore waters, also inside outer edge of continental shelf; often close to shore near deep canyons.

Range
From Amchitka Island in Aleutians, throughout Gulf of Alaska to tip of Baja California.

Comments
These animals may occur in herds of up to several thousand. As with all cetaceans, the maximum age is difficult to determine. Many cetaceans are known to have long life spans, and some have lived for 30 years. Captive Pacific White-sided Dolphins have lived for just over 10 years.

Harbor Porpoise
Phocoena phocoena
211

To 6' (1.8 m). Chunky; back dark brown or gray fading to lighter grayish brown on sides; often speckled in transition zone; white on belly extends up sides, especially in front of dorsal fin. Head small, rounded; beak very short, indistinct. Dorsal fin small, dark, triangular, tip blunt.

Habitat
Subarctic and cold temperate waters, usually inshore within 10-fathom curve, rarely to 100 fathoms offshore. Often in bays, harbors, estuaries, and river mouths.

Range
In Pacific from Gulf of Alaska and eastern Aleutian chain to S. California; uncommonly from Chukchi and Beaufort seas. In Atlantic from Davis Straits and southeastern Greenland to North Carolina.

Comments
This species tends to be wary of vessels and does not ride bow waves. It often swims quietly at the surface. Harbor Porpoises are known to feed on octopuses, squids, and fishes, including herrings. In turn they may be preyed upon by large sharks and by Killer Whales. Because they live mostly inshore, they are often adversely affected by human activities.

Short-finned Pilot Whale
Globicephala macrorhynchus
214

To 23' (7 m). Robust; black overall, anchor-shaped gray patch on chin, gray area on belly, sometimes light chevrons extend toward rear from each side of blowhole, gray saddle sometimes behind dorsal fin. Head thick, bulbous, sometimes flattened or squarish in front, especially in older males. Flippers relatively short, one-sixth body length. Dorsal fin crescent-shaped, low, with long base, far forward on back.

Habitat
Tropical and temperate waters from outer edges of continental shelves seaward, sometimes close to shore.

Range
In Pacific from Aleutian Islands, Alaska, to Guatemala. In Atlantic from New Jersey to Venezuela, including Gulf of Mexico; known from Delaware Bay.

Comments
These whales often occur in very large herds and are frequently stranded in masses. In the Lesser Antilles they are killed for both oil and meat, and hunted with harpoons from open boats. They feed on squids and fishes. Short-finned Pilot Whales have been reported to "spy-hop," or "pitchpole" (hang

vertically in the water with their heads out), but they rarely breach. They do not ride bow waves of boats. When resting on the surface, individuals position themselves side by side in lines. They "lobtail" or slap their flukes on the water.

Sperm Whale
Physeter catodon
215

To 69' (21 m). Head huge, one-quarter to one-third length; dark brownish gray, skin appears corrugated or shriveled; sometimes belly and front of head grayish and mouth area white. Snout blunt, squarish, projects far beyond lower jaw tip. Single blowhole well to left of midline and far forward on head; small bushy "spout" emerges forward at sharp angle. Row of large teeth on each side of lower jaw, small teeth buried in upper jaw. Distinct hump on back two-thirds of way back from snout tip, followed by series of crenulations or bumps. Keel present on underside. Flukes broad, triangular, not concave, deeply notched on rear edges.

Habitat
Mostly in temperate and tropical oceans; rarely at depths less than 100 fathoms and along edge of continental shelf.

Range
Worldwide. In Pacific from Bering Sea to equator; in Atlantic from Davis Straits to Venezuela, including Gulf of Mexico.

Comments
This species can be identified by its distinctive spout. It feeds primarily on squids (including giant species), and eats a variety of fishes. These whales were hunted extensively; the forehead contains spermaceti and a fine grade of oil, and the teeth were favored material for scrimshaw, the ivory objects carved by sailors and artisans. It was the search for an albino Sperm Whale that inspired the novel *Moby-Dick,* but today individuals of over 50' (15.2 m) are rare.

Sei Whale
Balaenoptera borealis
220

To 62' (18.9 m). Spindle-shaped, tapering toward rear; dark steel-gray, often appears galvanized, belly grayish white near grooves on throat and chest; right lower lip uniformly gray; baleen plates mostly grayish black; leading edges of flukes sometimes white. Snout slightly arched; rostrum not very pointed, with single median ridge along top; paired blowholes on top of head. Dorsal fin tall, strongly crescent-shaped, placed two-thirds of body length back from head. Grooves on underside extend midway between base of flippers and navel.

Habitat
Near shore and offshore, primarily in temperate open seas.

Range
In Pacific from Gulf of Alaska to vicinity of Islas Revillagigedo, off Baja California. In Atlantic from southern Arctic Circle to northeastern Venezuela, including northwestern and southern Gulf of Mexico. Seasonal distribution varies.

Comments

The Sei Whale derives its name from its association with the Sei fish, the Norwegian name for the Pollock (*Pollachius virens*). The Sei Whale feeds near the surface on plankton, krill, small schooling fishes, and squids. Like all of the baleen whales, it does not feed everywhere in its distribution—such as in the southern portions of its range—but only where food is abundant. The Sei Whale has been harvested intensively since the 1960s, and is processed for human consumption in Japan and Scandinavia.

Walrus
Odobenus rosmarus
223

Pacific race larger. Atlantic males 8'2"–11'10" (25–36 m) long. Atlantic females 7'6"–9'6" (23–29 m) long. Yellowish to reddish-brown hide, essentially hairless except on muzzle about 400 bristles up to 1' long. No external tail. Short, round head. Upper canines are 2 large tusks, up to 40" long in Pacific bulls; cows' tusks somewhat shorter, narrower, more curved in middle.

Habitat
Along continental shelf of northern seas, especially along edge of pack ice; preferred water depth less than 60' (18 m).

Range
Pacific race migratory, generally in Chukchi Sea off northeastern Siberia in summer, Bering Sea off SW. Alaska in winter; Atlantic race in Arctic seas around Greenland south to Hudson Bay.

Comments
Walrus are sociable animals, gathering in mixed herds of up to 2000 bulls, cows, and calves when feeding and migrating, as well as when hauled out on ice floes. The sexes segregate only during the breeding season. If a Walrus is attacked, neighboring animals will come to its defense, and injured herd mates are also helped from the water onto ice. Excellent swimmers, Walrus use hind flippers alternately for propulsion and can travel about 15 mph. They can dive to 300' and remain submerged about half an hour. The Pacific Walrus is migratory, riding pack ice whenever possible, though it will swim if its chunk of ice begins going in the wrong direction. Although ungainly on land, Walrus spend more time out of the water than other aquatic carnivores, sunbathing and resting on ice and beaches for long periods, but they will dive immediately if they scent man.
The size of tusks is important in helping bulls establish dominance, and all Walrus use tusks to defend themselves against predators. Tusks are also used like grappling hooks to help animals haul out onto ice.

Northern Elephant Seal
Mirounga angustirostris
224, 232

Males 14'9"–21'4" (45–65 m) long. Females 9'10"–11'6" (30–35 m) long. Largest aquatic carnivore in Northern Hemisphere. Brown or gray above, lighter below. Adult male with large snout drooping over muzzle; when inflated during mating season, it curves down and back into mouth. Hind flippers with 2 lobes, reduced claws.

Habitat
Temperate seas; subtropical sandy beaches for breeding and molting.

Range
Pacific coastal waters from Gulf of Alaska south to Baja California; breeds on islands from California's Farallon Islands south to San Benito Island off Baja California.

Comments
In the 1890s this seal was nearly exterminated by the whaling industry for the oil to be rendered from its great rolls of blubber. In 1892 a tiny colony of fewer than 20 animals was discovered on Guadalupe Island, off Baja California; they were protected, and the herd now numbers about 65,000 seals, which breed on offshore islands from Baja north to San Francisco. Limited to sandy beaches by its enormous bulk, the Elephant Seal has recently been forced onto mainland beaches owing to the increase in its population. The first birth on the mainland occurred in 1975, and by 1979 almost 100 cows had given birth in a new rookery at Ano Nuevo Point, near Santa Cruz, California.

Northern Fur Seal
Callorhinus ursinus
225

Males 6'3"–7'3" (19–22 m) long. Females 3'8"–4'8" (11–14 m) long. Bulls with greatly enlarged necks, blackish above with massive grayish shoulders, reddish below; females gray above, reddish below. Very large flippers. Tiny tail. Small head with short, pointed nose, large eyes, long whiskers.

Habitat
At sea most of the year; in summer breeds on rocky island beaches.

Range
Point Barrow, Alaska, on the Arctic Ocean south in winter to San Diego, California; in summer breeds on the Pribilof islands in the Bering Sea; Commander and Robben islands (USSR); and San Miguel Island, off California. Abundant off Washington coast from late November–June; occasionally seen in Puget Sound and Strait of Juan de Fuca.

Comments
One of the most oceangoing of the aquatic carnivores and the greatest traveler, sometimes migrating up to 6200 miles (10,000 km), this fur seal returns to land only during the breeding season. At sea it is rarely seen in groups of more than 3. This fur seal's major rookery on the Pribilofs is enormous, with more than a million seals within a 31-mile radius. The breeding grounds were discovered in 1786, and by 1834 overhunting had greatly reduced fur seal populations. As early as 1835, the seals were afforded some protection and the taking of females forbidden. Now the harvest of fur seals is

carefully managed and limited to excess males in bachelor
herds. The pelts are prized for their fine, soft fur; blubber is
rendered for oil; and flesh and bones are used for meal. Since
1973 there has been no hunting on 1 of the 2 major Pribilof
islands, which has been designated a study area.

Guadalupe Fur Seal
Arctocephalus townsendi
226

Males to 6'3" (19 m) long. Females 4'6" (14 m) long.
Brownish gray above, with silvery cast on yellowish-gray head
and neck; brownish black below, with chest lighter in adult
males. Snout pointed, rust-orange on sides; flippers large.

Habitat
Rocky coastal islands.

Range
California's Channel Islands to Cedros Island off Baja
California; only known to breed on Guadalupe Island.

Comments
Nearly exterminated by sealers in the 1880s, by 1892 only 7
individuals were known to exist. Although a fisherman sold 2
males to the San Diego Zoo in 1928, and 1 seal was seen on
San Nicholas Island in 1949, very few were found until 1954,
when 14 were sighted on Guadalupe Island. Today they are
protected, and the population numbers about 1000. This seal
prefers rocky caves as breeding sites, and while the male will
defend his territory, unlike other eared seals he occasionally
oversees his harem from the water.

California Sea Lion
Zalophus californianus
227

Males 6'6"–8'2" (20–25 m) long. Females 5'–6'6" (15–20
m) long. Slender. Buff to brown; appears black when wet.
Head becomes paler with age. Males much larger than
females, with high foreheads.

Habitat
Sandy or rocky beaches, occasionally caves, protected by high
cliffs; preferably on islands.

Range
Pacific Coast from Vancouver south to Baja California and into
Gulf of California; breeds on islands from California's Channel
Islands south through Gulf.

Comments
The trained seal of zoo and circus, this sea lion in the wild
often indulges in similar antics, throwing objects and catching
them on its nose and cavorting in the water. The fastest of the
aquatic carnivores, it can swim up to 25 mph when pressed. It
can descend to 450' and stay submerged for 20 minutes. It
uses sonar for underwater navigation and finding prey.
Once sold primarily for the oil rendered from their blubber
and also for dog food, and killed by commercial fishermen who
believed they hurt the industry, today the much-reduced
numbers of California Sea Lions are fully protected by law.

Steller Sea Lion
Eumetopias jubatus
228

Males 8′10″–10′6″ (27–32 m) long. Females 6′3″–7′3″ (19–22 m) long. Largest eared seal (males larger than any bear). Bulls buff above, reddish brown below; with dark brown flippers and massive necks and forequarters. Cows uniformly brown, one-third the size of males, and more cylindrical in shape. Snout and face otterlike; low forehead.

Habitat
Rocky shores and the coastal waters along them.

Range
Pacific Coast from S. Alaska and Aleutian and Pribilof islands south to S. California, and Channel Islands, off California.

Comments
These sea lions usually stay in the water during poor weather but otherwise spend much time on rocky shores; they will dive into the sea if a boat approaches. Occasionally they swim up rivers. They eat fish, including blackfish, rockfish, greenling, and—more rarely—commercially valuable ones, such as salmon, squid, clams, and crabs, generally feeding at night in water within 10–15 miles from shore.

Ribbon Seal
Phoca fasciata
229

Males to 6′ (18 m) long. Males dark brown with creamy-white rings around neck, rump, and base of front flippers. Females gray with rings indistinct. Males are slightly larger than females.

Habitat
Open sea and Arctic ice floes.

Range
Bering Sea from Alaska to Aleutian Islands; 1 taken near Morro Bay, California, in 1962.

Comments
As it seldom occurs near shore, this rare seal seems even less common than it is. Usually solitary, it molts, rests, and gives birth on pack ice and swims in the open waters of the Bering Sea when the ice is gone. It can remain submerged almost half an hour. Among seals its way of moving on ice is unique; it slithers along, alternating front flippers and throwing its head and body from side to side to stretch its flippers forward.

Ringed Seal
Phoca hispida
230

Males 4′3″–5′3″ (13–16 m) long. Smallest aquatic carnivore. Coloration highly variable, often brownish to bluish black above, streaked and marbled with black on back, often with irregular light rings on sides; whitish to yellowish below with scattered dark spots. Males slightly larger than females.

Habitat
Land-fast ice; seldom on shifting ice of open sea.

Range
Arctic seas from Point Barrow, Alaska, east to Labrador and Newfoundland.

Comments
Ringed Seals spend most of the year under thick ice, using the strong claws on their fore flippers to dig and maintain breathing holes; juveniles often move to open water near the edge of ice. Females also use their claws to dig a pupping den 10' long by 2' high in the snow by their breathing hole, although sometimes they use natural snow caves. The Ringed Seal dives to 300' and can stay submerged up to 20 minutes but usually surfaces in about 3 minutes. Feeding mostly on crustaceans and small fish, in deep water it eats the larger zooplankton. Besides the Polar Bear, Killer Whales and sharks prey upon it, and Arctic Foxes take pups in the den. Coastal Eskimos take great numbers, which they use for food, clothing, tools, and oil.

Pacific Harbor Seal
Phoca vitulina
231

4'–5'7" (12–17 m) long. Usually yellowish gray or brownish with dark spots above, but highly variable from cream to dark brown; spotted creamy white below. Males and females about same size.

Habitat
Coastal waters, mouths of rivers; some northern populations permanently inland in freshwater lakes.

Range
In West, southern Arctic from Yukon and N. Alaska south along California coast; in East, S. Greenland and Hudson Bay coasts south to Carolinas.

Comments
Harbor Seals spend much time basking on beaches and rocky shores in groups of several individuals to 500. At the first sign of danger, they give an alarm bark and dive into the water. They can dive to 300' and remain submerged up to 28 minutes. They feed when the tide comes in, sometimes ascending rivers with the tide, and haul out at low tide, sleeping high and dry until the next rising tide unless disturbed.

Bearded Seal
Erignathus barbatus
233

Males 8–11' (24–34 m) long. Large. Uniformly grayish to yellowish. Bearded with tufts of long, flat bristles at sides of snout. Fore flippers squared off, with third digit longer than others. Males larger than females.

Habitat
Arctic and subarctic continental shelf, in relatively shallow water up to 500' deep; moves seasonally with drift ice.

Range
Northern coastal waters and shallow seas from Alaska to Labrador, including Hudson Bay.

Comments
The nonmigratory Bearded Seal is generally solitary but during breeding season may congregate in groups of up to 50.

At this time, although bulls do not form harems, they may fight each other; they give a long warble to woo cows. This slow-growing species does not attain full size until 10 years old. Life span may exceed 25 years. They occasionally eat bottom-dwelling fish, but mainly feed upon whelks, clams, crabs, and octopus, using their sensitive bristles and strong claws to help locate and dig out prey. The Polar Bear, man, and an occasional Walrus are their chief predators. Bearded Seals have little commercial value, but 2000–4000 are taken annually by Eskimos for their flesh, and their rough hides are used for nonskid boot soles.

Sea Otter
Enhydra lutris
234

30–71¼" (7.6–18 m) long. Dark brown with head and back of neck yellowish or grayish. Old males may have white heads. Fairly short tail, thick at base, gradually tapering. Feet webbed; hind feet flipperlike. Males somewhat larger than females.

Habitat
Coastal waters within mile of shore; especially rocky shallows with kelp beds and abundant shellfish.

Range
Pacific Coast from California to Alaska.

Comments
Highly aquatic, the Sea Otter eats, sleeps, mates, and even gives birth at sea. Flipperlike hindlegs make it clumsy on land, and it takes to the beach only to wait out storms. By day it feeds while floating on its back, sculling with its tail; but if in a hurry, it swims on its belly, using feet and tail. It can remain submerged 4–5 minutes. Apart from primates, the Sea Otter is a greater user of tools than any other mammal. When it dives for food, it also brings up a small rock. It then floats on its back, places the rock on its chest, and cracks the shell against it. Abalone, sea urchins, crabs, mussels, and fish—as much as 15 lb per day—are its chief foods. The Sea Otter helps control the sea urchin population, thus allowing kelp beds to thrive. In some areas abalone fishermen consider these animals competitors for their catch. At night the Sea Otter wraps strands of kelp about its body to secure its position in the kelp beds where it sleeps. It watches for danger by standing in the water and shading its eyes with both forefeet; if it spots such predators as sharks and Killer Whales, it hides in kelp beds. Once abundant, the Sea Otter was so heavily hunted for its highly prized pelts that by 1911, when international treaty forbade its massacre, it had nearly become extinct. Not seen in California for almost a century, in the spring of 1938 a herd appeared in the sea south of Carmel; today the population there, designated as "threatened," is perhaps 1000, and even larger herds are found off the coast of southern Alaska and the Aleutian Islands.

FISHES

The fishes that dominate the underwater world of the Pacific Coast range from the mysterious, primitive-looking eels and rays to the more familiar rockfishes, salmons, and perches. Most marine fishes spend their lives in the ocean; a few ascend rivers inland to spawn or feed. Some are chiefly solitary; others travel in enormous schools. Many of these fishes—such as tuna and herring—are commercially important; a very few, such as the White Shark, pose a serious threat to swimmers and divers. This section describes many of the most frequently seen fishes along our western coast.

Brown Rockfish ⊗
Sebastes auriculatus
235

To 21½" (55 cm). Deep, fusiform, compressed; olive-brown above with light orange-brown mottling, lighter below, dark brown spot on rear of gill cover, pectoral, pelvic, and caudal fins pinkish. Snout moderately sharp; top of head flat between eyes; 6 pairs of head spines, including those on crown. Dorsal fins continuous, deeply notched, spiny portion longer-based, with incised membranes; spines and rays about same length; caudal fin squared off.

Habitat
Shallow, low-profile reefs; occasionally over soft bottoms to 70 fathoms.

Range
From Prince William Sound, Alaska, to Baja California.

Comments
The Scorpionfish family, which includes the rockfishes, has more members on the Pacific Coast than does any other family. Rockfishes are among the most difficult marine fishes to identify; there are 65 species in the genus *Sebastes* alone. Brown Rockfishes are born in the late spring, and after a short period during which they float with the plankton community, they settle to the bottom, usually in calm areas such as bays. Their spines are mildly venomous.

Grunt Sculpin
Rhamphocottus richardsoni
236

To 3¼" (8.5 cm). Deep, compressed; creamy yellow with brown bars and streaks; caudal peduncle and all fins except pelvics bright red. Snout long, sharp; mouth small, cirrus on upper lip of adults small, flaplike. Lowest pectoral rays free; spiny and soft dorsal fins separated by notch; caudal fin rounded. Scales reduced to plates bearing minute spines.

Habitat
Rocks and reefs in intertidal zone and below low tide level; over soft bottoms to depths of 90 fathoms.

Range
From Bering Sea to Santa Monica Bay, California.

Comments
The Grunt Sculpin is thought to spawn in the winter. It feeds on the larvae of both small crustaceans and fishes. An amusing aquarium pet, it uses its pectoral fins to crawl over rocks.

Giant Sea Bass
Stereolepis gigas
237

To 7' 5" (2.3 m). Heavy, robust, slightly compressed, greatest depth near head; dark gray, usually with large, black spots on sides; juveniles red with black spots. 2 spines on gill cover. Dorsal fin has more spines than soft rays. Caudal fin square to slightly indented.

Habitat
Rocky areas and kelp beds.

Range
From Humboldt Bay, California, to Gulf of California.

Comments
Giant Sea Basses spawn in the summer and do not mature
until about 11 to 13 years of age, when they weigh 50 to 60
lb (23 to 27 kg). Some may live as long as 100 years.
Increasingly rare, these huge fishes are highly prized by
anglers and divers. In recent years their numbers have declined
drastically, and their capture is prohibited in California.

Kelp Bass
Paralabrax clathratus
238

To 28″ (81 cm). Elongate, moderately compressed; greenish
brown above, belly white; white blotches between dorsal fin
and lateral line. Lateral line continuous to base of caudal fin.

Habitat
Reefs, wrecks, and kelp beds to depths of 25 fathoms.

Range
From mouth of Columbia River, Oregon, to Bahía Magdalena,
Baja California.

Comments
The Kelp Bass spawns from late spring through early fall. It is
one of the sport fishes most sought in southern California, and
the annual catch was recently estimated to have exceeded 1
million fishes. It feeds on crustaceans, squids, octopuses,
polychaete worms, and fishes. It is a slow-growing fish that
takes 4 to 6 years to reach 12″ (30 cm); a 24″ (61 cm) fish
might be 20 years old.

Blue Rockfish ⊗
Sebastes mystinus
239

To 30″ (76 cm). Fusiform, deep, elongate, compressed;
bluish black with light blue mottling on sides, fins dark, no
spots on dorsal fin membranes. Snout moderately sharp,
mouth and eyes small; up to 4 pairs of weak head spines.
Dorsal fins continuous, deeply notched, spiny portion longer-
based, with incised membranes; rear edge of anal fin vertical
or slightly indented; caudal fin notched.

Habitat
Over rocky reefs and soft bottoms, from the surface to 300′.

Range
From Bering Sea to Baja California.

Comments
In late winter, the Blue Rockfish bears its young, which spend
several weeks as part of the plankton community. Large
aggregations of adults occur in mid-water, where they feed on
small crustaceans, jellyfishes, salps, and algae. The Blue
Rockfish is usually the most abundant rockfish in the catches
of charter boat and skiff anglers. The dorsal and anal fins
contain mildly venomous spines.

Kelp Rockfish ⊗
Sebastes atrovirens
240

To 17″ (43 cm). Deep, fusiform, compressed; body and
fin membranes light gray and brown to golden brown with
mottling. Snout moderately sharp, lower jaw scaled; 5 or more

pairs of head spines; no spines on crown. Spiny and soft dorsal
fin portions same height; continuous, deeply notched, spiny
portion longer-based, with incised membranes. Caudal fin
rounded.

Habitat
Rocky reefs and kelp beds to depths of 25 fathoms.

Range
From Timber Cove, California, to Baja California.

Comments
Kelp Rockfishes occur singly or in large aggregations. They
feed on small crabs, shrimps, squids, and some fishes. They
form a small proportion of the catches of sport anglers and
scuba divers. The sharp head spines and the mildly venomous
dorsal and anal spines should be handled with caution.

Black Rockfish ⊗
Sebastes melanops
241

To 24" (61 cm). Deep, fusiform, compressed; black
with gray mottling on sides, gray to white stripe along lateral
line usually present; black spots on dorsal fin. Head convex
between eyes; head spines not prominent; no knob at tip of
lower jaw. Dorsal fin continuous, deeply notched, anal fin
rounded; caudal fin squared off to notched.

Habitat
Over rocks and soft bottoms to depths of 200 fathoms.

Range
From Amchitka Island, Alaska, to Huntington Beach,
California.

Comments
The Black Rockfish occurs both singly and in large groups
near the bottom or at mid-water. It feeds on crabs and other
crustaceans as well as on fishes, and may weigh as much as
10½ lb (4.8 kg). This species is an important sport and
commercial fish. The spines in the dorsal and anal fins are
mildly venomous.

Yellowfin Croaker
Umbrina roncador
242

To 18" (46 cm). Elongate, compressed, greatest depth under
origin of first dorsal fin; iridescent blue to gray above; sides
silvery with dark, wavy lines, fins yellowish. Snout bluntly
rounded; upper jaw projects beyond tip of lower; chin has
single barbel. Dorsal fins contiguous. Caudal fin notched.
Lateral line extends to tip of caudal fin.

Habitat
Over sand, in surf zone, near rocks or kelp, and to 25' (8 m)
in bays.

Range
From Point Conception, California, to Gulf of California.

Comments
Yellowfin Croakers spawn during the summer. They are

caught by surf anglers and speared by skin divers. This fish has been recorded to a length of 20" (51 cm). Their yellowish fins and the dark, wavy lines on the sides of the body help distinguish them from 10 other species of croakers in our area.

Yellowtail Rockfish ⊗
Sebastes flavidus
243

To 26" (66 cm). Deep, fusiform, compressed; olive to gray-brown washed with green, lighter on sides and white below, reddish-brown speckles on scales; pectoral, pelvic, anal, and caudal fins yellowish. Head spines not prominent; head convex between eyes. Dorsal fin continuous, deeply notched; spines and rays about same length; rear edge of anal fin straight, vertical; caudal fin slightly notched or forked.

Habitat
Over deep reefs and soft bottoms from surface to depths of 150 fathoms.

Range
From Kodiak Island, Alaska, to San Diego, California.

Comments
Yellowtail Rockfishes are born in January, February, and March. Large groups occur in mid-water, usually over deep reefs where they feed on crustaceans, squids, and small fishes. This species is one of the 3 most important rockfishes caught for sport in central and northern California. The dorsal and anal fins contain mildly venomous spines.

Widow Rockfish ⊗
Sebastes entomelas
244

To 21" (53 cm). Elongate, fusiform, compressed; brassy brown above, often whitish below, membranes of pectoral, pelvic, and anal fins black. Snout fairly sharp; mouth small, forehead rounded; head spines not prominent. Dorsal fins continuous, deeply notched; spines and rays about same length. Rear profile of anal fin straight; caudal fin notched.

Habitat
Low-profile reefs in sandy or silty areas to depths of about 200 fathoms.

Range
From Kodiak Island, Alaska, to Baja California.

Comments
Widow Rockfishes occur in huge groups in mid-water, where they feed on plankton. They contribute to the catches of anglers, and are now one of the most important commercial rockfishes on the Pacific Coast. A single trawler has been known to catch over 50 tons (45,359 kg) in one day. Mildly venomous spines are present in the dorsal and anal fins.

Bocaccio ⊗
Sebastes paucispinis
245

To 3' (91 cm). Elongate, fusiform, compressed; light olive-brown above, lighter below, sides pink; young have dark brown spots. Snout sharp, lower jaw projects beyond upper; head convex between eyes; 3 pairs of head spines not prominent. Dorsal fin continuous, deeply notched, spiny portion longer-based, with incised membranes. Caudal fin slightly forked.

Habitat
Adults over rocky reefs and soft bottoms, surface to 175 fathoms. Juveniles around shallow reefs and in bays.

Range
From Kodiak Island, Alaska, to Baja California.

Comments
A single Bocaccio female will release up to 2 million young in the winter. This species feeds on a variety of fishes, crabs, and squids. Small numbers are taken by ocean anglers. The dorsal and anal fins contain mildly venomous spines.

Kelp Greenling
Hexagrammos decagrammus
246, 250

To 21" (53 cm). Elongate, fusiform, slightly compressed; males dark gray with bright blue spots, occasionally black-edged; females gray-brown with golden or brown spots. Snout moderately sharp; mouth yellowish inside; lips fleshy; distinguished by pair of cirri over eyes with length less than three-fourths eye diameter, pair on nape very small, occasionally absent. Dorsal fin long, single, deeply notched; caudal fin slightly indented. 5 lateral lines, fourth extends well beyond anal fin origin. Spiny scales covering gill cover.

Habitat
Shallow reefs to depths of 25 fathoms.

Range
From Aleutian Islands, Alaska, to La Jolla, California.

Comments
The Kelp Greenling spawns in the fall. Its mass of blue eggs is attached to rocks and guarded by the male. This very colorful fish, popular among anglers, feeds on shrimps, small crabs, polychaete worms, fishes, and the siphons of clams.

Lingcod
Ophiodon elongatus
247

To 5' (1.5 m). Elongate, fusiform, almost round in cross section; gray-brown to green with darker spots and mottling. Snout sharp; mouth large; lower jaw projects beyond upper, jaws with very sharp teeth; cirrus over each eye. Dorsal fin long, continuous, deeply notched, caudal fin squared off. 1 lateral line.

Habitat
Over reefs and soft bottoms, in shallow and deep water to 233 fathoms.

Range
From Kodiak Island, Alaska, to Punta San Carlos, Baja California.

Comments
This fish is the only member of the Greenling family that has

a large mouth and large canine teeth. In the breeding process the male guards the eggs until they hatch. Lingcods feed on various large fishes, crustaceans, and mollusks. This voracious predator is one of the most highly esteemed sport fishes, primarily because it makes excellent eating. It is also a valuable commercial species.

China Rockfish ⊗
Sebastes nebulosus
248

To 17″ (43 cm). Deep, fusiform, compressed; blue-black with yellow mottling and yellow stripe extending from spiny dorsal fin down to and along lateral line, bluish-white spots below. Snout moderately sharp; head deeply concave between eyes; 5 pairs of head spines prominent. Fins dark; dorsal fin continuous, deeply notched, with incised membranes; some spines longer than rays. Caudal fin slightly rounded.

Habitat
Rocky areas with caves and crevices at 2–70 fathoms.

Range
From Prince William Sound, Alaska, to San Miguel Island, California.

Comments
This solitary rockfish spends most of its time in or near crevices or caves, where its large pectoral fins enable it to support itself on the cave floor and maneuver in crevices. Its food consists of brittle stars, crabs, and shrimps. China Rockfishes make up a minor portion of sport and commercial hook-and-line catches. The dorsal and anal fins contain mildly venomous spines.

Quillback Rockfish ⊗
Sebastes maliger
249

To 24″ (61 cm). Fusiform, deep, compressed; slate-brown with orange spots and blotches on back and dorsal fin, rear of head to pectoral fin insertion yellow with brown spots, orange spots below. Head flat between eyes; 5 pairs of spines on head. Pectoral and pelvic fins blackish. Dorsal fin continuous, deeply notched; spines cream-colored, longer than rays, membranes of spiny dorsal deeply incised.

Habitat
Rocky reefs with caves and crevices to depths of 150 fathoms.

Range
From Gulf of Alaska to Avila, California.

Comments
This is a common inshore, solitary rockfish north from British Columbia. It is caught in small numbers by anglers and commercial fishers. It has mildly venomous spines.

Buffalo Sculpin
Enophrys bison
251

To 15″ (38 cm). Elongate, tapering, almost round in cross section, greatest depth at pectoral fin insertion; dark gray, green, or brown above, often with light blotches. Snout rounded; head large; spine in front of gill cover long, sharp, reaches rear of gill cover. Pelvic fin with 1 spine, 3 soft rays; 2 dorsal fins; caudal fin squared off. Heavy bony plates on lateral line.

Habitat
Over shallow reefs and soft bottoms around piers and wrecks.

Range
From Kodiak Island, Alaska, to Monterey Bay, California.

Comments
Numerous members of the sculpin family (Cottidae), of which there are 111 species in North America, are commonly found in tide pools and around piers, reefs, and wrecks. They are all small, similar, and somewhat difficult to identify to species. Most have a large head and an elongate, tapering body partly covered with scales or prickles; the eyes are located high on the head. Buffalo Sculpins eat shrimps, crabs, and young fishes. This species lacks sufficient flesh to be edible.

Cabezon ⊗
Scorpaenichthys marmoratus
252

To 3'3" (99 cm). Elongate, slightly compressed; variably red to olive-green to brown with dark and light mottling. Snout moderately blunt, with large, fleshy cirri on midline of snout and over each eye. Pelvic fin with 1 spine, 5 soft rays; caudal fin squared off. No visible scales.

Habitat
Rocks and reefs in intertidal zone and below low tide level to 42 fathoms.

Range
From Sitka, Alaska, to Punta Abreojos, Baja California.

Comments
The Cabezon spawns in winter, and the male guards the mass of greenish to purplish eggs until they hatch. The eggs are poisonous if eaten. This large, tasty sculpin is highly desired by anglers, who catch it from the shore.

**California
Scorpionfish** ⊗
Scorpaena guttata
253

To 17" (43 cm). Elongate, rounded in cross section, slightly flattened; red to brown with spots overall. Head robust, with ridges; snout rounded. Spines present on gill cover and gill cover bone. Pectoral fin large, broad, rounded; dorsal fin continuous, notched; caudal fin squared off. Lateral line straight; scales large, spiny.

Habitat
Shallow reefs and kelp beds to depths of 100 fathoms.

Range
From Santa Cruz, California, to Uncle Sam Bank, Baja California; upper Gulf of California.

Comments
Unlike most other members of the family, this fish deposits

eggs embedded in transparent, pear-shaped cases. It is considered an excellent food fish and makes up a minor portion of the southern California sport and commercial catch. All of its spines are venomous.

Red Irish Lord
Hemilepidotus hemilepidotus
254

To 20" (51 cm). Elongate, tapering, almost round in cross section; body and fins red and brown with black mottling and spots. Head flattened; cirri present; snout moderately sharp; 2–3 pairs of simple spines in front of gill cover. Gill membranes united, narrowly joined to narrow part of breast between gill openings (isthmus). Dorsal fin single with 2 notches; caudal fin slightly rounded. Band of 4–5 scale rows below dorsal fin.

Habitat
Shallow, rocky reefs to 26 fathoms.

Range
From Bering Sea south to Monterey Bay, California.

Comments
The colorful Red Irish Lord lays its egg masses in intertidal areas during the spring. Adults feed on crabs, barnacles, and mussels. Anglers only occasionally catch this edible sculpin.

Snubnose Sculpin
Orthonopias triacis
255

To 4" (10 cm). Elongate, slightly compressed; brown with light and dark mottling and bright red patches. Head large, snout very blunt; spines in front of gill cover present. Pelvic fins with 1 spine, 3 soft rays; anus much closer to pelvic fin base than to anal fin; caudal fin rounded. Cirri along lateral line; scales between lateral line and dorsal fin.

Habitat
Rocks between high and low tide levels and reefs below intertidal zone to depths of 17 fathoms.

Range
From Monterey Bay, California, to Isla San Geronimo, Baja California.

Comments
This small sculpin is rarely caught by anglers, but is familiar to divers.

Shortspine Thornyhead ⊗
Sebastolobus alascanus
256

To 30" (76 cm). Elongate, fusiform; red with some black on fins. Head large, snout rounded; 7 pairs of head spines, very strong, sharp. Pectoral fins deeply notched in profile. Dorsal fin continuous, deeply notched, spiny portion longer-based, with incised membranes. Caudal fin squared off.

Habitat
Over deep, soft bottoms and sometimes around reefs to depths of 838 fathoms.

Range
From Bering Sea to N. Baja California.

Comments
This fish lays eggs that float in masses near the surface. The
Shortspine Thornyhead feeds on crustaceans and other
invertebrates. It is rarely caught by anglers, but makes up a
major share of the catches of commercial trawlers working
deeper than 100 fathoms.

California Sheephead
Semicossyphus pulcher
257, 264

To 3' (91 cm). Fusiform, deep, compressed. Males with
head, rear of body, and caudal fin black, mid-body brick-red,
chin white; females reddish brown; juveniles brick-red on
sides with white stripe; pectoral, dorsal, and caudal fins with
large black spots. Forehead steeply sloping in adults; large
canine teeth present. Single dorsal fin extends from pectoral
fin insertion to rear of anal fin base; caudal fin almost square.

Habitat
Reefs and kelp beds to depths of 48 fathoms.

Range
From Monterey Bay, California, to Cabo San Lucas, Baja
California; also in Gulf of California.

Comments
Adult California Sheepheads are female until they are 7 or 8
years old, when the ovaries become testes; fishes then function
as males for the rest of their lives. California Sheepheads
spawn in spring and summer and feed on crustaceans,
echinoderms, and mollusks. They are popular with anglers and
spear fishers, but the annual catch in California is no more
than about 50,000 fish.

Spotted Ratfish ⊗
Hydrolagus colliei
258

To 3'2" (96 cm). Elongate, head large, tapering to slender
caudal fin; bronze above, with metallic hues, silvery below
with numerous white spots; eyes green. Teeth pliable,
incisorlike. Males have spiny, club-shaped projection on head,
sharp retracting clasping organs, used in copulation, in front
of pelvic fins, and slender claspers with expanded ends
adjacent to each pelvic fin base. First dorsal preceded by long,
venomous spine; second dorsal has undulating outline. Lateral
line wavy, several branches on the head; no scales.

Habitat
Over soft bottoms to 500 fathoms.

Range
From SE. Alaska to Bahia San Sebastian Vizcaino, Baja
California; isolated populations found in upper Gulf of
California.

Comments
This fish is most easily recognized by its smooth skin, long,
tapering tail, and bulky snout. Males change color during
courtship. Ratfishes deposit their eggs, which are fertilized
internally, in elongate, ridged, brown cases during the late
summer. These distinctive fishes feed on clams, crabs,

shrimps, and fishes. They are not sought by either sport or commercial fishers. Care should be taken in handling a Ratfish, as the venomous spines can cause a painful wound, and the clasping organs are quite sharp.

Garibaldi
Hypsypops rubicundus
259, 260

To 14″ (36 cm). Deep, compressed; adults bright orange, juveniles have iridescent blue markings on head, body, and fins. 1 nostril on each side of snout. Dorsal fin has 11–13 spines, 12–15 rays; extends from above pectoral fin insertion to posterior of anal fin base; caudal fin forked, tips rounded. Lateral line ends under soft dorsal fin.

Habitat
Reefs and kelp beds to 16 fathoms.

Range
From Monterey Bay, California, to Bahía Magdalena, Baja California; rare north of Point Conception, California.

Comments
Garibaldis spawn from March through July. The male prepares the nest and guards the eggs until they hatch in 2 or 3 weeks. They feed on a variety of invertebrates. Garibaldis are protected by law in California, and may not be taken for either sport or commercial purposes.

Rainbow Seaperch
Hypsurus caryi
261

To 12″ (30 cm). Deep, very compressed; sides have red and blue stripes, about 10 red-brown bars on upper body, pelvic and anal fins usually red-orange, edges blue, dark blotch on soft dorsal fin. Anal fin base shorter than distance from pelvic fin insertion to anal fin origin.

Habitat
Reefs, piers, and kelp beds; bays and outer coast to depths of 22 fathoms.

Range
From Cape Mendocino, California, to Isla San Martin, Baja California.

Comments
Rainbow Seaperches gather in large aggregations to breed in the fall; the young are born the following summer. Members of this species occasionally act as cleaners, picking parasites off other fishes. Anglers catch 10,000 to 20,000 Rainbow Seaperches annually along the California coast. A similar species, the Striped Seaperch (*Embiotoca lateralis*), has dusky pelvic fins.

Yelloweye Rockfish ⊗
Sebastes ruberrimus
262

To 3′ (91 cm). Deep, fusiform, compressed; back red, becoming orange-yellow on sides, paler below, eyes bright yellow, fin edges black; juveniles have 2 silvery-white stripes on sides. Mouth at tip of snout, large; lower jaw unscaled, knob at tip broad, low, rounded; head concave between eyes,

with serrated ridges on older individuals; 6 or more pairs of
head spines. Dorsal fins continuous, deeply notched, spiny
portion longer-based, with incised membranes. Caudal fin
rounded.

Habitat
Reefs and caves at depths of 10–300 fathoms.

Range
From Gulf of Alaska to Baja California.

Comments
A female may release up to 3 million young in late spring.
The Yelloweye Rockfish feeds on fishes and crustaceans.
Because it is large and makes fine eating, this rockfish is
highly prized by both sport and commercial bottom fishers.
However, since it remains in a single location and is solitary,
not many catches are sizable. The dorsal and anal fins contain
mildly venomous spines.

Vermilion Rockfish ⊗
Sebastes miniatus
263

To 36 " (91 cm). Deep, fusiform, compressed; dark red
to orange with gray mottling on sides, mouth and fins
reddish, rear two-thirds of lateral line gray to white, fin edges
usually black. Rough scales on underside of jaw; head convex
between eyes; 6 pairs of head spines. Dorsal fin continuous,
deeply notched. Caudal fin squared off.

Habitat
Over rocky reefs and soft bottoms to depths of 150 fathoms.

Range
From Queen Charlotte Islands, British Columbia, to Baja
California.

Comments
The Vermilion Rockfish is popular with anglers because it is
large and makes good eating. It is also an important
commercial species caught with hook and line off southern
California. Mildly venomous spines in the dorsal and anal fins
can cause painful wounds.

Señorita
Oxyjulis californica
265

To 10" (25 cm). Elongate, cigar-shaped; yellow-orange above,
cream below; caudal fin with large black spot. Snout pointed;
mouth small; teeth small, protruding. Dorsal fin single,
elongate. Caudal fin squared off to slightly rounded. Scales
large.

Habitat
Reefs and kelp beds to depths of 55 fathoms.

Range
From Salt Point, Sonoma County, California, to Isla Cedros,
Baja California.

Comments
Señoritas occur in large aggregations and singly. They spawn

from May through August and feed on small snails, crustaceans, worms, and larval fishes. Some pick parasites from other fishes; they are the most common parasite-cleaners off southern California. Anglers catch Señoritas using very small hooks, but few are retained because they are not considered edible.

Giant Kelpfish
Heterostichus rostratus
266

To 24″ (61 cm). Slender, elongate, compressed; greenish yellow, green, or reddish brown with silver stripes; color varies with surroundings. Snout long, tip of lower jaw pointed, extends beyond upper jaw. Caudal fin forked.

Habitat
Rocky areas with eelgrass, leafy red algae, jointed coralline algae, or kelp beds to depths of 22 fathoms.

Range
From British Columbia to Cabo San Lucas, Baja California.

Comments
Giant Kelpfishes feed on small crustaceans, mollusks, and fishes. Occasionally caught by anglers but seldom retained, they are probably more familiar to scuba divers. There are four other species of Kelpfish in our area belonging to the genus *Gibbonsia*. They are difficult to identify to species.

Shiner Perch
Cymatogaster aggregata
267

To 8″ (20 cm). Elongate, depth one-third length, compressed; light greenish above, silvery below, 3 yellow bars on sides interspersed with black; breeding males nearly all black, with speckles covering yellow areas. Distance from pectoral fin insertion to dorsal fin origin one-third of standard length. Caudal peduncle slender; scales large.

Habitat
In bays around piers; on outer coast over soft bottoms, and near reefs and kelp beds to 80 fathoms.

Range
From Wrangell, Alaska, to Bahía de San Quintín, Baja California.

Comments
Anglers fishing from piers catch large numbers of these abundant perches.

Kelp Perch
Brachyistius frenatus
268

To 8½″ (22 cm). Elongate, compressed; golden above with elongate white blotches, silvery below. Snout long, pointed, upturned; tip of lower jaw projects beyond upper jaw. Caudal peduncle long; caudal fin shallowly forked.

Habitat
In kelp beds among fronds; near surface to 17 fathoms.

Range
From N. British Columbia to Bahía Tortugas, Baja California.

Comments
Kelp Perches breed in the fall and give birth to fully
developed young in the spring. These small perches are
cleaners; much of their food consists of ectoparasites picked off
other fishes. Kelp Perches are too small to be sought by
anglers.

Striped Seaperch
Embiotoca lateralis
269

To 15" (38 cm). Deep, very compressed; red, blue, and yellow
stripes on sides, pelvic fins dusky, caudal fin base orange.
Upper jaw extends beyond lower. Base of anal fin longer than
distance from pelvic fin insertion to anal fin origin.

Habitat
Reefs, piers, and kelp beds; in bays and offshore areas to
depths of 70' (21 m).

Range
From Wrangell, Alaska, to Punta Cabros, Baja California.

Comments
All members of this family bear live young. Anglers fishing
from rocky shores, piers, and small boats catch about 100,000
Striped Seaperches each year in northern and central
California. They are also harvested in small numbers by
commercial hook-and-line fishers.

Opaleye
Girella nigricans
270

To 26" (66 cm). Deep, compressed; dark olive-green, usually
with 2 yellow-white spots below dorsal fin, eyes blue. Snout
rounded. Rear profile of anal fin rounded; caudal fin almost
square in profile. Scales prominent.

Habitat
Shallow reefs and kelp beds to 16 fathoms.

Range
From San Francisco, California, to Cabo San Lucas, Baja
California.

Comments
Opaleyes spawn during April, May, and June and are mature
at 2 to 3 years, reaching 8–9" (20 cm–23 cm) in length. They
feed on algae and eelgrass, apparently taking most of their
nourishment from small animals living on the plants. Anglers
fishing from shore and skiffs take about 74,000 Opaleyes
annually. Commercial fishers using round haul nets or purse
seines catch only small amounts.

Rubberlip Seaperch
Rhacochilus toxotes
271

To 18" (46 cm). Deep, very compressed; brassy above, tan
below, occasionally with wide, tapering, light bar below
middle of dorsal fin. Lips large, pink, fleshy; lower lip with 2
fleshy lobes on underside. First dorsal fin ray shorter than
third; base of spiny part shorter than smooth part; spines
shorter than longest ray; origin of first dorsal fin above pectoral
fin insertion. Caudal fin moderately forked.

Habitat
Reefs, piers, and kelp beds, from shallow bays to 25 fathoms.

Range
From Russian Gulch State Beach, California, to Thurloe Head, Baja California.

Comments
A large female Rubberlip Seaperch produces about 20 young each summer. Adults feed on shrimp, amphipods, small crabs, and other crustaceans. Numbers of Rubberlip Seaperches are taken by anglers in California, and commercial fishers catch about 10 tons (9000 kg) each year on hook and line and in gill nets. A related species found in the same habitat, the Pile Perch (*R. vacca*), has black-tipped pelvic fins and a dark bar on the dorsal fin; its lips are not pink and fleshy like those of *R. toxotes*.

Redtail Surfperch
Amphistichus rhodoterus
272

To 16" (41 cm). Deep, very compressed; silver with light reddish bars on sides, caudal fin reddish. Lower edge of eye below top of upper lip. Longest dorsal fin spine longer than rays.

Habitat
Steeply sloping sandy beaches and other sandy areas to about 25' (8 m).

Range
From Vancouver Island, British Columbia, to Monterey Bay, California.

Comments
Redtail Surfperches feed on sand-dwelling crustaceans and mollusks. Highly sought by surf anglers in northern California, they also support a small, hook-and-line commercial fishery.

Walleye Surfperch
Hyperprosopon argenteum
273

To 12" (30 cm). Deep, very compressed; silver, back faintly dusky, pelvic fin tips black, caudal fin edge black.

Habitat
In surf, over sand, and around piers, reefs, and kelp beds; bays and outer coast to depths of 60' (18.3 m).

Range
From Vancouver Island, British Columbia, to Punta Rosarito, Baja California.

Comments
The Walleye Surfperch breeds from October through December, giving birth to 5–12 young in the spring. This species feeds on small crustaceans. Shore anglers in southern California bays and on the outer coast catch between 150,000 and 200,000 Walleye Surfperches annually. The species is also part of the commercial surfperch catch. Two related species found in similar habitats are the Spotfin Surfperch (*H. anale*),

which has a black blotch on the dorsal fin spines and anal fin soft rays; and the Silver Surfperch (*H. ellipticum*), which has a pinkish caudal fin and no black on the pelvic fin tips.

Bermuda Chub
Kyphosus sectatrix
274

To 20" (51 cm). Oval, compressed; bluish gray to dark gray with pale yellow stripes, horizontal yellow bands on head, upper part of gill cover membrane blackish; young have pale spots same size as eyes on head, body, and fins. Head short; snout blunt; mouth small, horizontal. Roots of incisorlike teeth horizontal, visible in mouth. Pectoral fin short; dorsal fin continuous, interrupted by shallow notch, spiny portion retractable into sheath of scales; caudal fin forked. Scales spiny, cover most of head, body, and all fins except spiny dorsal.

Habitat
Near shore on coral reefs and over rocks, occasionally in sargassum.

Range
In Atlantic from Massachusetts to Brazil, including Bermuda, Gulf of Mexico, and Caribbean.

Comments
A related Pacific species, the Blue-bronze Chub (*K. analogus*), ranges from Oceanside, California, to Peru. It occurs in shallow reefs and kelp beds to 16 fathoms, and is distinguished by brassy stripes on the sides and a prominent stripe under the eye.

Halfmoon
Medialuna californiensis
275

To 19" (48 cm). Compressed, deep; dark blue above, light blue below, dark spot above gill opening. Caudal fin distinctly crescent-shaped. Scales extend onto soft rays of dorsal fin.

Habitat
Reefs and kelp beds from near surface to depths of 22 fathoms.

Range
From Vancouver Island, British Columbia, to Gulf of California.

Comments
Halfmoons probably spawn during the summer and fall. At 2 years of age, most are mature and about 8" (20 cm) long; the maximum known age is 8 years. Halfmoons feed on small invertebrates, particularly those living among algae. The sport catch in California amounts to about 67,000 fishes annually with an average weight of about ½ lb (200 g).

Amercian Shad
Alosa sapidissima
276

To 30" (76 cm). Elongate, strongly compressed; top and bottom profiles evenly rounded; depth about one-fourth length. Back dark bluish or greenish, sides much paler, belly silvery, dusky spot behind gill cover usually followed by several small, less distinct dusky spots. Head one-fifth or less of length; mouth oblique; eye diameter much less than length of snout. Dorsal fin origin in front of pelvic fin insertion.

Habitat
Bays, estuaries, and fresh water.

Range
Introduced in Sacramento River, California, now Alaska to Mexico; from S. Labrador to St. Johns River, Florida.

Comments
All *Alosa* are schooling species that enter freshwater streams to spawn. None remain long in fresh water, nor do they go far out at sea.

Striped Mullet
Mugil cephalus
277, 287

To 18″ (46 cm). Elongate, cylindrical toward front, compressed toward rear; silvery, back olive- or bluish green, 6–7 darker stripes on sides. Head flat between eyes; transparent, membranous eyelid well developed; mouth small, wide, at tip of snout, lower jaw has fleshy knob at tip. Pectoral fins inserted high on shoulders; pelvic fins abdominal; dorsal fin has 4 weak spines well separated from soft dorsal; caudal fin forked. Scales cover body, top of head, and bases of soft dorsal and anal fins. No lateral line.

Habitat
Coasts, estuaries, and fresh water.

Range
In Pacific from San Francisco Bay, California, to Chile. In Atlantic from Cape Cod to Brazil, including Gulf of Mexico, Caribbean, and West Indies.

Comments
These important food fishes occur in schools. Striped Mullets are known to travel several hundred miles up rivers, but spawning always takes place in the sea.

Striped Bass
Morone saxatilis
278

To 6′ (1.8 m). Elongate, moderately compressed; back olive-green to dark blue, sides silvery, belly white, upper sides with 6–9 dark, uninterrupted stripes; dorsal, anal, and caudal fins dusky. Mouth large, lower jaw slightly projecting. Teeth small. Gill cover has 2 flat spines near rear edge. First dorsal fin with 8–10 strong spines, separated from second dorsal by deep notch. Scales extend onto all fin bases except spiny dorsal.

Habitat
Inshore over various bottoms; some permanently in fresh water.

Range
Introduced from Atlantic Ocean and associated rivers to coastal streams in Washington, Oregon, and California. Also widely introduced into rivers and lakes in much of Mississippi River system and Colorado River.

Comments
The Striped Bass is a very important sport fish, although commercial fishing in California and Oregon is prohibited. There is much concern about the survival of this species in Atlantic streams. It is anadromous, and spawns prolifically in fresh water.

Bonefish
Albula vulpes
279

To 3' (91 cm). Elongate, fusiform; bluish or greenish, silvery overall, occasionally with dusky side stripes and bars that fade upon death; base of fins often yellow. Upper jaw overhangs lower. Pelvic fins abdominal. Caudal fin large, deeply forked.

Habitat
Shallow waters over soft bottoms.

Range
In Pacific from San Francisco, California, to Peru; in Atlantic from Bay of Fundy to Rio de Janeiro, Brazil, most common in S. Florida, Bermuda, and Bahamas.

Comments
Bonefishes eat clams, snails, shrimps, and small fishes. Although they have been virtually ignored on the West Coast, they are prized game fishes on the East Coast, since they are easier to catch on shallow sand flats.

Ocean Whitefish
Caulolatilus princeps
280

To 3'4" (1 m). Fusiform, compressed, head profile blunt; yellow-brown above, whitish below, fins yellowish. Dorsal fin continuous. Anal fin long, has blue stripe.

Habitat
Over soft bottoms and reefs from surface to 50 fathoms.

Range
From Vancouver Island, British Columbia, to Peru. Not common north of Point Conception, California.

Comments
Ocean Whitefishes have become popular with southern California anglers. They are good fighters and their flesh is very tasty. They feed on other fishes, squids, shrimps, pelagic red crabs, and hermit crabs.

Yellowtail
Seriola lalandei
281

To 5' (1.5 m). Elongate, fusiform, compressed; olive-brown to brown above, yellow stripe along each side, fins yellowish. Head longer than body depth at dorsal fin origin. Dorsal fin spines shorter than soft rays. Lateral line lacks bony shields.

Habitat
Near surface around reefs, islands, and kelp beds.

Range
From British Columbia to Chile.

Comments
The Yellowtail feeds on anchovies, sardines, mackerels, squids, and pelagic red crabs. Second only to the elusive Albacore, it is one of the most popular gamefishes in southern California. Its migrations north into this area depend upon water temperature, so the annual catch fluctuates between 5000 and 400,000 fishes. Most are caught by hook and line, as it is illegal to use purse seines for Yellowtail in California.

Yellowfin Tuna
Thunnus albacares
282

To 6' (1.8 m). Fusiform, compressed; dark blue above, gray below, fins tinged yellow, finlets yellow, edges black. Snout moderately sharp, mouth at tip of snout. Pectoral fin tip not extending beyond second dorsal fin origin; dorsal fins about same height, second dorsal greatly elongate in large individuals; 8–9 dorsal and 7–9 anal finlets; caudal fin lobes slender, rear profile crescent-shaped.

Habitat
On surface and at mid-depths in open seas.

Range
In Pacific from Point Buchon, California, to Chile. In Atlantic from Massachusetts to Brazil.

Comments
This is the most valuable of all tunas worldwide. Schools of Yellowfin Tunas are pursued by fleets of purse-seine boats from around the world. Dolphins are frequently caught in large numbers with the tunas, and these large, expensive boats have had to modify their nets and fishing methods to resolve this problem. The Yellowfin Tuna is also a highly prized game fish. A similar species is the Albacore (*T. alalunga*), which has pectoral fins that extend beyond the anal fin origin.

Sockeye Salmon
Oncorhynchus nerka
283

To 33" (84 cm). Elongate, fusiform, moderately compressed. Marine coloration: greenish blue above, silvery below, with fine black speckling on back but no large, dark spots. Freshwater coloration: body and fins bright red, head pale green, jaws dark, pale below; females may have green and yellow blotches, in some populations bodies scarlet. Snout bluntly pointed, mouth large, at tip of snout; lips fleshy. Adipose fin present.

Habitat
Surface waters of open ocean, and freshwater streams, rivers, and lakes containing tributary streams for spawning over fine gravel.

Range
From Bering Strait to Sacramento River, California; introduced elsewhere in northern lakes.

Comments
The Family Salmonidae, which includes trouts and salmons, is one of the most important and well-researched fish groups.

There are 6 species of Pacific salmons in the genus
Oncorhynchus, 5 of which occur in our area. Sockeye Salmon
spawn during summer in small tributaries of lakes, where the
young spend 1–3 years before migrating to the ocean. After
living at sea for 2–4 years, maturing adults return to their
home streams. Sockeye Salmon have the greatest commercial
value of all the Pacific salmons, although few are caught by
anglers in the ocean because they rarely strike lures or trolled
baits.

Cutthroat Trout
Salmo clarki
284, 288

To 30″ (76 cm). Elongate, cylindrical or slightly tapering at
both ends, moderately compressed. Back dark olive; sides
variable: silvery, olive, reddish to yellow-orange; belly lighter;
dark spots on back, sides, and on dorsal, anal, and caudal fins.
Mouth extends beyond eye; bright red to red-orange slash
mark on each side of throat, particularly visible in breeding
males. Adipose fin present. Caudal peduncle narrow; caudal
fin slightly forked. Lateral line complete.

Habitat
Inshore marine and estuarine waters; lakes; coastal, inland,
and alpine streams.

Range
From S. Alaska south to N. California; inland from S. British
Columbia and Alberta south to New Mexico; E. California east
to central Colorado. Introduced in western United States.

Comments
There are more than 10 subspecies of Cutthroat Trouts, locally
called "native trout," which vary in coloration and size. The
largest specimen, caught in Pyramid Lake, Nevada, in 1925,
weighed 41 lb (18.6 kg), but this strain is now extinct. Other
cutthroats, while rarely over 15″ (38 cm), are sought by inland
and coastal fisheries, and by anglers.

Sablefish
Anoplopoma fimbria
285

To 3′4″ (1 m). Elongate, fusiform, almost round in
cross section; blackish gray above, gray to white below. Snout
moderately sharp. First dorsal fin rounded, second dorsal
triangular, wide space between them; anal fin has no spines;
caudal fin indented.

Habitat
Over soft bottoms in deep water to depths of 1000 fathoms.
Most abundant in water 1200–3000′ (365–915 m) deep, but
enter very deep water in winter months.

Range
From Bering Sea to Isla Cedros, Baja California.

Comments
The Sablefish spawns during the winter, and the eggs drift
near the surface. This species feeds on fishes, worms, and
crustaceans. Smoked and sold for food, it is very important
commercially, although of minor interest to anglers.

Chinook Salmon
Oncorhynchus tshawytscha
286

To 4' 10" (1.6 m). Elongate, fusiform. Marine coloration: greenish blue to black above, silvery white below, oblong, black spots on back and entire caudal fin; very dark overall in fresh water. Gums at base of teeth black. Adipose fin present; striations on caudal fin rays smooth.

Habitat
Ocean near surface and at mid-depths, may feed near bottom; spawns in fresh water in large rivers.

Range
Bering Strait south to S. California; in freshwater streams south to Sacramento River; widely introduced.

Comments
Chinook Salmon enter fresh water most months of the year, but their major spawning runs occur in the spring and fall. Bright red eggs are buried in gravel of river bottoms. Their diet, similar to that of the Coho Salmon, consists of a variety of crustaceans, and fishes such as anchovies, herrings, young rockfishes, and sand lances. Chinook Salmon are the most highly prized ocean game fishes on the West Coast.

Pacific Herring
Clupea harengus pallasi
289

To 18" (46 cm). Laterally compressed, fusiform; dark green above, silvery white below. No striations on gill covers. Plates on belly lack bony keel. Single dorsal fin located directly above pelvic fins.

Habitat
Inshore waters.

Range
From Gulf of Alaska to N. Baja California.

Comments
The Pacific Herring spawns during the winter and early spring. The eggs are deposited on objects, such as kelp, rocks, and eelgrass, in very shallow water and hatch in 10 days. Large quantities of eggs are harvested, often to be exported to Japan. Adult Pacific Herring feed on a variety of crustaceans and small fishes, and are themselves prey for many important commercial and sport fishes such as salmons. The related Pacific Sardine (*Sardinops sagax*), occurring in a similar habitat, has black spots and belly plates with bony keels.

Pacific Hake
Merluccius productus
290

To 3' (91 cm). Elongate, slightly compressed; back metallic silver-gray with black speckles, silvery below. Mouth large; lower jaw projects beyond upper; no barbel; gill cover and inside of mouth black. Distinguished by 2 dorsal fins, second fin and anal fin long and deeply notched; caudal fin squared off.

Habitat
Surface to bottom of open sea to 500 fathoms, occasionally inshore waters.

Range
From Gulf of Alaska south to Gulf of California.

Comments
The Pacific Hake, sometimes called Pacific Whiting, spawns from January to June. It feeds mostly at night, chiefly on other fishes, shrimps, and plankton. Anglers trolling for salmon commonly catch Pacific Hake, but rarely eat them. Russians eat large amounts of Pacific Hake, but in the United States these fishes are used chiefly for animal food.

Chub Mackerel
Scomber japonicus
291

To 25″ (64 cm). Elongate, fusiform, slightly compressed; dark green to blue-black above with many wavy, dark streaks extending to just below lateral line, silvery below with numerous dusky blotches. Head pointed, flattened between eyes; snout conical, shorter than rest of head; transparent, membranous eyelid present. 2 dorsal fins widely separated, first triangular, second slightly concave; 5 dorsal and 5 anal finlets. 2 small keels on each side of caudal peduncle, no large median keel. On front part of body, lacks girdle of scales; largest scales around pectoral fins.

Habitat
Warm coastal waters over continental shelf.

Range
In Pacific from Gulf of Alaska to Chile. In Atlantic from Nova Scotia south to Florida, Gulf of Mexico, and Venezuela.

Comments
Chub Mackerels, usually schooling fishes themselves, feed on other schooling fishes like anchovies and herrings, and on invertebrates. This species is an excellent food fish.

Pacific Tomcod
Microgadus proximus
292

To 12″ (30 cm). Elongate, moderately compressed; olive-green above, creamy white below, fin tips dusky. Small chin barbel, equal in length to pupil diameter. Lower jaw shorter than upper. 3 dorsal fins and 2 anal fins present. Anus below first dorsal fin.

Habitat
Over soft bottoms, around piers and jetties in bays, and to depths of 120 fathoms.

Range
From Bering Sea south to Point Sal, California.

Comments
Pacific Tomcod grow fast but live only about 5 years. During "runs" of occasional abundance, they are popular with pier and skiff anglers. They are considered fine food fishes. The related Pacific Cod (*Gadus macrocephalus*) has a larger chin barbel and occurs in deeper water from the Bering Sea to Santa Monica, California.

Jack Mackerel
Trachurus symmetricus
293

To 32" (81 cm). Fusiform, compressed; metallic blue to olive-green above; silvery below, but darkens with age. Pectoral fin extends to base of first soft ray in anal fin. Dorsal fins barely separated. Lateral line has bony shields toward rear.

Habitat
Offshore on surface and at midwater; around reefs and kelp.

Range
From SE. Alaska to Galapagos Islands.

Comments
Large Jack Mackerels are important commercially in southern California. They feed on krill, squids, anchovies, and lanternfishes, and are a major food source for seals, sea lions, porpoises, swordfishes, sea basses, and pelicans.

Topsmelt
Atherinops affinis
294

To 14½" (37 cm). Elongate, compressed; green-blue above with brilliant bar on each side, silvery below. Teeth forked in single row on each jaw. Anal fin origin under rear of first dorsal fin.

Habitat
Surface waters near shore, in bays, and around kelp beds.

Range
From Vancouver Island, British Columbia, to Gulf of California.

Comments
Topsmelts mature in 2 or 3 years and spawn during late winter and spring, often over estuarine mud flats. The large eggs are attached to kelp and other algae. Topsmelts and the larger Jacksmelts are caught by anglers from piers. The annual commercial haul of both species in California weighs about 250 tons.

Northern Anchovy
Engraulis mordax
295

To 9" (23 cm). Elongate, fusiform, slightly compressed; metallic blue to green above, silver below. Mouth large, snout short. Pectoral axillary scale more than half of pectoral fin length. Anal fin origin under or behind last few dorsal rays.

Habitat
Coastal surface waters.

Range
From N. British Columbia to Cabo San Lucas, Baja California.

Comments
The Northern Anchovy spawns during the winter and early spring, and the pelagic eggs take between 2 and 4 days to hatch. This anchovy rarely lives longer than 4 years. Tagging studies indicate that schools of anchovies move fairly large distances up and down the coast. An extremely important commercial fish, this species is also a major food source for other fishes, birds, and mammals.

Bay Pipefish
Syngnathus leptorhynchus
296

To 14" (36 cm). Very elongate, hexagonal in cross section toward front; green to brown and mottled, depending on habitat. Snout very long; mouth small, at tip of snout. No pelvic fins; caudal fin very small. Covered with bony plates. 53–63 rings.

Habitat
Eelgrass beds in bays.

Range
From Sitka, Alaska, to Baja California.

Comments
All pipefishes mate in early summer, and the female deposits the eggs in the brood pouch of the male. Bay Pipefishes feed on small crustaceans. Observers rarely notice these relatives of the seahorse unless they are seen swimming away from vegetation.

Pacific Lamprey
Lampetra tridentata
297

To 30" (76 cm). Eel-like. Marine coloration: adults steel-blue above, silvery below. Freshwater coloration: brownish red above, lighter below. Larvae yellowish. Eyes large; mouth without jaws, broad tooth plate above mouth with 3 cusps, 4 pairs of lateral teeth. No paired fins; dorsal fin deeply notched, divided into 2 parts.

Habitat
Close to shore; large inland streams.

Range
From Alaska south to S. California.

Comments
The Pacific Lamprey is parasitic on various ocean fishes for 1–2 years. After maturing it ascends streams in the late spring and early summer, and spawns over a gravel nest in shallow water. Adults die soon after spawning. The larvae live in streams for 5–6 years before entering the ocean to become parasitic. The Pacific Hagfish (*Eptatretus stouti*), a similar species, is a serious nuisance to fishing operations, affecting catches of Lingcod, salmon, and other commercially important food fishes. Pacific Lampreys, however, appear to have little impact on marine fish populations and do not feed when they move into streams to spawn.

California Grunion
Leuresthes tenuis
298

To 7½" (19 cm). Elongate, fusiform; greenish above, silvery below with stripe along side. Snout bluntly rounded; teeth minute or lacking. First dorsal fin spiny, origin slightly in front of anal fin origin.

Habitat
Off sandy beaches to depths of about 60' (18.3 m).

Range
From San Francisco, California, to Bahía de San Juanico, Baja California.

Comments
From March to September during spring high tides, the California Grunion spawns at night on beaches. The eggs are buried in the moist sand and hatch when the next spring tide occurs. Each female may spawn from 4 to 8 times during a season. Anglers are allowed to use only their hands to capture these fishes at this time.

Plainfin Midshipman
Porichthys notatus
299

To 15" (38 cm). Elongate, tapering; purple-bronze above, yellow-white below. Head large, broad; eyes widely separated, protrusible. Rows of light-emitting organs on underside; second row of light-emitting organs under head is V-shaped, with apex toward front. Pectoral, dorsal, and anal fins lack spots.

Habitat
Over sand and mud to depths of 200 fathoms.

Range
In Pacific from Sitka, Alaska, to the Gulf of California.

Comments
The Plain Midshipman comes into shallow water during the late spring to spawn. The male becomes emaciated while guarding the eggs and young, so that the mortality rate among egg-tending males tends to be high. This species feeds at night on other fishes and crustaceans. It often appears in the catches of sport and commercial anglers. The related Specklefin Midshipman (*P. myriaster*) has spots on its pectoral, dorsal, and anal fins, and occurs in the Pacific from Point Conception, California, to Bahía Magdalena, Baja California.

Blackeye Goby
Coryphopterus nicholsi
300

To 6" (15 cm). Elongate, almost round in cross section; tan to olive, usually with brown mottling and speckles, first dorsal fin edge black; iridescent blue spot beneath each eye. Snout rounded. Tips of pectoral fins reach anus; pelvic fins form sucking disk on underside; 2 dorsal fins, second long, almost reaches caudal fin; anal fin almost one-third length; caudal fin rounded. Scales large.

Habitat
Over sand and mud near reefs, in bays and off coast to depths of 70 fathoms.

Range
From Queen Charlotte Islands, British Columbia, to Punta Rompiente, Baja California.

Comments
Spawning occurs from April to October, when the males lure females into their resting cave. The eggs are guarded by the male. The related Arrow Goby (*Clevelandia ios*) occurs in estuaries, dwelling in the burrows of ghost and mud shrimps. This fish ranges from Vancouver Island, British Columbia, to the Gulf of California.

Spotted Cusk-Eel
Chilara taylori
301

To 14¼" (36 cm). Elongate, eel-like; light brown to cream with small, dark spots. No spines in fins; pelvic fins filamentous, located on throat. Dorsal fin single, long-based, continuous; anal fin similar in shape. Dorsal, anal, and caudal fins continuous around body.

Habitat
Over and in soft bottoms to depths of 133 fathoms.

Range
From Oregon to S. Baja California.

Comments
The Spotted Cusk-Eel burrows tailfirst into the sand or mud during the day, and comes out at night to feed. It is occasionally captured by divers and makes an interesting aquarium fish. A few are accidentally caught by commercial fishers in trawls and round haul nets.

Penpoint Gunnel
Apodichthys flavidus
302

To 18" (46 cm). Elongate, eel-like, compressed; green, yellow, light brown, or red. Head bluntly rounded; mouth at tip of snout, small. Pectoral fin length about twice eye diameter; no pelvic fins; dorsal fin contains only spines, extending from pectoral fin insertion to caudal peduncle, connected to caudal fin. Anal fin spine has deep groove.

Habitat
Intertidal areas over rocks and shallow eelgrass beds.

Range
From Kodiak Island, Alaska, to S. California.

Comments
The rarely seen Penpoint Gunnel spawns in January. Its diet consists of small crustaceans and mollusks.

Wolf-Eel ⊗
Anarrhichthys ocellatus
303

To 6'8" (2 m). Eel-like, elongate, compressed, tapering to pointed caudal fin; light gray or gray-brown with dark mottling and spots surrounded by lighter coloration. Snout blunt; front of jaws with large, strong, canine teeth. Pelvic fins absent; dorsal fin long, continuous, consists of spines. Lateral line absent.

Habitat
Reefs and wrecks with large crevices, to depths of 106 fathoms.

Range
From Kodiak Island, Alaska, to Imperial Beach, San Diego County, California.

Comments
The Wolf-Eel spawns during the winter, when the eggs are deposited in crevices or caves and are guarded by both parents. This large predator feeds on crabs taken from traps and on fishes, sea urchins, sea cucumbers, and snails. Anglers and

spear fishers catch a few Wolf-Eels. If molested, these fishes may bite and cause serious wounds.

California Moray ⊗
Gymnothorax mordax
304

To 5' (1.5 m). Elongate, eel-like; brown to green-brown. Mouth large, teeth strong, gill openings small, round; back of head elevated. Pelvic and pectoral fins absent. Skin thick, scaleless.

Habitat
Shallow, rocky reefs with crevices and caves to 22 fathoms.

Range
From Point Conception, California, to Bahía Magdalena, Baja California.

Comments
The only moray found north of Baja California, the California Moray eats crabs, shrimps, lobsters, and various fishes. Females deposit eggs that develop into transparent, floating, pelagic larvae. If disturbed, California Morays may bite divers.

Pacific Halibut
Hippoglossus stenolepis
305

To 8'9" (2.7 m). Elongate, highly compressed, diamond-shaped, eyes on right side; eyed side dark brown with fine mottling, blind side pigmented, lighter brown. Snout moderately sharp; mouth medium-sized, smaller than that of California Halibut; double row of teeth in upper jaw sharp, conical. Pelvic fins symmetrically placed; dorsal fin origin over middle of eye, longest soft rays of dorsal and anal fins at about middle of body; caudal fin slightly forked. Lateral line arched above pectoral fin; scales numerous, smooth.

Habitat
Over soft bottoms at 3–600 fathoms.

Range
From Bering Sea to Santa Rosa Island, California.

Comments
The Pacific Halibut supports one of the oldest and most valuable fisheries on the Pacific Coast. It is a highly desirable sport fish off Washington, British Columbia, and Alaska.

Pacific Sanddab
Citharichthys sordidus
306

To 16" (41 cm). Extremely compressed, deep, eyes on left side; eyed side brown, with darker brown mottling and sometimes dull orange spots; blind side off-white to pale brown. Snout moderately sharp; ridge between eyes concave; diameter of lower eye longer than snout length; gill cover bone visible. Pelvic fins asymmetrical, attached to ridge underneath eyed side; dorsal fin origin over eyes; anal fin origin below pectoral fin; anal and dorsal fins extend almost to caudal fin. Lateral line straight.

Habitat
Over soft bottoms to 300 fathoms.

Range
From Bering Sea to Cabo San Lucas, Baja California.

Comments
The Pacific Sanddab spawns during the winter; some females may spawn twice a season. Highly regarded as food, this flatfish is sought by anglers as well as commercial trawlers. Occurring in a similar habitat are the related Speckled Sanddab (*C. stigmaeus*), which ranges from Montague Island, Alaska, to Bahía Magdalena, Baja California, and the Longfin Sanddab (*C. xanthostigma*), which ranges from Monterey Bay, California, to Costa Rica.

Starry Flounder
Platichthys stellatus
307

To 3' (91 cm). Deep, compressed, almost diamond-shaped, eyes on either left or right side; eyed side dark brown to nearly black with vague blotches, blind side white to creamy white, occasionally blotched. Dorsal, anal, and caudal fins have distinctive black and white or black and orange bars. Mouth small. Dorsal and anal fin soft rays longest behind middle of body; caudal fin straight or rounded. Lateral line only slightly curved over pectoral fin, no dorsal branch; scales star-shaped, very rough to touch.

Habitat
In bays and estuaries over soft bottoms, and off open coast to 150 fathoms.

Range
From Arctic Ocean off Alaska to Santa Barbara, California.

Comments
The Starry Flounder feeds on crabs, shrimps, worms, clams, and small fishes. It can tolerate very low salinity and is often captured in major rivers, well away from the open ocean. Small numbers are taken by anglers and commercial trawlers.

English Sole
Parophrys vetulus
308

To 22" (56 cm). Deep, elongate, highly compressed, almost diamond-shaped, eyes on right side; eyed side dark to light brown, occasionally with brown spots, blind side pale yellow to white. Snout moderately long, sharp; mouth small; upper eye visible from blind side. Dorsal fin origin above middle of upper eye, longest dorsal soft rays at middle of body; caudal fin indented. Lateral line almost straight, with short dorsal branch; no scales on fins.

Habitat
Over soft bottoms to 300 fathoms.

Range
From Bering Sea to Bahía de San Cristobal, Baja California.

Comments
The migratory English Sole may travel up to 700 miles (1160 km). It ranks among the top 3 flatfishes in terms of pounds caught by commercial trawlers.

C-O Sole
Pleuronichthys coenosus
309

To 14" (36 cm). Deep, highly compressed, eyes on right side; eyed side brown with darker mottling, blind side creamy white; prominent C- and O-shaped marks on caudal fin. Snout rounded; mouth small, almost hidden by eyes when viewed from above. Dorsal fin origin in front of middle of upper eye; 4–6 front soft rays of dorsal fin extend onto blind side but not beyond mouth; caudal peduncle about one-fourth body depth; caudal fin rounded, smooth scales on both sides. Lateral line lacks abrupt arch over pectoral fin, dorsal branch extends toward rear to about middle of body.

Habitat
Over soft bottoms and rocks to depths of 190 fathoms.

Range
From SE. Alaska to Cabo Colnett, Baja California.

Comments
This flatfish probably spawns during late winter and early spring; its eggs float near the surface. Small numbers of C-O Soles are caught by anglers with hook and line and by commercial trawlers. Like all flatfishes, it is edible.

Rock Sole
Lepidopsetta bilineata
310

To 24" (61 cm). Moderately deep, compressed, eyes on right side; eyed side dark brown or gray with mottling, blind side whitish. Snout short, bluntly sharp; teeth in both jaws, better developed on blind side. Dorsal fin origin over eyes; caudal fins slightly rounded. Lateral line arched over pectoral fin, has short dorsal branch not extending beyond rear edge of gill cover. Scales spiny on eyed side, smooth on blind side, extend onto dorsal, anal, and caudal fin rays.

Habitat
Over rocks and soft bottoms at 2–200 fathoms.

Range
From Bering Sea to Tanner Bank, California.

Comments
The female Rock Sole releases between 400,000 and 1.3 million eggs during the spawning period from February to April. Adults feed on clam siphons, polychaete worms, shrimps, small crabs, brittle stars, and sand lances, all of which can be used as bait by anglers.

Diamond Turbot
Hypsopsetta guttulata
311

To 18" (46 cm). Deep, diamond-shaped, highly compressed, eyes on right side; eyed side dark gray with numerous blue spots, blind side not pigmented, yellow around mouth. Snout short, moderately sharp. Dorsal fin origin over eyes; middle soft rays of dorsal and anal fins longest; caudal fin rounded. Dorsal branch of lateral line extends more than halfway to caudal fin.

Habitat
Over soft bottoms at 1–25 fathoms.

Range
From Cape Mendocino, California, to Bahía Magdalena, Baja California.

Comments
This distinctively shaped flatfish is commonly encountered by divers off southern California.

California Halibut
Paralichthys californicus
312

To 5' (1.5 m). Elongate, deep, highly compressed; eyes usually on left side, occasionally on right. Eyed side light to dark brown with lighter mottling, blind side lighter. Snout moderately sharp; mouth large; numerous sharp teeth in jaws; gill cover visible. Dorsal fin origin over eye; caudal fin squared off or indented. Lateral line highly arched over pectoral fin.

Habitat
Over soft bottoms to 100 fathoms.

Range
From Quillayute River, Washington, to Bahía Magdalena, Baja California.

Comments
This is a very popular sport fish; the annual catch may exceed 300,000. It is also an important commercial species, with annual landings of 500 to 1000 tons.

Bat Ray ⊗
Myliobatis californica
313

To 6' (1.8 m) wide. Disk diamond-shaped, wider than long; wings long, blunt-pointed; brown, olive, or black above, white below. Head and eyes extend beyond front of disk. Tail whiplike, with 1 or more spines at base. Skin smooth.

Habitat
Shallow, sandy areas in bays and on coast to 25 fathoms; kelp beds.

Range
From Oregon to Gulf of California.

Comments
Anglers consider Bat Rays excellent fighters, but few are kept for eating. The young develop within the female and are released in late summer and fall. The venomous tail spines can cause a painful injury.

Round Stingray ⊗
Urolophus halleri
314

To 22" (56 cm) long. Disk almost circular; tail shorter than disk; gray-brown above, sometimes with small, light spots, yellow below. Lacks dorsal fin; long, venomous spine about halfway down tail.

Habitat
Over sand or mud in shallow bays and off coast to 70' (21 m).

Range
From Humboldt Bay, California, to Panama Bay.

Comments
All stingrays are ovoviviparous, the young developing within the female. They feed on shrimps, crabs, snails, and clams. Concentrations of them occasionally make some beaches in California unsafe for swimmers, as their venomous spines can cause painful wounds.

Big Skate
Raja binoculata
315

To 8' (2.4 m). Rhomboid-shaped disk, concave in front; olive-brown or gray above, whitish below. Distinguished by 2 large eyespots, one on each side of disk, and by pelvic fins with shallow notch. Thorns become more apparent as fish ages.

Habitat
Over soft bottoms at depths of 10–360' (3–110 m).

Range
From Bering Sea to Bahía de San Quintin, Baja California.

Comments
Big Skates lay eggs in individual horny cases. These fishes are occasionally captured by anglers but are rarely retained. They form a minor portion of the commercial trawl catch, but only the wings are used for food.

Thornback
Platyrhinoidis triseriata
316

To 3' (91 cm). Skatelike, disk wider than long; brown above, white below. Front of head rounded; gills on underside of disk. 3 rows of spines on back of adults; 2 small dorsal fins present; caudal fin squarish.

Habitat
Over sand and mud to 25 fathoms.

Range
From San Francisco, California, to Thurloe Head, Baja California.

Comments
Thornbacks eat sand-dwelling worms, snails, clams, crabs, and shrimps. They are ovoviviparous—they bear live young hatched from eggs held inside the mother's body.

Pacific Electric Ray ⊗
Torpedo californica
317

To 4'6" (1.4 m). Depressed, disk round, fused with head and pectoral fins; dark blue or gray-brown, often with black spots above, dirty white below. First dorsal fin above pelvic fins, second dorsal fin between caudal fin and rear of pelvic fins. Caudal fin large, rear profile nearly straight. Only ray in our range that lacks spines or prickles.

Habitat
Over mud and sand in shallow waters, and in kelp beds to 150 fathoms.

Range
From N. British Columbia to Bahía San Sebastián Vizcaino, Baja California.

Comments
The Pacific Electric Ray bears live young from eggs retained in the female's body. It feeds on fishes such as halibuts and herrings, capturing its prey by stunning it with a powerful electric charge. These rays have shown aggressive behavior towards divers off California and may be dangerous.

Pacific Angel Shark
Squatina californica
318

To 5' (1.5 m). Flattened, skatelike, but head and pectoral and pelvic fins separate; gray-brown above, body usually covered with brown spots; underside white. Mouth under head, as in skates, at tip of snout; barbels and spiracle present; 5 gills on sides in notch behind head. Dorsal fins behind rear of pelvic fins; caudal fin lobes about equal in size.

Habitat
On sand and mud bottoms, from shallow water to 100 fathoms.

Range
SE. Alaska to Gulf of California; not recorded in British Columbia.

Comments
Pacific Angel Sharks usually lie partially buried in sand waiting for prey such as Queenfishes and California Halibuts. They are occasionally caught by anglers, but are not highly prized. A small commercial gill-net fishery supplies fish markets.

Leopard Shark
Triakis semifasciata
319

To 6'6" (2 m). Elongate, fusiform; gray with black spots and bars, which may stretch across back. Snout moderately long, pointed; fourth and fifth gill slits over pectoral fin. First dorsal fin origin above rear of pectoral fin; second dorsal fin origin in front of anal fin.

Habitat
Over sand and mud in shallow bays and inshore waters, to depths of 50 fathoms.

Range
From Oregon to Gulf of California.

Comments
Leopard Sharks feed on fishes and crustaceans such as crabs and shrimps. These nomadic sharks are quite tasty, are very popular sport fishes, and form part of the commercial shark fishery.

White Shark ⊗
Carcharodon carcharias
320

To 21' (6.4 m). Elongate, fusiform; gray or brown above, dirty white below. Snout bluntly pointed; teeth triangular and serrate. Origin of first dorsal fin above rear of pectorals; anal fin beneath or behind second dorsal fin. Caudal peduncle has keel; caudal fin crescent-shaped, upper and lower lobes almost equal.

Habitat
Coastal surface waters.

Range
On Pacific Coast from Alaska south to Gulf of California; on Atlantic Coast south from S. Newfoundland to Brazil, including Gulf of Mexico.

Comments
White Sharks bear live young hatched from eggs held inside mother's body; the young are about 5' (1.5 m) long at birth. These savage predators feed on fishes, sea otters, seals, sea lions, and even crabs. This species is the most dangerous shark that occurs in North America and has attacked and killed humans on both the Pacific and Atlantic coasts. It is occasionally caught by commercial fishermen, and the flesh is reportedly quite palatable.

Ocean Sunfish
Mola mola
321

To 13' (4 m). Deep, almost round, highly compressed; back gray-blue, sides and belly metallic silver. Snout short, rounded; mouth small; gill openings small. No pelvic fins; dorsal and anal fins very long, consist of soft rays only, placed far back; caudal fin greatly reduced, rounded, flaplike. Covered with thick mucus; scaleless.

Habitat
Surface of open seas, occasionally near shore.

Range
In Pacific from British Columbia to South America. In Atlantic from Gulf of St. Lawrence to Argentina.

Comments
These fishes feed on jellyfishes, ctenophores, and salps. They are not sought by anglers or commercial fishers, but they are a familiar sight drifting lazily on the surface of the water during the late summer and inshore along California in the fall.

Blue Shark
Prionace glauca
322

To 12'7" (3.8 m). Very slender, fusiform; dark blue above, bright blue on sides, gray-white below; tips of pectoral, dorsal, and anal fins dusky. Snout long, narrowly rounded, longer than width of mouth. Teeth serrate, triangular and curved in upper jaw, narrower in lower jaw. Pectoral fins very long, narrow, and somewhat crescent-shaped. Dorsal fins relatively small, no ridge of skin. Keel on caudal peduncle weak; caudal fin crescent-shaped.

Habitat
In shallow coastal waters over sand or mud, and far out at sea. Common in surface waters during late summer.

Range
Worldwide; on Pacific Coast from Gulf of Alaska to Chile.

Comments
Blue Sharks bear live young, up to 60 developing within the

female. This species is common and well known to commercial fishers and whalers. Ordinarily they feed on small schooling fishes; however, they are known to follow vessels for days feeding on offal. They are not considered dangerous to people.

Spiny Dogfish
Squalus acanthias
323

To 5' (1.5 m). Elongate, slender; gray or brown above, dingy white below; young have light spots on back. Snout long, pointed. Spine in front of each dorsal fin; origin of first dorsal fin slightly behind rear of pectorals; origin of second dorsal fin behind rear of pelvics. Lacks anal fin; upper lobe of caudal fin larger than lower, tip rounded.

Habitat
In temperate and subtropical waters over soft bottoms, off coast to 200 fathoms.

Range
On Pacific Coast from Bering Sea to central Baja California; on Atlantic Coast from Newfoundland to North Carolina; a few stray to Cuba.

Comments
The fully developed young are born in broods of 2–20 and average 8–12" (20–30 cm) long at birth. Tagging studies off California suggest that Spiny Dogfishes are migratory. Though they are an important food fish in Europe and were once sought for their liver oils, these abundant sharks are considered pests in North America.

White Sturgeon
Acipenser transmontanus
324

To 12'6" (3.8 m). Elongate, rounded in cross section, head slightly flattened; gray above, lighter below. Snout short, broad, pointed; mouth on underside, below eye; 4 long barbels near tip of snout. 38–48 plates along side. Tail heterocercal.

Habitat
Over soft bottoms in ocean; in deep pools of large rivers.

Range
In Pacific from Gulf of Alaska south to N. Baja California; in fresh water south only to Sacramento River, N. California.

Comments
White Sturgeons spawn in rivers during the spring. Males do not mature until they are 11 to 22 years old; females mature between 11 and 34 years. These large game fish feed on small fishes such as Eulachon, and on crustaceans and mollusks. Sturgeons are highly regarded both commercially, for their caviar and meat, and for sport. The related Green Sturgeon (*A. medirostris*) has a concave profile, long snout, and 4 barbels that are closer to the mouth. It occurs in a similar habitat within the same range as *A. transmontanus*.

SEASHORE CREATURES

The intertidal areas and the nearshore waters of the Pacific Coast harbor a world of fascinating animal life. Hundreds of creatures—long and round, large and minute—find shelter among sand grains, burrow deep into the muddy bottoms of bays, or live attached to wave-lashed rocks. Crabs scuttle along the bottom of the sea, searching for a meal; jellyfishes drift by, a floating mass of tentacles. Many of these seashore creatures are so bushy that early biologists classified them as plants. To a visitor who is wading, swimming, or diving along these shores, the underwater world holds tremendous promise of discovery. This section describes some of the most interesting and beautiful of these seashore creatures.

Commensal Crabs
Pinnotheres spp.
325

⅝" (16 mm) wide, ½" (13 mm) long. Oval. White, salmon, brown, or blue, with or without white spots. Carapace round, smooth, soft, flexible. Pincers small; hand flat on inside, swollen on outside; fingers curve to meet; walking legs slender, last 2 joints of walking legs with fringe of hair. Female's abdomen wider than carapace.

Habitat
In mantle cavity of various bivalve mollusks, tubes of parchment worms, or pharynx of tunicates, or on sea stars.

Range
British Columbia to Peru; Massachusetts to Florida and Texas.

Comments
Phylum Arthropoda, Class Crustacea. These crabs live as commensals or parasites on the body or in the cavity of a host animal that feeds on organic particles that the crab shares.

Purple Shore Crab
Hemigrapsus nudus
326, 332

2¼" (57 mm) wide, 2" (51 mm) long. Round-bodied. Upper surface of carapace purplish black, sometimes reddish brown or greenish yellow; white beneath. Pincers covered with deep purple or red spots, purple or reddish above, fading to white below. Carapace oval-oblong, arched in front, smooth; 3 short teeth on margin between eye socket and side. Eyes far apart. Pincers large in male, equal, both fingers toothed, pincer tips bent toward each other, cup-shaped. Walking legs sturdy, flattened, not very hairy.

Habitat
On open rocky shores, among seaweeds, and in bays and estuaries.

Range
Alaska to Baja California.

Comments
Phylum Arthropoda, Class Crustacea. This crab feeds primarily on the film of small algae on rocks, but is also a scavenger of animal matter.

Black-clawed Mud Crab
Lophopanopeus bellus
327

1⅜" (35 mm) wide, ⅞" (22 mm) long. Small, fan-shaped. Upper surface brown, tan, reddish brown, white, or bluish, variously mottled; fingers of pincers black with reddish-brown tips. Carapace rounded across front, sides narrowing toward straight rear margin. Area between eye sockets bowed, notched in middle. 3 teeth on side margin, last 2 sharp-pointed. Pincers stout.

Habitat
Under rocks on mud or sand bottoms, in quiet bays and estuaries, in tide pools and kelp holdfasts on rocky shores; from low-tide line to water 240' (73 m) deep.

Range
Alaska to S. California.

Comments
Phylum Arthropoda, Class Crustacea. Unlike many crabs, the female of this species mates while hard-shelled, and usually produces 2 broods per year.

Flat Porcelain Crab
Petrolisthes cinctipes
328

1″ (25 mm) long, ⅞″ (22 mm) wide. Carapace oval, flattened, almost circular. Reddish brown, legs banded near tips. Pincers large, equal; length of joint next to hand less than twice width, margins not parallel, lobe on inner margin nearest body. Fifth pair of walking legs very small and folded up between carapace and abdomen. Abdomen turned under body.

Habitat
Under stones and in spaces between shells, in mussel beds, among sponges and tunicates; between high- and low-tide lines.

Range
British Columbia to S. California.

Comments
Phylum Arthropoda, Class Crustacea. This is one of the most common crustaceans between high- and low-tide lines, especially in mussel beds and under loose stones. Porcelain crabs are filter feeders.

Yellow Shore Crab
Hemigrapsus oregonensis
329

1⅜″ (35 mm) wide, 1¼″ (32 mm) long. Round-bodied. Upper surface of carapace yellow to gray, mottled with brownish purple or black; pincer tips yellow to white. Legs hairy. Otherwise similar to the Purple Shore Crab.

Habitat
On mud flats, in eelgrass beds, in bays and estuaries; between high- and low-tide lines.

Range
Alaska to Baja California.

Comments
Phylum Arthropoda, Class Crustacea. This crab, sometimes called the Oregon Mud or Mud-flat Crab, feeds most commonly at night, eating algae that it scrapes off rocks and shells. It can bury itself in the mud quickly when pursued.

Dungeness Crab
Cancer magister
330

9¼″ (23 cm) wide, 6⅜″ (16 cm) long. Fan-shaped. Upper side grayish brown, tinged with purple, cream-colored underneath, pincers not black-tipped. Carapace oval, surface granular; 5 unequal teeth between eye sockets; margin with 10 teeth from eye socket to side, last one largest. Pincers stout, fingers bent downward at tips; walking legs short.

Habitat
On sand bottoms; from low-tide line to water more than 300′ (91 m) deep.

Range
Alaska to S. California.

Comments
Phylum Arthropoda, Class Crustacea. The Dungeness Crab is the chief crab species taken commercially on the Pacific Coast. While it occurs mainly in water more than 100' (30 m) deep, it comes into shallow water to molt. The molted skeletons washed up on the beach have caused people to think the crabs were dying of some disease.

Striped Shore Crab
Pachygrapsus crassipes
331

1⅞" (48 mm) wide, 1½" (38 mm) long. Square-bodied. Upper surface of carapace brownish purple or blackish, with green cross-stripes, fading to white beneath. Pincers mottled reddish purple above, white below; upper joint of walking legs mottled green and purple; outer joints purplish brown above, whitish below. Carapace with shallow crosswise grooves, 1 tooth on side. Eyes almost at corners, far apart. Pincers heavy, equal; fingers with spoon-shaped tips; walking legs flattened, sturdy.

Habitat
On rocky and hard-mud shores; in tide pools, mussel beds, bays and estuaries; well above low-tide line.

Range
Oregon to Baja California.

Comments
Phylum Arthropoda, Class Crustacea. This crab spends time on land, but submerges to wet its gills and feed.

Thick-clawed Porcelain Crab
Pachycheles rudis
333

¾" (19 mm) long, ⅝" (16 mm) wide. Carapace oval, flattened, nearly circular. Dull brown. Granular pincers unequal, with scattered, long hairs. Fifth pair of walking legs folded up between carapace and abdomen; abdomen turned under body.

Habitat
Under rocks, in kelp holdfasts and holes left by boring clams, among mussels on pilings; low-tide line to 60' (18 m) deep.

Range
Alaska to Baja California.

Comments
Phylum Arthropoda, Class Crustacea. These little crabs are usually found in pairs, living in a nook from which they have grown too large to escape.

Shield-backed Kelp Crab
Pugettia producta
334

3¾" (95 mm) wide, 4¾" (121 mm) long. Smooth, shield-shaped. Olive or reddish brown with darker dots, paler below. Carapace smooth, squarish, extended forward to include V-notched beak and spine to inside of eye sockets, with distance between sockets one-third of total width of carapace; prominent spine on each side, one-third distance between widest point and eye socket; 2 more strong spines toward rear end. Pincers equal, moderate size. Walking legs moderately long, sturdy; second pair longest, 1½ times body length.

Habitat
Adults in kelp beds; young near low-tide line on rocks or inshore brown algae; from low-tide line to water 240' (73 m) deep.

Range
Alaska to Baja California.

Comments
Phylum Arthropoda, Class Crustacea. The color of this crab matches the color of the kelp that it eats and on which it lives. In Puget Sound, where kelps die back in winter, it is carnivorous, feeding on barnacles, bryozoans, and hydroids.

Oregon Cancer Crab
Cancer oregonensis
335

1⅞" (48 mm) wide, 1⅜" (35 mm) long. Oval, convex. Upper side dark red, underside paler; tips of pincers black. Carapace almost round, convex, coarsely granular; area between eye sockets with 5 unequal teeth; 10 teeth from eye socket to side, carapace widest at seventh and eighth tooth. Pincers stout, short, bent downward at tips, walking legs short, hairy.

Habitat
On rocks and pilings on rocky shores; from low-tide line to water 1335' (435 m) deep.

Range
Alaska to S. California.

Comments
Phylum Arthropoda, Class Crustacea. This species lives among beds of mussels and barnacles. It feeds chiefly on these, but also eats worms, small crustaceans, and scraps of green algae.

Red Crab
Cancer productus
336

6¼" (16 cm) wide, 4¼" (108 mm) long. Fan-shaped. Upper side brick-red, underside yellowish white. Carapace oval, smooth, area between eye sockets extended forward beyond side margins, with 5 equal teeth; 9 teeth from eye socket to side. Pincers stout, short tips bent down; walking legs short.

Habitat
Among rocks, in tide pools, bays and estuaries, and on open rocky shores; from low-tide line to water 260' (79 m) deep.

Range
Alaska to S. California.

Comments
Phylum Arthropoda, Class Crustacea. Although adults are uniformly brick-red, young Red Crabs are strikingly varied; white, brown, blue, red, or orange—either solid or patterned.

Turtle Crab
Crypotolithodes sitchensis
337

2″ (51 mm) long, 2¾″ (70 mm) wide. Oval. Carapace margin concealing legs, scalloped, wide; eye sockets notched into margin; beak squarish, widest at front end. Color variable: red or purplish red on gray, brown, or olive, with or without streaks or blotches.

Habitat
Around rocks in quiet water, from low-tide line to water 50′ (15 m) deep.

Range
Alaska to S. California.

Comments
Phylum Arthropoda, Class Crustacea. At rest, this little creature resembles an old shell more than a living animal, as its legs are concealed beneath the carapace.

Pacific Rock Crab
Cancer antennarius
338

4⅝″ (117 mm) wide, 2¾″ (70 mm) long. Fan-shaped. Upper side purplish red; underside cream-colored, with many red spots; tips of fingers black. Carapace oval, finely granular; 11 teeth from eye socket to side; length two-thirds width, widest at eighth–ninth tooth. Pincers stout, short, bent downward at tips; walking legs short.

Habitat
On rocky shores, kelp beds, gravel bottoms; from between high- and low-tide lines to water 130′ (39 m) deep.

Range
Oregon to Baja California.

Comments
Phylum Arthropoda, Class Crustacea. This crab is both a scavenger and a predator, successful at devouring hermit crabs. The crab inserts the fingers of both pincers into the shell containing the hermit, chips away until the hermit can retreat no farther, and then eats it.

Blue-handed Hermit Crab
Pagurus samuelis
339

¾″ (19 mm) long, ⅝″ (16 mm) wide. Living in snail shell. Pear-shaped. Olive-brown; bright blue bands present near tips of walking legs; pincer tips pale blue; antennae red. Carapace widest at rear, beak rounded and toothlike. Antennae retractable. Abdomen soft, cylindrical, long, with reduced appendages.

Habitat
On rocky shores in tide pools on gravel bottoms and under rocks; between mid- and low-tide lines, to water more than 50′ (15 m) deep.

Range
Alaska to Baja California.

Comments
Phylum Arthropoda, Class Crustacea. Adults of this species

show a marked preference for the shells of the Black Turban Snail. A species similar in size and habitat preference is the Little Hairy Hermit Crab (*P. hirsutiusculus*), which has hairy legs with several white cross-bands, and white pincer tips against a tannish-gray background. These species have the same range.

Sharp-nosed Crab
Scyra acutifrons
340

1½" (38 mm) wide, 1¾" (44 mm) long. Pear-shaped, encrusted. Reddish brown, mottled. Carapace widest near rear; narrowing in front to a beak of 2 flat horns; surface rough but not spiny. Pincers long, equal; second walking legs longest.

Habitat
Among seaweeds and sedentary animals, under rocks, on pilings; from low-tide line to water 300' (91 m) deep.

Range
Alaska to Baja California.

Comments
Phylum Arthropoda, Class Crustacea. The carapace of this crab is usually overgrown with sponges, tunicates, barnacles, bryozoans, or hydroids. When quiet, the crab usually sits with its beak down, making it very difficult to see.

Masking Crab
Loxorhynchus crispatus
341

3½" (89 mm) wide, 4" (102 mm) long. Pear-shaped, covered with growth. Grayish brown, covered with short, brownish hairs; fingertips white. Carapace widest in rear third; side margin without spines; beak notched at tip, thick, moderately long, bent down slightly; sharp spine above and 1 beside eye. Pincers long, slender; fingers short; second pair of walking legs longest, fifth shortest.

Habitat
On rocks, pilings, and kelp holdfasts; below low-tide line to water 505' (154 m) deep.

Range
N. California to Baja California.

Comments
Phylum Arthropoda, Class Crustacea. The Masking Crab, or Moss Crab, is a "decorator," camouflaging itself with seaweed, sponges, anemones, hydroids, or bryozoans, attaching them to the hooked hairs on its back.

Pacific Mole Crab
Emerita analoga
342

1⅜" (35 mm) long, 1" (25 mm) wide. Egg-shaped. Pale grayish or tannish, appendages whitish. Carapace convex, with fine crosswise wrinkles in front, smooth in rear half. First pair of antennae hairy. Second pair of antennae long, feathery, usually concealed under edge of carapace. Eyestalks long, slender. First pair of walking legs without pincers, broad, sturdy; second, third, and fourth pairs less sturdy, hairy, leaflike; fifth pair very slender. Abdomen broad at front, tapering rapidly, with pair of forked, leaflike appendages and long, spearhead-shaped tailpiece on last segment, bent forward underneath body.

Habitat
On open sandy beaches; between high- and low-tide lines.

Range
Alaska to Peru and Chile.

Comments
Phylum Arthropoda, Class Crustacea. These crabs often occur in dense populations on open beaches. They are sometimes called Sand Crabs.

California Fiddler Crab
Uca crenulata
343

¾" (19 mm) wide, ½" (13 mm) long. Square, with 1 large pincer. Pale tan to brown, with white hands. Carapace nearly rectangular, somewhat narrowed at rear, convex, tooth behind eye socket. Eyestalks long, antennae small. Pincers of male unequal, 1 greatly enlarged, with ridge on inner surface of hand; pincers of female small, equal.

Habitat
In burrows in sandy mud in bays and estuaries; near high-tide line.

Range
S. California to Baja California.

Comments
Phylum Arthropoda, Class Crustacea. This is the only fiddler crab found on the western coast of the United States, and its future is uncertain because of encroachment on its habitat by human construction.

Beach Ghost Shrimp
Callianassa affinis
344

2⅝" (67 mm) long, ½" (13 mm) high. Long, cylindrical. White to pink. Carapace ⅓ length of abdomen, longitudinal groove along each side. Eyestalks short, almost meeting in midline; beak small, rounded. First and second walking legs with pincers, first pair unequal, one walking leg huge in male.

Habitat
Burrowing in gravel near large rocks on protected shores; in mid-tidal zone.

Range
S. California to Baja California.

Comments
Phylum Arthropoda, Class Crustacea. These animals live in pairs in a permanent burrow, which they share with a pair of blind goby fish.

Bay Ghost Shrimp
Callianassa californiensis
345

4⅝" (117 mm) long, ¾" (19 mm) high. Long, slender. Whitish, with yellow swimmerets and yellow bristles. Carapace one-third length of abdomen, transparent on sides, gills visible. Base of antennae half as long as carapace, entire antennae as long as carapace. First pair of walking legs unequal, with pincers, one huge in adult male.

Habitat
Burrowing in mud on flats, in bays and estuaries; between high- and low-tide lines.

Range
S. Alaska to Baja California.

Comments
Phylum Arthropoda, Class Crustacea. This species burrows through loose sandy mud, and may dig down more than 24" (61 cm) from the surface. Its burrow attracts numerous commensals. Some oyster farmers in the Pacific Northwest consider this shrimp a pest, as its digging in the soft bottom makes the substrate less favorable for oyster culture.

California Rock Lobster
Panulirus interruptus
346

16" (41 cm) long, 4" (102 mm) high. Long, cylindrical, spiny. Reddish brown, spines red, underside lighter brown; legs with pale brown longitudinal stripe. Carapace with rows of strong spines, largest pair of spines above eyestalks, directed forward. First pair of antennae slender, branched, two-thirds body length; second pair of antennae longer than body, large, heavy, spiny, base with strong spines. No pincers on walking legs. Upper surface of abdomen pebbled.

Habitat
Among rocks in tide pools; at low-tide line and below to moderately deep water.

Range
Central California to Baja California.

Comments
Phylum Arthropoda, Class Crustacea. These lobsters are fished commercially in California and Baja California. Anyone handling them should wear gloves because of the spines.

Spiny Mole Crab
Blepharipoda occidentalis
347

2⅜" (60 mm) long, 1⅝" (41 mm) wide. Egg-shaped. Carapace and pincers gray. Carapace has 3 spines along front midline and 4 on border at each side and deep notch on rear margin. Front half has fine indentations; rear half smooth. First pair of antennae very slender, second pair of antennae heavier, feathery. Eyestalks slender, eyes small. First pair of walking legs with pincers, heavy, spiny, hairy. Remaining walking legs smaller, but strong, leaflike. Abdomen tucked under body.

Habitat
On open sandy beaches; from low-tide line to 30' (9 m) deep.

Range
Central California to Baja California.

Comments
Phylum Arthropoda, Class Crustacea. Young Spiny Mole Crabs comb tiny organisms and organic particles from the water with their feathery antennae, but do not migrate up and down the beach with the tides. The adults are scavengers, feeding mostly on dead mole crabs (*Emerita*) that abound in the same habitat.

Coon-stripe Shrimp
Pandalus danae
348

5¾" (146 mm) long, 1¼" (32 mm) high. Large. Pale red, with irregular longitudinal blue stripes and occasional white spots on body; legs striped brown and white. Beak curved upward, long, slender, continuing as ridge on carapace; many teeth above and below on beak; 4 teeth on ridge behind level of eye socket. Second walking legs unequal, end joint beaded with many constrictions. Tailpiece with 6 spines on each side.

Habitat
In bays, estuaries, and eelgrass beds, occasionally in tide pools; from low-tide line to water 600' (182 m) deep.

Range
Alaska to central California.

Comments
Phylum Arthropoda, Class Crustacea. The Coon-stripe Shrimp is a functional male when young, subsequently changing to a fertile female. Most species of *Pandalus* live in deeper water, often in vast numbers in shrimp beds on muddy or muddy sand bottom. They form the basis for an important commercial shrimp industry. *P. jordani* is the most important commercial species in the Pacific Northwest, especially Oregon. *P. borealis,* fished off the coast of New England, is caught off Alaska and British Columbia.

Mottled Tube-maker
Jassa falcata
349

⅜" (10 mm) long, ¹⁄₁₆" (2 mm) high. Arched, slender, nearly as wide as high. Reddish, mottled with paler spots. Antennae bristly, second pair nearly twice as long as first. Oval eyes beside base of first antennae. Second walking leg with huge hand nearly one-third body length, with large thumb and long, sharp claw opposite it; last 2 pairs bent along abdomen.

Habitat
In tubes on pilings, wharves, buoys, eelgrass, and hydroid stems; near low-tide line and below to water 33' (10 m) deep.

Range
British Columbia to S. California; Newfoundland to Florida and Texas.

Comments
Phylum Arthropoda, Class Crustacea. This amphipod builds a tube out of mud, debris, and mucus, attaching it to almost

any solid surface where there is good water flow. It feeds both by straining out suspended organic particles with its bristly antennae, and by preying on small invertebrates, grasping them with its huge second walking leg.

California Beach Flea
Orchestoidea californiana
350

1⅛" (28 mm) long, ¼" (6 mm) high. Arched, stout, broad. Ivory. Juveniles with dark butterfly-shaped marks on back. First pair of antennae short, second pair of antennae longer than body, orange in juveniles, rosy red in adults. Eyes round, medium-sized, black. 7 pairs of walking legs, second pair with thick hand and long claw, last 3 pairs heavy and strong, last 2 pairs bent back along abdomen.

Habitat
On wide, fine-sand beaches along open shore; near high-tide line and above.

Range
British Columbia to S. California.

Comments
Phylum Arthropoda, Class Crustacea. At night these beach fleas can be seen in hordes on the sand above the breaking waves, leaping about and eating washed-up seaweed as the tide ebbs. When the tide returns, they move up the beach toward the high-tide line and excavate new burrows.

Harford's Greedy Isopod
Cirolana harfordi
351

¾" (19 mm) long, ¼" (6 mm) wide. Elongate, oval, flattened. Pale gray, tan, brown, blackish, 2-toned, variable. Second pair of antennae slender, one-half body length. Black eyes near side of head. 7 thoracic segments behind head, each bearing pair of walking legs tucked under body, all similar. Rounded, triangular tailpiece plus pair of flattened 2-part appendages form tail fan.

Habitat
Under stones on sandy bottom; in mussel beds between high- and low-tide lines, and kelp holdfasts below low-tide line.

Range
British Columbia to Baja California.

Comments
Phylum Arthropoda, Class Crustacea. These scavengers occur in large numbers and quickly consume any dead creature in their vicinity. They are, in turn, preyed on by a number of inshore fishes.

Western Sea Roach
Ligia occidentalis
352, 353

1" (25 mm) long, ½" (13 mm) wide. Oval, flattened, roachlike. Tannish gray, mottled. Eyes at side of head. 7 clearly defined thoracic segments, each with pair of walking legs, all similar. Tailpiece short. Last pair of appendages measuring more than one-third body length, slender, extending backward from sides of tailpiece.

Habitat
On rocks and jetties; near high-tide line and above.

Range
Central California to Central America.

Comments
Phylum Arthropoda, Class Crustacea. These creatures are more commonly hidden in crevices during the day. They become active late in the afternoon, and continue until after dawn. They undergo a daily color change, from darker during the day to paler at night. Sea roaches are larger than most isopods. They are essentially terrestrial in habits.

Vosnesensky's Isopod
Idotea wosnesenskii
354

1⅜" (35 mm) long, ½" (13 mm) wide. Elongate, straight, flattened. Almost black, also light brown, red, or green. Body sturdy, second pair of antennae one-fourth body length, straight. Eyes at side of head, 7 pairs of thoracic legs, all similar. Tailpiece rounded, with small tooth at tip, one-fourth body length. Last pair of appendages form doors enclosing gill-like appendages under tailpiece.

Habitat
Under rocks, in mussel beds, and among seaweeds, in bays and exposed rocky shores; from between high- and low-tide lines to water 53' (16 m) deep.

Range
Alaska to S. California.

Comments
Phylum Arthropoda, Class Crustacea. This species is eaten by a number of shallow-water fishes. It was named after Russian zoologist I. G. Vosnesensky, who collected animals in Siberia, Alaska, and California in the mid-19th century.

Smooth Skeleton Shrimp
Caprella laeviuscula
355

2" (51 mm) long, ¼" (6 mm) wide. Long, slender, arched, jointed. Pale tan, greenish, or rosy. Head rounded at front, long, first antenna one-third body length, twice as long as second antenna. Eyes small, round. Body smooth. First and second thoracic appendages with grasping claw, second thoracic appendage much larger. Pair of saclike gills on next 2 segments. Last 3 segments with bristly grasping appendages directed backward.

Habitat
On hydroids, bushy algae, and other growth; near low-tide line and below in shallow water.

Range
British Columbia to S. California.

Comments
Phylum Arthropoda, Class Crustacea. This species eats detritus, 1-celled plants, small invertebrates, and carrion, and is in turn eaten by various fishes, shrimps, and sea anemones.

The California Skeleton Shrimp (*C. californica*) is larger, 1⅜″ (35 mm) long and ⅟₃₂″ (1 mm) high, and buffy; it lives on eelgrass in central and southern California. There are numerous other species of *Caprella* along the coast.

Clawed Sea Spider
Phoxichilidium femoratum
356

⅛″ (3 mm) long, ⅟₁₆″ (2 mm) wide. Slender, flattened, with long neck, tiny abdomen. Pale tannish gray. Proboscis cylindrical, rounded at tip, projecting from under long neck, about one-fourth length of body; pinchers longer than proboscis on each side, but no feelerlike appendages. 4 eyes on projection behind proboscis. 4 pairs of slender legs about ½″ (13 mm) long, with extra clawlet beside claw at tip. Only male has accessory legs.

Habitat
Among hydroids and other growth on rocks; near low-tide line and below to water 332′ (101 m) deep.

Range
Alaska to central California; Arctic to Long Island Sound.

Comments
Phylum Arthropoda, Class Pycnogonida. This sea spider is most commonly found among dense growths of tubularian hydroids, on which it feeds.

Stearns' Sea Spider
Pycnogonum stearnsi
357

½″ (13 mm) long, ⅛″ (3 mm) wide. Salmon-pink, ivory, or white. Surface smooth. Eyes lacking. 4 pairs of short, stout legs; male has pair of accessory appendages for carrying eggs.

Habitat
Under rocks, associated with sea anemones, hydroids, and tunicates; from midtidal zone to low-tide line.

Range
British Columbia to central California.

Comments
Phylum Arthropoda, Class Pycnogonida. This species preys chiefly on the Giant Green Anemone, but also on the Frilled Anemone, the Proliferating Anemone, and possibly the Ostrich-plume Hydroid. This sea spider sucks fluid and other food material from anemones by means of its proboscis, which it inserts into the tissue of its host.

Burrowing Brittle Star
Amphiodia occidentalis
358

Disk diameter ½″ (13 mm), arm length 6⅝″ (17 cm). Extremely long-armed. Gray to tannish gray, mottled, dark spot on disk at base of each arm. Disk almost circular, smooth, lacking spines or plates; jaws with 4–5 teeth. Arms 15 times width of disk, slender; vertical row of 3 blunt spines at side of arm joint.

Habitat
In sand under rocks, in algal and kelp holdfasts, on mud flats,

and among eelgrass roots; from low-tide line to water 1210' (369 m) deep.

Range
Alaska to S. California.

Comments
Phylum Echinodermata, Class Stelleroidea, Subclass Ophiuroidea. This brittle star's long, slender arms are sometimes lost to predators, and it is common to find specimens in the process of regenerating ends of arms.

Dwarf Brittle Star
Axiognathus squamata
359

Disk diameter ¼" (6 mm), arm length 1" (25 mm). Tiny, long-armed. Tan, gray, or orange; white spot at margin near base of each arm. Disk round, plump, surface covered with fine scales, 2 large scales at base of each arm; jaws with 2 rounded teeth on each side. Arms with oval plate on top of each joint, vertical row of 3 short spines on each side.

Habitat
Among rocks and gravel in tide pools, in crevices and algal holdfasts, on rocky shores; from between high- and low-tide lines to water 2716' (828 m) deep.

Range
Alaska to S. California; Arctic to Florida.

Comments
Phylum Echinodermata, Class Stelleroidea, Subclass Ophiuroidea. This little brittle star is bioluminescent, capable of emitting light. The Puget Dwarf Brittle Star (*A. pugetanus*), which ranges from British Columbia to southern California, has the same disk diameter, but longer arms, 1½" (38 mm), and is gray or banded with gray and white.

Panama Brittle Star
Ophioderma panamense
360

Disk diameter 1¾" (44 mm), arm length 10" (25 cm). Long-armed. Olive or grayish brown, with buff bands on arms. Central disk pentagonal, flat, granular above, mouth 5-pointed, closable; 2 slits into each respiratory pouch, 1 near mouth, 1 next to arm where it joins disk. 7–8 short spines in vertical row on side of each joint, held close against arm.

Habitat
Among rocks and seaweeds on sand bottoms; near low-tide line and below in shallow water.

Range
S. California to Peru.

Comments
Phylum Echinodermata, Class Stelleroidea, Subclass Ophiuroidea. This predatory brittle star can live successfully in marine aquaria for several years, feeding on bits of fish or clam meat. When the star senses food, it advances, sweeping the lead arms back and forth. As soon as it touches the food, it coils an arm around it, brings to the mouth, and swallows it.

Esmark's Brittle Star
Ophioplocus esmarki
361

Disk diameter 1¼" (32 mm), arm length 3¾" (95 mm).
Brown or red-brown. Arm spines very short; surface of disk
smooth.

Habitat
Under rocks and in crevices; from low-tide line to water 220'
(67 m) deep.

Range
N. California to S. California.

Comments
Phylum Echinodermata, Class Stelleroidea, Subclass
Ophiuroidea. This slow-moving species captures slower-
moving prey, or scavenges for particles of food. It is rugged
and does not fragment when handled.

Daisy Brittle Star
Ophiopholis aculeata
362

Disk diameter ¾" (19 mm), arm length 3⅝" (92 mm). Long-
armed. Red, orange, pink, yellow, white, blue, green, tan,
brown, gray, and black, in infinite variety of spots, lines,
bands, and mottlings. Central disk scalloped, a lobe
protruding between adjacent arms, covered with fine, blunt
spines and roundish plates. Plates on top of arms surrounded
by row of small scales; joints with 5–6 bluntly tapered spines
in vertical rows on side of arm.

Habitat
Under rocks in tide pools, among kelp holdfasts; from low-
tide line to water 5435' (1657 m) deep.

Range
Bering Sea to S. California; Arctic to Cape Cod.

Comments
Phylum Echinodermata, Class Stelleroidea, Subclass
Ophiuroidea. These elegant brittle stars are an exotic sight in
a tide pool, scrambling into hiding when one exposes them by
lifting away their rock.

Armored Sea Star
Astropecten armatus
363

Radius 6" (15 cm). Flattened. Gray to beige. Upper surface
covered with rosettes of small spines. 5 arms edged with row
of plates bearing movable spines; tube feet pointed and
lacking suckers.

Habitat
In bays and outer coasts on sand bottoms; from low-tide line
to water 200' (61 m) deep.

Range
S. California to Ecuador.

Comments
Phylum Echinodermata, Class Stelleroidea, Subclass
Asteroidea. This sea star feeds on the Purple Dwarf Olive and
other snails, sand dollars, and sea pansies. It also scavenges.

Spiny Brittle Star
Ophiothrix spiculata
364

Disk diameter ¾" (19 mm), arm length 6" (15 cm). Spiny. Orange, yellow, tan, brown, green; variously patterned. Long, thorny spines on margins of arms and disk.

Habitat
Under rocks, in crevices and mats of algae or invertebrates; from low-tide line to water 660' (200 m) deep.

Range
Central California to Peru.

Comments
Phylum Echinodermata, Class Stelleroidea, Subclass Ophiuroidea. *O. spiculata* occurs in large concentrations in favorable habitats. Kelp holdfasts and clumps of bryozoans and worm tubes are often writhing masses of *Ophiothrix* arms. Individuals anchor themselves with the spines of one or more arms, and extend the others into the water for filter feeding.

Pacific Comet Star
Linckia columbiae
365

Radius 3⅝" (92 mm). Long-armed. Gray, mottled with red or red-brown. 5 long arms usual, but may vary from 1–9; arms rarely symmetrical.

Habitat
On rocky shores; from low-tide line to water 240' (73 m) deep.

Range
S. California to Colombia.

Comments
Phylum Echinodermata, Class Stelleroidea, Subclass Asteroidea. *Linckia*'s powers of regeneration far exceed those of our other sea stars. A shed arm will regenerate a new disk and arms to complete a new star.

Pacific Henricia
Henricia leviuscula
366

Radius 3⅝" (92 mm). Disk small. 5 long, slender, tapering arms usual, but may vary from 4–6. Tan, yellow, orange, red, or purplish, usually spotted or mottled. Often has fine network of short spinelets.

Habitat
On and under rocks with growth of sponges, bryozoans, or algae, in protected places; from low-tide line to water 1320' (402 m) deep.

Range
Alaska to Baja California.

Comments
Phylum Echinodermata, Class Stelleroidea, Subclass Asteroidea. Breeding habits in this sea star vary with size. Smaller females brood their eggs in a depression around the mouth formed by arching the arms. Larger females discharge eggs directly into the water and do not brood them.

Broad Six-rayed Sea Star
Leptasterias hexactis
367

Radius 2" (51 mm). 6-armed. Green, black, brown, or red, sometimes mottled. Disk moderate-sized with 6 fairly broad arms; spines on upper surface dense and mushroom-shaped.

Habitat
On rocky shores; well above low-tide line and below in shallow water.

Range
British Columbia to S. California.

Comments
Phylum Echinodermata, Class Stelleroidea, Subclass Asteroidea. *L. hexactis,* also called the Six-armed Star, eats small snails, limpets, mussels, chitons, barnacles, sea cucumbers, and other species, including dead animals. It produces yellow, yolky eggs that stick together in a mass after fertilization. These are brooded under the disk of the female until they hatch as miniature sea stars after 6 to 8 weeks. The small 6-rayed sea stars of the West Coast are quite variable and have presented problems of identification. The only other species currently recognized is the Small Slender Sea Star (*L. pusilla*), which has sharp spines and longer, thinner arms than *L. hexactis,* and is a light gray-brown or reddish color. It also has a very limited range, from San Francisco to Monterey Bay.

Troschel's Sea Star
Evasterias troschelii
368

Radius 8" (20 cm). Slender. Orange to brown to blue-gray, sometimes mottled. Small central disk and 5 slim, tapering arms.

Habitat
On rock or sand bottoms, usually in quiet water; from low-tide line to water 230' (70 m) deep.

Range
Alaska to central California.

Comments
Phylum Echinodermata, Class Stelleroidea, Subclass Asteroidea. Like the Ochre Sea Star, from which it can be distinguished by its smaller disk and thin arms, Troschel's Sea Star does not do well in areas exposed to heavy wave action. The Fragile Scale Worm occurs as a commensal on this species, and may often match the color of its host.

Ochre Sea Star
Pisaster ochraceus
369

Radius 10" (25 cm). Heavy. Yellow, orange, brown, reddish, or purple. Central disk moderately large, with 5 stout, tapering arms; upper surface with many short, white spines in netlike or pentagonal pattern on central disk.

Habitat
On wave-washed rocky shores; well above low-tide line, and sometimes below.

Range
Alaska to Baja California.

Comments
Phylum Echinodermata, Class Stelleroidea, Subclass
Asteroidea. This is the commonest large, intertidal sea star,
and it occurs in great numbers on mussel beds on the coast.

Giant Sea Star
Pisaster giganteus
370

Radius 12″ (30 cm). Heavy. Red, brown, tan, or purple, with
blue rings around base of spines. Body tough, firm; arms
thick; spines large and well-spaced.

Habitat
On rocky shores and in shallow water on rock bottoms; near
low-tide line and below.

Range
British Columbia to Baja California.

Comments
Phylum Echinodermata, Class Stelleroidea, Subclass
Asteroidea. In southern California, Kellet's Whelk (*Kelletia
kelletii*) has been observed sharing food with *P. giganteus,* but
the whelk itself sometimes falls prey to the Giant Sea Star.

Bat Star
Patiria miniata
371

Radius 4″ (102 mm). Short-armed. Most commonly reddish
orange, but highly variable in color and pattern. Usually 5
but sometimes 4–9 broad, short arms; lacks spines and
pinchers.

Habitat
On rocks, among surfgrass, and on rock and sand bottoms;
from low-tide line to water 960′ (293 m) deep.

Range
Alaska to Baja California.

Comments
Phylum Echinodermata, Class Stelleroidea, Subclass
Asteroidea. This is the most abundant sea star on the West
Coast, where it is especially numerous in certain kelp forests.
It is sometimes called the Sea Bat.

Leather Star
Dermasterias imbricata
372

Radius 4¾″ (121 mm). Blue-gray network with red or orange
in the spaces between. Disk large and high, with 5 arms;
upper surface feels like wet leather; body has a strong garlic
odor.

Habitat
On rocky shores, in clean harbors on pilings and sea walls;
from low-tide line to water 300′ (91 m) deep.

Range
Alaska to S. California.

Comments
Phylum Echinodermata, Class Stelleroida, Subclass Asteroidea.
D. imbricata feeds on anemones, sea cucumbers, the Purple Sea

Urchin, and a variety of other invertebrates. The anemone Red Stomphia will release itself from its substrate and swim away when touched by the Leather Star.

Spiny Sun Star
Crossaster papposus
373

Radius 7" (18 cm). Many-armed. Scarlet above, with concentric bands of white, pink, yellowish, or dark red; white underneath. Central disk large, with netlike pattern of raised ridges; 8–14 arms, length one-half radius. Entire upper surface sparsely covered with brushlike spines; marginal spines larger. Mouth area bare. 2 rows of sucker-tipped tube feet in grooves.

Habitat
On rock bottoms; from low-tide line to 1080' (329 m) deep.

Range
Alaska to Puget Sound; Arctic to Gulf of Maine.

Comments
Phylum Echinodermata, Class Stelleroidea, Subclass Asteroidea. Among the most beautiful of echinoderms, these sea stars seem to be sunbursts of color. They are predatory on smaller sea stars, swallowing them whole.

Dawson's Sun Star
Solaster dawsoni
374

Radius 10" (25 cm). Radius of central disk one-third total radius. Many-armed. Upper surface gray, yellow, brown, or sometimes red, often with light patches. 8–13 arms.

Habitat
On variety of bottom types; from low-tide line to water 1200' (420 m) deep.

Range
Alaska to central California.

Comments
Phylum Echinodermata, Class Stelleroidea, Subclass Asteroidea. *S. dawsoni* often preys on sea stars, even cannibalizing its own species. It also feeds on some sea cucumbers and the Diamondback Nudibranch (*Tritonia festiva*). It is seen washed up on the beach after storms. Stimpson's Sea Star (*S. stimpsoni*) is a closely related species with a similar range, a radius of 3¼" (83 mm), and 9–11 arms, which are more slender. Its color is red, orange, yellow, green, or blue, with a blue-gray spot on the central disk continuing as a stripe down each arm.

Sunflower Star
Pycnopodia helianthoides
375

Radius 26" (66 cm). Many-armed. Purple, red, pink, brown, orange, or yellow. Disk broad, 24 arms; surface soft and flexible; spines, pinchers, and soft gills abundant.

Habitat
On rocky shores and soft bottoms; from low-tide line to water 1435' (437 m) deep.

Range
Alaska to S. California.

Comments
Phylum Echinodermata, Class Stelleroidea, Subclass Asteroidea. This is the largest, most active sea star on the Pacific Coast, and to see one in motion is an impressive experience. A large *Pycnopodia* has more than 15,000 tube feet that have to be coordinated in its stepping movements.

Eccentric Sand Dollar
Dendraster excentricus
376

3" (76 mm) wide, ¼" (6 mm) high. Disk-shaped. Light lavender-gray, brown, reddish brown, or dark purple-black. Test almost circular, flattened, 5 petal-shaped loops of tube feet on upper dorsal surface; both surfaces covered by short, fine spines. Mouth central on lower surface, anus at rear margin.

Habitat
On sand bottoms of sheltered bays and open coasts; from low-tide line to water 130' (40 m) deep.

Range
Alaska to Baja California.

Comments
Phylum Echinodermata, Class Echinoidea. The sand dollar most familiar to beachcombers is the dead, clean test of this species found along sandy shores. The 5 petal-shaped areas on the upper surface are the slits from which the respiratory tube feet emerge.

Heart Urchin
Lovenia cordiformis
377

3" (76 mm) long, 2⅜" (60 mm) wide. White, gray, yellow, rose, or purple. Heart-shaped. Outline indented at front end, extending as groove containing front petal. Upper surface convex, covered with numerous small spines and fewer long spines more than 2¾" (70 mm) long. Lower surface flat, mouth forward of center, anus at rear margin.

Habitat
On sand bottoms in bays and outer coasts; from low-tide line to water 460' (140 m) deep.

Range
S. California to Panama.

Comments
Phylum Echinodermata, Class Echinoidea. *Lovenia* lives in a burrow just below the surface of the sand. The tube feet extend up a vertical shaft to the surface and sift surface deposits for fine organic particles.

Giant Pacific Octopus
Octopus dofleini
378

Body plus longest arm 16' (5 m) long. Globe-shaped, with 4 pairs of arms. Reddish or brownish, with fine black lines; color changeable. Arms 3–5 times body length, with 2 alternating rows of suckers; tubular siphon under neck. Head as broad as body, with eyes high on each side. Skin wrinkled and folded.

Habitat
On rocky shores, in tide pools; from low-tide line to water 1650' (503 m) deep.

Range
Alaska to S. California.

Comments
Phylum Mollusca, Class Cephalopoda. This species is one of the largest known octopods, the heaviest on record weighing nearly 600 pounds (272 kg). It is fished commercially from Alaska to northern California. The Giant Pacific Octopus feeds on shrimps, crabs, scallops, abalones, clams, various fishes, and smaller octopods, and is eaten by seals, sea otters, sharks, and other large fishes.

Two-spotted Octopus
Octopus bimaculatus
379, 380

Body plus longest arm 30" (76 cm) long. Pear-shaped, with 4 pairs of arms. Usually gray, brown, olive, or reddish; mottled with black, mantle paler underneath, variable. Arms 4–5 times mantle length, with 2 alternating rows of suckers; web between arms. Head narrow, eyes high on sides of head; conspicuous black spot below each eye. Mantle with many prickly bumps.

Habitat
In holes, under rocks, and among kelps; from low-tide line to water 160' (49 m) deep.

Range
S. California to Baja California and Gulf of California.

Comments
Phylum Mollusca, Class Cephalopoda. In 1949 it was discovered that there were 2 closely related species of Two-spotted Octopods instead of one. The second was named the Mud Flat Octopus (*O. bimaculoides*). This is the species most commonly found between high- and low-tide lines, on mud flats as well as among rocks. Its arms are shorter, 2½–3½ times mantle length, and its eggs are larger. However, the first clue that there were 2 species instead of one was offered by the discovery that there were 2 different populations of kidney parasites (mesozoa) in the Two-spotted Octopus. It is noted that the males and females at breeding time have no trouble distinguishing between the species.

Opalescent Squid
Loligo opalescens
381

Mantle 7⅝" (20 cm) long, 1¾" (44 mm) wide. Cylindrical, tapered to point at rear. White, mottled gold, brown, or red; color changeable. Head with pair of large eyes, 4 pairs of arms about one-half mantle length, 1 pair of tentacles two-thirds mantle length; siphon under neck; triangular fin one-half mantle length on each side of rear.

Habitat
Ocean surface to bottom in open coastal waters; around outer fringes of kelp beds.

Range
British Columbia to Mexico.

Comments
Phylum Mollusca, Class Cephalopoda. Fast, agile swimmers, squid prey actively on small fish and invertebrates. Most frozen squid found in American fish markets and food stores are of this species. They are taken by net in large numbers when they enter shallow water to breed.

Beroë's Comb Jelly
Beroe cucumis
382

4½" (115 mm) high, 2" (55 mm) wide. Flattened, purselike, lacking tentacles and lobes. Translucent; pink to rust. Mouth broad, occupying entire oral end. 8 rows of comb plates extend over one-half length of body. Under each row lies a canal with abundant branches that end blindly.

Habitat
In nearshore waters and bays.

Range
Alaska to S. California; New Brunswick to Cape Cod.

Comments
Phylum Ctenophora. Beroë's Comb Jelly feeds chiefly on cnidarian medusae and other comb jellies. A West Coast species, Forskal's Comb Jelly (*B. forskali*), differs in having the branches of neighboring canals united into a network, but it is roughly triangular. It is the same size as *B. cucumis*.

Purple Jellyfish ⊗
Pelagia noctiluca
383

3" (76 mm) high, 4" (102 mm) wide. Bell hemispherical. Rose-pink to purple or yellow. Warty. Margin has 16 rectangular lobes that alternate with 8 long, rosy pink tentacles and 8 marginal sense organs. Feeding tube long, thick, extending far below the bell as 4 long, frilly, pink-edged lips surrounding the mouth. Four pink, ribbonlike gonads, placed horizontally. Luminescent at night.

Habitat
Surface of open ocean; sometimes washed ashore by storms.

Range
Warm waters off North and South America.

Comments
Phylum Cnidaria, Class Scyphozoa. Mildly toxic. *Pelagia noctiluca* occurs in large swarms, which appear as glowing white balls at night. The Purple Banded Jellyfish (*P. colorata*), a much larger form, 32" (80 cm) wide and 24" (61 cm) high, is a Pacific species that is sometimes seen in the tide pools and along the West Coast of the United States. It is a handsome creature, with deep purple radial bands on a silvery-white background. It is highly toxic.

Moon Jellyfish ⊗
Aurelia aurita
384

3" (76 mm) high, 16" (41 cm) wide. Saucer-shaped. Whitish, translucent. 8 shallow marginal lobes, sense organs in 8 clefts between lobes. Numerous short, fringelike tentacles. Feeding tube short, stout, expanding as 4 long oral arms with frilly margins. Numerous branching radial canals. Reproductive organs horseshoe-shaped or round. Ripe female organs: yellowish, pink, or violet; males': yellow, yellow-brown, or rose; immatures': whitish.

Habitat
Floats near surface; just offshore.

Range
Alaska to S. California; Arctic to Florida and Mexico.

Comments
Phylum Cnidaria, Class Scyphozoa. Mildly toxic. This is the jellyfish most commonly washed up on beaches during high tide or after a storm. Its sting causes a slight rash that may itch for several hours.

**Many-ribbed
Hydromedusa**
Aequorea aequorea
385

Medusa 1½" (38 mm) high, 7" (18 cm) wide. Saucer-shaped. Glassy-transparent with thick jelly. Radial canals narrow, 80 or more. Marginal tentacles long, numbers vary. Feeding tube short, wide; mouth with ruffled lips. Gonads slender, extending most of length of radial canals, bluish in male, rosy in female. Polyp stage unknown.

Habitat
Floating in open water, occasionally near shore.

Range
Alaska to California; Maine to Texas.

Comments
Phylum Cnidaria, Class Hydrozoa. This worldwide species of familiar jellyfish is frequently washed up on beaches. It is luminescent, and at night one can see the outline of its parts in "living light."

Penicillate Jellyfish
Polyorchis penicillatus
386

Medusa 1⅝" (41 mm) high, 1⅜" (35 mm) wide. Bell globular, transparent, with 90 tentacles on margin, each with a dark red base bearing an eyespot. 4 radial canals with numerous short side branches, and numerous long, slender gonads suspended below each canal; feeding tube short, with 4-cornered mouth at top. Polyp stage unknown.

Habitat
Floating in coastal and bay waters.

Range
British Columbia to S. California.

Comments
Phylum Cnidaria, Class Hydrozoa. This is among the largest of hydromedusae on the West Coast.

Sea Gooseberry
Pleurobrachia bachei
387

1⅛" (28 mm) high, 1" (25 mm) wide. Round to egg-shaped. Transparent, iridescent. 2 tentacles, each fringed on 1 side, can extend over 20 times body length or retract completely. 8 rows of comb plates, equally spaced, extend nearly full length of body. Pharynx, stomach and its branches, and tentacles and sheaths white, pink, yellow, or orange-brown.

Habitat
Near shore; usually in large swarms.

Range
Alaska to Baja California.

Comments
Phylum Ctenophora. Unlike many jellyfish, Sea Gooseberries (sometimes called "Cats Eyes") do not sting. The sticky filaments of the trailing tentacles capture small crustaceans, fish eggs and larvae, and other planktonic animals. The tentacles then contract and wipe the prey off on the mouth, which immediately swallows it. A voracious carnivore, swarms can decimate schools of young herring and cod. The Arctic Sea Gooseberry (*Mertensia ovum*) is more egg-shaped, flatter, and larger, 2" (51 mm) high and 1" (25 mm) wide. It occurs in central California, and from the Arctic to the Gulf of Maine, and sometimes in winter to Cape Cod.

Angled Hydromedusa
Gonionemus vertens
388

Medusa ½" (13 mm) high, ¾" (19 mm) wide. Dome-shaped. Transparent. Feeding tube not quite reaching bell margin, thickest where attached. Mouth has 4 slightly frilled lips. Ruffled sex organs extend along most of length of 4 radial canals, creating cross-shaped marking. 60 long marginal tentacles, each with spiral or ringlike clusters of stinging cells and an adhesive sucker near end. Feeding tube, gonads, and tentacle bases yellowish tan to reddish brown. Polyp stage unknown.

Habitat
Floating in shallow water; sometimes clinging to eelgrass.

Range
Alaska to central California; common in Puget Sound; Arctic to Cape Cod.

Comments
Phylum Cnidaria, Class Hydrozoa. When the medusa attaches itself to a rock or seaweed, the tentacles form an angle at the sucker, hence the species' name.

Lion's Mane ⊗
Cyanea capillata
389

24" (61 cm) high, 96" (244 cm) wide. Bell saucer-shaped, upper surface smooth. Color varies with age and, thus, size; pink and yellowish to 5" (127 mm), reddish to yellow-brown to 18" (46 cm), darker red-brown when larger. 16 marginal lobes. Shaggy clusters of more than 150 tentacles attached beneath 8 deep clefts between lobes, marginal sense organs in 8 shallower clefts. Feeding tube stout, extending as 4 much-folded, membranous lips around mouth. 4 highly folded, ribbonlike gonads suspended under bell alternate with lips.

Habitat
Floats near surface.

Range
Alaska to S. California; Arctic to Florida and Mexico.

Comments
Phylum Cnidaria, Class Scyphozoa. Highly toxic. This is the largest jellyfish in the world. Although most individuals are 1–2 feet in diameter, specimens 8 feet wide have been found. Contact with *Cyanea*'s tentacles produces severe burning and blistering. Prolonged exposure may cause muscle cramps and breathing difficulties. In Sir Arthur Conan Doyle's story, "The Adventure of the Lion's Mane," Sherlock Holmes solves a homicide caused by contact between the victim and this medusa in a tidepool.

By-the-wind Sailor
Velella velella
390

Float 4" (102 mm) long, 3" (76 mm) wide, 2" (51 mm) high. Float consisting of flat, oval, cartilagelike skeleton full of gas-filled pockets, with vertical triangular crest set diagonally across the top, serving as a sail. Blue, transparent. Single large-mouthed feeding tube, surrounded by rows of reproductive bodies. Numerous blue tentacles around the rim.

Habitat
Surface of the sea.

Range
Warm waters. As far north as central California from the tropical Pacific; in the East, driven ashore from the Gulf Stream by storms, as far north as Cape Hatteras, or occasionally farther.

Comments
Phylum Cnidaria, Class Hydrozoa. Although they contain stinging cells, the tentacles of the Sailor are harmless to man. The By-the-wind Sailor can "tack" in the manner of a sailboat. On the West Coast in the spring it is occasionally driven ashore in large numbers.

Bat Star Worm
Ophiodromus pugettensis
391

To 1½" (40 mm) long, ⅛" (3 mm) wide. Robust. Reddish brown to purple or black. Lobe above mouth with 3 antennae, 2 pairs of eyes; head with 6 pairs of tentacles. Appendages with long dorsal filaments.

Habitat
Free-living on mud bottoms or among marine growth; or commensal among the tube feet of sea stars, particularly the Bat Star; from above low-tide line out onto the continental shelf.

Range
Entire Pacific Coast.

Comments
Phylum Annelida, Subclass Errantia. These worms may be
free-living or live on sea stars. Those removed from a sea star
will readily return to it, and will also be attracted to a sample
of water that the star once occupied, scenting its presence.
The Bat Star host may have as many as 20 worms on it at
once, and worms will leave one star for another that
approaches. On the other hand, free-living worms are
oblivious to sea stars. Larvae can be found in the water at all
times of the year, with seasonal peaks in February and May in
southern California.

Polydora Mud Worm
Polydora ligni
392

1″ (25 mm) long, ¹⁄₁₆″ (2 mm) wide. In a mud-covered tube.
Slender, cylindrical. Translucent, reddish. Head with 2 long
antennae (which are easily lost), lobe above mouth forked in
front, with 4 eyes arranged in a rectangle; fifth bristle-bearing
segment with large group of long bristles pointing upward;
tail somewhat flared. 14 pairs of gills, usually beginning with
segment 12.

Habitat
In soft, fragile tubes covered with mud and attached to hard
objects in protected places on mud and clay bottoms; near
low-tide line and in shallow water.

Range
California; entire East Coast.

Comments
Phylum Annelida, Class Polychaeta, Subclass Sedentaria.
These worms are sometimes so abundant in oyster beds that
they bury the oysters in several inches of mud tubes. There are
many species in the genus *Polydora,* some of them boring into
oyster shells or snail shells occupied by hermit crabs.

**Sinistral Spiral Tube
Worm**
Spirorbis borealis
393

⅛″ (3 mm) long, ⅛″ (3 mm) wide. In limy tube coiled like a
snail shell, counterclockwise to left from opening toward
center. Tiny worm inside. Whitish, translucent. 9 feathery
gills; stalked lid; collar of 3 segments.

Habitat
Attached to kelps, Irish moss, and other algae, and to rocks
and shells; from above low-tide line to shallow depths.

Range
Entire Pacific Coast; Maine to Cape Cod.

Comments
Phylum Annelida, Class Polychaeta, Subclass Sedentaria.
These worms are unusual among polychaetes in being
hermaphroditic; the forward segments of the abdomen are
female and the rear ones male. The tube of the Dextral Spiral
Tube Worm (*S. spirillum*) coils to the right. The worm itself is
similar to *S. borealis* in measurements, habitat, and
distribution.

Common White Synapta
Leptosynapta inhaerens
394

6″ (15 cm) long, ⅜″ (10 mm) wide. Wormlike. Translucent pinkish to brownish white. Long, slender, smooth, fragile; 5 white longitudinal muscle bands visible through body wall. No tube feet. 10–12 retractable featherlike tentacles, each with 5–7 branches on opposite sides of stalk.

Habitat
On sand and sandy mud; from low-tide line to water 637′ (194 m) deep.

Range
Puget Sound to S. California; Maine to South Carolina and Bermuda.

Comments
Phylum Echinodermata, Class Holothuroidea. Its weight, when its digestive system is full of sand, and its delicate construction make this animal difficult to handle without breaking it. It can, however, regenerate pieces of its body.

Red Lineus
Lineus ruber
395

8″ (20 cm) long, ⅛″ (3 mm) wide. Slender, slightly flattened, head wider than adjacent part of body. Dark red, brownish, or greenish, pale at borders, sometimes ringed with faint, white lines, with 4–8 black eyespots and longitudinal sensory groove on each side.

Habitat
Under rocks and shells, and among mussels and algal growth on both sand and mud bottoms; above low-tide line and below to shallow depths.

Range
Washington to central California; Maine to Long Island.

Comments
Phylum Rhynchocoela, Class Anopla. The Red Lineus tolerates low salinities well. Some biologists regard the greenish form of this animal as a separate species.

Red Tube Worm
Serpula vermicularis
396

4″ (102 mm) long, ¼″ (6 mm) wide. In sinuous, limy tubes 4″ (102 mm) long. Collar prominent, abdomen tapered. Pinkish or red-orange; plume of 40 pairs of gills pink, orange, or red, with whitish bands. Lid funnel-shaped, with 160 fine notches on the border.

Habitat
Attached to rocks, pilings, floats, and shells in protected harbors and tide pools, and on open shores; from low-tide line to water more than 300′ (91 m) deep.

Range
Alaska to S. California.

Comments
Phylum Annelida, Class Polychaeta, Subclass Sedentaria. This worm's gills are used both for respiration and for plankton

feeding. When disturbed, they snap back into their tube with great speed, and the buttonlike operculum closes the entrance. This species was named in 1767 by the father of our modern system of classifying animals and plants, Carolus Linnaeus. Though he described it from specimens obtained in the North Atlantic, it does not occur on the eastern shores of the United States.

Tailed Priapulid Worm
Priapulus caudatus
397

3¼" (83 mm) long, ½" (13 mm) wide. Slender, cylindrical. Cream-colored, buff, yellowish, or tan. Trunk cylindrical, with numerous encircling, indented rings with tiny, wartlike nodules, especially on last few rings. Large, completely retractable, club-shaped proboscis one-third trunk length, with 25 longitudinal rows of fine spines; mouth at end, surrounded by 3 rings of large, brown, inward-directed hooks. Rear end with greatly stretchable tail appendage resembling bunch of grapes.

Habitat
Soft mud; from low-tide line to water 1650' (500 m) deep.

Range
Puget Sound to central California; Arctic to Maine.

Comments
Phylum Aschelminthes. While the rings on this worm's body look like segments, they are only superficial constrictions. *Priapulus* probes through soft mud by alternately extending and retracting its proboscis. When it encounters a prey organism, usually a polychaete worm, it grabs it with the hooks surrounding its mouth, retracts the proboscis, and swallows the prey whole.

Agassiz's Peanut Worm
Phascolosoma agassizii
398

4¾" (121 mm) long, ½" (13 mm) wide. Long and slender; no appendages. Trunk light to dark brown, sometimes with purplish or brown spots; extensible front end paler, with irregular dark rings. Trunk rough, cylindrical, tapered to a blunt point at rear, covered with papillae, largest ones at rear end; extensible front end narrow, armed with 25 rings of small, toothlike spines, mouth surrounded by ring of small, slender tentacles.

Habitat
In sand, under rocks, in roots of surfgrass, and in kelp holdfasts, mussel beds, and on pilings; above low-tide line.

Range
Alaska to Baja California.

Comments
Phylum Sipuncula. This is the most common species of sipunculid on the West Coast. The free-swimming plankton-feeding larvae are long-lived, enabling them to achieve wide dispersal by water currents before settling down as juvenile worms.

Innkeeper Worm
Urechis caupo
399

7¼" (18 cm) long, 1¾" (44 mm) wide. Sausage-shaped. Yellowish pink. Trunk smooth, cylindrical; pair of hooklike bristles near head end, circle of 11 strong bristles around anus. Short proboscis at front end, shaped like spoon with sides turned up.

Habitat
Sandy mud flats.

Range
N. to S. California.

Comments
Phylum Echiura. *Urechis* is called the Innkeeper Worm because its U-shaped burrow is also inhabited by many commensals, including a goby fish, a scale worm, and 2 species of crabs. A tiny clam succeeds in living a foot or more down in mud by the simple expedient of poking its siphons into the Innkeeper Worm's burrow, and drawing water from and expelling it into the burrow, rather than having to come to the surface.

Eyed Fringed Worm
Cirratulus cirratus
400

4¾" (120 mm) long, ⅛" (3 mm) wide. In mud tubes. Cylindrical. Orange to yellowish. Head bluntly pointed, with 2–9 pairs of eyes on top, arranged in an arc. Cluster of long filaments on first bristle-bearing segment, 1 or more pairs on most of the rest.

Habitat
Under rocks, mussel beds, and sponges; from near low-tide line to shallow depths.

Range
Entire Pacific Coast; Maine to Cape Cod.

Comments
Phylum Annelida, Class Polychaeta, Subclass Sedentaria. The Eyed Fringed Worm feeds by extending its filaments out of the tube and sweeping them over the bottom, picking up small organic particles for food. The filaments are fragile, and are easily broken off when the worm is handled.

Chevron Amphiporus
Amphiporus angulatus
401, 402

6" (15 cm) long, ⅜" (10 mm) wide. Thick, slimy. Reddish brown to purplish above, whitish or pinkish below, rounded head demarked by whitish sensory grooves, forming a rear-pointing chevron. Pale area with 12 small eyespots on each side in front of chevron; 20 larger eyespots along each side of front margin, separated from other eyespots by a thin, pale line; proboscis thick, pinkish.

Habitat
Beneath rocks in sandy or gravelly places; from above low-tide line to water more than 450' (140 m) deep.

Range
Washington to S. California; Maine to Cape Cod.

Comments
Phylum Rhynchocoela, Class Enopla. This species may be mistaken for a leech. There are at least 17 species of *Amphiporus* along the West Coast, making this the most common genus there. The Blood Nemertean (*A. cruentatus*), similar in shape to *A. angulatus,* is 1⅜" (35 mm) long and ⅛" (3 mm) wide, and is translucent yellow, pink, or orange, with 3 longitudinal vessels containing red blood. It ranges along the entire Pacific Coast, and from Massachusetts to both coasts of Florida; it is found among hydroids, bryozoans, and algae, on rock and shell bottoms, from low-tide line to water 240' (73 m) deep.

Opal Worm
Arabella iricolor
403

To 24" (60 cm) long, ¼" (6 mm) wide. Long, slender. Reddish brown, reddish yellow, or greenish, with brilliant metallic iridescence. 500 segments; head without antennae or tentacles; lobe above mouth bluntly conical, with 4 black eyes in a row at rear margin. Paired appendages simple, small.

Habitat
Burrowing in sand and sandy mud, in oyster and mussel beds, and among eelgrass roots, invading estuaries with low salinities; from low-tide line to water 275' (95 m) deep.

Range
Entire Pacific Coast; Massachusetts to Florida and Texas.

Comments
Phylum Annelida, Class Polychaeta, Subclass Errantia. The Opal Worm, iridescent as its name implies, will first contract into a ball, but glistens brightly in the sunlight once cleaned of the sand that usually adheres to its secreted mucus.

Two-gilled Blood Worm
Glycera dibranchiata
404

15⅜" (38 cm) long, ½" (13 mm) wide. Long, round. Pink. Lobe above mouth conical, with 4 tiny antennae at tip. Pharynx everts as long, bulbous proboscis with 4 black jaws at tip. Each appendage with red, fingerlike, nonretractable gill on upper and lower side.

Habitat
In mud, sandy mud, and sandy gravel bottoms in bays and open waters; from near low-tide line to water 1322' (403 m) deep.

Range
Central California to Mexico; Gulf of St. Lawrence to Florida and Texas.

Comments
Phylum Annelida, Class Polychaeta, Subclass Errantia. This worm is sometimes called a Beak Thrower because it can suddenly and forcefully shoot out its proboscis. It uses this mechanism for burrowing, for ingesting prey, and for nipping the unwary person handling them. This species is used as fish bait, and is shipped all over the United States by bait diggers

in Maine. The Tufted-gilled Blood Worm (*G. americana*) ranges along the entire Pacific Coast and from Cape Cod to Florida and Texas. It measures 14" (36 cm) long and ½" (13 mm) wide and differs from *G. dibranchiata* chiefly in having retractable gills on only the upper side of each appendage.

Clam Worm
Nereis virens
405

To 36" (95 cm) long, 1¾" (44 mm) wide. Thicker in head region, tapered toward rear. 200 segments. Iridescent greenish, bluish, or greenish brown above, usually with fine red, gold, or white spots; paler beneath; appendages red, showing blood vessels. Head with 4 pairs of tentacles of equal length; a fleshy lip on each side of mouth, lobe above mouth broad, rectangular, with pair of short tentacles; proboscis with pair of short tentacles; proboscis with pair of strong, black jaws. 2 pairs of eyes; body appendages 2-lobed, upper part of appendages broad and leaflike.

Habitat
In sand, sandy mud, mud, clay, and various peat bottoms, among roots of eelgrass, in protected waters and in brackish estuaries; high-tide line to more than 500' (160 m) deep.

Range
Entire Pacific Coast; Maine to Virginia.

Comments
Phylum Annelida, Class Polychaeta, Subclass Errantia. The Clam Worm is a swift and voracious predator, feeding on other worms and invertebrates, carrion, and certain algae. It has a keen sense of smell and in captivity can readily locate bits of fresh clam meat. Another large nereid found in Pacific waters, *N. brandti,* is very difficult to distinguish from *N. virens* and indeed may intergrade with it.

Six-lined Nemertean
Tubulanus sexlineatus
406

8" (20 cm) long, ⅛" (3 mm) wide. In a thin, parchmentlike tube. Cylindrical, head round. Upper surface brown or black. 6 white longitudinal stripes and up to 150 white cross-stripes. Lacks eyespots and sensory grooves.

Habitat
Among mussels, algae, and other growth on rocks and pilings; from low-tide line to a few feet below.

Range
Entire Pacific Coast.

Comments
Phylum Rhynchocoela, Class Anopla. This worm can stretch to lengths of more than 1 meter. The Tube Nemertean (*T. pellucidus*) also forms a tube of parchment, but is much smaller, measuring only 1" (25 mm) long and ⅛" (3 mm) wide. It is slender, cylindrical, and white, sometimes with a pale orange stripe down its back, and ranges from British Columbia to California, and from Cape Cod to Florida and Texas.

Lug Worm
Arenicola cristata
407

12" (30 cm) long, 1" (25 mm) wide. Firm and sturdy, thick in front, with tapering head and tail end; skin coarse and checkered. Greenish black. Head without appendages or eyes; mouth with bulbous proboscis covered with short, fingerlike projections. Each segment with 5 rings, the thickest with tufts of long bristles above and ridges furrows with shorter hooks below.

Habitat
Burrowing in sandy mud flats in protected places; near low-tide line and just below.

Range
Entire Pacific Coast; also on Atlantic Coast.

Comments
Phylum Annelida, Class Polychaeta, Subclass Sedentaria. To feed, the Lug Worm pumps water into its burrow, thus irrigating its gills and collapsing the muddy sand at the end of the burrow. It then eats that sand, from which it digests the organic matter. Periodically, the worm backs up to the surface to void the undigested sand and mud. This material somewhat resembles earthworm castings.

Leafy Paddle Worms
Phyllodace spp.
408

18" (46 cm) long, ⅜" (10 mm) wide. Long, slender. Whitish, tan, brownish, greenish, or gray, some with dark band down middle of back, or with cross-stripes. Head with 4 pairs of long tentacles; lobe above mouth heart-shaped, with 4 short antennae and 2 prominent eyes. Body segments with large, leaflike, oval paddles on upper side of appendages, smaller ones on lower side.

Habitat
Under rocks, among shells and gravel, and in algal holdfasts; from low-tide line to water 5000' (1524 m) deep.

Range
Alaska to Mexico; Arctic to Florida and Texas.

Comments
Phylum Annelida, Class Polychaeta, Subclass Errantia. These worms prey on other polychaetes, and on nemertean worms and other small creatures, and are themselves eaten by several species of fish, including cod, haddock, and plaice. Laboratory examination is usually necessary to determine the species.

Eighteen-scaled Worm
Halosydna brevisetosa
409

4⅜" (110 mm) long, more than ⅜" (10 mm) wide. Covered above with 18 pairs of grayish, brownish, or reddish-brown oval scales, each scale with a pale dot. 1 pair of antennae, and 1 unpaired.

Habitat
Free-living among mussels, algal holdfasts, or growth on rocks and pilings; or commensal in the tubes of several other polychaetes and the snail shell occupied by Baker's Hermit

Crab (*Paguristes bakeri*). From above low-tide line to water more than 1460′ (545 m) deep.

Range
Entire Pacific Coast.

Comments
Phylum Annelida, Class Polychaeta, Subclass Errantia. The commensal forms of this scale worm are typically about twice as big as their free-living relatives. When several of these worms are put together in a container, however, they attack one another, biting off scales and bits of flesh.

Fifteen-scaled Worm
Harmothoe imbricata
410

To 2½″ (65 mm) long, ¾″ (19 mm) wide. Thick, flattened. Covered above with 15 pairs of scales. Reddish, orange, tan, brown, green, gray, black, speckled or mottled, or with black stripe down the back. 2 pairs of eyes on frontal lobe; front pair on lower side, rear pair on upper side.

Habitat
From open shores to very brackish estuaries; in rocky tide pools. Free-living under rocks, among marine growth; or commensal in tubes of other polychaetes, or in shells occupied by hermit crabs. From above low-tide line to water more than 11,000′ (3350 m) deep.

Range
Alaska to S. California; Arctic to New Jersey.

Comments
Phylum Annelida, Class Polychaeta, Subclass Errantia. This ubiquitous scale worm is tolerant of great ranges of temperature, salinity, and depth. The Four-eyed Fifteen-scaled Worm (*H. extenuata*) is 3″ (75 mm) long, ¾″ (20 mm) wide, and likewise variable in color. It differs most obviously from *H. imbricata* in having both pairs of eyes on the upper surface of the frontal lobe. It has the same range as *H. imbricata*.

Twelve-scaled Worm
Lepidonotus squamatus
411

2″ (51 mm) long, ⅝″ (16 mm) wide. Stout. Grayish, tan, or mottled brown. Covered above by 12 pairs of oval scales, with tan, reddish, or greenish projections of several sizes; tentacles and antennae with dark bands, pointed tips.

Habitat
Under rocks, among marine growth, on pilings, and on gravel and shell bottoms; from above low-tide line to water more than 8000′ (2438 m) deep.

Range
Alaska to California; Labrador to New Jersey.

Comments
Phylum Annelida, Class Polychaeta, Subclass Errantia. The name *Lepidonotus* means "scaly back," and when this worm is disturbed it rolls up like an armadillo into a scale-covered ball. It is tough and does not easily lose its scales.

Tapered Flatworm
Notoplana acticola
412

2⅜" (60 mm) long, ¾" (19 mm) wide. Flat, tapered oval. Pale gray or tan, with darker spots along midlines; branches of digestive tract visible when full of food. Widest near front, tapering toward rear. No obvious tentacles, but position marked by round clusters of eyespots; 25 eyespots in longitudinal bands on each side of head over brain.

Habitat
Under rocks; between high- and low-tide lines.

Range
Entire coast of California.

Comments
Phylum Platyhelminthes, Order Polycladida. This is one of the most common flatworms on rocky shores, and is an aggressive predator, eating animals half its size, including limpets and small barnacles. Most specimens are hermaphroditic.

Oval Flatworm
Alloioplana californica
413

1½" (38 mm) long, ¾" (19 mm) wide. Oval, thick, firm. Bluish green to pale olive; radiating brown branches of digestive tract may show through. Nipplelike tentacles covered with eyespots; 2 patches of eyespots over brain. Mouth in middle of underside.

Habitat
Under large rocks resting on gravel or coarse sand, and in crevices; near high-tide line.

Range
California and Baja California.

Comments
Phylum Platyhelminthes, Order Polycladida. The Oval Flatworm feeds on tiny snails, whose tough, rasplike "tongues" can be found in its digestive tract.

Yellow-edged Cadlina
Cadlina luteomarginata
414

3¼" (83 mm) long, 1⅜" (35 mm) wide. Oval, convex. White or pale yellow, bright yellow band around margin. Comblike antennae; ring of 6 white, feathery gills near rear end; body covered with low, rounded, yellow-tipped projections.

Habitat
Under rocks, in tide pools; from low-tide line to water 65' (20 m) deep.

Range
British Columbia to Baja California.

Comments
Phylum Mollusca, Class Gastropoda, Subclass Opisthobranchia. This nudibranch's back feels gritty to the touch because supporting sharp spicules project through its surface. It feeds on several species of sponges.

**Blue-and-gold
Nudibranch**
Hypselodoris californiensis
415

2⅜" (67 mm) long, ⅝" (16 mm) wide. Long, oval; royal blue, with paler blue edge of mantle. 4 longitudinal rows of bright yellow spots. Rear end of foot not covered by mantle. Comblike antennae darker blue, as is ring of gills on back.

Habitat
On rocky shores; from low-tide line to water 95' (29 m) deep.

Range
Central California to Baja California.

Comments
Phylum Mollusca, Class Gastropoda, Subclass Opisthobranchia. Like many nudibranchs, this handsome species secretes a substance that protects it from predators.

**California Brown Sea
Hare**
Aplysia californica
416

16" (41 cm) long, 8" (20 cm) wide, 8" (20 cm) high. Plump, soft, with long, winglike flaps near the top on either side; shell small, internal. Reddish, brownish, or greenish, with mottled white and dark spots and lines; young usually reddish. Head with 1 pair of antennae low, near mouth, 1 larger pair above, farther back, eyes in front of them. Foot extends length of animal from head to beyond body mass.

Habitat
In sheltered places with few waves; from low-tide line to water 60' (18 m) deep.

Range
N. California to Baja California.

Comments
Phylum Mollusca, Class Gastropoda, Subclass Opisthobranchia. Sea hares are so called because of the fancied resemblance of the second pair of antennae to a hare's long ears, and the similarity of the animal's general shape to that of the crouched hare. Like their namesakes, sea hares are herbivorous, eating a variety of red, green, and brown algae—from whose pigment they derive their color—and eelgrass. The California Black Sea Hare (*A. vaccaria*) is perhaps the world's largest gastropod. It attains a length of 30" (76 cm), a width of 15" (38 cm), and weight of 35 lbs (16 kg). This animal is reddish brown to black, with white speckles, and ranges from southern California to Baja California.

Navanax
Navanax inermis
417

8" (20 cm) long, 2" (51 mm) wide, 2" (51 mm) high. Torpedo- or cigar-shaped. Velvety brown or black, with violet sheen and numerous yellowish or white speckles sometimes arranged in streaks; margin edged in bright blue. Head rounded at sides, with 1 pair of stumpy antennae; long flaps fold up over the back; rear end of foot with deep notch.

Habitat
In protected bays and on mud flats; from low-tide line to water 25' (8 m) deep.

Range
Central California to Baja California.

Comments
Phylum Mollusca, Class Gastropoda, Subclass Opisthobranchia. An active predator that follows the mucus trails of its prey, this animal is carnivorous, feeding mostly on bubble snails, but also on nudibranchs and sea hares.

Red Sponge Nudibranch
Rostanga pulchra
418

1¼″ (32 mm) long, ¾″ (19 mm) wide. Broadly oval. Yellow-red to scarlet, with tiny dark spots sprinkled over the surface. Comblike antennae short, stout; ring of 6–9 short, feathery gills on back near rear end. Velvety in appearance.

Habitat
On rocky shores with overhanging ledges or large boulders; from low-tide line to water 30′ (9 m) deep.

Range
British Columbia to Baja California.

Comments
Phylum Mollusca, Class Gastropoda, Subclass Opisthobranchia. This nudibranch feeds on several kinds of red sponges, whose pigments it incorporates into its own body. *Rostanga* matches the sponge in color, as does the spiral ribbon of eggs it lays on the sponge surface.

Salted Doris
Doriopsilla albopunctata
419

2¾″ (70 mm) long, 1″ (25 mm) wide. Oval, somewhat flattened; back covered with low projections. Bright yellow to reddish brown, small white dot on each projection. Comblike antennae usually reddish; ring of 5 whitish, feathery gills on back near rear end.

Habitat
On rocky shores; from low-tide line to water 150′ (46 m) deep.

Range
N. California to Baja California.

Comments
Phylum Mollusca, Class Gastropoda, Subclass Opisthobranchia. This nudibranch has no radula, but is able to feed on sponges by secreting a fluid from its mouth to soften the surface of the sponge, and then sucking up the soft matter. The white dots on the animal's back look like a sprinkling of salt, hence the common name.

Rough-mantled Doris
Onchidoris bilamellata
420

1″ (25 mm) long, ¾″ (19 mm) wide. Mixed pattern of chocolate- to rusty-brown and cream-color. Broadly oval. Back covered with many short, thick, knobby projections. Comblike antennae; 16–32 simple featherlike gills arranged in 2 half-rings on back near rear end.

Habitat
On rocks and pilings near mud bottoms; from well above low-tide line to water 25' (8 m) deep.

Range
Alaska to Baja California; Bay of Fundy to Rhode Island.

Comments
Phylum Mollusca, Class Gastropoda, Subclass Opisthobranchia. This nudibranch feeds on acorn barnacles. In New England it can frequently be found in large numbers, 20 or more per rock, under barnacle-covered boulders in quiet estuaries. Formerly known as *O. fusca.*

Monterey Doris
Archidoris montereyensis
421

2" (51 mm) long; ¾" (19 mm) wide. Oval. Covered with cone-shaped projections. Bright yellow to yellow-orange, with dark spots both on and between projections. Comblike antennae short and thick; ring of 7 yellowish, feathery gills on back near rear end.

Habitat
On rocky shores; from low-tide line to water 160' (50 m) deep.

Range
Alaska to S. California.

Comments
Phylum Mollusca, Class Gastropoda, Subclass Opisthobranchia. The Monterey Doris feeds chiefly on the Crumb of Bread Sponge. It lays its eggs in a long, yellow ribbon, which is attached in a spiral to a rock and may contain 2 million eggs.

Sea Lemon
Anisodoris nobilis
422

10" (25 cm) long, 3" (76 mm) wide. Elongately oval, covered on top with short, rounded projections. Orange to pale yellow, whitish at tips of projections, black spots between but not on projections. Antennae comblike, short. Ring of 6 white-edged, frilly gills on back near rear end.

Habitat
From low-tide line to water 750' (230 m) deep.

Range
British Columbia to Baja California.

Comments
Phylum Mollusca, Class Gastropoda, Subclass Opisthobranchia. This nudibranch is one of the largest on the Pacific Coast. It is known to feed on several different kinds of sponges and on dead organic matter. The Sea Lemon emits a strong, fruity odor that seems to discourage predators.

Ring-spotted Doris
Diaulula sandiegensis
423

3⅝" (92 mm) long, 1½" (38 mm) wide. Oval. Creamy white to gray or light brown, with a few black circles or spots of varying size on the back. Comblike antennae, ring of 6–7 gills on back near rear end. Velvety in appearance, gritty to the touch.

Habitat
On rocky shores; from low-tide line to water 110' (35 m) deep.

Range
Alaska to Baja California.

Comments
Phylum Mollusca, Class Gastropoda, Subclass Opisthobranchia. The Ring-spotted Doris lays a white spiral ribbon of eggs, attaching it to an overhanging rock ledge. Such a ribbon may contain 16 million eggs. Specimens of this animal in the northern part of its range generally have more rings and spots than those farther south.

Stiff-footed Sea Cucumber
Eupentacta quinquesemita
424

4" (102 mm) long, ½" (13 mm) wide. Cucumber-shaped. White or cream-colored with yellow tentacles. Body cylindrical, tapered at ends; 10 short, bushy tentacles around mouth; 5 rows of stiff, nonretractable tube feet.

Habitat
Under rocks and in crevices, in algal- and invertebrate-covered substrates; near low-tide line and below in shallow water.

Range
British Columbia to S. California.

Comments
Phylum Echinodermata, Class Holothuroidea. This species, common in the shallow water of both outer coasts and clean harbors, is eaten by several species of sea stars.

Dwarf Sea Cucumber
Lissothuria nutriens
425

¾" (19 mm) long, ⅜" (10 mm) wide. Oval, convex, soft. Upper surface red or orange; lower surface pink. Lower side flat, with 3 rows of tube feet; upper surface with many slender projections, mouth and anus directed upwards at opposite ends; 10 highly branched tentacles around mouth.

Habitat
On rocks, and among algal holdfasts, surfgrass roots, and encrusting invertebrates; low-tide line to 65' (20 m) deep.

Range
Central California to S. California.

Comments
Phylum Echinodermata, Class Holothuroidea. This interesting little sea cucumber broods its eggs in shallow depressions on its upper surface, and retains them until they develop into tiny juveniles with tube feet.

Red Sea Cucumber
Cucumaria miniata
426

10″ (25 cm) long, 1″ (25 mm) wide. Cucumber-shaped. Brick-red, bright orange, pinkish, or purple. Long, round, bluntly tapered at rear. Smooth, tough. 10 highly branched, orange, retractable tentacles of equal size. 5 rows of tube feet. 2 rows above, 3 below.

Habitat
Nestled in crevices and under rocks; near low-tide line and below to shallow depths.

Range
Alaska to central California.

Comments
Phylum Echinodermata, Class Holothuroidea. This animal's body is curved in the crevice it inhabits so that both the tentacular crown and the anus are exposed to moving water. The Peppered Sea Cucumber (*C. piperata*) is about half the size of *C. miniata,* and is yellowish white and speckled with brown or black. Found from British Columbia to Baja California.

Bushy-backed Sea Slug
Dendronotus frondosus
427

4⅝″ (117 mm) long, 1″ (25 mm) wide. Widest in middle, tapered to point at rear end. Grayish brown to rusty red mottled with white spots, or pure white. Head blunt, with 6 branched projections extending forward. Comblike antennae set in sheaths with whorl of branched projections; 2 rows of 5–8 bushy projections along back.

Habitat
On rocks and floats, and among seaweeds; from low-tide line to water 360′ (110 m) deep.

Range
Alaska to California; Arctic to New Jersey.

Comments
Phylum Mollusca, Class Gastropoda, Subclass Opisthobranchia. The Bushy-backed Sea Slug is commonly found wherever there is an abundance of the hydroids on which it feeds. It is also known to browse on bryozoans and colonial tunicates.

Hermissenda Nudibranch
Hermissenda crassicornis
428

3¼″ (83 mm) long, ⅜″ (10 mm) wide. Broadest just behind head, tapering to a fine point at the rear. Bluish white, with orange line down middle of back; margins with pale electric-blue lines; first pair of tentacles with blue lines, second pair bluish with raised rings. Numerous fingerlike projections, swollen in middle, with orange stripe just below white tip of each projection, in 2 clusters on each side of back.

Habitat
In tide pools, and on rocks, pilings, and mud flats; from low-tide line to water 110′ (34 m) deep.

Range
Alaska to Baja California.

Comments
Phylum Mollusca, Class Gastropoda, Subclass
Opisthobranchia. This is one of the most abundant
nudibranchs on the Pacific Coast. It feeds on hydroids and
other invertebrates, and is even cannibalistic; when 2
individuals meet they frequently fight.

Sea Clown Nudibranch
Triopha catalinae
429

6″ (15 cm) long, ¾″ (19 mm) wide. Almost cylindrical.
White or grayish tan, with orange-red tips to all projections,
antennae, and gills. Head broad, with 8–12 short, branching
projections directed forward; stumpy, branched projections
scattered over back. Comblike antennae and ring of 5 feathery
gills on rear half of back.

Habitat
In tide pools and kelp beds; from above low-tide line to water
110′ (34 m) deep.

Range
Alaska to Baja California.

Comments
Phylum Mollusca, Class Gastropoda, Subclass
Opisthobranchia. This white Sea Clown with orange spots is a
spectacular sight. When stranded in a tide pool with small
fish it is not attacked, perhaps because of some substance it
secretes. It feeds on bryozoans. The Spotted Triopha (*T.
maculata*), which ranges from northern California to Baja
California, is similar in size and structure, but is red to
reddish brown or black, with numerous white to bluish spots
and all appendages tipped bright red.

California Stichopus
Parastichopus californicus
430

16″ (41 cm) long, 2″ (51 mm) wide. Cucumber-shaped.
Brown, red, or yellow, often mottled. Upper surface with
large and small, red-tipped, conical projections. Tube feet on
lower surface only, numerous.

Habitat
On protected rocky shores and pilings in clean, quiet water;
from low-tide line to water 300′ (91 m) deep.

Range
British Columbia to Baja California.

Comments
Phylum Echinodermata, Class Holothuroidea. In Puget
Sound, natural populations of the California Stichopus
normally eject their internal organs in late fall and then
regenerate a new set for spring. *P. californicus* moves along the
bottom like an inchworm or flexes its body to "swim" when
approached by predatory sea stars. A related species, the
Parvima Stichopus (*P. parvimensis*) occurs from Monterey Bay
to Baja California. It is similar, but has a chestnut-brown
upper surface with short projections that are tipped with
black.

Elegant Eolid
Flabellinopsis iodinea
431

3⅝" (92 mm) long, ½" (13 mm) wide. Higher than wide.
Vivid purple. 2 pairs of antennae, the second pair bright red;
back covered with numerous orange, fingerlike projections.

Habitat
On pilings and rocks, and in kelp beds; from low-tide line to
water 110′ (34 m) deep.

Range
British Columbia to Baja California.

Comments
Phylum Mollusca, Class Gastropoda, Subclass
Opisthobranchia. This gaudily colored nudibranch has
flattened sides, and can drop from a surface and swim with a
series of quick, alternate, U-shaped bends of its body.

Hopkins' Rose
Hopkinsia rosacea
432

1¼" (32 mm) long, ½" (13 mm) wide. Oval. Deep rosy pink.
Covered by long, fingerlike projections, with comblike
antennae and ring of feathery gills on back near rear end.

Habitat
On rocky shores; near low-tide line and just below.

Range
Oregon to Baja California.

Comments
Phylum Mollusca, Class Gastropoda, Subclass
Opisthobranchia. The long, fingerlike projections on the back
of this beautifully colored nudibranch almost conceal the
antennae and gills. Hopkins' Rose feeds on a pink encrusting
bryozoan, and lays a pink spiral ribbon of eggs.

Green Sea Urchin
*Strongylocentrotus
droebachiensis*
433

3¼" (83 mm) wide, 1½" (38 mm) high. Spiny, oval. Test
brownish green, spines light green, gray-green or, more
rarely, brownish green or reddish green; tube feet brownish.
Spines not greatly variable in length, never over one-third
diameter of test. Area around anus with many scalelike plates
of different sizes. 10 clusters of gills.

Habitat
On rocky shores and in kelp beds; from low-tide line to water
3795′ (1157 m) deep.

Range
Alaska to Puget Sound; Arctic to New Jersey.

Comments
Phylum Echinodermata, Class Echinoidea. These urchins are
so abundant in certain protected bays that it is impossible to
walk through a bed of them without stepping on some.

Purple Sea Urchin
Strongylocentrotus purpuratus
434

4″ (102 mm) wide, 1¾″ (44 mm) high. Spiny, oval. Adults vivid purple; juveniles greenish. Domed above and flattened beneath. Area around anus with many scalelike plates.

Habitat
On rocky shores with moderately strong surf; from low-tide line to water 525′ (160 m) deep.

Range
British Columbia to Baja California.

Comments
Phylum Echinodermata, Class Echinoidea. Above the low-tide line, these urchins often live in rounded depressions in the rock, which they slowly erode with their teeth and spines. This species is one of the best known in the world.

Red Sea Urchin
Strongylocentrotus franciscanus
435

5″ (127 mm) wide, 2″ (51 mm) high. Spiny, oval. Red, red-brown, or light to dark purple. Spines abundant, variable, largest 3″ (76 mm) long. Area around anus with many scalelike plates.

Habitat
On rocky shores of open coasts; from low-tide line to water 300′ (91 m) deep.

Range
Alaska to Baja California.

Comments
Phylum Echinodermata, Class Echinoidea. This large urchin is eaten by the California Sea Otter, and is in low abundance in the otter's range. A fishery in southern California processes the urchin's ovaries and ships them to Japan as a delicacy.

Northern Red Anemone
Tealia crassicornis
436

5″ (127 mm) high, 3″ (76 mm) wide. Columnar, smooth. Red, sometimes mottled, occasionally with dull green spots. Approximately 100 thick, blunt tentacles arranged in several rings around the mouth; white, frequently ringed with red, white, or dark pigment. Particles of shell and gravel often attached to column.

Habitat
Firmly attached to rocks, usually in protected places shaded by seaweeds or overhanging rocks; near low-tide line and below in shallow water.

Range
Alaska to central California; Arctic to Cape Cod.

Comments
Phylum Cnidaria, Class Anthozoa, Order Actiniaria. Specimens found above low-tide line are usually small; larger ones are subtidal. This handsome anemone is listed in some references as *T. felina*. In this species size is more a function of food availability than of age.

Club-tipped Anemone
Corynactis californica
437

1¼" (32 mm) high, 1" (25 mm) wide. Cylindrical, short, with flared crown of tentacles. Red, pink, orange, buff, purple, brown, or nearly white. Oral disk surrounded by many club-tipped tentacles, usually white, in radial rows. Column smooth. Flat, adhesive basal disk with tissue usually continuous with that of its neighbors.

Habitat
On rocks, ledges, and pilings, on open shores and in bays; from low-tide line to water 95' (30 m) deep.

Range
N. California to Baja California.

Comments
Phylum Cnidaria, Class Anthozoa, Order Corallimorpharia. These are not true anemones, but are more closely related to the stony corals. Their knobby tentacles contain the largest stinging cells known, but they are not toxic to humans.

Proliferating Anemone
Epiactis prolifera
438, 441

1½" (40 mm) high, 2" (50 mm) wide. Cylindrical, squat. Solid, spotted, or striped, gray, green, blue, brown, orange, or reddish; base usually with white vertical lines. 96 short, tapered tentacles around oral disk; column smooth, with pits near base where young develop. Basal disk flat, adhesive, spread wider than trunk.

Habitat
Attached to rocks, large algae, and eelgrass, on unprotected coasts and in bays; from between high- and low-tide lines to water 30' (9 m) deep.

Range
Alaska to S. California.

Comments
Phylum Cnidaria, Class Anthozoa, Order Actiniaria. This anemone has unusual breeding habits. At any time of the year, half the animals observed in nature will be brooding and may have several young developing around the base of the column.

Aggregating Anemone
Anthopleura elegantissima
439

Aggregating individuals 6" (15 cm) high, 3⅛" (80 mm) wide; solitary individuals 20" (50 cm) high, 10" (25 cm) wide. Cylindrical. Column pale gray-green to white; pale, variously colored tentacles with pink, lavender, or blue tips, in 5 rings around oral disk, numerous, thick, pointed; ring of knobs with stinging cells just under tentacles. Column covered with vertical rows of adhesive projections.

Habitat
Either in dense populations or solitary, on rock walls, boulders, or pilings; from between high- and low-tide lines to low-tide line.

Range
Alaska to Baja California.

Comments
Phylum Cnidaria, Class Anthozoa, Order Actiniaria. Aggregation in this species is not a matter of many individuals coming together, but the result of many asexual longitudinal divisions of 1 founding anemone. Groups started from different founding individuals will not mix, but will fight if too close together.

Giant Green Anemone
Anthopleura xanthogrammica
440

12" (30 cm) high, 10" (25 cm) wide. Cylindrical. Column greenish brown; tentacles green, bluish, or white; oral disk green, grayish, or bluish green. Numerous short, thick, tapered tentacles in 6 or more rings around flat oral disk; basal disk adhesive, flat. Column covered with scattered adhesive projections.

Habitat
On exposed coastline and in bays and harbors, on rocks, seawalls, and pilings; in tidepools; from above low-tide line to water more than 50' (15 m) deep.

Range
Alaska to Panama.

Comments
Phylum Cnidaria, Class Anthozoa, Order Actiniaria. Each Giant Green Anemone is solitary, but is often in tentacle-tip contact with another in favorable tide pools and channels. Individuals living in open daylight are bright green, partly from symbiotic algae in their tissues and partly from pigment. Those living in heavily shaded areas are paler. These are the main large anemones seen in tide pools and rocky channels along our coast. They feed on animals they can sting and engulf, including crabs, fishes, and detached mussels.

Orange Cup Coral
Balanophyllia elegans
442, 443

⅜" (10 mm) high, ⅜" (10 mm) wide. Cylindrical, solitary. Orange or yellow. Oral disk surrounded by 36 long, tapered, translucent tentacles dotted with masses of stinging cells. Base set in stony, cup-shaped skeleton into which the polyp can retract. Skeleton has radial plates showing pattern of internal septa.

Habitat
In shaded places on and under ledges and boulders along open coast and in bays, from above low-tide line to water 70' (21 m) deep.

Range
British Columbia to Baja California.

Comments
Phylum Cnidaria, Class Anthozoa, Order Scleractinia. This is the only stony coral to occur between the high- and low-tide lines on the Pacific Coast. Its orange color is a fluorescent pigment and even at depths of 30' (9 m) or more, where red light is lacking, it shows the same bright hue.

Frilled Anemone
Metridium senile
444

18" (50 cm) high, 9" (25 cm) wide. Smooth. Reddish brown to olive-brown or lighter, to cream-colored and white; paler forms may be mottled. Oral disk lobed; tentacles slender and very abundant, 1000 in large specimens, producing a frilled appearance. Long, white threads of stinging cells discharged when animal is disturbed.

Habitat
Attached to rocks, wharf piles, and other solid objects; near low-tide line and below in shallow water.

Range
Alaska to S. California; Arctic to Delaware.

Comments
Phylum Cnidaria, Class Anthozoa, Order Actiniaria. These anemones reproduce either sexually or asexually, the latter by dividing lengthwise or by leaving behind, as they creep over a surface, bits of tissue from the pedal disk that regenerate into complete anemones. This species and the Giant Green Anemone are favorite specimens in public aquaria because of their size, color, availability, and hardiness. They live many years.

Ghost Anemone
Diadumene leucolena
445

1½" (40 mm) high, ½" (15 mm) wide. Translucent, whitish, pink, or olive. Columnar. Mostly smooth, but with low, scattered projections. 60 slender, pale tentacles, ½" (13 mm) long, surrounding mouth. White threads of stinging cells discharged when animal is disturbed.

Habitat
On or under rocks, among marine growth on pilings and jetties; in shallow water of bays and other protected areas.

Range
California; Maine to North Carolina.

Comments
Phylum Cnidaria, Class Anthozoa, Order Actiniaria. This little anemone is easily confused with immature forms of the Frilled Anemone. It lacks the vertical stripes of color found on certain other small anemones of similar habitat, such as the Striped Anemone (*Haliplanella luciae*).

Red Soft Coral
Gersemia rubiformis
446, 451

6" (15 cm) high, 3" (76 mm) wide. Soft, fleshy, with stout, club-shaped branches or cluster of pear-shaped lobes rising from main stem. Red to orange. Branches terminate in clusters of polyps set close together, each with 8 short, featherlike tentacles.

Habitat
Attached to rocks, pilings, and other solid objects; below low-tide line.

Range
Alaska to N. California; Arctic to Gulf of Maine.

Comments
Phylum Cnidaria, Class Anthozoa, Subclass Octocorallia. The
needlelike limestone spicules imbedded in the Red Soft Coral's
stem lend support to its structure. This soft coral is very
commonly associated with the young of the basket star
Gorgonocephalus eucnemis.

**Trumpet Stalked
Jellyfish**
Haliclystus spp.
447

1″ (25 mm) high, ½″ (13 mm) wide. Translucent, with red,
orange, yellow, or tan. Widely flared when expanded, with
each of 8 short arms ending in a pompom of 100 knobbed
tentacles. Notches between arms spaced equally, each notch
with trumpet-shaped anchor that has small tentacle in middle
and ridged ring around base. Mouth has 4 lips. Reproductive
organs situated along length of arms.

Habitat
Attached to eelgrass, kelp, rockweed, other seaweeds, and
occasionally rocks; near low-tide line and below in shallow
water.

Range
British Columbia to N. California; New Brunswick to Cape
Cod.

Comments
Phylum Cnidaria, Class Scyphozoa. These jellyfish are traps for
small crustaceans, and when one of these comes into contact
with a tentacle, it is immediately put into the mouth and
swallowed.

Gurney's Sea Pen
Ptilosarcus gurneyi
448

18″ (46 cm) high, 4″ (102 mm) wide. Stout, plumelike.
Tannish yellow to orange, translucent. Midrib bearing 20
pairs of flat, wide side branches with rows of polyps along
both edges, and swollen base for anchorage.

Habitat
Anchored in soft bottoms; from below low-tide line to water
more than 100′ (30 m) deep.

Range
British Columbia to central California.

Comments
Phylum Cnidaria, Class Anthozoa, Subclass Octocorallia.
When disturbed, this plumy colony can contract and
completely withdraw into the muddy bottom by releasing
large amounts of water from a system of internal canals. It
displays brilliant bioluminescence when disturbed in
the dark.

**Monterey Stalked
Tunicate**
Styela montereyensis
449

10″ (25 cm) high, 2″ (51 mm) wide. Shaped like long bowling
pin. Yellow to reddish brown. Thick, leathery tunic, ridged
longitudinally; openings close together, near tip, 1 pointed
down.

Habitat
On rocks in both exposed and protected habitats; from low-tide line to water 100' (30 m) deep.

Range
British Columbia to Baja California.

Comments
Phylum Chordata, Class Ascidiacea. This is a common, easily recognized, and broadly distributed solitary tunicate. An individual observed in Monterey grew to 2" (51 mm) high in less than 3 months and over 9" (23 cm) in 3 years.

Club Hydroid
Clava leptostyla
450

⅜" (10 mm) high, 1" (25 mm) wide. Unbranched, rising from a network of creeping horizontal stems. Pink to reddish orange. 30 threadlike tentacles scattered over top quarter of club-shaped heads. Clusters of reproductive organs just below tentacles. No medusa stage.

Habitat
Usually attached to rockweeds and knotted wrack, occasionally on rocks; just above low-tide line and in bays and shallow water.

Range
Central California; Labrador to Long Island Sound.

Comments
Phylum Cnidaria, Class Hydrozoa. These hydroids can be found growing in velvety clusters in tide pools.

Slipper Sea Cucumber
Psolus chitonoides
452

4¾" (121 mm) long, 2½" (64 mm) wide. Scaly, flat-bottomed, oval. Orange. Body covered with large, granular plates. Bright red oral tentacles.

Habitat
On rocks; from low-tide line to water 50' (15 m) deep.

Range
Alaska to Baja California.

Comments
Phylum Echinodermata, Class Holothuroidea. This animal adheres very firmly to a rock and is difficult to dislodge. Its chief predators are sea stars.

Giant Feather Duster
Eudistylia polymorpha
453, 454, 456

10" (25 cm) long, ½" (13 mm) wide. In sturdy, parchmentlike tubes. Body tannish, gills maroon, reddish, orange, or brown, usually with cross-bands of lighter and darker shades. Cylindrical, slightly flattened, tapered; collar at head end; large plume of featherlike gills 2½" (64 mm) across when expanded.

Habitat
Attached to boulders or pilings, or wedged into crevices on

open rocky shores; from near low-tide line to water 1400'
(430 m) deep.

Range
Entire Pacific Coast.

Comments
Phylum Annelida, Class Polychaeta, Subclass Sedentaria.
These worms frequently occur in large numbers in a tide pool,
presenting a handsome sight that resembles a flower garden.
They retract into their tubes with remarkable speed when
touched, or even when a shadow passes over them. The gills
have numerous eyespots, which mediate this "shadow reflex."

Banded Feather Duster
Sabella crassicornis
455

2" (50 mm) long, ⅛" (3 mm) wide. In stiff, leathery tube 4"
(102 mm) long. Tapered. Creamy pink to orange-tan. 4-lobed
collar at head end, head with plume of 24 straight, feathery
gills, united at base, banded with various shades of red, each
with 2–6 paired, dark red eyespots, evenly spaced in rows
across plume.

Habitat
Attached to rocks and shells; from near low-tide line to water
170' (52 m) deep.

Range
Entire Pacific Coast; Maine to Cape Cod.

Comments
Phylum Annelida, Class Polychaeta, Subclass Sedentaria.
Living in a dead-end tube presents a problem in voiding fecal
pellets. Sabellids have a ciliated groove that runs the length of
the body and carries the pellets to the top of the tube so the
worm can dump them outside.

Red Tube Worm
Serpula vermicularis
457, 458

4" (102 mm) long, ¼" (6 mm) wide. In sinuous, limy
tubes 4" (102 mm) long. Collar prominent, abdomen tapered.
Pinkish or red-orange; plume of 40 pairs of gills pink, orange,
or red, with whitish bands. Lid funnel-shaped, with 160 fine
notches on the border.

Habitat
Attached to rocks, pilings, floats, and shells in protected
harbors and tide pools, and on open shores; from low-tide line
to water more than 300' (91 m) deep.

Range
Alaska to S. California.

Comments
Phylum Annelida, Class Polychaeta, Subclass Sedentaria. This
species was named in 1767 by Carolus Linnaeus. Though he
described it from specimens obtained in the North Atlantic, it
does not occur on the eastern shores of the United States.

**Red-striped Acorn
Barnacle**
Megabalanus californicus
459

2″ (51 mm) high, 2⅜″ (60 mm) wide. Almost cylindrical, flat-topped. White, with longitudinal red stripes. Sides composed of 2 pairs of limy plates overlapping 1 of 2 unpaired plates. 2 pairs of plates at top with gape between. Side plates with 12–15 ribs of many sizes converging to point at top. Base limy.

Habitat
On rocks, pilings, kelps, and other hard-shelled animals; from low-tide line to water 30′ (9 m) deep.

Range
N. California to Mexico.

Comments
Phylum Arthropoda, Class Crustacea. Because of their gregarious habits, these barnacles get much longer than wide. Splendid clusters are cleaned and sold in shell shops.

Common Goose Barnacle
Lepas anatifera
460

6″ (15 cm) long, 2¾″ (70 mm) wide. Flattened, lance-shaped, stalked. Enclosed in 5 strong, limy, white, orange- or yellow-edged plates; stalk purplish brown. 6 pairs of feathery feeding appendages extendible through gape between plates. Stalk one-half total length, thick, rubbery. Surface of plates almost smooth, with fine lines; stalk smooth.

Habitat
Floating; attached to drifting objects, buoys, bottles, tar masses, and the Common Purple Sea Snail.

Range
Washed ashore on both coasts of the United States.

Comments
Phylum Arthropoda, Class Crustacea. The Common Goose Barnacle is a creature of the high seas. Its swimming larvae are attracted by the shaded undersides of floating objects, where they settle gregariously. Anything long afloat, such as a buoy, may be completely covered below with barnacles.

Leaf Barnacle
Pollicipes polymerus
461, 465

3¼″ (83 mm) long, 1⅛″ (28 mm) wide. Cylindrical, stout, stalked, scaly. Enclosed in 6 major white plates surrounded by many smaller, overlapping plates. Stalk grayish or brownish. 6 pairs of feathery appendages extend through gape between plates, forming a feeding net. Stalk thick, tough, covered with fine spines. Surface of plates smooth.

Habitat
Attached to wave-swept boulders; between high- and low-tide lines.

Range
British Columbia to Baja California.

Comments
Phylum Arthropoda, Class Crustacea. The Leaf Barnacle

frequently occurs in vast, dense populations, sometimes mixed with the California Mussel on steep or vertical rock surfaces.

Giant Acorn Barnacle
Balanus nubilis
462, 466

3½" (89 mm) high, 4⅜" (111 mm) wide. Conical, flat at top. Whitish. Sides composed of 2 pairs of limy plates overlapping only 1 of 2 unpaired plates. 2 pairs of plates at top with gape between. Side plates heavy, rough, but without definite ribs; top plates without grooves, 1 pair of top plates with long projection extending upward.

Habitat
On rocks, pilings, and hard-shelled animals; from low-tide line to water 300' (91 m) deep.

Range
Alaska to S. California.

Comments
Phylum Arthropoda, Class Crustacea. This large barnacle is sometimes confused with the Eagle Barnacle (*B. aquila*), which gets even larger, 5⅜" (136 mm) high and 5¼" (133 mm) wide. *B. aquila* is also white and rough, but has grooved top plates. These large barnacles are roasted and eaten by Indians in the Northwest.

Volcano Barnacle
Tetraclita rubescens
463

2" (51 mm) high, 2" (51 mm) wide at base. Conical, volcano-shaped. Brownish or brick-red. Wall consists of 4 plates, almost indistinguishably fused. 2 pairs of plates at top with gape between pairs. 6 pairs of bristly appendages extend through gape when feeding. Plates highly ribbed, sometimes eroded. Young barnacles proportionally less high. Base consists of limy plate.

Habitat
On rocks, on open wave-swept shore; between high- and low-tide lines and sometimes below.

Range
Central California to Baja California.

Comments
Phylum Arthropoda, Class Crustacea. This genus is chiefly tropical and is the only nonstalked barnacle with a wall of 4 plates.

Thatched Barnacle
Semibalanus cariosus
464

2" (51 mm) high, 2⅜" (60 mm) wide. Conical, rough. Gray. Wall of 6 plates; surface appears thatched, with many slender, tubular ribs. 2 pairs of plates at top with gape between; base membranous (seen only by prying animal off rock).

Habitat
On rocks, along exposed shores; above low-tide line.

Range
Alaska to S. California.

Comments
Phylum Arthropoda, Class Crustacea. This species grows in crowded colonies in the northern part of its range, but is more solitary in the southern part. *S. cariosus* broods its young in the winter, and in spring liberates larvae that then settle on a rocky surface. These barnacles may live as long as 15 years.

Little Striped Barnacle
Balanus amphitrite
467

¾" (19 mm) high, ¾" (19 mm) wide. Conical, flat at top. White, with reddish-brown or purple stripes, cluster of 3–4 stripes in middle of each side plate. Sides composed of 2 pairs of limy plates overlapping 1 of 2 unpaired plates. 2 pairs of plates at top with gape between. Side plates smooth, bluntly pointed at top. Top plates smooth. Base limy.

Habitat
On rocks, pilings, and shells in bays and estuaries; from low-tide line to water 60' (18 m) deep.

Range
Central California to Panama; Cape Cod to Florida and Texas; Mexico.

Comments
Phylum Arthropoda, Class Crustacea. This species is commonly found on the bottoms of ships, which have carried it to many parts of the world. Though it can survive in colder waters, it requires at least 68°F (20°C) to breed.

Bay Barnacle
Balanus improvisus
468

¼" (6 mm) high, ½" (13 mm) wide. Conical, flat at top. White. Sides composed of 2 pairs of limy plates overlapping only 1 of 2 unpaired plates. 2 pairs of plates at top with gape between. Side plates smooth. Base limy.

Habitat
On rocks, pilings, oysters and other hard-shelled animals, in brackish estuaries; from low-tide line to water 120' (37 m) deep.

Range
Oregon to Ecuador; Nova Scotia to Florida and Texas; Mexico.

Comments
Phylum Arthropoda, Class Crustacea. This estuarine form was introduced from the East Coast to the West Coast before the middle of the 19th century along with the Eastern Oyster. It can tolerate fresh water at least part of the year, and has been found attached to freshwater crayfish.

Crumb of Bread Sponge
Halichondria panicea
469

More than 12" (30 cm) wide, 2" (51 mm) high. Thin crust. Yellow to greenish. Pores prominent on low "volcanoes." Texture like bread crumbs.

Habitat
Protected undersides of stones, wharf piles, and other solid

substrata; also in mussel beds and on kelp stems and holdfasts; from low-tide line to water more than 200′ (61 m) deep.

Range
Alaska to S. California; Arctic to Cape Cod.

Comments
Phylum Porifera, Class Demospongiae. Like most sponges, the Crumb of Bread Sponge has a strong odor. Although distasteful to most predators, it is fed upon by various dorid nudibranchs and by at least one species of sea star. Bowerbank's Crumb of Bread Sponge (*H. bowerbanki*), which is distinguishable from *H. panicea* only by its spicules, is similarly distributed on both coasts.

Boring Sponge
Cliona celata
470

One or more ⅛″ (3 mm) wide, ¹⁄₁₆″ (2 mm) high yellowish pores protruding from holes in mollusk shells or coral. Sponge may overgrow the host entirely.

Habitat
In living and dead mollusk shells and corals.

Range
Washington to California; Gulf of St. Lawrence to Gulf of Mexico.

Comments
Phylum Porifera, Class Demospongiae. The larvae of these sponges settle on shells and coral, develop into tiny sponges and, secreting sulfuric acid, excavate pits and galleries, loosening chips of the shell or coral, which are then ejected. The host is weakened to the point of disintegration, and the sea bottom is thus kept free of accumulating shells.

Purple Sponge
Haliclona permollis
471

36″ (91 cm) wide, 1⅝″ (41 mm) high. Encrusting, with raised "volcanoes," each with a pore up to ¼″ (6 mm) wide. Pink to lavender to purple. Smooth; soft but not slimy.

Habitat
Encrusted on rocks in protected places; on floating docks and in tide pools; from midtidal zone to water 20′ (6 m) deep.

Range
Washington to central California; New Brunswick to lower Chesapeake Bay.

Comments
Phylum Porifera, Class Demospongiae. The classification of this widespread species is still under investigation. On the West Coast it occurs higher up on rock faces than any other sponge. The nudibranch Ringed Doris feeds on the Purple Sponge, among others.

Purple Stylasterine
Allopora porphyra
472

6" (15 cm) wide, more than ⅛" (3 mm) high. Colony encrusting, limy. Vivid purple. Covered with scalloped pits, each containing up to 12 feeding polyps surrounded by mouthless stinging polyps.

Habitat
On protected, shaded faces of exposed rocks; near low-tide line and below.

Range
British Columbia to central California.

Comments
Phylum Cnidaria, Class Hydrozoa. Members of this genus seem to thrive best on vertical surfaces where they are not silted or overgrown by algae. They are often found in old sea urchin excavations.

Velvety Red Sponge
Ophlitaspongia pennata
473

More than 36" (91 cm) wide, ¼" (6 mm) high. Flat, encrusting. Coral-red, occasionally red-brown to mustard. Velvety; pores starlike, close together.

Habitat
Attached to overhanging rocks in shaded crevices, from between high- and low-tide lines to water 10' (3 m) deep.

Range
Washington to California.

Comments
Phylum Porifera, Class Demospongiae. The red nudibranch Crimson Doris is almost invariably present on the Velvety Red Sponge, on which it preys and lays coiled, red egg-masses that match the sponge in color.

Taylor's Colonial Tunicate
Metandrocarpa taylori
474

Colony ¼" (6 mm) high, 8" (20 cm) wide. Individuals ¼" (6 mm) high, ⅛" (3 mm) wide. Clusters of globes. Bright red, orange, yellow, or greenish. Individuals separate, but joined by a thin basal tunic.

Habitat
On protected rock faces; from low-tide line to water 72' (22 m) deep.

Range
British Columbia to S. California.

Comments
Phylum Chordata, Class Ascidiacea. This species grows when individuals produce buds, which separate from the parent but remain connected by a thin sheet of tunic that spreads on the substrate. The Fused Tunicate (*M. dura*) is a related, bright red species, occurring only below the low-tide line in the same range as *M. taylori*. It can be differentiated by its much thicker basal tunic and much larger colonies, which grow to ⅜" (10 mm) high and to more than 24" (61 cm) wide.

Heath's Sponge
Leucandra heathi
475

3½" (89 mm) wide, 4⅜" (111 mm) high. Globular to pear-shaped, with 1 large pore at top, giving volcanolike appearance. Whitish to cream-colored. Surface bristly with protruding limy spicules, those around pore are ¼" (6 mm) in length.

Habitat
Attached to rocks in crevices or protected places; from just above low-tide line to water more than 50' (15 m) deep.

Range
British Columbia to S. California.

Comments
Phylum Porifera, Class Calcispongiae. Despite their forbidding prickly appearance, the chalky spicules of Heath's Sponge crush easily when touched. The sponge sometimes takes the shape of the rock crevice in which it grows.

Red Beard Sponge
Microciona prolifera
476

Varies from a thin encrusting layer less than ⅛" (3 mm) high and covering a few square inches to 8" (20 cm) wide and 8" (20 cm) high with many fanlike branches. Red to orange. Pores inconspicuous.

Habitat
On rocks, pilings, oysters and other shells, and hard objects in protected bays and estuaries; below low-tide line.

Range
Washington to central California; Nova Scotia to Florida and Texas.

Comments
Phylum Porifera, Class Demospongiae. The Red Beard Sponge was the first animal shown to reorganize its form from experimentally separated cells. Cells divided by squeezing the sponge through a fine mesh cloth into a bowl of sea water creep about on the bottom, stick to each other, and finally form a mass that reorganizes into a sponge. This sponge tolerates both the pollution and the reduced salinities of bays and estuaries. It is preyed upon by nudibranchs such as the Crimson Doris (*Rostanga pulchra*).

Smooth Red Sponge
Plocamia karykina
477

More than 10" (25 cm) wide, 1" (25 mm) high. Encrusting, forming patches. Bright red to salmon-orange. Smooth, firm; pores large, variable in size, far apart.

Habitat
Attached to rocks in protected places; from between high- and low-tide lines to just below low-tide line.

Range
British Columbia to Baja California.

Comments
Phylum Porifera, Class Demospongiae. This sponge is thicker

and smoother than the Velvety Red Sponge, with fewer but larger pores. The red nudibranch Crimson Doris also feeds on this species.

Luxurious Fringed Worm
Cirriformia luxuriosa
478

6" (15 cm) long, ¼" (6 mm) wide. Nearly uniform in diameter. Yellowish, shading to orange or red. Head conical, no eyes; segments in front quarter each with 1 pair of red filamentous gills without grooves; segments 5–7 with 40 pairs of long, reddish-orange, grooved tentacles; segments farther back with fewer tentacles.

Habitat
In crevices in tide pools, in mussel beds, and among roots of surfgrass; from above low-tide line to water 65' (20 m) deep.

Range
Central California to Baja California.

Comments
Phylum Annelida, Class Polychaeta, Subclass Sedentaria. This worm is named *luxuriosa* because of the abundance of its long tentacles. It burrows just below the surface of the sand or mud, and extends its gills and tentacles into the water for oxygen and small organic food particles.

Curly Terebellid Worm
Thelepus crispus
479, 480

11¼" (28 cm) long, ¾" (19 mm) wide. In a tough, membranous, sand-encrusted tube. Reddish pink. Wide thorax, narrower abdomen. Head with numerous tentacles; 3 pairs of curly gills, each consisting of a cluster of red, unbranched filaments.

Habitat
Under rocks on exposed, rocky shores; above low-tide line.

Range
Entire Pacific Coast.

Comments
Phylum Annelida, Class Polychaeta, Subclass Sedentaria. This is the most common terebellid worm on the rocky shores of the West Coast, where its tough tube enables it to withstand the strong wave action.

Tubularian Hydroid
Tubularia crocea
481

Polyp colony large, tangled, more than 12" (30 cm) wide. Single pink polyps 5" (127 mm) high on sparsely branched stems rising from a creeping horizontal stem. Head pear-shaped, with whorl of short, threadlike tentacles around mouth, longer ones around base; 24 tentacles in each whorl. Grapelike clusters of reproductive organs, attached above basal whorl, hang down below it. No free-living medusa stage.

Habitat
Attached to almost any solid object continuously submerged in shallow water.

Range
Alaska to Baja California; Nova Scotia to Cape Hatteras,
possibly to Florida.

Comments
Phylum Cnidaria, Class Hydrozoa. These hydroids commonly
encrust boat hulls. Related species are the Ringed Tubularian
(*T. larynx*), 2″ (51 mm) high, which has highly branched
stems with circular constrictions; the Tall Tubularian (*T. indivisa*), with about 40 tentacles per whorl and polyps up to
12″ (30 cm) high; and the Sparsely-branched Tubularian (*T. spectabilis*), distinguished from *T. crocea* only by details of its
reproductive organs.

Bushy Wine-glass
Hydroids
Obelia spp.
482

Colony 8″ (20 cm) high, 4″ (102 mm) wide. Bushy. Whitish.
Colony highly branched, each branch with rings just above
attachments to stem. Feeding polyps at ends of branch tips
throughout upper part of colony; reproductive buds in lower
part of colony.

Habitat
Attached to rocks, shells, pilings, floats, and other solid
objects; found from low-tide line to water about 165′ (50 m)
deep.

Range
Both coasts of the United States.

Comments
Phylum Cnidaria, Class Hydrozoa. The old bushy colonies die
back in winter to the bases attaching them to the substrate.
New colonies may also grow back from these bases the next
spring. Recent work on the classification of the genus *Obelia*
suggests that there are only 2 species of Bushy Wine-glass
Hydroids, *O. bidentata* and *O. dichotoma*. They cannot be
distinguished in the field. The Double-toothed Bushy Wine-
glass Hydroid (*O. bidentata*) ranges from Puget Sound to S.
California and from Cape Cod to Florida and the West Indies,
and the Two-branched Wine-glass Hydroid (*O. dichotoma*) is
found from Alaska to Baja California.

Fern Garland Hydroids
Abietinaria spp.
483

Polyp colony 12″ (30 cm) high, 6″ (15 cm) wide. Bushy.
Whitish, yellowish, orange, or reddish brown. Stems stout,
stiff, branches alternate all in 1 plane. Polyp encased in flask-
shaped tube with narrow neck, tubes alternate on sides of
branch; polyp small, with 12 slender tentacles. Reproductive
structures are oval cases with smooth, ringed, or ridged walls.
No medusa stage.

Habitat
On ledges, rocks, and shells; from low-tide line to water
1440′ (439 m) deep.

Range
Alaska to S. California; Labrador to Cape Cod.

Comments
Phylum Cnidaria, Class Hydrozoa. The arrangement of branches in 1 plane gives these hydroids a fernlike appearance. The largest specimens occur well below low-tide line, and are collected by dredging or by scuba diving. The small size of structures used for identification makes laboratory examination necessary for accurate determination of species.

Halecium Hydroid
Halecium halecinum
484

Polyp colony 3" (76 mm) high, 1" (25 mm) wide. Erect, rigid. Grayish white. The few primary branches cemented together. Head sheath reduced to a slight flare. Feeding head small, with 12 short, rather thick tentacles. Sheath of reproductive organ pouchlike, attached directly to stem. Female has opening at one side of end bearing 2 small feeding heads. Reproductive organs reduced to saclike structures bearing gonads. No medusa stage.

Habitat
Attached to rocks, shells, and seaweed; from low-tide line to water 40′ (12 m) deep.

Range
British Columbia to central California; Arctic to Cape Hatteras.

Comments
Phylum Cnidaria, Class Hydrozoa. The Flared Halecium Hydroid (*H. tenellum*), an Atlantic Coast species, has been reported on the West Coast, as have a few others. *H. tenellum* is sparsely branched, ⅝" (16 mm) tall and ¼" (6 mm) wide.

Feathery Hydroids
Aglaophenia spp.
485, 486

Polyp colony ⅝–24" (16 mm–61 cm) high, ⅛–4" (3–102 mm) wide. Featherlike. Whitish, yellowish, tannish, or reddish. Stem simple or branching, usually in clusters rising from creeping base; upright stems jointed, with parallel jointed branches in 1 plane like a feather. Head sheaths on upper side of branch only, tubular, flared, 1 side fused to branch. Row of reproductive buds on branches, covered by pairs of leaflike structures bordered by knobs of stinging cells. No medusa stage.

Habitat
Attached to rocks, shells, or seaweeds; from low-tide line to water more than 8000′ (2438 m) deep.

Range
Alaska to S. California; Cape Cod to Florida and Texas.

Comments
Phylum Cnidaria, Class Hydrozoa. Most of the many species described for this genus occur in warm, subtropical Atlantic waters. It is possible that upon further study some of the hydroids described will no longer be considered separate species, since the differences cited in some cases are very small.

SEAWEEDS AND ALGAE

The sandy and rocky bottoms along the Pacific coast support a wide variety of marine algae—commonly known as seaweeds. Some grow close to the high-tide line, while others, like the giant Bull Kelp, which reaches 100 feet in size, are usually found farther out in deeper water. These plants provide shelter and food for a large number of different kinds of organisms, from fishes to tiny diatoms. This section includes descriptions of some of the seaweeds most frequently seen along these shores.

Turkish Towel
Gigartina exasperata
487

12–20″ (30–50 cm) long, 4–8″ (10–20 cm) wide. Blades broad, densely covered with minute projections that give the appearance of a turkish towel. Blades range from deep red to purplish red; iridescent when submerged. Stipe small, sometimes branched with more than 1 blade.

Habitat
On rocks in the lower intertidal and subtidal zones.

Range
British Columbia to California.

Comments
Gigartina species are an important source of carrageenan, which is used in many food products as a thickening agent.

Iridescent Seaweed
Iridaea cordata
488

Blades 1–3′ (.25–1 m) long. Blades dark bluish purple and iridescent; broad; smooth or with an undulating margin; frequently split or lobed.

Habitat
Lower rocky intertidal zone; also in upper subtidal.

Range
Alaska to California.

Comments
In the lower intertidal zone, this plant forms distinct bands. It contains carrageenan, and studies are currently underway to establish the feasibility of harvesting it commercially.

Winged Kelp
Alaria spp.
489

Main blade 6–10′ (2–3 m) long, 2–10″ (5–20 cm) wide. Olive-green to rich brown. Each blade has a midrib and arises from a short stipe. At base of main blade are 2 opposite rows of reproductive blades called sporophylls.

Habitat
In the lower intertidal zone on moderate to exposed shores.

Range
Gulf of Alaska to central California.

Comments
There are several *Alaria* species on the Pacific Coast. These are choice sea vegetables and can be added to soups, stir-fried, or, like grape leaves and cabbage leaves, used to wrap foods. When harvesting Winged Kelp, do not remove the sporophylls; they should be left to ensure that the plant reproduces.

Giant Perennial Kelp
Macrocystis spp.
490, 491

Plants to 200′ (60 m) or longer. Individual blades 10–15″ (25–35 cm) long, 2″ (5 cm) wide. Leaflike blades are gold to rich brown, with pointed tips, rounded bases. Blades fastened to rounded floats that rise from the stipe. Hundreds of blades grow from a repeatedly branched stipe, rising from a massive, rhizomelike base.

Habitat
In the subtidal zone, in areas exposed to open sea, but somewhat sheltered from the full force of heavy wave action.

Range
Alaska to California.

Comments
This is our largest kelp; it can grow more than 18" a day. Vast forests grow off the coast of southern California; they are harvested by underwater mowing machines mounted on barges. State laws regulate this harvesting. Algin is extracted from the kelp, then used in food products, drugs, and in the processing of textiles, beer, paints, ice cream, and paper products. The profitable kelp industry was at one time brought to near collapse due to a combination of factors, one of the most important the demise of the sea otter population. As the sea otter became hunted to near extinction by fur traders, sea urchins, on which the sea otters had preyed, rapidly increased their numbers. The urchins, in turn, increasingly harvested the kelp, tearing the plants loose from their holdfast. As soon as new shoots were formed, the urchins ate them. At first, the sea urchin population was regulated by the application of lime. Later, as the sea otter population slowly increased in size again, a natural balance was reestablished.

Feather Boa
Egregia menziesii
492

Blade to 30' (10 m) long, 4–7" (10–15 cm) wide. Usually dark brown to olive-green. Blade broad, stout, sturdy, and flattened, arising from sturdy holdfast; many branches arise from one holdfast. Stipe and blade rough, with blunt projections. Many small blades ⅜–¾" (1–2 cm) wide and many small, oblong floats.

Habitat
On rocks in the lower intertidal and subtidal zones in moderately exposed waters; on more exposed shores, slightly higher.

Range
British Columbia to California.

Comments
Like many kelps, *Egregia* species have been used as mulch and fertilizer by farmers.

Bull Kelp
Nereocystis luetkeana
493

To 100' (30 m) long. Visible portion is an inflated float 4–6" (10–15 cm) in diameter. Float supports a number of long, strap-shaped blades, each several feet in length, that trail in the water. Long, hollow stipe is usually 6–20' (2–6 m) long; stipe anchored to rocks by massive holdfast.

Habitat
Upper subtidal zone.

Range
Alaska to California.

Comments
Also known as Bull Whip Kelp or Ribbon Kelp, *Nereocystis* is one of the largest seaweeds. Most plants do not survive winter storms and grow to their massive size in a single season. The inflated float proves a platform for great blue herons as they fish, and the submerged portions of the plant provide a habitat for many fishes and marine invertebrates. Bull Kelp is an excellent edible.

Sugar Wrack
Laminaria saccharina
494

Blades 2' (0.6 m) or longer. Blade is long, brown, and often split along lines of mucilage ducts. Surface may be smooth or ruffled. Stipe is 1–3' (.25–1 m) long.

Habitat
On rocks, wharfs, or shells in the intertidal and subtidal zones.

Range
From the Aleutian Islands to Coos Bay, Oregon; also found on North Atlantic shores.

Comments
There are a number of commonly encountered *Laminaria* species that flourish in cool waters. At least 40 grow along the Pacific Coast, where they provide food and shelter for a variety of marine animals. This kelp was once an important source of potash, used in making soap and other products; iodine was also extracted from it. It is edible, and used as a flavoring in soups and stews.

Sea Lettuce
Ulva lactuca
495

4–20" (10–50 cm) long. Single, moderately large, oblong blade, often ruffled along the margin. Light to dark green.

Habitat
On rocks; also epiphytic on other algae in the upper intertidal zone; often found floating on mud flats.

Range
Bering Sea to Chile.

Comments
There are a number of *Ulva* species that grow on the Pacific Coast. When fertile, reproductive cells are released from the edges of the plants, occasionally forming pale green clouds in tide pools. Because these algae are high in vitamins and minerals, in many countries they are used as a food.

Sea Palm
Postelsia palmaeformis
496

To 20″ (15–50 cm) tall. Distinctive appearance: resembles a small, olive to brown palm tree. Grooved, strap-shaped blades up to 10″ (25 cm) long located near the top of stipe. A large plant may have as many as 100 blades.

Habitat
On exposed portions of the outer coast, often associated with mussels and barnacles.

Range
British Columbia to central California.

Comments
Sea Palms are annuals. They have sturdy holdfasts and grow tightly fastened to the most exposed rocks in the high intertidal zone, where they resemble a grove of tiny palm trees. They are delicious eaten fresh, stir-fried, or in soups, but care should be taken to leave enough plants attached to the rocks to ensure that reproduction will occur the following season.

Sea Staghorn
Codium fragile
497

To 16″ (10–40 cm) long. Dark green, with cylindrical segments about ¼–⅓″ (0.5–1 cm) in diameter that branch repeatedly. Cylindrical segments are erect, spongy, hairy, and forked.

Habitat
Middle to lower intertidal zone and subtidal regions of rocky shores.

Range
Alaska to Mexico.

Comments
This alga also grows in other parts of the world. In New England, it has become a nuisance to commercial fishermen because scallops, oysters, and mussels all attach themselves to the plants, then are carried out to sea when strong waves surge over the algae, ripping them from the ocean floor. The plant's distinctive appearance has given it the alternate common name Dead Man's Fingers. In Japan, *Codium fragile* is bleached then soaked, sugared, and eaten as a delicacy. Because it is rich with vitamins plus iron and other minerals, it is also added to soups or used as a garnish.

Sea Sack
Halosaccion glandiforme
498

6″ (15 cm) long, 1″ (2–3 cm) wide; occasionally larger. Pale yellow to dark purplish red. Forms clumps of hollow, thin-walled, sausage-shaped sacs. Each sac filled near the top with gas.

Habitat
On rocks in the mid-intertidal zone, in both sheltered and exposed areas.

Range
Alaska to Mexico.

Comments
The gases that are trapped in the sacs are a result of rapid photosynthesis. When the sacs are gently squeezed, a fine spray of water squirts out of them.

Rockweed
Fucus distichus
499

4–20″ (10–50 cm) long. When wet, olive-green to yellowish; when dry, darker, sometimes almost black. Thick, flattened repeated and equal branches have midrib. Mature, fertile plants have swollen branch tips called receptacles on which male and female gametes (sex cells) are produced.

Habitat
On rocks in the mid-intertidal zone in temperate waters.

Range
Alaska to California.

Comments
Rockweed is also known as Bladder Wrack. *Fucus* species are common worldwide in temperate seas. Used as mulch, cattle fodder, and as a source of algin, they are also fit for human consumption.

Little Rockweed
Pelvetiopsis limitata
500

2½–6″ (6–18 cm) long. Resembles *Fucus* but smaller, without veins. Olive-green to brownish and repeatedly and equally branched. Mature tips swollen with sex organs and spores.

Habitat
Very high in the rocky intertidal zone on exposed coasts.

Range
British Columbia to central California.

Comments
Little Rockweed often grows along with *Fucus* species in the intertidal zone, where it forms extensive bands. It is a choice sea vegetable and may be used in stir-fried dishes and in soups.

Fir Needle
Analipus japonicus
501

2–10″ (5–25 cm) long. Light tan to deep olive or dark brown to forest-green. Shoots are tall and erect. Several plants arise from one encrusting holdfast.

Habitat
On rocks along moderately exposed shores in the mid-intertidal zone.

Range
Alaska to central California.

Comments
Like all brown algae, *Analipus japonicus* contains chlorophyll. The green pigment is masked by the presence of gold or brownish pigments. This plant is high in protein and also rich

in vitamins and minerals. It may be eaten fresh or sun dried, then salted and cooked with soy sauce. In Japan it is preserved in combination with mushrooms.

Nail Brush
Endocladia muricata
502

In clumps 2–4" (4–8 cm) tall. Dark brownish red to purple or black. Wiry. When dry, hard; when wet, softer, more flexible.

Habitat
On moderately exposed to very exposed rocky shores in the high intertidal zone.

Range
Alaska to Mexico.

Comments
Endocladia muricata forms a distinct association with the barnacles in the genus *Balanus* in the high intertidal zone. Animals that live in this zone are exposed to air much more than they are submerged in water, but some receive some wave splash. Many small animals and algae find shelter in this *Endocladia-Balanus* association.

Black Pine
Rhodomela larix
503

Strands to 12" (30 cm) long. Strands dark reddish brown to black, ropelike. Several branches arise from 1 holdfast; these branches have a dense covering of short branchlets arranged radially.

Habitat
On rocks in the mid- to lower intertidal zone.

Range
Alaska to California.

Comments
This plant is often found growing in association with another red alga, *Odonthalia,* which it somewhat resembles. The two algae often form a dark brown, purplish, or black band growing on rocks in the intertidal zone. A brown, sac-shaped alga, *Soranthera,* often grows on *Rhodomela.* Small herbivorous crustaceans feed upon Black Pine.

Tar Spot
Ralfsia pacifica
504

Crust ½" (.5–1 mm) thick, 1–4" (2–10 cm) in diameter. Minute filaments, tightly packed together, rise from cell layer located next to rock; together they form a thick, dark brown, circular crust that resembles tar. May have fine ridges radiating from central point; circular ridges parallel to edge may also be present.

Habitat
High in the intertidal zone on rocks and on other solid substrates.

Range
Alaska to Baja California.

Comments
Brown algae occur in all oceans but are most characteristic of temperate to cold waters. Some other species of brown algae resemble *Ralfsia* and, in certain stages, some red algae, such as *Petrocelis*, also form dark crusts on intertidal rocks. These algae seem able to survive temperature extremes and exposure better than tubular or bladelike species.

Coralline Algae
Corallina spp.
505, 506

2–4″ (4–10 cm) high, ¼″ (.7–1 mm) wide. Bright pink and very tough, with jointed, cylindrical branches encrusted with calcium carbonate (lime).

Habitat
Frequent in tide pools in the lower intertidal and upper subtidal zones.

Range
Alaska to Mexico.

Comments
These heavily calcified and highly articulated algae were once thought to be animals related to corals. There are several species common on the Pacific Coast. They are not tolerant of the drying effects of air. Clusters of coralline algae feel stiff and gritty when they are pinched. Their branches provide an excellent habitat for a variety of small invertebrate animals. When they are washed ashore, they dry out and, bleached by the sun, they turn white.

Encrusting Coral
Lithothamnium pacificum
507

Minute. Bright pink, forming extensive circular crusts; crusts may overlap.

Habitat
On rocks in tide pools in the lower intertidal and subtidal zones.

Range
British Columbia to California.

Comments
These plants are easily overlooked because they appear to be rock coloration or a mineral coating rather than living organisms. Encrusting coralline algae are important reef builders in tropical waters, where they build thick crusts of calcium carbonate.

Eelgrass
Zostera marina
508

Blades to 4′ (3 m) long, ⅛–¼″ (2–12 mm) wide. Leaves alternate, with parallel veins or only a midvein. Flowers sessile, in 2 rows on 1 side of flattened spadix.

Habitat
In quiet protected bays with muddy bottoms.

Range
From Alaska to Mexico.

Comments
Sea grasses are not true grasses. Instead, they are flowering plants related to certain pond weeds that live in fresh waters. The sea grasses have evolved an ability to live in saline waters. The flowers themselves are inconspicuous and resemble oddly shaped spikes of wheat. Eelgrass forms rich meadows in protected waters and is an important food and habitat for many animals, including sea turtles and waterfowl. The outer half of each blade is usually coated with a wide variety of minute marine plants and animals. The roots and extensive rhizomes bind the plants into the mud. Currents distribute both pollen and the small fruits; propagation also occurs by means of the rhizomes. The Seri Indians of the Gulf of California once harvested Eelgrass seeds, then ground them into a kind of flour. The blades have been used as insulation and as mattress stuffing. A red Alga, *Smithora naiadaum*, grows as an epiphyte on Eelgrass.

Surf Grass
Phyllospadix spp.
509

Blades to 6′ (2 m) long. Strap-shaped leaves resemble those of Eelgrass, but are narrower; leaves arise from prostrate rhizomes and roots. Bright green blades grow in tremendous beds approximately 30′ by 100′.

Habitat
On exposed rocky shores.

Range
Alaska to Mexico.

Comments
Several *Phyllospadix* species occur along the Pacific Coast. *P. scouleri* has broad, flat leaves and grows in the lower intertidal and upper subtidal zones. *P. torreyi* has thinner, wiry leaves, and grows in deeper waters. *P. serrulatus* resembles *P. scouleri,* but its leaves are thinner. Red coralline algae and brown algae grow as epiphytes on *Phyllospadix* species. The green alga *Monostroma zostericola* also grows as an epiphyte on both Surf Grass and Eelgrass.

Enteromorpha Green Algae
Enteromorpha spp.
510

To 8″ (1–20 cm) long. Usually hollow and tubular and occurring in groups. Plant mass is bright green to yellowish green.

Habitat
Usually attached to rocks in the upper intertidal zone, especially in tidal pools or areas with freshwater seepage.

Range
Worldwide.

Comments
Green algae are distinguished from other groups of algae by their bright green color, which is due to the presence of certain chlorophylls. These algae contain starch food reserves and cellulose cell walls similar to those found in green land

plants, and may be their ancestors. *Enteromorpha* species are worldwide in distribution. Of those that occur on the Pacific Coast, two of the most conspicuous are *E. intestinalis* and *E. linza*. *E. intestinalis* is quite tubular and *E. linza* is more flattened, somewhat resembling species in the genus *Ulva*. Compared with *Ulva* species, plants in the genus *Enteromorpha* are delicate. They are composed of a single layer of cells and consequently thin—so thin that it is possible to see your fingerprints through them. In contrast, plants in the genus *Ulva* are composed of more than one layer of cells. These plants are tolerant of brackish conditions and of pollution and grow rapidly. Occasionally bubbles of oxygen become trapped in their tubular bodies, buoying the plants to the surface. When the plants die, they quickly turn white; dried, their delicate structure crumbles and disintegrates. *Enteromorpha* species are very nutritious and may be eaten. However, when the water in which they grow has been polluted, they should be avoided.

BIRDS

No visit to the seashore is complete without the pleasure of watching birds in action. As tight little flocks of Sanderlings race up and down at the water's edge, terns and gulls cry out and dive for food. Farther out, over the water, cormorants glide evenly along, searching for fish just below the water's surface, while the large shearwaters and the songbird-sized storm-petrels may be seen well out to sea over the open ocean. In fall and spring, the air is rich with the calls of migrating ducks and geese. And from time to time, a Bald Eagle may be seen, swooping down from the sky for fishes. This section describes some of the most frequently seen birds that occur along the Pacific shores.

Arctic Loon
Gavia arctica
511

23–29″ (58–74 cm). Small loon with slender bill. In summer, similar to Common Loon but light gray head and neck contrasts with darker gray back; black shield on throat flanked with white stripes marks the elegant breeding plumage of both sexes. In winter, 2-toned like all loons, darker above than Red-throated Loon. Its straight bill also distinguishes it from Red-throated Loon and its smaller size from Common Loon.

Voice
Largely silent except on breeding grounds, where a barking *caw wow* is uttered. Also a variety of wailing and honking notes.

Habitat
Lakes in woods or tundra; winters along seacoast.

Range
Circumpolar. Breeds in the western and central Arctic of North America. Winters along the Pacific Coast to the Gulf of California.

Comments
This loon is believed to migrate only during the day. It flies in loose formations, presenting a long, slender gray outline, with the feet stretched backward and the neck held straight or bent downward in an arc.

Red-throated Loon
Gavia stellata
512

24–27″ (61–69 cm). Smallest loon. Slender upturned bill. In summer, gray above with a chestnut throat patch; in winter, mottled gray on back (lighter than other loons) with white throat and foreneck. Sexes look alike.

Voice
Silent except on breeding grounds, where it utters a rather long series of quacking notes.

Habitat
Small, shallow, partly vegetated lakes; generally seen along seacoasts in winter.

Range
More completely circumpolar than other loons. In America it breeds in Aleutians and along Arctic coasts, also inland on tundra, and south along Pacific Coast to S. British Columbia. Winters on both coasts and also on the Great Lakes.

Comments
These loons often gather in flocks of several dozen. They sit very low in the water with the head and bill tilted upward, and are the only loons that can take flight directly from water; others require a running start. In Arctic Alaska, Eskimo ceremonial cloaks are made from their skins, alternated with skins of the Yellow-billed Loon. In 1763 the Danish naturalist Erik Pontoppidan imagined that he saw a brilliant red star in the throat patch of this loon and named it *stellata*, meaning "the starred one."

Red-necked Grebe
Podiceps grisegena
513

18–22" (46–56 cm). Medium-sized, stocky grebe. Rufous neck in summer with black crown and gray face outlined in white. 2 small black ear tufts are visible where crown and nape meet. In winter gray neck and face with white crescent from throat to ear. Afloat, it looks short-bodied and heavy-headed, with rather long, stout yellow bill. In flight it shows double white patch on inner wing. Sexes look alike.

Voice
Generally silent except on breeding grounds, where a sharp *kack* and wailing courtship call may be heard.

Habitat
During summer marshy ponds and bays of lakes; in winter deeper open waters, especially along the coast.

Range
Mainly a northwestern bird, nesting on lakes from the Aleutians and Alaskan coniferous forest and northern tundra, east to Minnesota and south from central Washington to S. Wisconsin. In winter common on the Pacific Coast south to central California; less common on the Atlantic Coast.

Comments
The Red-necked Grebe migrates from its coastal wintering grounds to inland lakes, dispersing to nest on the vegetation in larger ponds. It eats small aquatic vertebrates such as fish, tadpoles, and newts. Like other grebes it swallows feathers, probably to strain out fish bones and other undigested remnants, which it periodically regurgitates.

Western Grebe
Aechmophorus occidentalis
514

22–29" (56–74 cm). Largest North American grebe. Long neck. Head, neck, and body slate-blackish above, white below; long, yellow bill. Long white wing stripe shows in flight. Sexes look alike year round.

Voice
A rolling *kr-r-rick!*, given most often on its breeding grounds, but frequently heard from wintering birds as well.

Habitat
Large lakes with marshy regions for breeding; in winter, mainly an inshore seabird.

Range
Breeds on prairie lakes and other big lakes of the West from British Columbia south to S. California and sparsely to Mexico, east to Lake Winnipeg. Winters from the central British Columbia coast south to central Mexico, and on some inland waters.

Comments
The mating display of these grebes is spectacular. Hundreds of paired birds display together, both sexes dancing and posturing like mirror images as they race across the surface of the water. In migration, they fly in loose flocks but spread out to feed during the day. These grebes are very susceptible to oil

spills and to insecticides that have accumulated in their food and thus affected their breeding success.

Eared Grebe
Podiceps nigricollis
515

12–14″ (30–36 cm). Teal-sized bird, a bit smaller than the Horned Grebe. Breeding birds rufous below with black head and neck, golden ear tufts (neck of Horned Grebe is rufous). In winter plumage, dark neck and dark ear region contrasting with whitish face distinguish it from the Horned Grebe; bodies of both dusky above, white below. At close range, bill upturned; that of Horned Grebe is straight. Both have red eyes.

Voice
On the breeding grounds, a loud *keryeep!*

Habitat
Large lakes and sloughs where part of the water is overgrown with emergent vegetation.

Range
Southwestern Canada through the western United States south to the desert belts. Also in the Old World. Winters south to Mexico.

Comments
Adult and young alike feed on insects. These birds migrate at night, and large congregations may be seen at lakes or seaside coves, where they dive for tiny crustaceans. Breeding in colonies is thought to provide a synchronized timetable for mating, egg laying, and rearing of young. So many eggs and chicks available simultaneously provide an oversupply of food for predators, allowing most eggs to escape predation.

Horned Grebe
Podiceps auritus
516

12–15¼″ (30–39 cm). Breeding birds of both sexes have rufous lower parts and neck, black head, and 2 buffy tufts on head. In winter gray above, white below; short, thin neck and much white on face, ear area, and neck, contrasting with blackish cap. Straight bill.

Voice
A high squeal and a sharp *ka-raa* heard on the nesting grounds. Otherwise generally silent.

Habitat
Small lakes and ponds. Bays, estuaries, and seacoasts in migration and winter.

Range
From the Yukon Delta east to Hudson Bay, and east-central Ontario, and North Dakota west to Idaho, Washington, and British Columbia. Winters on both coasts.

Comments
In contrast to the Eared Grebe, whose range it overlaps, this bird primarily eats fish and tadpoles rather than insects. Horned Grebes are solitary or form loose aggregations.

Common Loon
Gavia immer
517

28–36" (71–91 cm). Large bird, about the size of a Canada Goose. Breeding birds have dark bodies spotted with pearl-white marks, especially visible on back; head and neck glossy green-black with white necklace. Iris red, legs and feet blackish, webs pink. In winter, gray-brown above, white below. Dark bill heavy and straight, whereas similar Yellow-billed Loon has upturned bill.

Voice
Yodeling call given on breeding grounds; less commonly, on migration. Its tremolo, uttered at night in the still northern woods, is a thrilling sound. Silent on its wintering grounds.

Habitat
Coniferous forest belt of the North, lakes or rivers with deep water, and vegetation reaching the waterline to hide the nest. In winter loons are found on lakes and large rivers as well, but the majority prefer bays and coves along the seacoast.

Range
Aleutians, Alaska, Canada, northern border states of the United States, Greenland, and Iceland. Winters along all coasts of North America.

Comments
In the words of naturalist Sigurd Olson, the loon's wild, laughing tremolo is "the sound that more than any other typifies the wilderness." Loons are powerful divers and have been caught in fishermen's nets 200 feet below the surface. Seldom do dives last more than 30 seconds, but these birds have been known to stay under as long as 2 or 3 minutes. Their legs are set far back and within the body, so that only the ankles are visible. Unlike most other birds, they have almost solid bones with a specific gravity close to that of water, enabling them to submerge effortlessly.

Pied-billed Grebe
Podilymbus podiceps
518

12–15" (30–38 cm). Small, drab brown grebe with thick, short, chickenlike bill, no crest. White beneath tail; black bill ring and throat in summer, white throat and bill in winter. Very rarely seen in flight. Sexes look alike.

Voice
A low, hollow, yelping *eeow-eeow-eeow-keeowm-kowm-kowm*.

Habitat
Marshes, ponds, and ditches with shallow water and dense marsh vegetation; open water of any size in winter or on migration.

Range
Breeds throughout the Americas, except the subarctic and subantarctic regions. Winters in central British Columbia and all western and southern states with open water. Also on seacoasts.

Comments
The Pied-billed Grebe may mix with other waterfowl, but

it is usually solitary; breeding pairs are secretive and sometimes only one pair is found on a pond. It is able to sink with barely a ripple, only its head popping up, like a periscope, at a distance before it dives again.

White-winged Scoter
Melanitta fusca
519

19–23½" (48–60 cm). One of the largest ducks. Male black with white eye patch that curves back and up; female dark brown with 2 light cheek patches, much like female Surf Scoter. Both sexes have a white patch on inner flight feathers, usually visible even when wings are folded.

Voice
A hoarse croak.

Habitat
Muskeg and bogs of the boreal forest belt in summer; seacoasts in winter.

Range
Across Scandinavia, the Siberian taiga, Aleutian Islands, and on ponds from forested Alaska to Manitoba and North Dakota. Winters on the coasts and, rarely, on the Great Lakes.

Comments
Scoters dive for shellfish. At sea, where they winter, this species seems more solitary than other sea ducks. White-winged Scoters, Surf Scoters, Black Scoters, scaups, and Oldsquaws fly in long, wavering lines over water. Such a formation, when settled on the water, is called a "raft." When a raft disperses and starts to dive, the White-winged Scoters seem to drift apart, while the other species of scoters stay together.

Black Scoter
Melanitta nigra
520

17–20½" (43–52 cm). Medium-sized sea duck. Male black overall with bright orange spot on upper mandible. Female dark brown, head light grayish with contrasting dark cap.

Voice
More vocal than other scoters; during display male gives a peculiar whistling note, *coar-loo*.

Habitat
Tundra and boreal woodland interspersed with lakes or rivers; in winter, along seacoasts and in inshore waters.

Range
Circumpolar; in North America it breeds in the coastal regions of far W. Alaska and inland in northeastern Canada. Winters on both coasts, although it is uncommon south of N. California. Judging from subtle differences in the bill, Pacific Coast birds come only from Alaska.

Comments
Black Scoters, like Surf Scoters, are gregarious; the 2 species often feed near each other, but separately, in coves along the Pacific Coast. The mating display of both occurs on sunny

days during the winter. Whereas the male Surf Scoter dives and flies up while displaying around the female, the male Black Scoter splashes and whistles.

Surf Scoter
Melanitta perspicillata
521

17–21″ (43–53 cm). Male black with white patches on forehead and nape. Big swollen bill has a bright white-black, red-orange pattern. Female dark brown with 2 light cheek patches like those of White-winged Scoter, but white wing patches distinguish the latter.

Voice
A low grating croak and other grunting notes. Usually silent on winter grounds. In courtship flight, wings produce a whirring sound.

Habitat
Tundra and forest bogs during breeding season; coastal waters during winter.

Range
From Aleutian Islands and W. Alaska to W. Labrador, but its distribution is not completely known. Winters on both coasts and, rarely, on the Great Lakes.

Comments
The commonest scoter of the Pacific Coast in winter, it spends most of the year there and only a short season on its Arctic breeding grounds. These scoters stay some distance from shore, taking shellfish, especially mussels. In deeper water the colorful males and dark brown females dive with their wings partially open, and swim underwater with feet and wings, using the alula, a false wing, as a stabilizer. Displays of several males around a single female may be seen from early winter on, especially in sunny weather. Single birds, usually young males, may spend their second summer on the sea.

American Wigeon
Anas americana
522

18–23″ (46–58 cm). Male has brown body, grayish head, white crown (hence the popular name "Baldpate") and green face patch. Extensive flashing white forewing of male distinguishes the species; patch on inner flight feathers green. Female is drab brown, with finely flecked grayish head.

Voice
Males give a distinctive softly whistled *wheew-whew;* females quack.

Habitat
Open marshy areas, tundra, and prairie.

Range
Alaska and the Northwest Territories south to the central Canadian mountain provinces and the western states. On the Pacific Coast it winters in tidal and valley marshes from Vancouver Island south through Mexico, and in Hawaii. Also winters along the East Coast and in the Gulf Coast states.

Comments
In many parts of their range, flocks of wigeons and coots
winter together. Both feed on bottom vegetation, wigeons
dabbling in the shallows, coots diving in deeper waters. When
food that the wigeons reach becomes scarce, they steal food out
of the bills of the coots, causing the latter to work double-
time to satisfy themselves as well as the ducks. Wary and
alert, wigeons present a delightful sight on an open marsh,
whole flocks rising in unison at the slightest disturbance. In
the air they form tight, swiftly turning flocks and their
whistling calls enliven the scene.

Greater Scaup
Aythya marila
523

15½–20″ (39–51 cm). Medium-sized duck. Midbody of male
is white below, and light with wavy gray lines above. Head,
breast, and tail are black with green sheen on head. In flight,
its long, white wing stripe distinguishes it from Lesser Scaup.
Bill bluish gray. Female is dull brown with white facial patch
encircling base of bill.

Voice
Females give a low *arrr;* courting males, a soft, cooing
whistle.

Habitat
Wet tundra, lakes and rivers; boreal forests south of tundra. In
winter on the sea near the coast.

Range
Circumpolar; in North America, in low arctic tundra marshes
in a belt from western and central Alaska through northern
Canada. Winters on all 3 coasts, at some of the Great Lakes
and the Mississippi valley.

Comments
For most birders the Greater Scaup is either a winter duck or a
rarity. It is found in flocks, or rafts, often mixed with other
diving ducks.

Bufflehead
Bucephala albeola
524

13–15½″ (33–39 cm). Smallest North American duck.
Breeding male white with shiny black back and with large
white patch on head conspicuous against green- and purple-
glossed black forehead and nape. Female dark overall with pale
breast, blackish head with well-defined white oval below and
behind eye. Both sexes show white patch on inner wing in
flight.

Voice
Male gives a squeaky whistle; female, a low quack.

Habitat
Northern coniferous forest with small ponds and bogs
surrounded by open water and trees.

Range
Alaska to N. Ontario and south through British Columbia to

N. California. In winter, in most of America where waters remain open and on Pacific and Atlantic coasts.

Comments
These sprightly, beautiful ducks fly fast and usually close to the water. They are quite tame; when flushed, they often circle back and settle in their original places. In winter they visit even the smallest ponds or ditches as long as there is sufficient animal food. They also like rocky shores. Displaying males float high, alternating forward rushes with head-bobbing and chin-up displays with the head feathers erected.

Harlequin Duck
Histrionicus histrionicus
525

14½–21" (37–53 cm). Rather small. Breeding male is slate-blue with bright chestnut flanks and bold white markings outlined in black—as on a clown or harlequin—most conspicuous on head and wings. Female and nonbreeding male dark with 2 or 3 small white patches on head; male also shows some white on wing.

Voice
Mostly silent. Male utters high, squealing notes; female, a harsh croak.

Habitat
Near rushing water around boulders; in mountain streams during the nesting season and, in winter, around partly submerged ledges of rocky seashores.

Range
Breeds from W. Alaska, N. Yukon, British Columbia, and S. Alaska to Alaskan Peninsula, Vancouver Island, E. Oregon, and western states; and along North Atlantic coast. In the West, it winters along Pacific Coast south to central California.

Comments
In the Georgia Strait–Puget Sound area of Washington and British Columbia, these ducks may be seen all year among rocky headlands and islets where currents have created great surges. They dive daily for snails, chitons, and crabs. The earliest breeders leave for coastal streams on the nearby mainland in April. The males return at the end of June or later, when other males are still courting their females at sea, and wait for their Rocky Mountain home streams to thaw, at which time they can nest.

Oldsquaw
Clangula hyemalis
526

19–22½" (48–57 cm). Medium-sized sea duck, but male looks larger due to long central tail feathers. Most variable of all American ducks, wearing 3 plumages annually. Winter male is white on head, back, underside, and elongated shoulder feathers and has black on ear, breast, wing, and central tail feathers; in late spring mainly black, with chestnut-buff on mantle, white flanks, gray patch surrounding eyes; summer male has, in addition, gray flanks and sides, more buff on wings. Female corresponds to male but with shorter tail; black crown in winter plumage, white semicollar in spring and summer plumages. In flight, both sexes show dark wings.

Voice
The displaying male has a repertoire of gurgling, gabbling calls, some sounding like *ow-owly, owly, owly* or *ah, ah, ah,* and *ong.*

Habitat
Breeds on tundra ponds and marshes; winters on inshore waters with shallow mussel banks.

Range

Circumpolar on the Arctic coasts of northern continents with extensions southward. In the West, breeds on Aleutian Islands and Alaskan and Canadian tundra. Winters along Pacific Coast, south mainly to Washington.

Comments
When they arrive at wintering waters, Oldsquaws search for mussel banks where they will feed. Studies show that adults lead the immatures to feeding grounds; eventually the young learn the locality. In courting, several males display around a female, calling noisily. This phase of the courtship behavior gave rise to their American name; the British call them "Long-tailed Ducks."

Northern Pintail
Anas acuta
527

Male 25–29" (64–74 cm), female 20½–22½" (52–57 cm). Long-necked slender duck. Male has brown head and white neck and underparts, grayish back and sides and long black pointed central tail feathers. Patch on inner flight feathers metallic brown and green with white rear border that shows in flight. Feet gray. Female has brownish head, gray bill, and somewhat pointed tail.

Voice
As in most ducks, the male has the higher-pitched voice, uttering a high *dreep-eep;* females give a low quack.

Habitat
Marshes of the tundra and boreal forests as well as prairie marshes; in winter most freshwater marshes and lakes, as well as brackish water.

Range

Throughout the Northern Hemisphere; in North America breeds from Aleutians, Alaska to Hudson Bay and south to California and Colorado.

Comments
A banding project on the Hawaiian Islands revealed that the few thousand Pintails that winter there hatched as far away as California's Sacramento Valley, a Saskatchewan marsh, and even the Siberian tundra. Pairing takes place in late fall and winter in the southern wintering areas. The male then follows

his new mate to her breeding area, regardless of where he was born or spent the previous summer. Thus the Pintail population undergoes a steady mixing, keeping the species uniform everywhere.

Brant
Branta bernicla
528

23–26" (58–66 cm). Mallard-sized goose. On water it seems entirely dark except for a white collar; in flight it shows a black-and-white pattern. Head, neck, chest, back, wings, and tail black; sides of chest appear lighter; lower belly, flanks, and undertail snow-white.

Voice
A series of soft *ruk-ruk* calls.

Habitat
An entirely marine bird breeding on coastal tundra. Bays and estuaries in winter.

Range
Circumpolar on the Arctic shores of Eurasia and North America. On the Pacific Coast it winters from Vancouver Island to Baja California. Concentrations occur in winter in Washington's Puget Sound and in California's Humboldt and Morro bays.

Comments
The small size of these geese and their black-and-white appearance are unique. Many are shot by hunters each year, but a greater danger to the species is the steady loss of winter habitats to encroaching civilization.

Emperor Goose
Chen canagica
529

26–28" (66–71 cm). As large as Snow Goose or White-fronted Goose. Body and wings silver-gray: black-and-white feather margins give a scaled, bluish appearance. White head, hindneck, and tail, black throat and foreneck, flesh-colored bill, bright orange legs and feet. Juveniles gray overall.

Voice
Loud musical notes, *cla-ha, cla-ha, cla-ha.*

Habitat
Seacoasts, mud flats, marshes, and tundra.

Range
Islands and marshy coasts of the Bering Sea, Aleutian Islands. In winter, frost and pack ice drive it south of the Aleutian chain. Casual winter visitors appear south along the North Pacific coast and in inland valleys.

Comments
The head and neck of these geese take on a deep rust stain from the iron in stagnating waters, for they feed with head and neck submerged, grazing on bottom vegetation. The black pattern on the throat distinguishes this species from the "Blue Goose" (the blue phase of the Snow Goose), which is relatively rare in the West.

Tundra Swan
Cygnus columbianus
530

47–58″ (119–147 cm). Large white swan; habitually holds neck straight and stiff; black bill usually with a small yellow spot near eye. Immatures light gray-brown, with pinkish bill.

Voice
A high-pitched, whistling *wow-wow,* often heard long before the birds can be seen in the sky.

Habitat
Tundra in nesting season; in winter, tidal and freshwater marshes.

Range
Breeds near the Arctic coast between the Bering Sea and Hudson Bay and in the central Canadian Arctic. Winters on the Pacific Coast.

Comments
In one study, swans were marked with colored neck bands at Chesapeake Bay and their migration was followed to their Alaskan breeding grounds. One "Whistler," banded on the Atlantic seaboard the previous winter, was sighted in the Central Valley of California in March 1974. This Arctic breeder alternately visited the Atlantic and Pacific coasts of the huge North American continent, surely something of a record for birds.

Brown Pelican
Pelecanus occidentalis
531

45–54″ (114–137 cm). Large, heavy seabird. Huge, dark bill and large throat pouch; adults grayish brown with white head; immatures dark-headed, pale below. In flight, it is easily recognized by its alternate flapping and gliding of broad powerful wings, short tail, and S-shaped neck. Breeding birds have dark chestnut hindneck extending to crested nape.

Voice
Groaning and screaming sounds are uttered by young around breeding colonies. Adults generally silent.

Habitat
Oceans, inshore waters; stands on pilings or rocks.

Range
In the United States, Pacific and southeastern coastal areas. Also Central and South America. Occasionally reaches Vancouver Island.

Comments
These social, colonial birds fly in single file low over the water; on sighting prey they plunge from heights of up to 30 feet but surface to swallow fish. They also use their pouch, which expands under water, to suck in small fish. Pelicans have a history of at least 30 million years but were threatened with extinction in the early 1970s because they are sensitive to chemical pollutants, absorbed from the fish they eat. The pollutants affect calcium metabolism, resulting in thin-shelled eggs that break when moved by the incubating bird. Breeding improved sharply after DDT was banned.

Pelagic Cormorant
Phalacrocorax pelagicus
532

25–30" (64–76 cm). Smallest of Pacific Coast cormorants. Slim bill with hook at tip; slender head and neck. All black. At the onset of the courtship period, it acquires a bright white patch on its flanks. 2 crests visible at close range. Red pouch under bill, green eyes, and blue-green mouth lining. In flight it is long-necked, black with a green gloss. Immatures dark brown.

Voice
Groaning and hissing notes around the breeding colonies.

Habitat
Coastal waters, bays. Nests in colonies on sea cliffs and rocky islets, and may feed inshore or far offshore.

Range
A North Pacific seabird; breeds from Japan around the Pacific arc to central California, and into the Bering Strait.

Comments
In Alaska the Pelagic Cormorant's range overlaps with that of the very similar, slightly larger and stockier Red-faced Cormorant (*Phalacrocorax urile*). When all three cormorant species breed together, the Pelagic nests on a cliff face, while Brandt's often selects a gentle slope, and the Double-crested a cliff top. Pelagic Cormorants nest on ledges so narrow that they must alight and take off facing the cliff. By contrast, Double-crested and Brandt's colonies nest on broader ledges and can turn and face the sea in taking off.

Double-crested Cormorant
Phalacrocorax auritus
533

30–36" (76–91 cm). Goose-sized. Adults black; immatures light brownish, lightest on breast and neck; bill straight, with hooked tip. Adults and young have bare patch of orange skin underneath bill. Breeding adults have 2 inconspicuous tufts (white in 1 western race) on both sides of crown.

Voice
Usually silent, except for grunting calls in the nesting colony.

Habitat
Freshwater lakes, rivers, and the sea; generally requires trees for nesting but does well on treeless islands such as those in the Gulf of California; settles only around large, deep bodies of water that provide good fishing.

Range
Widespread in North America. In the West it breeds on islands along Pacific Coast and on inland lakes. Winters on seacoast and on inland waters.

Comments
The only cormorant nesting inland in the West. Cormorants perch upright and often dry their wings by spreading them. Double-cresteds following a coastline often take shortcuts over land whereas Brandt's and the Pelagic always fly over water.

Brandt's Cormorant
Phalacrocorax penicillatus
534

33–35" (84–89 cm). Almost as big as Double-crested Cormorant. Dark, somewhat iridescent seabird, but lacks crest. Cobalt-blue throat pouch visible only in breeding season, but is difficult to observe. Buffy band around pouch is more easily discernible. Both sexes have slender white plumes on face and back early in breeding season. Immatures dark brown with lighter underparts.

Voice
Guttural croaks and grunts around the breeding grounds. Otherwise generally silent.

Habitat
Colonial seabird; nests on coastal or offshore rocks next to the waters where it fishes.

Range
Restricted to northeastern Pacific Coast, from S. British Columbia to Baja California.

Comments
This is the commonest cormorant from Oregon south to California. Brandt's Cormorants often gather in flocks of several hundred and fly to feeding grounds in long straggling skeins. They dive together, forming a living net.

Common Murre
Uria aalge
535

16–17" (41–43 cm). One of the larger members of the auk family. A black-and-white seabird. Cheek, throat, and neck white in winter with thin black downcurved line curving down behind the eye and extending into white portion of cheek. Entire head and neck black in summer; always white below. On land it stands upright, penguin-fashion. In flight, slender head and pointed bill suggest a small loon.

Voice
Its common name echoes its call: its breeding colony resounds with a "murring" noise, a moaning *aarr-r-r*, among other calls.

Habitat
Open sea and gulfs. Murres fish away from land and return only for nesting.

Range
All coasts of the Northern Hemisphere where cold currents or upwellings nourish a multitude of fish. In the West they nest in colonies in western Aleutians and from Arctic Alaska to central California.

Comments
When half grown, the young jump 30 to 50 feet into the sea, and accompany the parents, first swimming, then flying, often hundreds of miles, to wintering waters. Apart from having their nests plundered for the eggs, murres of the Pacific Coast have been safe from human intrusion, though potential oil spills now pose a threat to whole colonies.

Pigeon Guillemot
Cepphus columba
536

12–14" (30–36 cm). Pigeon-sized. In breeding plumage, black with large white wing patch interrupted by 2 black stripes. In winter head and upperparts lighten slightly, giving dusky mottled effect; underparts are white with buffy barring on flanks. In all seasons the feet and bill lining are brilliant red.

Voice
Quite vocal around its breeding cliffs in spring; high thin whistles given singly.

Habitat
Rocky coastal areas, with shallow inshore waters as its feeding grounds; rock crevices and earthen holes serve as nest cavities. Also nests under docks and piers.

Range
A common inshore member of the auk family along the Pacific Coast from Aleutian Islands and Alaska to S. California. Winters well offshore.

Comments
The least social of all auks. Where coastal cliffs allow only one nesting cavity, only one pair will occupy it. Elsewhere, territories are laid out like beads on a string. They feed by diving, taking mostly small fish. Its eastern relative the Black Guillemot (*Cepphus grylle*), which has a large white wing patch, has been found nesting along the arctic Alaskan coast.

Xantus' Murrelet
Synthliboramphus hypoleucus
537

9½–10½" (24–27 cm). Robin-sized but slender, resembling a tiny murre. Black above, with no distinctive pattern; white cheek, throat, and underparts. Underwing linings white. Bill is thin, narrow pincers, good for catching small fish or shrimp. No seasonal change in plumage.

Voice
High thin whistles, usually in a quick series.

Habitat
Ocean; nesting in colonies on rocky sea islands.

Range
Breeds on offshore islands of Baja California and S. California, occasionally wanders north to Vancouver Island.

Comments
Murrelets are so called because they resemble tiny murres. At sea, they are often seen in pairs. This species was named for its discoverer, Hungarian explorer John Xantus, who pioneered on the West Coast in the 1860s.

Ancient Murrelet
Synthliboramphus antiquus
538

9½–10½" (24–27 cm). Quail-sized. Black head, gray back, white below, white plume over eye, and small white-barred area at side of neck. Bill white. In winter, wide white area on throat and face, back solid slate-gray; similar Marbled Murrelet has white patch on flanks, dark bill.

Voice
A low shrill whistling note; may give a piping whistle at sea.

Habitat
Open ocean; nesting on oceanic islets with enough soil for a burrow, often under heavy timber.

Range
Offshore islets of the North Pacific and mainland shores south to central British Columbia. Some winter there, but others occur south to S. California.

Comments
Russian explorers who discovered this bird thought its white plumes similar to an old man's white locks; hence its Latin (*antiquus*) and English names. By moving to and from land at twilight, these birds escape most predators with the exception of Peregrine Falcons. Ancient Murrelets are not strong flyers, and heavy storms may carry them as far inland as the Great Lakes or wash masses of dead bodies ashore on the Pacific Coast.

Horned Puffin
Fratercula corniculata
539

14½" (37 cm). Pigeon-sized. Chunky, tailless body. Black above, white below. White face makes head appear big; large, parrotlike bill bright yellow with brilliant red at tip. Red eyelids and small, black upturned "horn" above eye visible at close range. In winter face darker, feathers brownish, bill smaller, and base sooty-colored. Juveniles are even darker-faced, with narrow, sooty-brown bills.

Voice
Usually silent, but utters harsh notes from its burrow.

Habitat
Cold ocean waters, sea cliffs, and rocky or grass-covered islets and rocks.

Range
Bering Sea and its islands, North Pacific coasts to Japan and the Alaskan panhandle. Winters irregularly south to California.

Comments
The relatively huge bill is useful in catching and holding small fish, enabling the parents to bring 3 or 4 fish at a time to the young. It is also used as a signal to mate or neighbor, especially during breeding time in crowded colonies. The colonies may contain thousands of these birds, yet in the Aleutians and other places where they nest among the Tufted Puffins, they are lost among the tens of thousands of the latter species.

Tufted Puffin
Fratercula cirrhata
540

14½–15½" (37–39 cm). Pigeon-sized. Mostly seen sitting upright on a sea cliff. Black stubby body, white face, downcurved yellowish tufts hanging behind eyes, and large, orange-red, parrotlike bill. In winter colored bill plates are molted and bill is smaller, duller, face turns dusky, tufts disappear. Immatures dusky above, light gray below, with small bill. In flight, the large, webbed, red feet serve as brakes.

Voice
Silent except for occasional growling notes uttered around the nest site.

Habitat
Vertical sea cliffs; in colonies or singly. Feeds at sea.

Range
Sizable colonies nest on Siberian, Alaskan, and British Columbian coasts. A few nest on the California coasts. Winters offshore from S. Alaska and south to California.

Comments
In most mixed seabird colonies a strict social order prevails within each species. Each seems to have adapted to a specific niche, occupying the terrain most suited to it, thus reducing competition between species but sharpening it within each species.

Rhinoceros Auklet
Cerorhinca monocerata
541

14½–15½" (37–39 cm). Pigeon-sized. Dark above with lighter gray throat and breast, white underparts. Slender, pale yellow bill, white eye. In breeding plumage, short, upright "horn" at base of bill with white drooping whiskers at either side; white plume above eye. Immatures dark gray above, light below with duller, smaller bill and dark eye. Some may have orange-red bills.

Voice
Growling and mooing cries of adults and shrill piping of young are heard on the breeding grounds at night.

Habitat
Feeds on fish offshore; digs deep burrows in grassy or timbered headlands.

Range
Japan and SE. Alaska south to central California. Winters off the West Coast south to Baja California.

Comments
"Auklet" is a misnomer, since this bird is not a close relative of the small, plankton-feeding seabirds called auklets, but is actually related to the brighter-colored, parrot-billed puffins. These birds feed on the open sea during the day but may be seen at sunset in summer among Pacific Coast inlets and islets. They swim and bob with a beakful of fish.

Cassin's Auklet
Ptychoramphus aleuticus
542

8–9" (20–23 cm). Stocky, Robin-sized seabird. Dark, slate-gray above, lighter gray below, white belly. Eyes dark brown during first year, they then lighten and are white in breeding adults. Stubby bill has white spot at base of each side of lower mandible. No seasonal change in plumage.

Voice
Their weak, croaking song becomes a mighty chorus on windy, foggy nights.

Habitat
On islands in burrows in the ground (breeding); mostly pelagic, also along rocky seacoasts. Open ocean. Nests on sea cliffs and isolated headlands.

Range
Aleutians to central Baja California. Colonies irregularly distributed; over 100,000 birds nest on the Farallon Islands, near San Francisco.

Comments
The parents take 24-hour watches while incubating the chick. During the nesting season they grow a pouch under the tongue and fill it with food. The island birds fly to sea long before dawn, after which they run the risk of being pursued and devoured by Western Gulls. They feed on planktonic shrimp by day and approach the colony only after dark. Most seabirds abandon the nest site as soon as the young fledge, but on the Farallon Islands, Cassin's Auklets remain. From December to March, birds occupy the island so densely that vacated burrows (the owners presumably dead) are promptly taken over by others. It is believed that this "housing shortage" compels the auklets to defend burrows year round.

Leach's Storm-Petrel
Oceanodroma leucorhoa
543

7½–9″ (19–23 cm). Blackbird-sized black petrel, with black body and forked tail. North Pacific populations breeding south to central California are identified by white rump. Farther south, in S. California, white on rump virtually disappears. Wings have brown crossbar.

Voice
Silent at sea, but can be detected at night by subdued ticking and trilling notes and twitterings coming from the rock piles where they nest and, at courtship time, from the air when they circle over the nesting burrows.

Habitat
Open ocean.

Range
Pacific Ocean is the center of its distribution. Nests widely in scattered colonies on both sides of the North Pacific south to Japan and Baja California. Winters mainly in tropical seas.

Comments
Until recently called "Leach's Petrel." Storm-petrels flutter close to the water to pick up tiny fish, crustaceans, or other surface plankton. In a colony at night and against a moonlit sky, storm-petrels look like bats.

Short-tailed Shearwater
Puffinus tenuirostris
544

13–14″ (33–36 cm). Dark shearwater, appearing black
overall, including bill and feet. Wing linings vary from light
gray-brown to dusky, usually lacking flashing silvery color of
those of the similar Sooty Shearwater. Bill and tail are smaller
than in the Sooty; also, in winter, darker than Sooty; generally
difficult to distinguish from Sooty at any range.

Voice
Silent at sea. Hoarse calls heard sparingly even on the
breeding grounds.

Habitat
High seas.

Range
Breeds in Tasmania and neighboring islands off the Australian
coast; visits the northeastern Pacific, where it is common in
the Aleutian, Alaskan, and British Columbian waters; seen
farther south along the California coast in late fall, on return
migration to its breeding grounds.

Comments
In Tasmania and Australia, the young of this shearwater are
exploited for oil and meat on the breeding grounds. (This
species is known there as the "Mutton Bird".) Its post-
breeding migration resembles a great figure 8: first through
the Micronesian islands toward Japan, then up to the Alaskan
area; in fall it flies southward along the Pacific Coast of North
America to central California, and crosses its northward path
at the Fiji Islands before returning to Tasmania.

Sooty Shearwater
Puffinus griseus
545

16–18″ (41–46 cm). Black except for pale silvery wing
linings seen in flight.

Voice
A din of nasal, squealing, and crooning notes is heard on the
breeding grounds; otherwise silent.

Habitat
Open oceans, but in stormy weather they are driven landward,
approaching prominent coastal points such as Point Roberts,
Washington.

Range
From its breeding grounds in southeastern Australia, New
Zealand, and southern South America to the North Pacific,
where it spends the nonbreeding season and perhaps the first 2
years of life. Millions of these birds migrate or summer off the
coast from Alaska to California.

Comments
Although shearwaters feed during daylight, they are strictly
nocturnal in their breeding colonies. They are the "Moaning
Birds" that sailors on South Sea islands heard after dusk as the
birds sat outside their burrows and wailed and yammered in
territorial disputes. Most shearwaters leave their single
offspring before it fledges, but the chick has been fattened and

overfed to give it the resources necessary to grow, develop flight feathers, and leave the colony. Adult and young thus fly north separately, yet all follow the ancestral routes to the Pacific Coast.

Pink-footed Shearwater
Puffinus creatopus
546

20″ (51 cm). Gull-sized. Dark gray-brown above, white below; underwings white with dark borders. Straw-colored, black-tipped bill and pink feet.

Voice
Silent except on southern breeding grounds, where it utters grunts and moaning calls.

Habitat
Open ocean, seldom seen from the shore.

Range
Off the Pacific Coast of North America in migration; breeds on smaller islands off the Chilean coast.

Comments
Shearwaters occur from spring to fall, but are seen most commonly in fall, when thousands congregate at favored places, such as Monterey Bay or outside San Francisco's Golden Gate. They fly close to the water, using several deep wingbeats followed by a long glide, searching for surface food such as small fish and crustaceans. They alight and dip their bills or even dive.

Buller's Shearwater
Puffinus bulleri
547

16½–18″ (42–46 cm). Gull-sized with wedge-shaped tail. Dark gray above, with a darker cap, white below and underwing. In flight, dark bar on upper wing and lower back creates M-shaped pattern of darker color, the points of the M coming at the bend of the wing.

Voice
Silent when at sea. A mewing chorus is heard in the colony at night.

Habitat
Open ocean, seen offshore where attracted by food concentrations.

Range
Nests in New Zealand, and after the nesting season ranges in the North Pacific, especially from Monterey Bay in central California north to Washington and British Columbia, where it is rather common.

Comments
Its flight, somewhat slower than that of the other shearwaters, is characterized by less frequent wing flapping and longer gliding periods with wings arched.

Black-footed Albatross
Diomedea nigripes
548

28–36" (71–91 cm). Wingspan: 78–84" (2 m). Large seabird. Dusky black overall with white area encircling dark bill and light streaking in outermost flight feathers; some adults have white undertail coverts. Long narrow wings; stiff shearwater-like wingbeat and gliding pattern.

Voice
Screeches and grunts. In courtship display, whistles, quacks, and bill-clapping noises.

Habitat
Open ocean, rarely seen near shore.

Range
Along the entire Pacific Coast of North America. Breeds on mid-Pacific islands, including northwestern Hawaiian Islands.

Comments
Albatrosses take 10 to 12 years to mature. The young roam the Pacific, seldom returning to their birthplace before they are 6 or 7 years old. These birds take squid and surface fish; they often follow ships and feed on refuse.

Great Skua
Catharacta skua
549

20–22" (51–56 cm). Stocky with short, broad, wedge-shaped (not elongated) tail. Adults and juveniles resemble a stocky juvenile Western Gull: overall dark brown, but with bill heavier and more hooked than in a gull. In light phase, body gray-brown, head pale. Central band of white across base of outermost flight feathers visible on the open wings.

Voice
A scream transcribed as *skerr;* on the breeding ground it utters another call, *uk uk uk.* Otherwise silent.

Habitat
Open ocean when visiting Pacific Coast.

Range
Uniquely bipolar. One population nests on the coasts of northern Europe, several others on and around Antarctica. Ours are visitors from Antarctica and do not nest in the regions covered by this book. Many believe that these "South Polar Skuas" are a species distinct from the North Atlantic breeders.

Comments
This is the largest and most predatory of northern skuas. At sea off the North American coasts it robs other seabirds of their prey. On its southern breeding grounds it is a coastal scavenger and preys on seabird eggs and young. This large bird is deceptively fast; it can outfly any gull and often forces it to drop or disgorge its food.

Parasitic Jaeger
Stercorarius parasiticus
550

16–21" (41–53 cm). Resembles medium-sized long-tailed gull, but flies like a falcon. Light phase brown above, white below; black cap, yellowish cheeks; gray-brown wash on chest.

Dark phase uniformly brown. Both phases show white flash near tip of wing formed by white bases of primaries. There are 3 species of jaegers best distinguished (in adults) by tail shape. Parasitic has 2 long central tail feathers extending 2–4 inches beyond tip of tail. The dusky, barred immatures of the 3 species—predominating among fall and winter visitors—lack longer central tail feathers and are difficult to distinguish.

Voice
On the tundra, it utters a wailing cry, *ka-aaow* or *ya-wow.* When attacking a seabird or a flock, piercing *tok-tok* or *tick a tick tick* cries frighten the intended victims.

Habitat
Tundra for nesting; open ocean during the rest of the year.

Range
Circumpolar Arctic breeder of the North American and Eurasian tundra. In winter it roams the seas, including the North Pacific; north to California, but mostly in Southern Hemisphere.

Comments
The American name for these birds, jaeger, comes from the German word for hunter. During the short Arctic summer this species feeds mainly on birds and lemmings. Upon leaving the Arctic, jaegers become pirates, robbing seabirds by harassing them until they disgorge their captured prey. They can often be seen pursuing flocks of terns on migration.

Pomarine Jaeger
Stercorarius pomarinus
551

20–23″ (51–58 cm). Largest jaeger, stockier than Parasitic Jaeger, but similar in coloration. Light phase dark above, white below, dark cap, yellow wash on face. Often shows strong to incomplete dark breast band; coarse barring on flanks. White wing flash larger than in other species. Dark phase uniformly blackish except for wing flash. Broad, twisted central tail feathers extend 3–5 inches beyond rest of tail in adults. Immatures brownish, strongly barred with black.

Voice
Various squealing and squeaky notes, a harsh *which-you,* and a querulous chatter. Generally silent during migration.

Habitat
Tundra breeder; on the open ocean after the breeding season.

Range
Circumpolar on Arctic tundras. In the West it may be seen on its breeding grounds in western and N. Alaska and northern Canada. It is common off the Pacific Coast during fall and spring. Winters on open ocean from Hawaii and California south to South America.

Comments
Its flight is steadier, with slower, heavier wingbeats, than that of the Parasitic Jaeger; in pursuit of gulls or terns, however, it makes lightning-fast dives, chasing them until they disgorge

their food, which it then catches in the air. Along the West Coast the Pomarine is the most common jaeger. On the tundra it feeds almost exclusively on lemmings.

Osprey
Pandion haliaetus
552

21–24½" (53–62 cm). Large hawk. Dark brown above, white below. Head is white with dark line through eyes. In flight, shows a distinctive bend in its wing at the elbow.

Voice
High, whistled *k-yewk, k-yewk, k-yewk* calls.

Habitat
Coasts and inland lakes and rivers.

Range
Truly cosmopolitan; occurring on every continent, at least as a winter visitor. Nests throughout North America. Winters from southern United States, south.

Comments
Called the "Fish Eagle" in many countries because, unlike other birds of prey that feed on small mammals and birds, it feeds entirely on fish. It catches fish by hovering, then plunging talons-first into the water. Like the Bald Eagle, its nesting success has decreased in many areas because the fish it eats are contaminated with toxic chemicals. It requires active measures to ensure its conservation.

Bald Eagle
Haliaeetus leucocephalus
553

30–43" (76–109 cm). Wingspan: 78–96" (2–2.4 m). Adult, over 5 years old, has snow-white head, neck, and tail; brownish-black body: Yellow bill. Immatures brown, except for whitish wing linings and, usually, whitish blotches on underparts. Head and tail gradually whiten with each molt as birds attain adulthood.

Voice
A thin, chittering note, quite weak for so magnificent a bird.

Habitat
Most often on or near seacoasts; also large lakes and rivers where fish are abundant.

Range
Formerly bred throughout North America, but now breeds only in Aleutians, Alaska, parts of northern and eastern Canada, northern United States, and Florida. In winter, along almost any body of water, especially larger rivers in the interior of the continent.

Comments
Although the Bald Eagle eats carrion and sometimes catches crippled waterfowl, it is primarily a fish-eater. Its beachcombing role has been its downfall, for it accumulates pesticides in its own body from contaminated fish and wildlife. Hunting, poaching, and the encroachment of civilization have diminished its populations drastically except

in the rain forest coasts of Alaska and northern and central British Columbia.

Common Raven
Corvus corax
554

21½–27″ (55–69 cm). Large, black bird. Thick bill, shaggy ruff at throat, and wedge-shaped tail. Alternately flaps and soars like a hawk, flapping less and soaring more than the American Crow.

Voice
Utters a hoarse, croaking *kraaak* and a variety of other notes, including a hollow, knocking sound and a melodious *kloo-klok*, usually in flight.

Habitat
A great variety, including Pacific Coast beaches, deserts, mountains, canyons, northern or high-elevation forests.

Range
Aleutians and throughout Alaska and Canada to Greenland. South, in the West, to Central America and east to the foothills of the Rockies.

Comments
A very "intelligent" bird, it seems to apply reasoning in situations entirely new to it. Its "insight" behavior at least matches that of a dog. It is a general predator and opportunistic feeder, like other members of the crow family, and often feeds at garbage dumps.

American Crow
Corvus brachyrhynchos
555

17–21″ (43–53 cm). Smaller than Raven, with shorter, less powerful bill. Black overall.

Voice
The *caw* call is not as hoarse as that of the Raven.

Habitat
Deciduous growth, along rivers and streams; orchards and city parks. Also mixed and coniferous woods, but avoids closed coniferous forests and desert expanses.

Range
Coast to coast wherever trees grow, thus from the northern treeline to the desert belt; but not in the Pacific Northwest.

Comments
An opportunist in its feeding, it will consume a great variety of plant and animal food: seeds, garbage, insects, mice. In orchards and fields it destroys many injurious insects. Its nest plundering is decried; however, the labeling of birds as either "harmful" or "useful" is misleading and antiquated. Crows do destroy many eggs and nestlings of woodland and meadow birds, but they also weed out the weak and feeble and they alert the animals of a neighborhood when danger approaches. The related Northwestern Crow (*C. caurinus*) ranges along the Pacific Coast from S. Alaska to Puget Sound.

Black Oystercatcher
Haematopus bachmani
556

17–17½" (43–44 cm). Large shorebird. Black with long, stout, red bill; flesh-colored legs and feet; light eyes. Sexes look alike.

Voice
Their loud ringing notes carry above the crashing of the surf; a whistled *wheeee-whee-whee-whee.*

Habitat
Rocky seacoasts.

Range
Cool Pacific shores from the Aleutians south to Baja California.

Comments
Before nesting, the birds undertake conspicuous long courtship flights, screeching loudly as they turn and twist, emphasizing each cry with a peculiar wingbeat, as if flying in slow motion. The flat, strong bill is used to open oysters or pry limpets off rocks. After breeding, the birds may flock together, up to 40 or 50 gathering on a flat rock at low tide.

Belted Kingfisher
Ceryle alcyon
557

11–14½" (28–37 cm). Large head; very long, heavy bill; crest. Male bluish gray above with white underparts and bluish-gray breast band. Female similar but with rufous band below the bluish-gray one.

Voice
A loud, dry rattle, often prolonged.

Habitat
Banks of rivers and lakes; seashore; near clear fishing waters.

Range
Aleutians, central Alaska, across Canada, south to Mexico and the Gulf Coast. Winters north to the limit of unfrozen fresh water and south to Central America and Caribbean islands.

Comments
While searching for fish, it perches conspicuously on a limb over a river or lake. On sighting a fish it flies from its post and hovers over the water before plunging after its prey. When flying from one perch to another, often a good distance apart, it utters a loud rattle.

Great Blue Heron
Ardea herodias
558

42–52" (107–132 cm) and 48" (122 cm) tall. A large blue-gray heron. Back and wings blue-gray; underparts whitish with black streaking on belly, head white with black stripe ending in black plumes behind eye; black-and-white foreneck and chest end in gray plumes in the breeding adult. Juveniles lack plumes and are more brownish.

Voice
Herons call mainly when startled or alarmed, uttering a loud, raucous *grak* or *kraak.*

Habitat
Coastal cliffs, brackish lagoons, and freshwater lakes; wetlands where tall trees, rock ledges, or extensive reeds provide a safe site for the heronry. It readily makes 20- to 30-mile round trips to feed.

Range
Widespread in North America except the northern tundra and forest belts, and extending to northern South America. Migratory where waters freeze.

Comments
Because of the gray body and long legs and neck, Great Blue Herons are often miscalled cranes, but herons have a longer bill and fly with neck folded back on the shoulder, extending it only when about to alight or when under attack. Herons stand in water or on a bank; cranes stand in marshes or dry fields, and are more wary. In late summer, young herons disperse widely and may be encountered at small ponds, mountain waters, or even in backyard pools, wherever fish are plentiful.

Red-necked Phalarope
Phalaropus lobatus
559

6½–8″ (17–20 cm). Bluebird-sized. In spring male dark gray with white throat and buffy neck; female has bright rusty neck. Bill dark, thinner than in Red Phalarope. In fall and winter darker backed than Red Phalarope with dark ear and crown markings contrasting with white head. Shows pronounced wing stripe in flight.

Voice
A high, sharp *kip*.

Habitat
Breeds near ponds on wet tundra; winters on high seas.

Range
Circumpolar; in North America on tundra from Aleutians and Alaska to Labrador. In migration, common off Pacific Coast; also occurs on lakes of all western states and provinces. Majority winter on oceans of Southern Hemisphere, but some stay in extreme S. California.

Comments
Red-necked Phalaropes, like the Red Phalarope but unlike other shorebirds, prefer to swim rather than wade, which enables them to spend the winter on the high seas. They float buoyantly and pick small creatures from the surface.

Red Phalarope
Phalaropus fulicaria
560

7½–9″ (19–23 cm). A slim shorebird with smallish head and dainty bill. In spring bright rust-red below with buffy mottled back and white face. Female has black lores and crown; male smaller and less colorful. Bill yellow with black tip. In fall and winter unstreaked gray above, head and underparts white, bill darker; dark eyeline is common in all phalaropes in winter plumage.

Voice
A sharp *kip*.

Habitat
A tundra-breeding seabird, it passes offshore along the coast in fall and spring. Winters on high seas.

Range
Circumpolar; in North America breeds on Arctic coasts from Alaska across Canada to Greenland. Winters in open oceans of both hemispheres, but usually not in very cold regions; rarely north of central California on the Pacific Coast.

Comments
Phalaropes feed on the surface; they swim in tight circles with the body held high, the head bobbing, paddling with lobed toes, in search of plankton or small marine invertebrates.

Virginia Rail
Rallus limicola
561

8½–10½" (22–27 cm). Long-billed, small rail. Quite colorful but the colors blend in a camouflage effect: gray face with white throat; cinnamon wings and breast; back cinnamon with black mottling; belly barred black-and-white. White undertail area conspicuous when tail is raised; this seems to be an important signal among rail-like birds.

Voice
Attracts attention with its loud calls, usually described as a grunting, descending *wak-wak-wak,* or *kick, kick, kid-ick, kid-ick, kid-ick.*

Habitat
Found mostly in freshwater and brackish marshes; it also inhabits salt marshes in winter.

Range
Wetlands from coast to coast; from southern Canada to the southern United States. Winters mainly in southern United States and Mexico, but may be found throughout range where marshes do not freeze.

Comments
The best time to see this rail is in a marsh in a blind or boat at dawn, for it is then and at dusk that rails forage briefly in the open. In California it has been found nesting as high as 6800 feet.

Clapper Rail
Rallus longirostris
562

14–16½" (36–42 cm). Chicken-sized. Grayish brown with tawny breast and barred flanks, long legs, and fairly long, slightly downcurved bill.

Voice
A loud *kik-kik-kik-kik* that carries far even in dense reeds.

Habitat
Densely vegetated salt marshes; locally in fresh or brackish marshes.

Range
From the central California coast south to Baja California and to South America; also along the Atlantic and Gulf coasts.

Comments
Rails are secretive, seldom coming out into the open. The population in the western United States has been endangered by the gradual destruction of marsh habitat. Its stronghold is San Francisco Bay (with fewer than 3000 birds in the early 1970s). A freshwater population (Yuma Clapper Rail), containing fewer than 1000 birds, is found along the lower Colorado River of California, Arizona, and Mexico.

Whimbrel
Numenius phaeopus
563

15–18¾" (38–48 cm). Large gray-brown sandpiper with long, downcurved bill, crown striped; legs and feet blue-gray.

Voice
Flight call is a loud, whistled *whi whi whi whi whi*.

Habitat
Nests on the tundra; during migration mainly on sea beaches, tidal flats, and large, partly flooded fields.

Range
Breeds in Alaska and Canada. Regularly winters from California and Florida coasts south to southern South America.

Comments
In migration they occur along sandy beaches, in salt marshes, and even on rocky coasts. The larger the bird, the more space it needs. Thus a lone Whimbrel usually stands amid several dowitchers and numerous smaller birds; however, when feeding or resting in salt marshes and coastal meadows Whimbrels occur in flocks. This species feeds on large insects, berries, and aquatic invertebrates while on its tundra nesting grounds.

Marbled Godwit
Limosa fedoa
564

16–20" (41–51 cm). Large, long-legged shorebird. Long, slightly upturned bill. Mottled buffy brown above; with pale, fine wavy lines below, giving marbled impression; cinnamon wing linings; bill flesh-colored at base, with black at tip; feet bluish gray.

Voice
A loud *karrack* and a laughing *ha-ha*. Also a rapid *ratica, ratica, ratica*.

Habitat
Prairie grasslands and meadows around lakes; coastal wetlands, beaches in winter.

Range
Western interior provinces of Canada south to Montana and the Dakotas. Winters from California and Gulf Coast to northern South America.

Comments
In spring, the aerial displays and noisy calls of godwits are conspicuous. They favor prairie meadows for nesting. After breeding they migrate to coastal beaches.

Short-billed Dowitcher
Limnodromus griseus
565

10½–12″ (27–30 cm). Snipelike, long-billed shorebird with white lower back and rump, black-and-white-checkered tail, dark bill, green legs. Smaller than the Long-billed Dowitcher. In summer: salmon below, with dark spotting on breast. In winter: gray overall except for light eyebrow stripe, white lower back and rump.

Voice
Its call distinguishes it from its long-billed cousin; a mellow *tu-tu-tu,* as opposed to the thin *keek* of the latter.

Habitat
Marshes or edge of wet tundra in summer; mud flats and shallow ponds the rest of the year.

Range
S. Alaska through northern coniferous forest region of Canada east to Labrador. Winters locally along the southern coasts of United States and south to South America.

Comments
These are among the first shorebirds to migrate south, the adults leaving as early as July and the young following in August. In fall and winter, this species is found mainly on coastal mud flats, whereas the Long-bill prefers freshwater ponds.

Red Knot
Calidris canutus
566

10–11″ (25–28 cm). Among the largest of beach sandpipers, with bill as long as head. Breeding birds mottled gray-brown above, reddish below. In fall and winter pale gray on back, white belly. Immatures buffy gray. Best identified by stout proportions, moderate-sized bill. Rump and tail grayish at all seasons.

Voice
A low-pitched *tu-whit.* Also a nonmusical *wunt wunt.*

Habitat
For nesting, drier tundra; in winter, mud flats, estuaries, and open areas in coastal salt marshes.

Range
Circumpolar in the High Arctic tundra. Migrants from N. Alaska or Siberia go south along the Pacific Coast in August and September, returning in April or early May. Winters locally along the coast of California and south to southern South America. Also found in migration along the Atlantic Coast.

Comments
This species, the dowitchers, Willet, and Marbled Godwit are

the large birds most commonly seen on mud flats. The Red
Knot resembles the small sandpipers in shape and coloration,
but is much larger. Formerly called the "Knot."

Western Sandpiper
Calidris mauri
567

6–7" (15–18 cm). Long black bill, slightly downcurved at the
tip. Rusty red above in spring, white below; some reddish on
shoulders even in fall. Legs and feet are black. In fall, gray
above, white below.

Voice
A grating and rather high *keeep* note, often with a squeaky
quality.

Habitat
Upland tundra in summer; in mud flats, beaches, and
seashores in winter.

Range

Breeds in the coastal tundra of Alaska. Winters on the Pacific
Coast from California to Peru and on the Atlantic Coast from
New Jersey to Venezuela. Great numbers move through
British Columbia, Washington, and Oregon, mainly along the
coast, rare in the interior states.

Comments
This is the western counterpart of the Semipalmated
Sandpiper, the common "peep" of the Atlantic and Gulf
coasts. The flocks of these "peeps" that spread out on mud
flats during fall and winter take to flight readily when an
intruder nears. When the tide covers their shallow feeding
grounds, the flocks move to higher ground; there they preen
themselves and wait for the next low tide.

Least Sandpiper
Calidris minutilla
568

5–6½" (13–17 cm). Smaller than Western Sandpiper. Short
thin dark bill, yellowish legs, light brown breast, and striped
brown underparts. Least Sandpipers appear warm brown; in
winter they look drab or gray; but leg color does not change.

Voice
A high *preeep* or *pree-rreeep*.

Habitat
Nests in tundra marshes, bogs; tidal mud flats, grassy pools,
and flooded fields in winter.

Range

Low Arctic tundra from Alaska to Labrador, even bogs in the
Maritime Provinces. Visits the Pacific and other coastal states
in great numbers in winter, though some flocks proceed south
to Central and South America.

Comments
A very common sandpiper of mud flats and wet grassy areas. It
is tame in the presence of man. As a tightly bunched flock
twists and turns in unison, the birds alternately flash white
bellies and dark backs.

Rock Sandpiper
Calidris ptilocnemis
569

8–9" (20–23 cm). Small sandpiper; most frequently seen in winter. Slate-gray head, breast, and upperparts with indistinct white eye stripe, chin, and wing stripe, dark rump and tail. Feet yellowish or greenish. Indistinct white wing bar. Spring breeding plumage resembles that of Dunlin; brown mottled crown and less rust color on back, higher and smaller dusky-black breast blotch, and less breast streaking.

Voice
Trilling calls on the nesting grounds.

Habitat
Breeds on upland tundra; rocky shores in winter.

Range
The High Arctic of the Bering Strait, Aleutians, areas of Alaska and Siberia. Winters along the northern Pacific shores of North America; common in British Columbia and Washington, scarcer in California.

Comments
Dark gray birds feeding in loose flocks at the waterline or on exposed, alga-covered surfaces at low tide may be Rock Sandpipers, Black Turnstones, or Surfbirds. All are similarly camouflaged to match wet, dark rocks. In flight, the 3 are easily distinguished: the Rock Sandpiper has a dark tail, the Surfbird has a white tail terminating in a black triangle, and the Black Turnstone has its checkered black-and-white pattern.

Sanderling
Calidris alba
570

7–8¾" (18–22 cm). Small, plump sandpiper. In breeding plumage, back, head, and upper breast are mottled gray-and-white with rust-colored tones, white on belly. Easy to recognize in winter plumage, when it is the palest of all small sandpipers: light gray above, white below; bill and feet black. In flight, shows bold white wing stripe.

Voice
A sharp, high *kit,* sometimes given in series.

Habitat
Nests on dry, stony tundra; migration and through winter, sandy beaches.

Range
Circumpolar; on the tundras of North America. Sandy beaches of all continents during the winter.

Comments
On their Arctic Canadian or Greenland nesting grounds, incubating Sanderlings may be observed from as close as 2 or 3 feet. Unlike most sandpipers, they are quite tame even during winter and are a delight to watch as they retreat and advance with the breaking waves. Sanderlings generally feed by probing, but also take small invertebrates that wash ashore. Whereas "peeps" such as the Western Sandpiper feed in large loose flocks on the mud flats, flocks of Sanderlings feeding on

the beach spread out in long lines along the water's edge and run in small groups of twos or threes.

Lesser Yellowlegs
Tringa flavipes
571

9½–11″ (24–28 cm). Smaller version of the Greater Yellowlegs, with shorter, straight dark bill. Mottled gray above, white tail with dusky bars, white rump, and dusky wing; faint white eyeline; long, bright yellow legs. Birds in spring plumage are generally much darker than those seen in the fall.

Voice
1 or 2 whistles, *yew* or *yew-yew,* without loud, ringing quality of Greater Yellowlegs' voice. On nesting ground it utters a torrent of such calls as long as an intruder is near.

Habitat
Marshes, mudflats, tundra and muskegs (breeding); marshes, ponds, wet meadows, lakes, and mudflats (nonbreeding); bogs, ponds in coniferous woodlands.

Range
From Alaska to James Bay in the forest and forest-tundra zones. Migrates southeastward through the West Indies to South America. Transient in the West, mainly on coastal mud flats and flooded fields. Some remain in the Southwest in winter.

Comments
This bird is fearless not only on its nesting grounds but even on migration. It was formerly considered a delicacy and hunted widely, but now enjoys full protection.

Greater Yellowlegs
Tringa melanoleuca
572

12½–15″ (32–38 cm). Large sandpiper. Long neck and slightly upturned bill; long bright yellow legs. Grayish overall with black-and-white mottling above, white below; white rump and barred tail.

Voice
A ringing *kyew-kyew-kyew,* the second note often emphasized.

Habitat
During the breeding season, swampy bogs, wet meadows in the northern or high-elevation forests of Canada; in winter, marshes, edges of large inland bodies of water, along irrigation canals.

Range
All along the northern fringes of the taiga belt, from Alaska to Newfoundland. In winter Oregon, California, S. Arizona, and the Gulf and south Atlantic states, but a common transient in most western wetlands, indeed in all of North, Central, and South America.

Comments
Yellowlegs gathered for fall migration at a Canadian lake were observed in this display: each showed the white rump and tail

pattern to a rival whom the bird wanted to supplant on the feeding ground. Each turned the tail slightly toward his rival and lowered the wing closest to the other; both held this posture for several seconds.

Willet
Catoptrophorus semipalmatus
573

14–17" (36–43 cm). Large, long-legged, and fairly long-billed, light sand-gray bird with gray legs. When flushed, it shows startling broad white wing bar and white base of tail contrasting with black band at the rear edge of its wings. In spring, mottled brown on chest; in fall and winter, grayish.

Voice
A loud *kreer-reer-reerr* or *pee-wee-wee.*

Habitat
Beaches, marshes, mud flats and lakeshores.

Range
Breeds in Great Basin and northern prairie states and Canadian provinces and along Atlantic and Gulf coasts. Winters on southern coasts of United States and south to South America; very common on California beaches and adjacent salt or freshwater marshes.

Comments
These are conspicuous and noisy birds, with several distinctive calls. They separate when feeding but remain in loose contact. If several are forced into the air by the approach of bathers, they usually fly together, calling back and forth, landing farther along the beach.

Spotted Sandpiper
Actitis macularia
574

7½–8" (18–20 cm). Small sandpiper. Flesh-colored or yellowish legs; white wing stripe shown in flight. In autumn unmarked olive-brown above, with olive wash across sides of upper breast, white below, with light eye stripe and white eye-ring. In spring, underparts are heavily marked with large, dark spots. Almost always first identified by teetering habit and manner of flight.

Voice
Utters a sharp *peet-weet* or a repeated *weet-weet-weet.*

Habitat
Streams, lakes, reservoirs, or almost any body of water that is surrounded by vegetation and woods.

Range
Very widespread; breeds in almost all of North America except the southeastern seaboard. In the southern part of its range, it breeds in mountains. Winters in milder areas of United States south to South America.

Comments
Often when disturbed, the small birds fly out from underfoot, make an arc over water on stiffly vibrating wings, alight a little farther on, and make jerky dashes along the shore,

bobbing almost continually. These are the Spotted Sandpipers, or their Old World counterpart, Common Sandpipers (*Actitis hypoleucos*). Some consider them one species.

Surfbird
Aphriza virgata
575

10" (25 cm). Slightly larger than Black Turnstone, with which it mixes. In winter, dark gray head, breast, and upperparts; white rump; white tail with black triangular pattern at tip; white wing stripe. Light lores, throat, and belly with gray-streaked flanks. Bill and legs yellow. In breeding plumage, heavy black-brown mottling above, and strong black mottling on white underparts.

Voice
On their winter grounds they utter a shrill *ke-week* in flight.

Habitat
Nests above timberline in dry open areas of the alpine tundra zone; in winter, rocky shores, headlands, and islets.

Range
Breeds on the mountain tundra of Alaska. Winters along the Pacific Coast from S. Alaska to southern South America.

Comments
When two such distantly related shorebirds as the Surfbird and Black Turnstone have similar plumage, it is attributed to a similar need for camouflage in the same environment. The bright wing stripe is a signal, perhaps helping to keep the flying flock in formation.

Wandering Tattler
Heteroscelus incanus
576

11" (28 cm). Medium-sized sandpiper. In winter uniformly dark gray above, paler below; light areas at throat and belly; dark bill slightly longer than head. Summer tattlers have fine black cross-barring below. Dark eyeline framed by lighter eye stripes above and yellow legs remain constant in all seasons.

Voice
Call is 3 to 4 clear whistles in rapid succession, usually as it takes to flight.

Habitat
Mountain streams in summer; coastal rocks, shell beaches, and rocky coves from fall to late spring.

Range
Breeds in mountain areas of south-central Alaska and NW. British Columbia. Winters on both Pacific Coasts (in U.S. from S. California southward).

Comments
The Surfbird, Bristle-thighed Curlew, Kittlitz's Murrelet, and Wandering Tattler all breed scattered about above the timberline in Alaska's rugged mountains, and their nests were among the latest to be discovered; the Tattler's nest was first found in 1922. They are easier to approach in their wintering places on the southern coasts, because they do not fear man.

When very low tides expose rocky bottoms, several tattlers come into sight but each feeds alone.

Black Turnstone
Arenaria melanocephala
577

9″ (23 cm). In breeding plumage upperparts, head, and breast black; large white spot in front of, and white line above, the eye; fine white spotting from nape across side of breast; white belly. Winter plumage is dusky black with unstreaked white belly. Legs dark. Bill short and slightly upturned. In flight, flashes a black-and-white pattern.

Voice
A distinctive grating *kr-re-e-e-e-r* uttered in flight.

Habitat
Nests in marshy, coastal tundra in summer; visits seaweed-covered rocky shores of the Pacific Coast in fall and winter.

Range
Breeds on western and southern coasts of Alaska. Winters all along the coast south to Baja California and Sonora.

Comments
Turnstones are territorial only on the breeding grounds. On the coast they live in flocks, the bright wing pattern probably aiding in keeping the group together in flights from one rocky islet to another. They turn over pebbles with the bill in search of crabs, beach hoppers, and sand fleas.

Dunlin
Calidris alpina
578

8–9″ (20–23 cm). Medium-sized sandpiper. Smaller than Red Knot but larger than Western Sandpiper. Bill longer than head and slightly curved. In spring and summer, cinnamon-red back, white below with black belly. In winter uniform gray upperparts and gray breast. Immatures brown above, buff below with brownish streaks on breast and sides.

Voice
A low, grating *kerrr*.

Habitat
Wet tundra in summer; seacoasts in winter.

Range
Holarctic; in North America along coast from Alaska to Hudson Bay. Winters on coasts; in the West from British Columbia to Baja California.

Comments
Large flocks are found on mud flats from autumn to spring. They spread out at low tide, but if a hawk flushes them, they cluster in a tight group of several hundred birds, twisting and swirling in the air. Few birds of prey would risk entering this flying mass, but an old, sick, or handicapped bird may lag behind to become easy prey.

Black-bellied Plover
Pluvialis squatarola
579

10½–13½″ (27–34 cm). In spring, top of head and back checkered gray and buff; face, neck, breast, and belly black. Broad white stripe from eye to side of breast. In winter, mottled grayish-buff upperparts, pale grayish underparts. In all plumages, whitish wing stripe, rump, and tail, and black patch under the wing visible in flight.

Voice
A rising and falling whistle of haunting quality: *ker-loo-ee*. The Lesser Golden utters a loud, falling *que-e-e-a*.

Habitat
Tundra; winters on seashores, mud flats, and coastal marshes.

Range
Northern Siberian, Alaskan, and Canadian tundra. Winters in southern continents, but enough remain on North America's Pacific Coast to be common in winter there.

Comments
When the tide recedes and a broad mud flat is exposed, shorebirds spread out to feed. The smaller sandpipers, such as the Least, Western, Dunlin, and Sanderling, remain in loose flocks, while the plovers spread out along the beach. The wary Black-bellied Plover is the first to take flight when an observer approaches; on its tundra nesting ground it allows a close approach. It does so not because it trusts man, but because on the tundra the safest course is to remain still and well camouflaged, whereas on a tidal flat the surest escape is flight.

Semipalmated Plover
Charadrius semipalmatus
580

6½–8″ (17–20 cm). Larger than a plump sparrow. Short neck and rounded head; dark sandy brown above, white below with single black breast band. Black eye stripe, white forehead and eyebrow; legs dark yellow; bill dark yellow with black tip.

Voice
A mellow whistled, *chu-whee*.

Habitat
Breeds on tundra; winters on seashore, favoring sandy beaches and tidal flats.

Range
North American tundra from Alaska to Labrador, south along the Pacific Coast to the Queen Charlotte Islands. Winters from central California coast to southern South America.

Comments
When feeding, these birds hunt littoral life exposed by the tide. Their feeding method is a quick run, followed by a sudden stop, and a lightning-swift jab at a tiny crab or beach hopper. The front toes are joined by a small web; hence the name *semipalmated,* meaning "possessing half a palm."

Killdeer
Charadrius vociferus
581

9–11" (23–28 cm). Robin-sized, larger than Semipalmated Plover. Grayish brown above, white below with 2 black breast bands and long, predominantly tan tail, most evident in flight or in distraction display.

Voice
Repeats its name, a shrill *kill-deer, kill-deer.*

Habitat
Fields, pastures, and mud flats, occasionally breeding on flat graveled roofs. After breeding, frequents coastal fields, inland beaches, or lawns.

Range
Throughout temperate North America. Migratory; winters inland where climates are mild; common along the East and West coasts.

Comments
If a predator approaches, the Killdeer performs a conspicuous distraction display, dragging itself, often on one foot, with its wings appearing broken and with tail fanned toward the intruder. This "injury-feigning" is effective in leading the predator away from the vicinity of nest or young.

Snowy Plover
Charadrius alexandrinus
582

6–7" (15–18 cm). A small pale plover with an incomplete breast band; also an incomplete eyeline; bill and feet dark as compared with dark yellow feet of the Semipalmated Plover.

Voice
A low-pitched *krut.* Also a whistled *ku-wheet.*

Habitat
Beaches, dry mud or salt flats, and sandy shores.

Range
In North America, nests on Pacific Coast from S. Washington, Oregon, California south to S. Baja California.

Comments
This small, sand-colored plover has a perfect camouflage on sandy shores. As soon as it stops running it seems to disappear, blending into its surroundings. The eggs also blend with dry sand or salty barren soil, and are almost impossible to find once the incubating bird slips off them.

Forster's Tern
Sterna forsteri
583, 588

14–16¼" (36–41 cm). Medium-sized tern. White with light silvery-gray mantle, primaries silvery; tail light gray. In summer black cap, bright orange-red bill with black tip. In winter black cap molts to white but black patch remains around eye; bill black.

Voice
A low, nasal *ky-yarr* and a harsh, buzzy *zraa.*

Habitat
Marshes near open shallow water.

Range
From the Canadian prairies south to south-central California (and San Diego) and across to Colorado; also on the southeastern Atlantic and Gulf coasts. Winters to Central and South America.

Comments
Terns have forked tails and longer, more slender wings than gulls. They feed almost entirely by plunge-diving on fish, pointing the bill downward, whereas gulls do not dive but usually feed from the surface of the water.

Elegant Tern
Sterna elegans
584

16–17″ (41–43 cm). Medium-sized tern. Orange; white with gray mantle and wings; black cap ending in long crest; deeply forked tail. In nonbreeding plumage forehead becomes white, but crown, crest, and eye area remain black.

Voice
A loud, grating *kar-eek*.

Habitat
Lagoons and beaches.

Range
Breeds in Gulf of California and at San Diego. Winters both to the south and north, some going down to Chile and Peru but others regularly visiting the northern California coast.

Comments
The nesting of the Elegant Tern is restricted mostly to Isla Raza, a small flat island in the northern part of the Gulf of California, where it has several colonies of hundreds of nests. Since terneries are crowded, with each female just out of bill range of her neighbors, and coastal winds obliterate landmarks that help adults find their nests, the individual color and markings of the single egg help parents recognize their own. When the eggs hatch, the color pattern of the hatchling serves the same purpose. The population was seriously depleted by Mexican egg-dealers; the breeding island is now protected.

Common Tern
Sterna hirundo
585

13–16″ (33–41 cm). Grayish seabird with long forked tail, black cap, red bill with black tip. Long wings with dark tips. In nonbreeding plumage forehead is white; dark smudge on nape and crown. Resembles Forster's, which has silvery primaries; Arctic Tern has all-red bill in breeding season.

Voice
Call is a loud, distinct, rolling *tee-arr* or *kree-err*. When a predator or bird-watcher approaches, this chorus changes to a screaming, rattling *kik kik kik*.

Habitat
Seacoasts, marshes, lakes, and rivers.

Range
Nearly circumpolar. In the West, in the prairie provinces of

Canada and in adjacent states. Migrates along the Pacific Coast to winter south of the United States. Also common on Atlantic Coast.

Comments
This bird flies with deliberate wingbeats over the water, head turned down at a right angle to the body. When it sights a fish or tadpole, it dives much like a booby to catch its aquatic prey.

Caspian Tern
Sterna caspia
586

19–23" (48–58 cm). North America's largest tern. Resembles medium-sized gull, with black cap and oversized red bill; moderately forked tail. Cap has slight crest; white streaking on forehead and crown in winter; undersurface of wings extensively blackish.

Voice
Loud, grating *kar-rreeow* or *ga-ga-gaaah;* immature birds utter a high, whistled *whee-you.*

Habitat
Inland lakes and rivers; coastal waters.

Range
Virtually cosmopolitan from the tropics to the Far North, but discontinuously distributed. Breeds in nesting sites on several lakes in west-central Canada and in the Great Basin area and California. Winters from the southern Pacific Coast of United States to Central America; also southern Atlantic and Gulf coasts.

Comments
A lone fisher, it patrols a chosen area, suddenly plunging headlong after its prey. Its courtship is typical of terns. The male seizes a fish crosswise in his bill and offers it to the female or lays it beside her. She may ignore it or join him in a courtship flight, during which she follows him as he carries the fish and rises high into the air. In winter it is often seen resting on sandbars along with Royal and other terns.

Least Tern
Sterna antillarum
587

8½–9½" (22–24 cm). Wingspan: 19–21" (50–55 cm). Smallest North American tern. White with gray back and wings. Crown black, forehead white; in winter, crown also white. Outermost flight feathers dusky; feet yellow; yellow bill tipped with black. Tail slightly forked. Immatures have blackish outermost flight feathers and white inner flight feathers; back dusky rather than pearl-gray.

Voice
A sharp *kit, kit* or *kseek.* Frequently repeats a 2-syllable *dee-dee* at the ternery.

Habitat
Seacoasts, beaches, bays, estuaries, lagoons, lakes, and banks of rivers and lakes.

Range
Cosmopolitan; in North America it breeds along the coast of California and Baja California, along major rivers in the interior United States, and along the Atlantic and Gulf coasts.

Comments
Due to the destruction of its habitat by human activities, it is an endangered species in California; along the coast south of San Francisco, only 20 colonies with a total of fewer than 700 pairs remained in 1973.

Sabine's Gull
Xema sabini
589

13–14″ (33–36 cm). Small gull (smaller than Black-legged Kittiwake), with gray back and upper surface of wing, white body and forked white tail. In summer, head of adult slate-gray. Black outermost flight feathers, and white triangle in midwing create a striking pattern in flight. Bill black with yellow tip, feet black. Winter adults and juveniles lack dark head. Juveniles retain the pattern of adult plumage, but have pale brown back and upper surface of wings and black, triangular band on tip of tail.

Voice
A single loud, harsh grating note, described as *kier*.

Habitat
Wet tundra and coastal wet meadows during breeding season; a bird of the open ocean when not breeding.

Range
The extreme High Arctic tundra in North America as well as in Siberia. On migration, fairly common off the West Coast, rarely recorded inland. Winters on the open ocean at tropical latitudes.

Comments
In flight the Sabine's Gull resembles a tern in that it seldom sails, and it swoops down, in the fashion of a tern, to pick food from the surface of a marsh. It runs around on mud flats like a shorebird.

Bonaparte's Gull
Larus philadelphia
590

12–14″ (30–36 cm). Small white, gray-backed, black-headed gull. In winter head is white with only ear patch dark; feet bright red in summer, pale pink in winter; bill blackish in both plumages; long triangle of white on leading edge of outer wing. Juveniles resemble winter adults but have diagonal brownish-black lines across inner wing and dark bands near end of tail.

Voice
A low, nasal *cherr* contact call, constantly uttered.

Habitat
In summer muskegs and lakes; in winter at sea.

Range
Boreal forest belt from Alaska and the Yukon and from British

Columbia to Hudson Bay. Passes through the Northwest in fall and spring. Winters off Pacific Coast of the United States and Mexico. Also Atlantic and Gulf coasts.

Comments
Flocks of these dainty gulls make a graceful spectacle as they fly ternlike along the seashore or over salt ponds. When swimming, they float high with wing tips crossed over the tail. Along the Pacific Coast, at peak migration time, jaegers accompany them and rob them of fish.

Heermann's Gull
Larus heermanni
591

18–21" (46–53 cm). Medium-sized gull. Predominantly dark. Bill red; snow-white head blends into gray on neck, back, and rump; slate-black on wings and tail, and white at tip of tail and inner flight feathers. Juveniles dusky with throat lighter and with tail trimmed with white; bill dark.

Voice
A high *see-whee.* Also a low-pitched *kuk-kuk-kuk* or a laughing *ah-ah-ah-ah.*

Habitat
Coastal waters, islands, and beaches.

Range
Breeds on islands (mainly Isla Raza) in the Gulf of California and on the San Benito Islands off the west coast of Baja California. Some migrate northward from July to October, spending the winter on the Pacific Coast north to Vancouver Island; others migrate southward as far as Panama. Nonbreeders are found year-round on the coast of California, but adults leave by January.

Comments
This gull demonstrates that all migration is not necessarily southward in fall and northward in spring in the Northern Hemisphere. On its breeding grounds, Heermann's Gull commonly follows fishing boats and robs fish from Brown Pelicans. Farther north, it scavenges along beaches and feeds on herring eggs.

Thayer's Gull
Larus thayeri
592

22½–25" (57–64 cm). Almost identical to Herring Gull. Back and upper surface of wings slightly darker gray, and black area of wing tips smaller, paler, with larger white "windows" and tips. Yellow bill with red spot on lower mandible; brown eye, with purple-red ring around it; pink feet. In immature plumages, very similar to Herring Gulls of the same age but slightly smaller with proportionately smaller bill; overall coloration somewhat paler, especially the wing tips.

Voice
A long, mewing call, *hiyah,* and a warning call, *gah-gah-gah,* like those of the Herring Gull.

Habitat
Seabird of the Arctic; coastal rocks and rocky headlands. In winter, among other gulls on the Pacific Coast.

Range
Central Canadian Arctic archipelago and adjacent areas. Winters from British Columbia to Baja California.

Comments
The Herring, Thayer's, Glaucous, Glaucous-winged, and Western gulls arose from the splitting up of a single northern gull species during glacial epochs. Experienced birders cannot positively identify all these gulls to species. These birds occasionally hybridize where their ranges meet, yet different eye, eye-ring, and foot colors usually keep them from interbreeding.

Black-legged Kittiwake
Rissa tridactyla
593

16–18″ (40–46 cm). Small gull of the open ocean. White with gray back and gray wings with ink-black wing tips; wing linings white. Yellowish bill similar to that of Mew Gull, but its black legs are distinctive. In winter, has large gray patch on back of head. Juveniles have black band at tip of tail that emphasizes the slight fork of the tail; dark bill, dusky nape band, and black zigzag "M" across open wings.

Voice
Among its many cries the commonest is *kittiwake,* which gives the bird its name.

Habitat
Open waters of Arctic Ocean and neighboring seas; bays and estuaries; with cliffs on islands or headlands for nesting.

Range
Circumpolar. Breeds on coastal cliffs of Arctic Ocean and neighboring seas. In winter, migrates southward; many get as far as Mexico.

Comments
Commonest gull of the Arctic. Colonies of many thousands occupy the steepest cliffs, the breeding pairs looking like pearls on a necklace. They may be so tightly packed that there is room for only one parent at the nest at a time. In one colony on Alaska's Pribilof Islands, rock walls 1000 feet high were covered with these nests on every ledge for 5 miles—probably totaling several million birds. They feed at sea even in the roughest weather, since they can snatch food from the top of the water.

Glaucous-winged Gull
Larus glaucescens
594

24–27″ (61–69 cm). Large white gull with pearly gray back and wings. Gray outermost flight feathers show a white "window" near tip of each feather; yellow bill with red spot on lower mandible, light brown or silvery eyes, pink feet. In winter red spot on bill becomes a diffuse black; head and nape look dusky. First-year birds gray-brown overall, with wing tips same color as mantle. Black bill, dark eyes and feet. Second-year birds acquire more gray and are generally paler.

Voice
Similar to the "long call" of the Western Gull: a raucous series of similar notes on 1 pitch. Other calls include a series of dull *ga-ga-ga* notes uttered when intruders appear, as when a boat approaches the breeding colony.

Habitat
Rocky or sandy beaches, harbors, dumps, open ocean.

Range

From the Aleutians and Bering Sea south to Oregon, where it mingles and hybridizes with the Western Gulls in a few colonies along the boundary area, particularly British Columbia and Washington; it hybridizes with the Herring Gull in parts of Alaska.

Comments
Like other large gulls, this species feeds mainly along the shore. Over water it picks up edibles such as dead or dying fish and squid; over the beach it feeds on dead seabirds, seals, whales, starfish, clams, and mussels. In most seabird colonies it is the main predator on eggs and chicks. In harbors and towns it scavenges on garbage. One banded female was observed to make daily trips from her nest to a garbage dump over 42 miles away.

California Gull
Larus californicus
595

20–23″ (51–58 cm). Similar to Herring Gull, but smaller, with darker gray mantle, dark eye, reddish eye-ring, and yellowish legs and feet; bill of breeding birds has red spot overlapped by black. Winter and immature birds have black subterminal bar on bill and lack eye-ring of adults. A common inland gull.

Voice
A shuddering, repetitive *kee-yah*.

Habitat
In breeding season, on interior lakes and marshes; in winter, mostly on seacoast.

Range

Northern prairie provinces east to North Dakota, south to NW. Wyoming and Utah, west to NE. California. Winters mainly on the Oregon, California, and Baja California coasts; in lesser numbers inland.

Comments
The California Gull attained fame when great numbers arrived at the Mormon colony near the Great Salt Lake and devoured a locust swarm that threatened the settlers' first crop. A statue in Salt Lake City commemorates the event.

Western Gull
Larus occidentalis
596

24–27" (61–69 cm). Large gull. Snowy white, with dark slaty back and wings. Yellow eye and bill; breeding adult has a red dot near tip of lower mandible. Pinkish or flesh-colored feet. In winter, head and nape light dusky. First-year immatures are dark gray-brown with dark, almost black outermost flight feather, contrasting with lighter areas on nape and rump; bill dark.

Voice
Most commonly utters a raucous series of similar notes. Also loud squealing calls.

Habitat
Coastal waterways, beaches, harbors, dumps; open ocean.

Range
Nests on the Pacific Coast from Washington to Baja California and through the Gulf of California. Regularly occurs in winter along the coast of British Columbia.

Comments
The large gulls of the Pacific Coast had a common ancestor but evolved separately in isolation during past Ice Ages. The Glaucous-winged Gull resembles the Western Gull in size and habits, but its coloration is extremely light, as befits a gull living among the ice floes of Alaska today or among glaciers of the Pacific Northwest in the past. A distinct population of Western Gulls that breeds through the Gulf of California has bright yellow feet; it wanders to the Salton Sea in small numbers in summer. It is now considered a distinct species, the Yellow-footed Gull.

Herring Gull
Larus argentatus
597

22½–26" (57–66 cm). Large white bird with gray back and wings. Wing tips black with white spots; bill yellow with red spot on lower mandible, feet pink. Eyes pale yellow with yellow eyelid ringing eye. In winter red spot on bill darkens to dusky, and head is suffused with dusky color. Juveniles similar to those of Western Gull, but slightly paler; they gradually acquire lighter plumage of the adult.

Voice
A loud series, *ke-yah, ke-yah* . . . Various squealing cries.

Habitat
Tundra, other wetlands, and coasts as long as nesting islets or cliffs are nearby; coastal areas in winter.

Range
In North America from central Alaska east to north-central Canada and south to British Columbia, the Great Lakes, and Long Island. In winter along the Pacific Coast to northern Mexico, and along the Atlantic and Gulf coasts. Cosmopolitan in Northern Hemisphere and overlaps with many gull species; hybridizes with Glaucous-winged, Glaucous, and other gulls.

Comments
Originally a beach scavenger and surface-fishing bird, this gull

greatly increased its Atlantic Coast populations by availing itself of man-made sources of food such as harbors, seafood canneries, and city dumps. In the West, the wintering population from the Far North forms a minority among the other large gulls.

Mew Gull
Larus canus
598

16–18″ (41–46 cm). Medium-small gull. White with gray back and upper surface of wing, black wing tips, and greenish-yellow legs. Bill is small compared to that of larger gulls and is unmarked greenish yellow. Juvenile similar to young Ring-billed Gulls but generally darker with less crisply marked tail band.

Voice
A high mewing *kee-yer.*

Habitat
Seacoasts, beaches, bays, and mud flats along rocky or sandy coasts; inland along lakes and rivers.

Range
Alaska east to central Mackenzie and south to N. Saskatchewan and along the coast to S. British Columbia. Winters on Pacific Coast.

Comments
This small gull is as versatile a feeder as the larger species of gulls, but its egg-stealing in seabird colonies is less destructive. It often eats insects, sometimes from swarms in the air.

Ring-billed Gull
Larus delawarensis
599

18–21″ (45–53 cm). Reddish eye-ring, greenish-yellow legs, and a blackish band ringing both mandibles of yellow bill. Adult plumage is acquired in 3 years, with mottled brown juvenile plumage gradually lightening and losing black band near end of tail.

Voice
High, shrill squeals; a shrill *ky-eow.*

Habitat
Breeds on islands in inland lakes; in winter along seacoasts.

Range
Prairie and lake country in Canada and midwestern states; also sparsely in the northern Great Basin area down to the northeastern corner of California. In winter, in the West it is found on the Pacific Coast and on reservoirs of the Southwest.

Comments
Misnamed "sea gull," this bird follows farm plows or scatters over meadows after heavy rains to feast on drowning earthworms. The eye of the slightly larger, darker-mantled California Gull is dark brown, whereas the eye of the Ring-bill is yellow.

Northern Fulmar
Fulmarus glacialis
600

17–20″ (43–51 cm). Resembles a medium-sized gull, but stockier. Rounded yellow bill with fused tubelike nostrils. Sexes look alike. 2 color phases. Light phase: head and underparts white; otherwise light gray above. Legs vary, but are never pink. Dark phase: overall smoky gray with light patch at base of outermost flight feathers visible in flight.

Voice
A grunting *kek kek kek*. Usually silent on winter grounds.

Habitat
Open ocean.

Range
Circumpolar on Arctic coasts. In winter along Pacific Coast south occasionally to Baja California.

Comments
The Northern Fulmar is stockier than its shearwater relatives and seems to have somewhat shorter wings, but the stiff-winged flight of both is similar. The fulmar's flight pattern, several flaps and a glide, banking and skimming in stiff-winged fashion low over the water, is quite different from the steadier flapping of the gull. This buoyant swimmer has pushed its breeding stations southward in the North Atlantic to Canada and the British Isles, responding to increased human activity in those areas. Fulmars consume offal and follow whaling ships for spoils of blubber and flesh.

WILDFLOWERS

From time to time, especially in the warm summer months, the dunes and rocky highlands of the Pacific Coast are emblazoned with a bright display of color as the local wildflowers come into bloom. Beach Strawberry and Beach Silvertop lend a touch of pure white to dunes and bluffs, while various shades of pink, lavender, and red come into play with Beach Morning Glory and Sea Rocket. This section describes some of the most common and beautiful wildflowers of the Pacific beaches.

Tree Lupine
Lupinus arboreus
601

A large, round, bushy plant with palmately compound leaves and showy, sweet-scented, conelike racemes of usually yellow "pea flowers" held just above the foliage at ends of short branches. Flowers occasionally violet or blue.
Flowers: over ½" (1.3 cm) long, in dense racemes 4–12" (10–30 cm) long; top petal (banner) hairless on back.
Leaves: 6–12 leaflets, each to 2½" (6.3 cm) long, arranged like wheel spokes.
Height: 2–9' (60–270 cm).

Flowering
March–June.

Habitat
Sandy areas and canyons near the Pacific Coast.

Range
Along the coast of the northern two-thirds of California; introduced as a sand binder in Oregon and Washington.

Comments
Lupines were once believed to be "wolflike," devouring soil nutrients (the genus name comes from Latin *lupus,* meaning wolf). In fact, they "prefer" poor soil, which they do not further deplete. Tree Lupine, one of the most handsome species in the genus, grows rapidly, and its deep roots make it an effective and beautiful stabilizer of shifting coastal dunes; portions of San Francisco that were once unstable sand were reclaimed by Tree Lupine.

Giant Coreopsis
Coreopsis gigantea
602

Resembles a small tree, with a soft, woody stem that branches near the top, where feathery leaves grow and large yellow flower heads bloom in clusters at the ends of long leafless stalks.
Flowers: heads up to 3" (7.5 cm) wide, with bracts in 2 series, outer lanceolate and shorter, inner ones broader; rays 2-tone yellow, more deeply colored at the base.
Leaves: up to 1' (30 cm) long, broadly ovate, repeatedly pinnately divided into fine, fleshy, very narrow lobes. Stems about 4" (10 cm) thick.
Height: 1–10' (30–300 cm).

Flowering
March–May.

Habitat
Coastal dunes and bluffs.

Range
Los Angeles County to San Luis Obispo County, California.

Comments
Another species, Sea Dahlia (*C. maritima*), stout but not woody, with heads borne singly on stalks, grows in coastal San Diego County. It is not a true Dahlia, a popular ornamental developed from wildflowers (species of *Dahlia*) found in the mountains of Mexico.

Narrow Goldenrod
Solidago spathulata
603

Generally several stems in a clump with largest leaves at the base and many small yellow flower heads in a narrow, long cluster.
Flowers: heads about ¼" (6 mm) long with 5–10 (usually 8) rays surrounding the small disk.
Leaves: to 6" (15 cm) long, lanceolate, smooth, tapered to a smooth stalklike base.
Fruit: seedlike, topped with a tuft of fine white bristles.
Height: 2–32" (5–80 cm).

Flowering
June–September.

Habitat
Coastal sand dunes and open mountain slopes and valleys.

Range
Canada south to the coast of central California.

Comments
These plants occupy a wide range of habitats and are variable. Although they occur well into the mountains, in alpine regions they are generally replaced by Alpine Goldenrod (*S. multiradiata*), which is similar but with bristly hairs on edges of the leafstalks.

Northern Dune Tansy
Tanacetum douglasii
604

A leafy, lightly hairy plant that grows in patches; leaves feathery, aromatic when crushed; stems topped by an open cluster of small, buttonlike yellow flower heads.
Flowers: heads about ½" (1.3 cm) wide, with disk and inconspicuous ray flowers.
Leaves: 2–8" (5–20 cm) long, pinnately divided, the lobes again pinnately divided 1 or 2 times.
Fruit: seedlike, tipped with a minute crown of tiny scales.
Height: 8–24" (20–60 cm).

Flowering
June–September.

Habitat
Sand dunes along the Pacific Coast.

Range
British Columbia to N. California.

Comments
This is closely related to the similar Seaside Tansy (*T. camphoratum*), densely hairy and lacking rays, which grows only near the San Francisco Bay. Tansy (*T. vulgare*), with no hairs and a cluster of 20–200 heads, was widely used medicinally; it was brought from Europe to the New World, where it was planted in colonial gardens, from which it escaped into the wild. Tansy's poisonous oil caused abortions, whereas a tea made from its steeped leaves was used to prevent miscarriage, and crushed leaves were used to poultice sprains and bruises.

Yellow Sand Verbena
Abronia latifolia
605

Many yellow, trumpet-shaped flowers in hemispherical heads bloom atop long stalks in leaf axils of trailing stems.
Flowers: head 1–2″ (2.5–5 cm) wide; 5 lobes on end of "trumpet."
Leaves: ½–2½″ (1.3–6.3 cm) long, opposite, fleshy, roundish.
Fruit: with 3–5 wings.
Height: creeper, with flower stalks to 6″ (15 cm) high, but stems to 3′ (90 cm) long.

Flowering
May–August.

Habitat
Dunes along the Pacific Coast.

Range
S. California to British Columbia.

Comments
This is the only yellow Sand Verbena. Two similar species, each differing primarily by flower color, grow along the Pacific Coast. Beach Pancake (*A. maritima*), from southern California to Mexico, has wine-red flowers, and Beach Sand Verbena (*A. umbellata*), from British Columbia to Baja California, has flowers varying from deep pink to white.

Menzies' Wallflower
Erysimum menziesii
606

A few short branches at base, and one short erect stem, end in dense, thick racemes of bright orange-yellow flowers.
Flowers: ½–¾″ (1.3–2 cm) wide; petals 4.
Leaves: largest at base, 1¼–3½″ (3.1–8.8 cm) long, spatula-shaped, sometimes very shallowly lobed, blunt at tip.
Fruit: slender pod 1½–3″ (3.8–7.5 cm) long, flat, stiffly standing out from stem.
Height: 1–8″ (2.5–20 cm).

Flowering
Mostly March–May.

Habitat
Coastal dunes.

Range
Northern two-thirds of California.

Comments
This lovely coastal wildflower will form low, conical mounds of solid yellow-orange when in full bloom.

Beach Primrose
Oenothera cheiranthifolia
607

Leafy stems lie on the sand, radiating from a central rosette of grayish leaves, with bright yellow flowers facing upward near the ends.
Flowers: ½–1¼″ (1.3–3.1 cm) wide; petals 4, nearly round; stamens 8.
Leaves: ½–2″ (1.3–5 cm) long, ovate, covered with grayish hairs.

Fruit: slender pod, 4-sided.
Height: creeper, with branches to about 6″ (15 cm) high, and stems 2–4′ (60–120 cm) long.

Flowering
April–August.

Habitat
Beach sands along the Pacific Coast.

Range
S. Oregon to Baja California.

Comments
The large knob on the end of the style, as well as several technical characteristics, show that this is a fairly close relative of Desert Primrose (*O. brevipes*). It is also known as *Camissonia cheiranthifolia*.

Beach Strawberry
Fragaria chiloensis
608

A low plant connected to others by "runners," at least when young, often growing in patches, with white flowers on stalks slightly shorter than the leaves.
Flowers: about ¾″ (2 cm) wide; sepals 5, green, pointed, with little bracts between; petals 5, broadly ovate, each with a short stalk at base; stamens many.
Leaves: compound; 3 broad, leathery leaflets, each ¾–2″ (2–5 cm) long, toothed at end, shiny, dark green on top, hairy and grayish on lower side, on stalk 2–8″ (5–20 cm) long.
Fruit: berry, ⅝–¾″ (1.5–2 cm) wide, enlarges from a cone-shaped flower center that has many pistils.
Height: creeper, with floral stalks 2–8″ (5–20 cm) high.

Flowering
March–August.

Habitat
Coastal dunes and bluffs.

Range
From Alaska south through the northern two-thirds of California.

Comments
The word "strawberry" comes from the Anglo-Saxon *streawberige*, and refers to the berries "strewing" their runners out over the ground. Chilean plants of this species were used as parents in the production of hybrid, domestic strawberries. Several species of wild strawberries in the West strongly resemble the Beach Strawberry but have thin leaflets.

Beach Silvertop
Glehnia leiocarpa
609

This low, spreading plant has rosettes of pinnate leaves that lie on the sand, and from the center, on very short stems, are a number of small, tight, round umbels with numerous tiny white flowers.
Flowers: umbels 3–4″ (7.5–10 cm) wide, with a few stout woolly branches; conspicuous bracts beneath flower clusters.

Leaves: 1–6″ (2.5–15 cm) long, fleshy, hairy on underside, divided 3 times into 3-lobed leaflets.
Fruit: ¼–½″ (6–13 mm) long with corky wings on edges and both faces.
Height: 2½″ (6.3 cm).

Flowering
May–July.

Habitat
Beach sands and dunes.

Range
Along the Pacific Coast from Alaska to N. California.

Comments
Glehnia probably honors P. von Glehn, 19th-century curator at the St. Petersburg Botanic Garden.

Powdery Dudleya
Dudleya farinosa
610

Whitish flower stalks and clusters of yellow flowers grow from dense rosettes of ovate, succulent leaves often covered with whitish powder.
Flowers: about ⅜″ (9 mm) wide, narrow; sepals 5, short, triangular; petals 5, narrow; flowers erect on individual stalks ¼–½″ (6–13 mm) long on main branches of cluster.
Leaves: 1–2½″ (2.5–6.3 cm) long, pointed, those on flower stalk much smaller.
Height: 4–14″ (10–35 cm).

Flowering
May–September.

Habitat
On bluffs near the Pacific Coast.

Range
S. Oregon to S. California.

Comments
This plant often grows in large matlike clusters. In the northern part of its range it is the only coastal species; to the south there are several.

Beach Morning Glory
Calystegia soldanella
611

Trailing stems growing from deep rootstocks have thick, kidney-shaped leaves and funnel-shaped pink or rose flowers on short stalks from axils.
Flowers: corolla 1½–2½″ (3.8–6.3 cm) wide, with 5 short, blunt points. 2 bracts ½″ (1.3 cm) long partially hide calyx.
Leaves: 1–2″ (2.5–5 cm) wide.
Height: creeper, with branches to 3″ (7.5 cm) high, and stems to 20″ (50 cm) long.

Flowering
April–September.

Habitat
Common on beach sands.

Range
Along the Pacific Coast from British Columbia to S.
California.

Comments
This fleshy plant does not seem very similar to the garden
Morning Glory, but the resemblance of its flower is
unmistakable. In the cool, humid, coastal climate it remains
open most of the day.

Sea Rocket
Cakile edentula
612

Low, fleshy, branching beach plant with pale lavender flowers.
Flowers: ¼" (6 mm) wide, 4-petaled.
Leaves: 3–5" (7.5–12.5 cm) long, ovate to lanceolate, wavy-
toothed or lobed.
Fruit: 2-jointed seed pod, to ¾" (2 cm) long, the upper joint
longer than the lower, ovoid, with a short beak.
Height: 6–20" (15–50 cm).

Flowering
July–September.

Habitat
Beaches.

Range
Pacific Coast.

Comments
This annual, found on the ridge of windblown sand behind
the high-tide line of beaches, gets its common name from the
rocketlike shape of the seed pods. The succulent young stems
and leaves have a pungent taste, somewhat like horseradish.

Common Ice Plant
Mesembryanthemum
crystallinum
613

A succulent plant with branched, reclining stems, covered
with tiny glistening beads; white or reddish flowers in the
upper axils.
Flowers: 1" (2.5 cm) wide, with many narrow petals ¼–⅜"
(6–9 mm) long, and many stamens.
Leaves: ¾–4" (2–10 cm) long, wavy, ovate or spatula-shaped.
Height: creeper, about 3" (7.5 cm) high, with stems 8–24"
(20–60 cm) long.

Flowering
March–October.

Habitat
On sandy flats and slopes in open areas near the coast; also in
deserts.

Range
Southern half of California to Baja California.

Comments
Found also in southern Europe and Africa, this plant was
probably introduced to North America from the Old World.
The beads on the stems are actually swollen with water; they

are easily crushed, exude their contents, and give the plant a moist feel.

Seaside Daisy
Erigeron glaucous
614

Bristly-hairy, sticky stems grow from a basal rosette, each long branch topped by a flower head with many narrow pale pink or lavender rays surrounding a yellowish disk.
Flowers: heads 1½–2½" (3.8–6.3 cm) wide; about 100 rays; bracts shaggy-hairy.
Leaves: to 5" (12.5 cm) long, broadly spatula-shaped, sometimes with teeth on the edges near the top, tapered to a broad, flat stalk.
Fruit: seedlike, with numerous fragile, fine bristles at top.
Height: 4–16" (10–40 cm).

Flowering
April–August.

Habitat
Coastal bluffs, hills, and old dunes.

Range
Oregon to S. California.

Comments
Succulence is a common feature of seaside plants, and this Daisy is unusual in its genus, for it, too, is slightly succulent.

Sea Fig
Mesembryanthemum chilense
615

A mat-forming plant with trailing, rooting stems, bearing large deep reddish-lavender flowers nestled among the erect, narrow, succulent leaves.
Flowers: 1½–2½" (3.8–6.3 cm) wide; sepals of different lengths, the larger like leaves; petals numerous, very narrow.
Leaves: 1½–3" (3.8–7.5 cm) long, mostly opposite, straight, 3-sided.
Fruit: green, fleshy, plump, flat at top, with 8–10 chambers.
Height: creeper, with trailing stems up to 3' (90 cm) long and flowering branches to 5" (12.5 cm) high.

Flowering
April–September.

Habitat
Coastal sands and bluffs.

Range
From S. Oregon to Mexico.

Comments
The tongue-tangling genus name means "blooming at midday"; flowers open only in full sun. A similar species, Hottentot Fig (*M. edule*), introduced from South Africa, is used to stabilize dunes. It has 3-sided curved leaves with fine teeth on the lower angle, and yellow petals that become pinkish. The fruit is edible. Other cultivated species have "escaped" in parts of California. They have flat or nearly cylindrical leaves.

Salt-marsh Club-flower
Cordylanthus maritimus
616

A softly hairy, loosely branched, low plant with pinkish and white bilaterally symmetrical corollas nearly hidden within the tubular calyx and leafy racemes.
Flowers: corolla ¾" (2 cm) long, lower end a slender tube, the upper end swollen, blushed with pink or dull red-violet, opening almost closed by the very short, pale yellow, beaklike upper lip and the equally short, 4-toothed lower lip; stamens 4.
Leaves: ¼–1" (6–25 mm) long, broadly lanceolate.
Height: 8–16" (20–40 cm).

Flowering
May–September.

Habitat
Salt marshes along the Pacific Coast.

Range
S. Oregon to N. Baja California.

Comments
Although hardly pretty, the curious Salt-marsh Club-flower always attracts attention. The genus name, from the Greek *kordyle* ("club") and *anthos* ("flower"), describes the corolla's shape.

Silky Beach Pea
Lathyrus littoralis
617

This silky-hairy, gray plant grows in low patches, with pink and white "pea flowers" in dense racemes among pinnately compound leaves.
Flowers: ¾" (2 cm) long; upper petal usually rose-pink, the lower ones white or pale pink.
Leaves: 2–10 broadly lanceolate leaflets, each ¼–¾" (6–20 mm) long.
Fruit: pod about 1¼" (3.1 cm) long.
Height: 8–24" (20–60 cm).

Flowering
April–June.

Habitat
Sand dunes along the Pacific Coast.

Range
Washington to central California.

Comments
This beautifully colored plant forms dense patches among yellow and pink Sand Verbenas and Beach Morning Glories, adding to the spectacular natural garden of coastal dunes. A relative, Beach Pea or Sand Pea (*L. japonicus*), differs in having smooth stems and leaves, 2–8 flowers, each ¾–1¼" (2–3.1 cm) long, with reddish-purple petals; it grows on sand dunes from northern California to Alaska.

California Thrift
Armeria maritima
618

A low plant with a basal cluster of many narrow leaves and, atop a slender, leafless stalk, a globe of pale lilac flowers, beneath which are several broad, purplish, papery bracts.
Flowers: head ¾–1″ (2–2.5 cm) wide; flower with calyx in the form of a funnel of pinkish parchment; 5 lobes on corolla joined at base.
Leaves: 2–4″ (5–10 cm) long.
Height: 2–16″ (5–40 cm).

Flowering
March–August.

Habitat
Beaches and coastal bluffs, or slightly inland on prairies.

Range
Pacific Coast from British Columbia to S. California; Arctic North America; Eurasia.

Comments
It resembles a small onion, but the two families are not closely related.

AN INTRODUCTION TO MARINE INVERTEBRATES

The term invertebrate is vaguely familiar to most people but somewhat mysterious to many. The word actually describes what certain animals lack—a backbone or spinal column. Fishes, amphibians, reptiles, birds, and mammals are vertebrates. All other animals lack a backbone and are, by definition, invertebrates.

Marine invertebrates are among the most fascinating animals on earth. They include creatures as diverse as sponges, jellyfishes, worms, snails, clams, squids, shrimps, lobsters, crabs, sea stars, and sea urchins. Many of the less familiar kinds of invertebrates, such as sponges, sea anemones, or hydroids, may be mistaken for plants. Closer investigation, however, reveals that they are animals.

The following essays and illustrations explain the principal anatomical features of the major phyla of marine invertebrates. A familiarity with the basics of invertebrate anatomy will help you identify the animals you encounter as you explore the Pacific Coast.

Sponges: Phylum Porifera

Sponges are the simplest many-celled animals. Their shapes vary from tiny cups, broad branches, and tall vases to encrustations and large, rounded masses. Sponges come in a variety of colors. Grays and browns predominate in deeper waters; brighter hues in the shallows. With differing growing conditions a species may vary greatly in size, shape, and color, and so can be difficult to identify.

A sponge consists of a cooperating community of individual cells, each performing a specific function. The cells surround a system of canals through which water is carried, providing the basis for all the sponge's life functions. Water enters the canals through minute pores (ostia) that dot the surface of the sponge. It then passes into chambers lined with collar cells, each with a fine-meshed funnel-shaped collar. Out of each collar extends a flagellum, a hairlike structure whose beating creates a current. The combined action of all the collar cells drives water through the canals and out of the sponge through a larger pore, the osculum. The collar cells trap food particles brought in with the water, and either digest them or pass them to other cells to be digested. This flow of water through the animal also brings in oxygen and removes carbon dioxide and other waste products. A simple sponge has just one chamber and one osculum; more complex sponges have many of each.

Most sponges have a skeleton that is a meshwork of tough protein (spongin), or of clusters of microscopic hard geometric objects (spicules), or a combination of both. Spicules are either limy (calcareous) or glasslike (siliceous) and appear in many different forms.

The Phylum Porifera is divided into three classes: the Calcispongiae, or Calcarea, which have limy spicules; the Hyalospongiae, or Hexactinellida (glass sponges), which are found only in deep waters; and the Class Demospongiae, which comprises all the remaining sponges and may have skeletons of glasslike spicules or of spongin or both, or may lack a skeleton entirely.

Cnidarians: Phylum Cnidaria

The Phylum Cnidaria includes hydras, hydroids, jellyfishes, sea anemones, and corals. Members of this phylum are nearly all found in marine and brackish water.

The cnidarian body is radially symmetrical, and consists of a tube or sac with a single opening, the mouth, surrounded by tentacles. The body wall consists of an outer layer, the epidermis, which is separated from the gastrodermis, the layer lining the digestive cavity (coelenteron), by a middle layer, the mesoglea, which varies from a thin, noncellular film to a thick layer that, in some forms, has so many cells that it resembles connective tissue or muscle. The epidermis includes cells specialized for production of nematocysts, a distinctive characteristic of cnidarians. Nematocysts provide an effective means of snaring prey animals and also offer protection against predators. The nematocyst is a capsule containing a long thread that is forcefully everted when triggered by contact with prey or other animals. Some nematocysts are sticky, some wrap around prey, but most inject venom into other creatures. People coming into contact with certain cnidarians may sustain reactions ranging from a mild rash to severe blistering and, in extreme cases, will suffer fatal congestive respiratory failure.

Generally, the cnidarian body is an asexual polyp—a tube with a mouth surrounded by tentacles, specialized for a sedentary (sessile) life attached to some solid object—or a saucer- or bowl-shaped sexual medusa that floats free in the water and swims by pulsating contractions. The life cycle of a cnidarian may include one or both of these forms. Polyps may be solitary or colonial, increasing colony size by budding, the process of forming outgrowths that develop into new individuals. In a colony, polyps may be specialized for various functions, such as trapping food, defense, digestion, or reproduction. The body or bell of a medusa is umbrella-shaped. An extension (manubrium) bearing the mouth is suspended from the underside. Tentacles are generally located on the margin of the bell and trail behind as the medusa swims.

Class Hydrozoa

This class includes hydroids, hydromedusae, chondrophorans, siphonophorans, and hydrocorallines. These animals are characterized by a noncellular mesoglea, a gastrodermis lacking nematocysts, and, with a few exceptions, gonads, or reproductive organs, in the epidermis. They may have either the polyp or the medusa body form, and a number of species pass through both stages in the life cycle. The medusa-stage animal is usually small and simple in form. The polyp stage of marine forms is often marked by a variety of specialized individuals in a colony, including feeding, defensive, and reproductive polyps. Usually the polyp stage is dominant in size and longevity, and in some species is the only stage.

Class Scyphozoa

Forms commonly known as jellyfish are included in Class Scyphozoa. The medusa is the dominant and in some cases the only stage. The small polyp stage (scyphistoma), when present, buds off small, lobed medusae (ephyrae) by a series of transverse constrictions. Scyphozoan medusae have a thick, firm mesoglea. The coelenteron is subdivided into a number of chambers and canals. Its lining is equipped with nematocysts. The manubrium—the extension bearing the mouth—may be long or short, with some species possessing oral arms surrounding the mouth. Gonads are located in pouches of the coelenteron.

Class Anthozoa

This class includes the soft corals, the sea anemones, and the stony corals, animals that also have a thick, firm mesoglea. All anthozoans are sexual polyps with no known medusa stage. The coelenteron is subdivided into chambers by radial partitions, the septa or mesenteries, which extend from the body wall toward the center. The mouth is situated on an oral disk, surrounded by tentacles. It is generally slitlike and may have one or two siphonoglyphs, ciliated grooves in the wall of the pharynx, at one or both ends; the pharynx opens into the coelenteron. The gastrodermis contains nematocysts and gonads. Sexes are usually separate. Some species are oviparous, shedding their eggs into the water. Others are viviparous, with fertilization taking place in the body of the female. After fertilization, the egg develops into a minute planula larva. Some sea anemones brood their young beyond the planula stage and release them as polyps, while others bud off new individuals asexually. Nearly all other anthozoans are colonial and undergo extensive budding.

Subclass Octocorallia. These colonial animals are sometimes called soft corals because of the tough, elastic matrix they secrete, into which the polyps can retract. The sea whips and sea fans have a horny core over which the softer tissues lie. Colonies may be bushy, whiplike, or fanlike. Their polyps have eight pinnately branched tentacles.

Subclass Zoantharia, Order Actiniaria. Sea anemones are solitary, sessile cnidarians, generally cylindrical in form when fully extended. The anemone body consists of a column, at the bottom of which is a pedal disk that attaches the animal to the substrate and at the top of which is an oral disk that bears the slitlike mouth and is surrounded by one or more rows of tentacles that vary in size and number from one species to another. The fully retracted animal is hemispherical, with only an indentation at the site of the retracted oral disk. While some anemones live with the entire body exposed, others bury themselves in a sandy or muddy bottom, exposing the oral disk only when fully extended, and retracting into the bottom when disturbed at low tide. Many anemones are capable of creeping slowly about on the pedal disk.

Order Scleractinia. The stony corals are mostly warm-water creatures and are structurally similar to sea anemones. They deposit a skeleton of calcium carbonate at their base. The skeleton conforms to the configuration of the base of the polyp, including its pattern of internal septa. The deposited skeleton extends partially up the column of the polyp and forms a cup in which the polyp sits. Most species of coral are colonial, reproducing by budding and branching. The entire skeletal structure of the colony is called the corallum. The corallum of different species varies in form from highly branched or bushy outgrowths to solid, massive boulders. Many reef corals are nourished by symbiotic algae that live within their tissues.

Order Corallimorpharia. Cnidarians in this order resemble true corals, but lack skeletons. They are colonial, have a basal disk and radially arranged tentacles.

Comb Jellies: Phylum Ctenophora

Like cnidarians, comb jellies have differentiated tissues without true organ systems, but they possess a modified radial symmetry. Unlike cnidarians, comb jellies do not sting. Body form varies, but is commonly globular or somewhat compressed. Water makes up more than ninety-five percent of the comb jelly's body weight. Some species have a pair of tentacles equipped with adhesive cells, some have oral lobes (two large flaps around the mouth), and some have neither. The comb jelly's mouth leads into a gullet, or pharynx, which in turn opens into a digestive cavity, the stomach. From the stomach, numerous canals extend throughout the animal, and digested food thus reaches all parts of the body. Ctenophores are carnivorous, feeding on a large variety of planktonic prey.

The comb jelly's comb plates (ctenae) consist of transverse rows of cilia fused together by a thin membrane and arranged in eight lines down the long axis of the animal. The beat of the comb plates by progressive waves, or metachronal rhythm, moves the animal through the water, mouth-end forward, coordinated by a sensory structure, the apical organ—a dome-shaped cyst containing a heavy granule, the statolith. All species found in American waters swim feebly, and thus are at the mercy of ocean currents. Refraction of light upon the comb plates imparts a jewel-like quality to ctenophores seen in the sunlight. In the dark, many comb jellies are bioluminescent, and their whole form, including the rows of comb plates, can be seen outlined in flashes of light.

Flatworms: Phylum Platyhelminthes

Of all animals that have a head, flatworms have the simplest body plan. As their name suggests, flatworms' bodies are compressed, their thickness small compared with their length and breadth. As with cnidarians, the mouth is the only opening into the digestive cavity; through it food is taken in and wastes discharged. Unlike cnidarians, flatworms have well-defined nervous, muscular, excretory, and reproductive systems, which lie within a solid matrix of tissue (parenchyma). Distribution of digested food is achieved by a digestive cavity that in some of them branches into all parts of

the body. Because of the worms' flatness, all cells are close
enough to the surface for exchange of oxygen and carbon
dioxide with the environment. The flat body—capable of
great contortion—also enables these creatures to hide in
narrow crevices or enter the body openings of other animals.
The phylum includes three classes: the Turbellaria,
Trematoda, and Cestoidea. The latter two parasitize various
vertebrate animals and will not be considered here. The Class
Turbellaria includes mostly free-living forms, of which only
the order Tricladida and Polycladida have members large and
obvious enough to catch the eye of the shore visitor. Triclads
have a digestive cavity with three major branches, one toward
the head and two toward the rear. Polyclads have numerous
branches radiating from the central digestive cavity. Members
of both orders have an epidermis covered with cilia, simple
eyespots (ocelli), and sensory structures for taste and smell on
the head end, as well as a mouth situated toward the rear on
the underside, and a muscular, sucking pharynx. Locomotion
is achieved by rippling contractions of body muscles aided by
the action of cilia, allowing the worm to glide smoothly over a
surface. Both groups include predators and scavengers that
feed on the bodies of dead animals. Some species are
commensals, living in close relation with another kind of
animal.

Nemertean Worms: Phylum Rhynchocoela

Most nemerteans are long, slender, and somewhat flattened.
Color varies greatly; many are highly colored—red, orange,
yellow, brown, or green—some patterned above with stripes
or spots, and paler underneath. Nemerteans range in size from
less than an inch (a millimeter) to several feet (30 meters)
long. They are remarkably elastic and can stretch many times
longer than their relaxed body length. They may be equipped
with eyespots and sensory grooves, are covered with cilia, and
consist internally of a solid mass of tissue, without a body
cavity. Their nervous systems and excretory systems are like
those of flatworms, and the digestive tract includes mouth and
anus. Soft-bodied and seemingly vulnerable, nemerteans are in
fact poisonous predators. They have a long sharp-tipped
proboscis, which can be thrust out accurately to a distance
almost as great as the animal's body length to capture prey—
usually small annelid worms and crustaceans—with abundant
mucus or paralyzing venom. The proboscis lies in a fluid-filled
sac above the mouth; in all species it is coated with glandular
secretions and in some species may be equipped with a
dartlike barb through which toxic substances are injected.

Segmented Worms: Phylum Annelida

The Phylum Annelida includes about 9000 known species
belonging to three classes: the Hirudinea, Oligochaeta, and
Polychaeta. The Hirudinea are leeches, of which only a few
species are parasitic on the gills, fins, and bodies of marine
fishes. The Oligochaeta include the earthworms and most
freshwater annelids, but only about 200 marine species. The
Polychaeta are nearly all marine, and include over 5000

species, two-thirds of all annelids. Our discussion will deal
only with the polychaetes.

An annelid's body is usually elongate, more or less cylindrical,
and consists of a series of segments. The body wall is covered
with a thin, elastic cuticle, beneath which lie layers of circular
and longitudinal muscles. These surround a fluid-filled body
cavity (coelom), which is usually divided between segments by
cross-walls (septa). A series of elongations and contractions
of the segments propels the worm forward.

The body plan is more advanced than that of phyla previously
discussed. Annelids have a complete digestive system
extending from the mouth on the first segment to the anus at
the hind end of the body. Above the mouth is a lobe, the
prostomium, a probing organ that often bears sensory
structures and is useful in feeding and burrowing. Most
annelids have well-developed circulatory, nervous, and
excretory systems. Respiration is carried on through the
cuticle, and some forms have specialized gills. All annelids are
equipped with glands that produce abundant mucus that helps
keep the cuticle moist and is used in some species to catch
food, build tubes, or form egg-masses.

The Polychaeta are divided into two subclasses, the Errantia
and the Sedentaria. The Errantia are worms that move about,
while the Sedentaria remain in a tube or burrow. Errant
polychaetes generally have well-developed, paired appendages
(parapodia), standard trunk segments, good locomotory
ability, and a head with eyespots and sensory appendages.
They are predators, browsers, or bottom-dwelling deposit
feeders. Sedentary polychaetes usually have a head without
eyes or sensory appendages, but sometimes with many gills
and feeding tentacles; a trunk divided into a thick thorax
followed by a slender abdomen—the segments of each quite
different; and appendages reduced and modified for adhering
to the inside of the tube or burrow.

Peanut Worms: Phylum Sipuncula

The small Phylum Sipuncula includes the peanut worms, a
group with certain features in common with annelid worms,
but several other characteristics that are unique. Both have
similar developmental and reproductive patterns, a similar
nervous system, and similar layers in the body and the walls of
the digestive tract. In sipunculids, however, there is no sign of
segmentation, and the digestive tract is U-shaped, doubling
over and terminating in an anus in the upper midline, well
toward the front end. These worms can extend and retract a
large part of the front end into and out of the trunk and, when
disturbed, contract into a plump, taut, elongate oval, in some
species resembling a peanut kernel. The mouth and
surrounding parts are the last to be seen when the worm
extends fully, and the first to roll in and disappear as it
retracts. The mouth is surrounded by tentacles. Animals with
short tentacles feed on organic matter taken in with mud or
sand; those with longer, branched tentacles filter organic
particles from the water.

Spoon Worms: Phylum Echiura

The Phylum Echiura is a small group of worms, similar in many ways to the Annelids, but lacking any suggestion of segmentation. Their digestive and nervous systems, body wall structures, reproductive patterns, and even bristles (setae) are similar. Echiurids are plump-bodied, sausage-shaped, fluid-filled creatures with a nonretractable proboscis that has a deep groove or trough on the underside, leading into the mouth. One or more rings of bristles encircle the rear end of the worm, justifying the name Echiura, which means "snake tail" in Greek.

Mollusks: Phylum Mollusca

In addition to the approximately 50,000 known living mollusk species, some 35,000 fossil mollusks have been described. The fossil record for this phylum extends over 600 million years and is extremely rich because the mineralized molluscan shell, or valve, fossilizes readily.

The body consists of three regions: a head, bearing the mouth and sense organs and containing the brain; a visceral mass surrounded by the body wall, containing most of the internal organs; and a foot, the muscular lower part of the body on which the animal creeps. A membranous extension of the body wall, the mantle, secretes the shell and encloses a mantle cavity containing the gills, anus, and excretory pores. The mouth in most groups is equipped with a long, tough, toothed, ribbonlike structure, the radula, by means of which the animal rasps food. Mollusks have well-developed organ systems—nervous, muscular, digestive, circulatory, respiratory, excretory, and reproductive—but, unlike annelids and arthropods, they lack body segmentation.

Class Polyplacophora

Chitons are flattened, oval creatures with a row of eight broad but short valves along the back. Surrounding the eight valves, and in some cases covering them, is a margin of the mantle called the girdle. On the underside is a large foot with which the animal clings tenaciously to a solid surface; when pried loose, it usually curls into a ball like a pill bug or a hedgehog. On each side of the foot in the mantle cavity lie paired gills. At the front of the foot is the head, bearing the mouth with its radula, but without tentacles; eyes are rare or absent. Most chitons feed by rasping fine algal growth from the surface of rocks and, in some cases, also prey on sedentary animals such as bryozoans, sponges, and protozoans.

Class Gastropoda

The Class Gastropoda contains about eighty percent of all living molluscan species, and includes the snails, limpets, abalones, sea slugs, and sea hares. Garden slugs and pond and land snails also belong to this group.

The general body plan of a gastropod includes a spiral shell into which the animal can retract, a head equipped with tentacles, eyes, and mouth, and a large foot. Forms such as sea hares have only a vestigial, internal shell.

Nudibranchs, or sea slugs, have shells in the larval stage, but lose them on maturing. Terrestrial slugs have no shell at any stage of the life cycle.

The snail shell is basically an elongate cone wound around an axis. Each turn around the axis is a whorl. The body whorl is the most recently formed and largest, and contains most of the snail's soft parts. The remaining whorls constitute the spire, which terminates in the apex. The apex is actually the original shell of the larval stage, and is called the nuclear whorl or protoconch; in most snails the nuclear whorl is worn off during growth. The inner side of the shell immediately adjacent to the axis about which it spirals is called the columella.

The columella may be hollow, opening in an umbilicus at the end opposite the apex, or may be closed over by a shell growth, the umbilical callus. The groove between adjacent whorls is called a suture. The outer surface of the whorls may be smooth or variously sculptured with small beads, larger nodules, sharp spines, ribs which run parallel to the axis, or heavy cords, finer threads, or very fine grooves or lines, all running spirally. A prominent spiral ridge on a whorl is termed a shoulder. The surface may be coated with a tough, horny layer, the periostracum.

The opening of the body whorl through which the head and foot are extended is the aperture. The aperture has an outer lip and an inner lip. In some snails the aperture may have a slender forward extension, the siphonal canal, in which lies a tubular fold of the edge of the mantle, the siphon, through which the animal takes water into the mantle to aerate the gills and carry off waste products. Many species have a horny, leathery, or limy lid, or operculum, attached to the side of the foot. When the head and foot are completely retracted, the operculum neatly seals off the aperture.

By far the majority of snails are dextral, coiling to the right. A few species are sinistral, coiling to the left, and occasionally an individual of a normally dextral species will be sinistral. To make sure which "handedness" a snail exhibits, hold the shell with the apex up and aperture toward you. If the aperture is on your right, the snail is dextral; if it is on your left, the snail is sinistral.

In cited measurements, the term "length" represents that of the axis, even though anatomically it would be more correct to call this the height. In a few low, flattened forms, such as limpets, slipper snails, and abalones, the term "length" will designate true length, the distance from front to rear, and the term "height," the distance from top of shell to surface of substrate. The width is always the broadest dimension at right angles either to the axis or to the true length.

In an active marine snail the opening of the mantle cavity is above the head, not at the rear as the generalized molluscan body plan would indicate. This change in position is achieved during embryological development—when it is bilaterally symmetrical—by a process called torsion, a 180-degree counterclockwise rotation of the visceral mass during larval development. Having the mantle open forward improves water flow over the gills. Torsion also makes the snail asymmetrical internally. The paired nerve cords are twisted about each other, and organs from the original right side, such as the gill, auricle of the heart, and excretory opening, are diminished or eliminated. Torsion must occur before coiling of the shell can commence. In some groups, especially the Opisthobranchs, "detorsion" has taken place.

The Class Gastropoda contains three subclasses: the Prosobranchia (meaning "gill forward"), the Opisthobranchia ("gill behind"), and the Pulmonata ("with a lung"), which are predominantly terrestrial and freshwater species. Of these subclasses, only the Opisthobranchia and Prosobranchia will be considered here.

Subclass Prosobranchia. The snails, limpets, and other gastropods in this group all possess a mantle cavity, gills, and openings to organ systems at the front of the body, having twisted around from the rear during embryonic development. The result is a U-shaped intestinal tract and once-parallel nerves now assume a figure-eight. The apparent advantage is to provide clean water to essential organs in an animal whose body is tucked away in a shell and whose ancestors had these organs toward the rear of its body. While prosobranchs are considered more primitive than opisthobranchs, their variety of form and habit is far larger and comprises the most abundant group of marine gastropods.

Subclass Opisthobranchia. The Opisthobranchia include a variety of hermaphroditic gastropods with gills located toward the rear as a result of detorsion in development, following torsion. This subclass includes both shelled forms and shell-less animals such as sea hares and the colorful sea slugs, or nudibranchs.

Class Bivalvia

The bivalves known to most people are those commonly used as food: clams, oysters, mussels, cockles, and scallops. The Class Bivalvia (also known as Pelecypoda) includes mollusks whose shells consist of two parts, or valves, hinged together along the upper midline. There are about 15,000 species of bivalves, more than eighty percent of them in the sea, and the others in fresh water.

The basic body plan of a bivalve is well adapted to a life of burrowing through the bottom. The two valves that enclose the rest of the body are convex, giving the animal a wedgelike or hatchetlike shape. (Pelecypoda means "hatchet foot" in Greek.) The foot usually is bladelike and can be protruded forward from between the valves. The mantle, which completely lines the shell, forms two openings at the rear end: a lower one, the incurrent siphon, to admit water into the mantle cavity, and an upper one, the excurrent siphon, for its escape. The siphons may be merely two slitlike openings between the two parts of the mantle, or two separate extensible tubes, or the two tubes may be united into a single neck which contains the two passages. The gills, meshworks of strands united into large sheets, are suspended on either side of the visceral mass within the mantle cavity. They are used both for respiration and for food collecting. The gills secrete mucus which traps food from the water—mostly one-celled plants and fine particles of organic matter. The thin layer of food-laden mucus is moved down the gills, then forward along their edges, where long, flaplike palps transfer it to the mouth. The head of a bivalve is little more than a bump with a mouth and a pair of palps. It is probable that bivalves evolved from gastropods, for in the seas of Japan there is a transitional form—a gastropod with its shell divided into two valves.

For purposes of identification, bivalve shells exhibit the most obvious and stable species characteristics. To determine the left valve from the right, hold the animal hinge-side upward and front end away from you. (The front end is the one from which the foot protrudes.) The right valve is then on your right and the left valve on your left. In some species you will find a gap between the valves for foot protrusion. Of course, if the live bivalve obligingly extends its foot, the question is settled. Alternatively, the protrusion of the siphons between the valves at the rear end lets you know indirectly which end is the front. For bivalves that typically lie with one valve down and one up, such as oysters, jewel boxes, and scallops, we refer to the upper and lower valves.

Concentric growth lines can be seen on the shell surface in most bivalves. The center area surrounded by the lines is the oldest part of the shell, and is known as the umbo (plural umbones), or beak. It is usually located nearer the front end than the back, or bent forward. Many characteristics used by conchologists in identification of bivalves—such as teeth, by means of which the two valves interlock near the hinge line; muscle scars, where muscles that close the shells attach; and the pallial line, which marks the internal attachment of the mantle to the shell—are exhibited on the inner surface of the shell. Since these features cannot be observed on living animals, little reference will be made to them. In determining dimensions, the length of the shell is measured as a straight line between its front and rear edges. The height is the distance between uppermost (hinge line) and lowermost edges. However, in oysters the length is commonly considered as the distance from the umbo to the opposite end (the height by our previous definition).

Class Cephalopoda

Members of the Class Cephalopoda—the squids, octopods, and nautiluses (the latter not included in this book)—are specialized variations on the molluscan theme. The visceral mass is surrounded by a mantle enclosing gills and body openings. Cephalopods have a head—with a brain, sense organs, and a mouth with a radula—and a foot specialized into a numer of arms surrounding the mouth and equipped with suckers. Some people refer to the arms as tentacles, but biologists reserve that term for a special pair of long appendages found in squids, and used for capturing prey. The mouth is equipped with a sharp beak, like a parrot's, with which the animal kills and tears apart its prey.

Squids have thin flexible internal shells made of a horny substance, and octopods have none at all. Both use their mantle cavities and siphons for locomotion. Water is admitted into the mantle cavity through slits behind the head, and jetted with great force out the siphon beneath the neck. An ink gland opening into the mantle cavity enables cephalopods, when threatened, to squirt out a cloud of ink and, in the confusion, make their escape. Squids living in ocean depths where the only light is "living light," or bioluminescence, confuse their enemies not with ink, but with a cloud of luminescent particles.

Class Scaphopoda

A relatively small group of mollusks found worldwide, consisting of approximately 350 living species in four genera and two families; in our range all four genera and about ninety species occur. They live in water 10,000 to 10,500 feet (3000 to 3200 meters) deep, although most species are found in water more than 100 feet (30 meters) deep. These mollusks first appeared in the Devonian period, about 300 million years ago. Their tubular shells are 1/8–5" (0.3–12.7 cm) long and open at both ends, with the front end, or aperture, larger than the hind end, or apex; the middle is either evenly tapered or swollen. The apex may have one or more slits or notches in the margin, or a projecting tube. The exterior is smooth, longitudinally ridged, or has circular rings.

Tusk shells live partially buried in sand or mud; water is drawn in and waste products are eliminated through the apex, which protrudes above the surface of the ocean floor. The foot is reduced in size and adapted for digging. The head bears no tentacles or eyes, and the mouth, furnished with a radula, is surrounded by lobes and threadlike appendages with which it captures the foraminifera and minute bivalves on which it feeds. Tusks lack gills and absorb oxygen through the mantle skin.

Arthropods: Phylum Arthropoda

Of all the major groups of invertebrate animals, by far the largest and most familiar are the arthropods. More than 1,000,000 species are known, of which all but about 85,000 are insects—invertebrates familiar to us all.

Only a very few species are associated with the sea, but many occur along shorelines. These animals include the preponderantly marine Crustacea, a class of more than 31,000 species, and the entirely marine Pycnogonida, or sea spiders (500 species). One other class, the Merostomata, includes the Horseshoe Crab, which is found along the eastern shores of North America.

An arthropod's most obvious characteristic is the tough encasement of armor, or exoskeleton, which gives the animal rigidity and protects its soft insides. This armor is made principally of a substance called chitin. The exoskeleton has

joints, regions where the chitin is thin and flexible,
permitting movement. Such joints are particularly obvious on
the legs, and give the phylum its name, Arthropoda, which
means "jointed foot" in Greek.

The presence of an exoskeleton prevents increase in body size.
Growth can be achieved only by a series of molts, the periodic
shedding of the exoskeleton. Before an arthropod molts, a
new, soft exoskeleton is deposited beneath the old one. The
old exoskeleton splits, the soft animal slowly climbs out, and
increases in size by taking in water or air. The new
exoskeleton soon hardens, and the animal's size is again fixed
until the next molt. During this process, the animal is soft
and defenseless and thus vulnerable to predators; it usually
goes into hiding while it molts.

The arthropods share a number of characteristics with the
annelids. Both are segmented and have a similarly organized
nervous system, and a heart that lies above the gut. Unlike the
annelids, however, the segments of arthropods are not all
alike, but are usually grouped together in functional regions:
head, thorax, and abdomen. In some groups the head and
thorax are fused and covered with a single plate, the carapace.
Arthropods are bristly, with nearly all their bristles sense
organs—some sensitive to touch, currents, taste, odor, or
sound. They have eyes that may be simple, with one lens and
retina, or compound, composed of many lenses and nerve
cells. Their circulatory system is said to be "open," that is,
with blood coursing from large blood vessels into open spaces
or sinuses to bathe the tissues, rather than through fine
capillaries among the tissues. All marine forms, except very
small ones, have gills for respiration.

Class Pycnogonida

The sea spiders, or pycnogonids, are a strange group of small-
bodied, long-legged marine arthropods. Though they walk on
eight legs, they are not spiders, which belong to a quite
different group of arthropods. The pycnogonid body consists of
a thorax of four segments, each with a pair of side projections
bearing the legs. The first segment has a necklike projection
with a single four-part eye on the top, and a sucking proboscis
with a mouth at the tip. Beside the proboscis there may be
paired accessory mouthparts in the form of pinchers and
feelers. A given species may have one, both, or neither of these
appendages. The rear end of the animal has a very small
projection, the abdomen, the sole function of which is to bear
the anus. In fact, there is so little room for organs in the body
cavity of a pycnogonid that the sex organs are located in the
long joints of the legs. In some pycnogonids, usually on
the male, there is an extra pair of slender legs curled under
the first body segment. It is on these that the female attaches
her eggs.

Class Crustacea

The crustaceans include a number of animals familiar because
they are edible: shrimps, lobsters, and crabs. They also
include a variety of other forms seen along the shore—

amphipods including beach fleas, isopods including sea roaches, and barnacles—as well as many tiny marine and freshwater creatures too small to be seen with the naked eye. A crustacean is an arthropod that usually possesses five pairs of appendages on five head segments: two pairs of antennae, one pair of jaws, or mandibles, one on each side of the mouth, and two pairs of manipulatory mouthparts, or maxillae. The number of segments in the body varies, depending on the group. In some forms the body may simply be a trunk. In more advanced types it may be divided into a thorax and an abdomen. The thorax has a maximum of eight segments, and the abdomen six, or, rarely seven. Each segment may bear a pair of basically Y-shaped appendages that have different forms and functions. The first three pairs on the thorax may be auxiliary mouthparts, or maxillipeds. The remaining five thoracic appendages may be walking legs, the first two or three ending in pincers. The first five segments on the abdomen bear forked, flattened appendages called swimmerets, and the last segment ends in a flattened tailpiece, or telson, flanked by a pair of broad, flat appendages (uropods) that together make up the tailfin. In crabs, the abdomen is folded forward and is recessed under the thorax.

Echinoderms: Phylum Echinodermata

The Phylum Echinodermata is an entirely marine group of animals including sea stars, brittle stars, sea urchins, sand dollars, sea cucumbers, and sea lilies, whose most obvious feature is their radial symmetry. The echinoderm body is nearly always arranged in five parts, or multiples thereof. There is a body axis with the mouth at one end and anus at the other. In some forms the mouth faces up, in others, down or to the side. Echinoderms have an internal limy skeleton, covered by skin, and may also have spines, some movable, some fixed, variable in size and shape. The unique characteristic of the phylum is an internal hydraulic system, termed the water vascular system, that operates numerous tube feet (podia). These are slender, fingerlike appendages, arranged in rows, which the animal extends by pumping full of fluid, and retracts with muscles within the tube foot itself. Tube feet are used in locomotion and feeding. Many echinoderms have tube feet equipped with suction disks at their tips, enabling them to cling tenaciously to a surface. Inside the body is a complex system of canals, filled with sea water (in sea cucumbers it is filled with body fluid) that operates the tube feet. Water passes back and forth between the canals and the sea through a sieve plate, a perforated disk through which the echinoderm can draw or expel filtered sea water as needed.

The phylum is divided into four classes: the Class Stelleroidea, the starlike echinoderms, which is divided into the Subclass Asteroidea, the sea stars, and the Subclass Ophiuroidea, the brittle stars; the Class Echinoidea, the sea urchins, sand dollars, and sea hearts; the Class Holothuroidea, the sea cucumbers; and the Class Crinoidea, the sea lilies.

Class Stelleroidea

Subclass Asteroidea. The asteroids include the sea stars, also called starfish. The asteroid body has the form of a somewhat flattened star, with arms (rays) usually numbering five or a multiple of five, rarely six or some other number, each in contact with adjacent arms where it joins the central disk. The surface of the central disk has the anus in the center, the sieve plate near the junction of two arms, and openings of sex ducts at each juncture of adjacent arms. The upper surface of each arm has the spines and other features of the species, and an eyespot, usually red, at the tip. The underside of a sea star has the mouth in the middle of the central disk, and an open groove from the mouth to the tip of each arm. Two or four crowded rows of tube feet lie in each groove. In some sea stars there is a special skeletal structure for pinching small objects, a modification of two or three spines. These pinchers (pedicellariae) may be shaped like small tweezers or pliers, or flattened like the jaws of a vise.

Sea stars travel on their tube feet. Tube feet with suckers reach ahead and attach, drawing the star in that direction while others detach, reach farther forward, attach, and so progress. Tube feet of burrowing sea stars lack suckers, and merely push the animal along.

Subclass Ophiuroidea. The brittle stars and basket stars make up the Subclass Ophiuroidea. In ophiuroids the base of an arm does not meet that of its neighbor as it does in a sea star; instead, a portion of the free border of the oral disk lies between them. The central disk may be round, pentagonal, or scalloped, its upper surface leathery or scaly. The mouth on the underside is shaped like a five-pointed star, an arm joining the disk at each star point alternating with a triangular pointed jaw with toothed margins. At the base of each jaw is a plate that may be perforated to form the sieve plate of the water vascular system, the number of sieve plates ranging from one to five. Beside the base of each arm are one or two slits that open into a large respiratory pouch. The arms are long, jointed, and flexible, unbranched in brittle stars, extensively branched in basket stars. The segments commonly bear spines, a feature used in identifying species. While there is no groove on the underside of the arm, as there is in a sea star, there is a double row of active, suckerless tube feet that serve as sense organs, are used in feeding, and may be of some use in locomotion. Arms are used for locomotion and grasping food.

Class Echinoidea

The Class Echinoidea includes the sea urchins, cake urchins, sand dollars, and heart urchins. Unlike sea stars and brittle stars, these creatures do not have arms, or rays. The skeleton, called a test, consists of rows of radially arranged plates immovably joined to one another. Movable spines, each with a concave base, fit on correspondingly convex bumps on each plate. Muscle fibers attached to each spine enable it to swing about in any direction.

Regular species, such as the sea urchins, are almost perfectly radially symmetrical, while irregular species, the cake urchins, heart urchins, and sand dollars, have a bilateral symmetry superimposed upon a radial pattern. In sea urchins, the middle of the upper surface has a circular area, usually with scaly plates, bearing the anus. It is surrounded by five petal-shaped plates, each with a large pore, the opening of a sex duct. One of these plates is also full of small pores, and is the sieve plate. Alternating with these plates are five other plates which may or may not touch the area bearing the anus. Beyond these ten plates are twenty longitudinal rows of firmly united plates extending toward the mouth, five pairs of rows perforated for tube feet alternating with five unperforated pairs. All plates bear spines. The long needlelike spines of one reef species bear a toxin that causes a painful sting.

Tube feet on an urchin are arranged in five pairs of rows that extend longitudinally around the test. They are tipped with suckers, and are long enough to reach beyond the spines. Urchins also have numerous stalked pinchers about the size of the tube feet; all of the pinchers have three jaws, and some have poison glands. These structures are defensive, protecting against predators and discouraging larval animals from settling on the urchins.

The body wall on the lower side extends beyond the border of the rows of plates as a flexible tip surrounding the mouth. Around the mouth are large tube feet, which can attach to the substrate and pull the mouth against it for feeding. In all cases, feeding involves gnawing with a toothed organ called Aristotle's lantern. This remarkable structure consists of a set of skeletal rods and muscles arranged to open and close five teeth, like the jaws of a drill chuck. The lantern can be protruded partially and completely retracted back into the mouth. The area around the mouth is usually adorned with ten frilly gills.

Cake urchins, heart urchins, and sand dollars are modified for burrowing in sand. They have shorter and more numerous spines than do sea urchins; tube feet are confined to the upper and lower surfaces, absent from the sides; and they have assumed a bilateral symmetry while retaining most of the general pattern of an echinoid. In heart urchins the mouth is well forward, and the anus at the rear end. In cake urchins and sand dollars the mouth remains central, but the anus is to the rear. The upper surface of the test shows the pattern of five sets of tube feet, one directed forward, two to the left, and two to the right. Though the anus is to the rear, the plates with reproductive pores and sieve plates remain at the upper center. Aristotle's lantern is not well developed in these irregular echinoids.

Class Holothuroidea

Members of the Class Holothuroidea are generally called sea cucumbers, though some of them bear no particular resemblance to the vegetable. They are elongated, with the axis running horizontally from mouth to anal end. More primitive forms have five well-developed longitudinal rows of tube feet equally spaced around the circumference, but since such long animals must lie with one side down, many of them have well-developed tube feet on the three rows in contact with the substrate, and the other two rows reduced or missing. This imposes an almost bilaterally symmetrical pattern on these radially symmetrical animals.

The mouth is surrounded by a row of tentacles, which may be fingerlike, stalked with a buttonlike tip, or branched. Tentacles are actually modified tube feet, part of the water vascular system. They are used in feeding. The holothuroids differ from the echinoderms previously discussed in having a water vascular system full of body fluid rather than sea water; no sieve plate communicates with the sea.

Bryozoans: Phylum Bryozoa

The Phylum Bryozoa, or Ectoprocta, includes more than 4000 species of colonial sedentary animals. Individuals (or zooids) in the colony are seldom as large as $\frac{1}{32}''$ (1 mm), though the colony itself may be several feet across.

The individual lies within a body-covering that is continuous with or fused to the body-covering of adjacent colony members. The covering may be gelatinous, membranous, rubbery, chitinous (made of the same tough material found in the exoskeleton of an insect or shrimp), or limy. The form of the colony may be branching, creeping, bushy, leafy, tubular, fleshy, or encrusting.

The case around the individual has an opening through which a crown of tentacles can be extended. The tentacles are ciliated and surround the mouth. The anus lies outside the crown of tentacles. The extended tentacles are funnel-shaped. Cilia drive water and food particles, mostly one-celled plants and bacteria, into the funnel. Some species draw food into the mouth with their tentacles.

A colony increases in size asexually by budding, and new colonies are established by sexual reproduction. Most bryozoans are hermaphroditic, but in some species the sexes are distinct.

There are three classes of bryozoans: the Stenolaemata, which are all marine, and are tubular and limy, with circular openings for the crown of tentacles; the Gymnolaemata, which are mostly marine, and are either tubular, encrusting, gelatinous, membranous, chitinous, or limy, with individuals specialized for specific functions; and the Phylactolaemata, which are all freshwater species.

Entoprocts: Phylum Entoprocta

The Phylum Entoprocta includes about sixty species of small sedentary animals, known as nodding heads, most of which are marine and colonial. An entoproct has an oval body mounted on a stalk. Its upper surface is surrounded by a crown of six to thirty-six ciliated tentacles. Within the crown lies the mouth at one end and the anus at the other; in this, entoprocts differ from bryozoans, whose anus is outside the crown of tentacles. The ciliated tentacles create a current of water, and organic particles are trapped on a coating of mucus on the tentacles and moved by cilia into the mouth and the U-shaped digestive tract consisting of esophagus, stomach, and intestine. When the feeding animal is disturbed, its tentacles retract by shortening and curling to the center.

Colonial entoprocts have an attached creeping stem from which arise a number of stalks, sometimes branched, with individuals at the tips. Within the stems are muscle fibers which cause the stalk to bend or "bow" at times, and then, as quickly, to straighten up again.

Brachiopods: Phylum Brachiopoda

The Phylum Brachiopoda includes about 260 living species of shelled animals, but over 30,000 fossil species have been described from as far back as 600 million years ago. The genus *Lingula* is the oldest genus of animal life of which there are still living species, and dates back over 425 years.

The brachiopod shell consists of two valves and superficially resembles that of the bivalve mollusks. Unlike those of mollusks, however, the valves are upper and lower instead of left and right. Brachiopods are sizable animals, with shells usually 1–3" (25–76 mm) long. They have a stalk that anchors them to the substrate. The phylum contains two classes: Inarticulata and Articulata. These names refer to the nature of articulation, or joining, of the two valves.

Classes Inarticulata and Articulata

The valves of inarticulates are the same size and are joined to each other only by muscles, with the stalk emerging from between them at that juncture. The articulates have a larger lower valve to which the upper is hinged. The stalk emerges through a hole in the lower valve to the rear of the hinge line. The bowl-like lower shell with its hole looks like an ancient Roman oil lamp, giving the group its common name of "lampshells."

The interior of the valves is lined with a mantle that secretes shell material. As the valves gape, they expose a large crescentic structure with a coiled arm at either side bearing a double row of long tentacles directed toward the gape. Cilia on the tentacles drive water over them, trapping fine organic particles and moving them to the mouth in the middle of the crescent. Inarticulates have a digestive system that ends at an anus; articulates have an intestine that ends as a blind pouch, and undigested matter, bound by mucus into small pellets that do not foul the tentacles, is expelled through the mouth. Articulate brachiopods have a short, muscular stalk that is attached to rocks or other solid objects. They are capable of twisting about on the stalk.

Inarticulate brachiopods have a long stalk with a tuft of fibers at the tip by which the animal is anchored in a mud or sand bottom. The stalk can contract or extend, permitting the animal to gape its valves at the surface of the bottom, or retreat under the surface at low tide or when disturbed. In some Asiatic countries these stalks are cooked and eaten.

Nearly all brachiopods have separate sexes, with ovaries or testes in the rear part of the body cavity. Eggs or sperm are discharged through the kidney ducts. Most species are spawners, with development to swimming larvae taking place in the sea, but a few brood the developing eggs. None is capable of asexual reproduction.

Acorn Worms: Phylum Hemichordata

The acorn worms are burrowing forms with a three-part body consisting of a muscular proboscis, usually short and cone-shaped, attached by a stalk to a short collar which bears the mouth just below the proboscis stalk, and a long trunk, the first part of which has many paired gill slits on the upper surface. These slits permit the escape of water taken in through the mouth and passed over gills in the walls of the foregut, or pharynx. The pharynx continues into the midgut, where digestion takes place, and subsequently into the hindgut, which terminates in the anus at the rear tip of the worm.

Chordates: Phylum Chordata

If it were not for the existence of sea squirts and lancelets, the Phylum Chordata would consist only of vertebrate animals—those with a vertebral skeleton or backbone; but sea squirts and lancelets necessitate a broader view of the Phylum Chordata. This phylum takes its name from the notochord, a stiffened rod consisting of a fibrous sheath around translucent cells whose turgid condition provides both firmness and flexibility. No member of any other phylum has a notochord. Possession of a notochord prevents a chordate's body from telescoping when its longitudinal muscles contract. Instead, it bends from side to side. Lancelets retain the notochord throughout life, whereas sea squirts and vertebrates possess one only during larval or embryonic stages of development. Above its notochord, a chordate has a tubular dorsal nerve cord. Chordates have a pharynx perforated with a number of paired gill slits in aquatic species.

Subphylum Urochordata

The Subphylum Urochordata includes tunicates, salps, and larvaceans. Many are sedentary animals whose body is enclosed in a jacket or tunic.

Urochordates have a large pharynx with slits in its walls and a food groove in its floor. The pharynx functions both in respiration and in filtering food. The adult shows no evidence of notochord or tubular nerve chord, which are found only in the tadpole-shaped larva and which the larva loses, along with its muscular tail, as it matures.

Class Ascidiacea. The tunicates or sea squirts (Class Ascidiacea) are attached forms, either solitary or colonial, the latter with many individuals produced by budding. They have a continuous tunic covering the body which is attached to a solid. At the end opposite this attachment there is one opening through which water enters the animal and another nearby through which water escapes. These are called the incurrent and excurrent siphons, respectively. The incurrent siphon opens into a large pharynx with slitted walls, surrounded by a cavity, the atrium, opening to the outside through the excurrent siphon. Water is thus moved by cilia into the pharynx through the incurrent siphon and the slits, into the atrium, and out of the atrium through the excurrent siphon. The pharynx is continuous with the rest of the digestive tract, which loops about the terminates in an anus situated just inside the excurrent siphon. The tadpole-shaped larva, with its notochord and muscular tail, is believed to have played an important role in the evolution of elongated chordates which, in turn, gave rise to fishlike forms. It is probable, then, that sea squirts were important members of our own evolutionary tree.

Class Thaliacea. Salps are small barrel-shaped, almost transparent members of the plankton that swim by taking water in the front end and forcing it out the rear by contractions of visible bands of body muscles. After storms large numbers of salps may be found on beaches.

Subphylum Cephalochordata

Of all the invertebrates, those most similar to the vertebrate animals are the cephalochordates, or lancelets. Adult lancelets clearly show the three chordate characteristics: pharyngeal slits, a tubular nerve cord above the digestive system, and notochord, the latter extending from the tip of the head to the tip of the tail. Lancelets, like urochordates, differ in having a chamber around the pharynx to receive and remove water coming through the slits, and they lack the brain, eyes, and internal ears common to vertebrates. The segmented muscles arranged along each side of their bodies, however, are similar to those of vertebrate fishes.

Phylum Porifera
Sponge

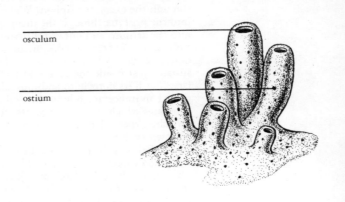

osculum

ostium

Phylum Cnidaria
Hydrozoan Polyp

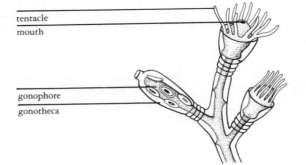

tentacle
mouth

gonophore
gonotheca

Phylum Cnidaria
Scyphozoan Medusa

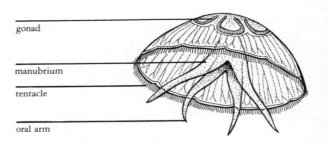

gonad

manubrium

tentacle

oral arm

Phylum Cnidaria
Sea Anemone

tentacle

oral disk
siphonoglyph
mouth

acontium

column

pedal disk

Phylum Ctenophora
Comb Jelly

apical organ

comb plate

mouth
oral lobe

Phylum Platyhelminthes
Flatworm

ocellus

tentacle

mouth

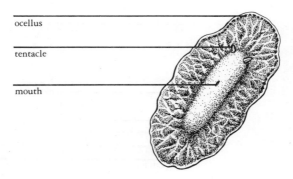

Phylum Rhynchocoela
Ribbon Worm

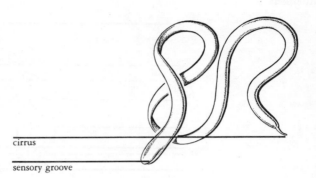

cirrus

sensory groove

Phylum Annelida
Clam Worm

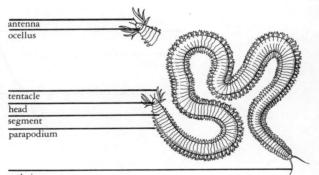

antenna
ocellus

tentacle
head
segment
parapodium

anal cirrus

Phylum Annelida
Parchment Worm

tube

head

cup
thorax
abdomen
parapodium

Phylum Sipuncula
Peanut Worm

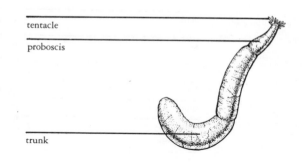

tentacle
proboscis

trunk

Phylum Echiura
Echiurid Worm

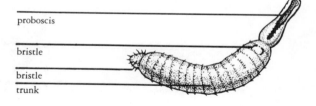

proboscis

bristle

bristle
trunk

Phylum Mollusca
Chiton

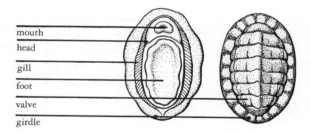

mouth
head

gill

foot

valve

girdle

Phylum Mollusca
Snail

spire

axial rib

spiral cord

body whorl

inner lip • aperture

outer lip

columella

siphonal canal

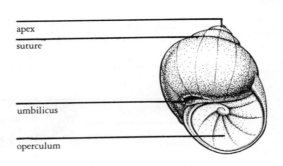

Phylum Mollusca
Snail

apex

suture

umbilicus

operculum

Phylum Mollusca
Nudibranch

tubercle

antenna

foot

Phylum Mollusca
Nudibranch

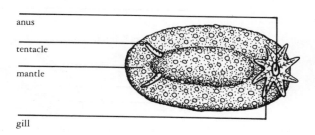

anus

tentacle

mantle

gill

Phylum Mollusca
Clam

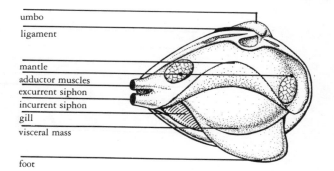

umbo

ligament

mantle
adductor muscles
excurrent siphon
incurrent siphon
gill
visceral mass

foot

Phylum Mollusca
Clam

umbo
ligament
lateral tooth

muscle scars

pallial line

Phylum Mollusca
Squid

fin

mantle

tentacle

siphon
eye

arm

Phylum Arthropoda
Sea Spider

proboscis
pincher
palp
eye
thorax
abdomen

leg

Phylum Arthropoda
Shrimp

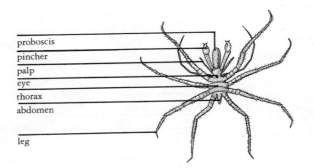

abdomen
carapace
beak
eye
antenna

walking leg

pincer
swimmeret
telson
tail fan

Phylum Arthropoda
Crab

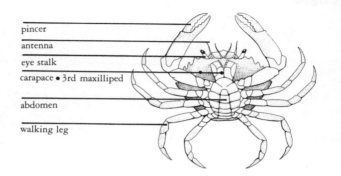

pincer
antenna
eye stalk
carapace • 3rd maxilliped
abdomen
walking leg

Phylum Echinodermata
Sea Star

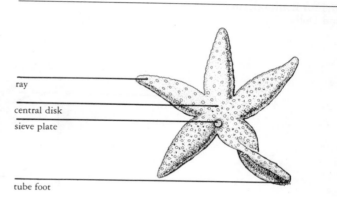

ray
central disk
sieve plate
tube foot

Phylum Echinodermata
Brittle Star

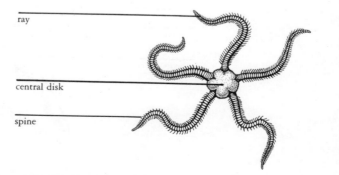

ray
central disk
spine

Phylum Echinodermata
Sea Urchin

spine

test

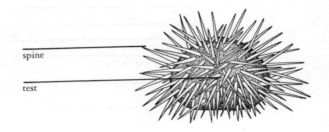

Phylum Echinodermata
Sand Dollar

spine

tube foot

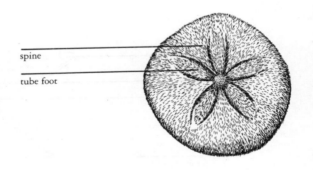

Phylum Echinodermata
Sea Cucumber

tentacle

tube foot

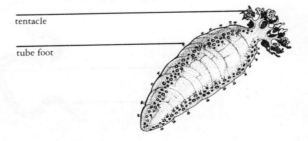

Phylum Bryozoa
Bryozoan

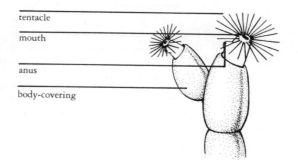

tentacle
mouth
anus
body-covering

Phylum Entoprocta
Entoproct

tentacle
anus
mouth
stalk
stem

Phylum Brachiopoda
Lampshell

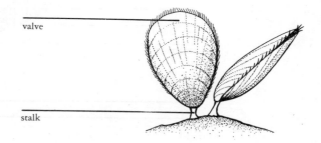

valve
stalk

Phylum Hemichordata
Acorn Worm

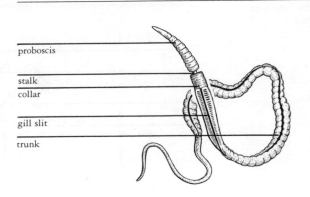

proboscis

stalk
collar

gill slit

trunk

Phylum Chordata
Tunicate

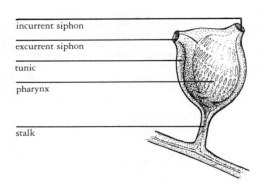

incurrent siphon

excurrent siphon

tunic

pharynx

stalk

Phylum Chordata
Lancelet

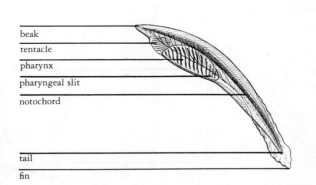

beak
tentacle
pharynx
pharyngeal slit
notochord

tail
fin

GLOSSARY

Abdomen In insects, spiders, and marine invertebrates, the hindmost division of an animal's body.

Accidental A species whose normal range is in another area, and has appeared in a given area only a very few times.

Adipose fin A fleshy fin, without supporting rays, behind the dorsal fin in some fishes.

Aestivation Dormancy during summer or the dry season.

Alveolar weathering Erosion caused by periodic wetting and drying, with resultant pitting and fretting. Also called salt-spray fretting.

Anal fin The median fin behind the anus.

Aperture In gastropods and tusk shells, the opening through which the animal's foot and head protrude.

Aristotle's lantern The chewing mechanism of a sea urchin, consisting of 5 teeth operated by a complex system of levers and muscles.

Auriculars Feathers covering the ear opening and the area immediately around it; often distinctively colored. Also called ear coverts.

Autotomy The capacity of some animals to shed a part of the body or to break into several pieces, in the absence of external force.

Axial In gastropods, running parallel to the shell's axis, or from spire to base.

Axillary process An enlarged, elongated scale at the insertion of the pectoral or pelvic fins of some fishes.

Axis The straight line with respect to which a body is symmetrical.

Baleen In some whales, the fibrous plates in parallel rows on each side of the upper jaw.

Beak In many toothed whales, the elongated forward portion of the head, consisting of the rostrum and the lower jaw.

Bilateral symmetry A body plan in which paired body parts lie on either side of a midline, so that each side is a mirror image of the other.

Bioluminescence Light produced by a living organism through a biochemical reaction.

Blow In cetaceans, the expulsion of air at the surface through the blowhole(s), or nostril(s), during exhalation; also called the spout.

Blowhole In cetaceans, the single or paired respiratory opening.

Body whorl The last whorl of a snail's shell, ending at the aperture and containing the bulk of the animal.

Brackish Somewhat salty, but less salty than seawater.

Breach To leap through the water surface.

Budding A mode of asexual reproduction in which an outgrowth of an organism develops and forms a new individual.

Byssal gap In certain bivalves, the opening between the margins of the valves through which the byssus passes.

Byssal threads Tough, silken threads secreted by certain bivalve mollusks as a means of attachment to a substrate.

Byssus In many bivalves, a bundle of hairlike strands used for attachment to objects.

Calcareous Composed of calcium carbonate; shelly.

Callus In gastropods, a thick or thin calcareous deposit extending over a portion of the shell.

Canal In gastropods, an open channel or a tube on the outer lip or base of the shell, containing the living animal's siphons.

Capillarity The tendency of a liquid (such as sea water) to adhere to a solid (such as sand grains); loosely, the ability of sand to retain moisture.

Carapace That part of the exoskeleton of a Horseshoe Crab or higher crustacean extending over the head and thorax, but not the abdomen. The upper part of a turtle's shell.

Casual A species whose normal range is in another area, but has occurred in our area somewhat more frequently than accidentals.

Caudal Pertaining to the tail.

Caudal fin The fin on the hindmost part of the body.

Caudal peduncle The part of the body of a fish between the posterior end of the anal fin base and the caudal fin base.

Cirrus A tactile projection that varies in shape according to the phylum; may be tentaclelike, fingerlike, or hairlike. (Plural, cirri.).

Claspers Modified parts of the pelvic fins of male sharks, rays, and skates; used in copulation.

Cloaca The chamber into which the digestive, urinary, and reproductive systems empty, opening to the outside through the anus.

Columella That part of the spiral shell of a snail surrounding the axis, about which the shell coils.

Comb plate A comblike membrane of fused cilia in a ctenophore; a ctena.

Commensalism An intimate relationship between animals of two species, in which each lives without obvious harm or benefit to the other.

Compressed Flattened from side to side so that the fish is higher than wide.

Coverts Small feathers that overlie or cover the bases of the large flight feathers of the wings and tail, or that cover an area or structure (e.g., ear coverts).

Cusp A pointed projection on a tooth.

Delta A fan-shaped alluvial estuarine deposit at a river's mouth.

Detritus Fine particles of plant, animal, or inorganic matter; an important part of marine food cycles.

Dextral In snails, having the aperture on the right-hand side of the columella.

Diatom A microscopic, unicellular plant living either attached to a solid or as plankton, and capable of photosynthesis.

Diurnal Active during daytime hours.

Dorsal Pertaining to the back or upper surface of the body.

Dorsal fin The fin along the midline of the back, supported by rays; often notched or divided into separate fins.

Ears In scallops and file shells, triangular or oblong projections at the ends of the hinge line.

Embayment Formation of a bay (as by faulting); a bay.

Escutcheon In bivalves, an elongate pointed area on the upper margin behind the umbones, set off by an angle or impressed line, and including the ligament.

Estuary A zone of meeting between river (or stream) and sea, especially the tidal mouth of a river, an environment under the influence of both systems.

Finlet One of several small, isolated fin rays behind the dorsal or anal fins.

Flange An erect, projecting flattened ridge.

Flight feathers The long, well-developed feathers of the wings and tail, used during flight. The flight feathers of the wings are divided into primaries, secondaries, and tertials. See also rectrix.

Flippers In cetaceans, the forelimbs.

Flukes In cetaceans, the horizontally positioned tail fin, resembling the tail of a fish, but not vertical.

Foot In mollusks, a muscular organ used in moving, adhering to a surface, or digging into sand or mud.

Gape A region of incomplete closure between the two valves of a bivalve mollusk.

Genus A group of very closely related species which share many structural features and ecological characteristics, and whose scientific names all begin with the same word, the generic name. (Plural, genera.)

Gill A respiratory organ that extracts dissolved oxygen and salts from the water.

Girdle In chitons, a band of muscular tissue that surrounds the valves and holds them together.

Gonad Sex gland; ovary or testis.

Gravid Bearing eggs or developing young; pregnant.

Growth line In both gastropods and bivalves, the line that marks former resting stages in the growth of the shell.

Halophyte Plant adapted to grow under saline conditions.

Heterocercal fin A caudal fin in which the upper lobe is considerably larger than the lower; it contains the vertebral column.

Holdfast The rootlike part of an alga attaching to the substrate.

Horny Made of horn, a brown, fibrous organic substance.

Hybrids Offspring of two different varieties, races, species, or genera.

Infauna Those animals that live burrowed in the substrate of a bay, marsh, or coastline.

Inner lip The inner margin of the aperture of a snail, bounded by the columella.

Insertion In fishes, the point at which each paired fin is joined to the body.

Intergrades Animals of related and adjoining subspecies that may resemble either form or exhibit a combination of their characteristics.

Keel A ridge on individual dorsal scales of some snakes; longitudinal ridge on the carapace or plastron of turtles; the raised edge along the upper edge of the tail in some salamanders.

Krill Shrimplike crustaceans occurring in huge numbers in the open seas, and eaten by baleen whales.

Larva A post-hatching immature stage that differs in appearance from the adult and must metamorphose before assuming adult characters (Plural, larvae.)

Lateral line A series of tubes or pored scales associated with the sensory system; usually extending from just behind the opercle to the base of the caudal fin.

Ligament In bivalves, a horny elastic structure located on the exterior or interior of the shell's hinge line, connecting the valves.

Littoral zone The marginal shore area covered by the tides (intertidal zone) and including the splash zone. It may be divided into the lower littoral zone, which remains submerged except during spring tides; the middle littoral zone, submerged by most high tides and exposed during most low tides; and the upper littoral zone, submerged only by spring tides.

Lore The space between the eye and the base of the bill, sometimes distinctively colored.

Lunule In certain bivalves, a heart-shaped or elongate depression in front of the umbones.

Mantle A fleshy organ enveloping the vital organs of mollusks, usually containing glands that secrete the shell.

Mantle cavity The space enclosed by the mantle of mollusks containing the gills and the visceral mass.

Maxilla The rear and usually larger of 2 bones forming the upper jaw.

Median fins The unpaired fins—dorsal, anal, and caudal.

Medusa One of the body forms of a cnidarian, cup-shaped or bowl-shaped with a mouth on a stalk on the underside, and capable of swimming by rhythmic contractions.

Microhabitat A small, often highly specialized and effectively isolated habitat.

Mucus A slippery protective substance secreted onto the exposed surfaces of many animals.

Muscle scar The attachment mark of a muscle on the interior of a shell.

Naris The external nostril; in birds located near the base of the upper mandible. (Plural, nares.)

Nearshore The zone of a beach made up of the underwater area from the low-tide line seaward; the subtidal region.

Nocturnal Active at night.

Nucleus The earliest part of a spirally organized structure such as an operculum or coiled shell.

Operculum A lid that closes an aperture; found in many snails and in certain tube-dwelling annelid worms.

Oral disk The flattened area around the mouth of an anthozoan polyp.

Origin The point at which the front of the dorsal or anal fin is attached to the body.

Outer lip In coiled gastropods, the outer margin of the aperture; the edge farthest from the columella.

Paired fins The fins that occur in pairs—the pectorals and the pelvics.

Pallial line In bivalves, the scar on the interior of the shell that marks where the mantle was attached.

Pallial sinus In bivalves, the shallow or deep embayment at the hind end of the pallial line.

Papilla A small, nipplelike projection; papillae often occur in groups.

Parasite An animal living in or on the body of an organism of another species, to the detriment of the latter.

Parietal callus In gastropods, a shelly thickening or deposit on the parietal wall.

Pectoral fins The paired fins attached to the shoulder girdle.

Pedal disk The flat base of a sea anemone, by which it adheres to a solid surface.

Pelvic fins The paired fins on the lower part of the body, usually just below or behind the pectoral fins.

Periostracum The tough coat of organic material on the outside of a mollusk's shell.

Photosynthesis The process by which plant cells use light energy to produce organic compounds from carbon dioxide and water, catalyzed by the green pigment chlorophyll, with free oxygen as a byproduct.

Pincer A term used to designate the nipperlike appendage of crustaceans; the chela.

Pinnate Featherlike; with two rows of simple branches rising in one plane from opposite sides of an axis.

Plankton A collective term for all organisms living suspended in water, either unable to swim or swimming so feebly as to be at the mercy of water currents.

Plastron The lower part of a turtle's shell.

Polyp One of the body forms of a cnidarian, usually cylindrical, with a mouth surrounded by tentacles at one end and with the other end attached.

Pored scale One of a series of scales with a small opening into a sensory system; usually found along the lateral line.

Porosity The ratio of the volume of space between sand grains to the volume of the mass of those sand grains; porosity is a crucial factor governing the lives of many burrowing animals.

Prehensile Adapted for grasping or wrapping around.

Primaries The outermost and longest flight feathers on a bird's wing. Primaries vary in number from nine to eleven per wing, but always occur in a fixed number in any particular species.

Proboscis An extensible or permanently extended structure on the head, commonly associated with the mouth of an animal, used in feeding or sensing food or other chemical substances.

Radial canal A canal branching from the central digestive cavity of a medusa, and extending to the margin of the bell.

Radial symmetry A body plan in which repeated body parts are arranged around a central point, as in a wheel.

Radula An organ located in the mouth cavity and consisting of minute teeth, either on a flexible muscular ribbon or unattached; used by snails, chitons, tusk shells, and cephalopods in feeding.

Ray The arm, or radiating appendage, of an echinoderm.

Ray One of the supporting structures in the fin membranes, either flexible (soft ray) or stiff (spine).

Rib A ridgelike sculptural element that is usually axial in gastropods and radial in bivalves.

Rostrum In fishes, a forward projection of the snout; in cetaceans, a forward extension of the upper jaw.

Salinity The salt concentration of a solution; salinity of seawater is expressed in parts per thousand rather than in percent. The average salinity of seawater is thirty-five parts per thousand.

Scapulars In birds, a group of feathers on the shoulder or along the side of the back.

Sculpture The ornamentation on the shells of mollusks.

Secondaries The large flight feathers located in a series along the rear edge of the wing, immediately inward from the primaries.

Segment One of the serially repeated divisions of the body of an annelid or arthropod.

Shield In gastropods, a thickened, distinctly margined callus on the body whorl near the inner lip.

Sinistral In snails, having the aperture on the left-hand side of the columella.

Siphonal canal In snails, a short channel, sometimes tubelike, at the lower end of the aperture, through which the siphon protrudes.

Spawn To release eggs and sperm into the water.

Species A population of animals or plants whose members are at least potentially able to interbreed with each other, but are reproductively isolated from other populations.

Speculum A distinctively colored area on the wing of a bird, especially the metallic patch on the secondaries of some ducks.

Spicule A small structure, often needlelike or dartlike, supporting the tissues of various sponges, soft corals, and compound tunicates.

Spine A usually rigid, unsegmented, unbranched structure that supports the thin membrane of a fin; a sharp, bony projection, usually on the head.

Spiracle In certain fishes, a respiratory opening, varying in size, on the back part of the head above and behind the eye; in whales, the blowhole.

Spire In gastropods, the whorls above the body whorl.

Spout A visible cloud expelled by a cetacean during exhalation at the water surface; also called the blow.

Stipe Stem or stalk, as for kelp or other seaweed.

Substrate The surface on which an organism lives.

Sucking disc An adhesive structure; a disc formed by a jawless mouth, the union of paired fins, or a modification of the dorsal spines.

Surf zone The area affected by wave action, extending from the high-water mark to the point where waves break.

Suture In spiral gastropods, the line or space that separates adjoining whorls.

Suture The seam between adjacent whorls of a snail's shell.

Symbiosis An intimate biological relationship between two species; includes parasitism, where one lives at the expense of the other; commensalism, where the presence of one neither helps nor damages the other; and mutualism, where both gain from the relationship.

Tadpole The larva of a frog or toad.

Tail fan A fanlike structure at the tip of the tail of some crustaceans, consisting of a telson, or tailpiece, and a pair of flattened abdominal appendages.

Tail stock In cetaceans, the tapered rear part of the body, just in front of the flukes.

Tarsus The lower, usually featherless, part of a bird's leg.

Telson The unpaired terminal structure attached to the last abdominal segment of a crustacean.

Tentacle An elongated extension on the head of gastropods, on the mantle of bivalves that serves as a sensory organ or around the mouth of an invertebrate, used for grasping or feeding, or as a sense organ.

Tertials The innermost flight feathers on a bird's wing, immediately adjacent to the body. They are often regarded simply as the innermost secondaries. Also called tertiaries.

Test The skeleton of an echinoid echinoderm, consisting of rows of fused plates.

Thorax In insects and marine invertebrates, the division of an animal's body between the head and the abdomen.

Tooth In gastropods, a small triangular or elongated protuberance on the columellar or parietal wall or on the inside of the outer lip; in bivalves, a ridge along the hinge line.

Trend Extend in a particular direction.

Tube foot One of the numerous small appendages of an echinoderm, hydraulically operated and used in feeding or locomotion, or as a sense organ; often tipped with a suction disk.

Tubercle A bump, node, or low, rounded projection on the surface of an animal.

Tunic The covering of a sea squirt's, or tunicate's, body; in compound tunicates, a thick mass in which many individuals are imbedded.

Umbilicus The hollow within the axis around which the whorls of a snail's shell coil; it may be closed by an overgrowth of shell material (the umbilical callus).

Umbo In bivalves, the earliest part of the shell (plural, umbones).

Umbonal ridge In bivalves, an angled or rounded ridge beginning at the umbo and usually extending to the hind end of a valve.

Valve In chitons, one of the eight plates comprising the shell; in bivalves, one of the two parts of the shell.

Vent Anus; opening of the cloaca to the outside of the body.

Visceral mass That part of the molluscan body containing the visceral organs.

Viviparous Live-bearing; a term applied to animals whose eggs develop inside the body of the female, and in which larvae are born in an advanced stage.

Vocal sac An expandable pouch on the throat of male frogs and toads that becomes filled with air and acts as a resonating chamber when they vocalize during courtship; the sac collapses at the end of the call.

Water table The upper limit of water contained in the ground.

Whorl One of the turns of a snail's shell.

Wing In certain bivalves, a flattened projection located at one or both ends of the hinge line.

Wing bar A conspicuous crosswise wing mark.

Wing stripe A conspicuous mark running along the opened wing.

BIBLIOGRAPHY

Abbott, I. A. and G. J. Hollenberg.
Marine Algae of California.
Stanford, California: Stanford University Press, 1976.

Abbott, R. Tucker.
American Seashells.
Princeton, New Jersey: D. Van Nostrand, 1954.

Angell, Tony and Kenneth C. Balcomb.
Marine Birds and Mammals of Puget Sound.
Seattle: University of Washington Press, 1982.

Brown, Vinson.
Sea Mammals and Reptiles of the Pacific Coast.
New York: Collier Books, 1976.

Carefoot, Thomas.
Pacific Seashores: A Guide to Intertidal Ecology.
Seattle: University of Washington Press, 1977.

Carson, Rachel.
The Edge of the Sea.
Boston: Houghton Mifflin Company, 1979.

Clemens, W. A. and C. V. Wilby.
Fishes of the Pacific Coast of Canada. Bulletin 48.
Ottawa, Canada: Fisheries Research Board of Canada, 1967.

Dawson, E. Yale and Michael S. Foster.
Seashore Plants of California.
Berkeley, California: University of California Press, 1982.

Gotshall, Daniel W.
Pacific Coast Inshore Fishes.
Los Osos, California: Sea Challengers, Western Marine
Enterprises, 1981.

Haley, Delphine, ed.
Marine Mammals of the Eastern North Pacific and Arctic Waters.
Seattle: Pacific Search Press, 1978.
Seabirds of the Eastern North Pacific and Arctic Waters.
Seattle: Pacific Search Press, 1984.

Hart, J. L.
Pacific Fishes of Canada. Bulletin 180.
Ottawa, Canada: Fisheries Research Board of Canada, 1973.

Kelley, Don Greame.
Edge of a Continent: The Pacific Coast from Alaska to Baja.
Palo Alto, California: American West Publishing Company,
1971.

Kozloff, Eugene N.
*Illustrated Guide to the Natural History of Western Oregon,
Washington and British Columbia.*
Seattle: University of Washington Press, 1978.
*Keys to Marine Invertebrates of Puget Sound, the San Juan
Archipelago and Adjacent Regions.*
Seattle: University of Washington Press, 1974.

Plants and Animals of the Pacific Northwest: An Illustrated Guide.
Seattle: University of Washington Press, 1976.
Seashore Life of Puget Sound, the Strait of Georgia, and the San Juan Archipelago.
Seattle: University of Washington Press, 1973.
Seashore Life of the Northern Pacific Coast.
Seattle: University of Washington Press, 1983.

Levinton, Jeffrey S.
Marine Ecology.
Englewood Cliffs, New Jersey: Prentice-Hall, Inc., 1982.

Light, S. F. et al.
Intertidal Invertebrates of the Central California Coast. 3rd edition.
Berkeley, California: University of California Press, 1970.

Maser, Chris et al.
Natural History of Oregon Coast Mammals. Report PNW-133.
Portland, Oregon: Department of the Interior, Bureau of Land Management, 1981.

McConnaughey, B. H. and Robert Zottoli.
Introduction to Marine Biology. 4th edition.
St. Louis: C. V. Mosby Company, 1983.

Morris, Robert H., Donald P. Abbott, and Eugene C. Haderlie.
Intertidal Invertebrates of California.
Stanford, California: Stanford University Press, 1980.

Nybakken, James W.
Marine Biology: An Ecological Approach.
New York: Harper and Row, 1982.

Power, D. M., ed.
California Islands.
Santa Barbara, California: Santa Barbara Museum of Natural History, 1980.

Ricketts, E. F. and J. Calvin.
Between Pacific Tides. 4th edition, ed. by Joel Hedgpeth.
Stanford, California: Stanford University Press, 1968.

Scagel, R. F.
Annotated List of Marine Algae of British Columbia and Northern Washington. With keys to genera.
Ottawa, Canada: Canadian Department of Northern Affairs and Natural Resources, 1957.
Guide to Common Seaweeds of British Columbia. Handbook No. 27.
Victoria, British Columbia: British Columbia Provincial Museum, 1967.
Marine Algae of British Columbia and Northern Washington. Bulletin No. 207.
Ottawa, Canada: National Museum of Canada, Queen's Printer, 1966.

Scheffer, V. B.
Natural History of Marine Mammals.
New York: Scribner's Sons, 1976.

Schwartz, Maurice L., ed.
Beaches and Coastal Environments (Encyclopedia of Earth Sciences).
Stroudsburg, Pennsylvania: Hutchinson Ross Publishing
Company, 1982.

Simmerman, Nancy Lange.
Alaska's Parklands—The Complete Guide.
Seattle: The Mountaineers, 1983.

Snively, Gloria.
*Exploring the Seashore in British Columbia, Washington and
Oregon: A Guide to the Shorebirds, Intertidal Plants and Animals.*
5th printing 1983.
Vancouver, British Columbia: Gordon Soules Book Publishers,
1978.

Stephenson, T. A. and Anne.
Life Between Tidemarks.
San Francisco: W. H. Freeman and Company, 1972.

Sumich, James L.
Introduction to the Biology of Marine Life. 2nd edition.
Dubuque, Iowa: William.C. Brown Company, 1980.

The Coastal Access Guide.
Coastal Commission, State of California.
Berkeley, California: University of California Press, 1983.

Waaland, J. Robert.
Common Seaweeds of the Pacific Coast.
Seattle: Pacific Search Press, 1977.

White, James Seeley.
Seashells of the Pacific Northwest.
Portland, Oregon: Binford and Mort, 1976.

Wiedemann, Alfred M., La Rea J. Dennis, and Frank H.
Smith.
Plants of the Oregon Coastal Dunes.
Corvallis, Oregon: Oregon State University Bookstore, Inc.,
1974.

CREDITS

The numbers in parentheses are plate numbers. Some photographers have pictures under agency names as well as their own. Agency names appear in boldface.

William H. Amos (393, 447)
Dennis Anderson (602, 605, 607, 609)

Animals Animals
Anne Wertheim (390, 462) Jack Wilburn (332)

Ardea Photographics
S. Roberts (543) J. S. Wightman (549)

Charles Arneson (108, 179, 240, 242, 253, 294, 306, 311–314, 316, 344, 345, 383, 403, 412, 413, 466–468, 491, 492, 497, 504, 505, 510

Peter Arnold, Inc.
Bob Evans (317)

Ron Austing (581)
Stephen F. Bailey (547, 563, 576)
Frank S. Balthis (22)
Fred Bavendam (373, 387, 389, 401, 405, 411, 436, 444, 494)
David W. Behrens (129, 417, 485, 493)
Hans Bertsch (419)
Edward B. Brothers (276)
Fred Bruemmer (228)
P. A. and F. G. Buckley (567)
James H. Carmichael, Jr. (25–37, 39–52, 54–75, 77–106, 109–119, 121–127, 130–176, 180–185, 189–192, 460)
Craig Cary (321)
Alfred Castro (372, 454)
David Cavagnaro (17)
Tony Chess (243, 249, 257, 262, 268)
Herbert Clarke (515, 521, 534, 542, 561, 577)
Anna-Jean Cole (618)

Click/Chicago
Tom J. Ulrich (225)

Bruce Coleman, Inc.
William Amos (482) Jen and Des Bartlett (550) Edward R. Degginger (379) Jeff Foott (186, 426) Lee Foster (617) R. N. Mariscal (355, 397, 438) M. Timothy O'Keefe (279) Joy Spurr (615) Kim Taylor (349) Ron and Valerie Taylor (320, 322)

Bruce Coleman, Ltd.
Jane Burton (469)

Stephen Collins (612)
Ed Cooper (12, 13, 608, 610, 614)
Helen Cruickshank (595, 596)
Harry Darrow (574)
Thomas H. Davis (520, 545, 589)
Edward R. Degginger (325, 333, 376, 377, 380, 398, 421, 428, 455, 461)

Jack Dermid (76, 407, 558)

Design Photographers International
Charles Seaborn (327, 340, 350, 375, 430, 443, 474)

John de Visser (1–3)
Townsend P. Dickinson (200)
John DeMartini (451)
Larry Ditto (554)
Jack Drafahl, Jr. (347, 434)
Susan Drafahl (341, 453, 456, 457)

DRK Photo
Stephen J. Krasemann (14, 512, 535, 593)

Earth Images
Terry Domico (269) Doug Maier (247) Al Salonsky (319)

Harry Engels, (552)
Douglas Faulkner (368, 370, 374)
Kenneth W. Fink (511, 525, 528, 529, 539, 564, 566, 575, 578, 591, 600)
Jeff Foott (2nd frontispiece, 5th frontispiece, 15, 234, 296, 298, 357, 361, 364, 365, 409, 415, 425, 432, 440–442, 458, 553, 579)
Kathryn Frost (229, 233)
Laurel Giannino (277, 323)
D. A. Gill (592)
Jeff Gnass (7)
François Gohier (3rd frontispiece, 19, 226, 231)
Daniel W. Gotshall (120, 235, 244, 246, 248, 251, 255, 256, 259, 261, 263–267, 270–273, 280, 285, 286, 290, 293, 301, 304, 308–310, 363, 386, 414, 416, 449, 475, 498)
Al Grotell (477)
Arthur Guppy (337)
David Hatler (538, 556)
Phil and Loretta Hermann (260)

Hubbs Sea World Research Institute
Stephen Leatherwood (199) Bob Pitman (204) Scott Sinclair (202) Randall S. Wells (203)

Paul Humann (236, 238, 254, 274, 318, 486)
Joseph Jehl (546)
Charles C. Johnson (604)
G. C. Kelley (518, 540, 580)
Richard Lang (275)
Paul D. Langer (356, 402)
Wayne Lankinen (568)
Calvin Larsen (531)
Tom and Pat Leeson (522)
Kenneth E. Lucas (237, 239, 241, 281, 299, 303, 307, 331, 338, 339, 346, 371, 378, 399, 422, 423, 429, 435, 463, 471)
Norman Meinkoth (38, 53, 107, 177, 328, 351, 359, 360, 391, 394, 418, 470)

Anthony Mercieca (523, 530, 562, 599)
C. Allan Morgan (197)
David Muench (Cover, 4th frontispiece, 4–6, 8–11, 20, 21, 24)
Tom Myers, (283, 324)

National Audubon Society Collection/Photo Researchers, Inc.
John Bova (585) William Curtsinger (196) Robert Dunne (362) Richard Ellis (205–222) Bob Evans (459) Gary Gibson (128, 187, 297, 326, 330, 334–336, 354) François Gohier (201) James Hancock (597) Walter Harvey (431) Russ Kinne (292) Al Lowry (439) Tom McHugh (342, 348, 353, 396, 541) Tom McHugh/Marineland of the Pacific (278) Tom McHugh/Pt. Defiance Aquarium (288, 289, 302) Tom McHugh/Seattle Aquarium (424, 452, 479) Tom McHugh/Steinhart Aquarium (245, 295, 300, 381, 382) Allan Power (287) Noble Proctor (465) William Ray (571) James Simon (230) William E. Townsend (367) George Whiteley (404)

Robert T. Orr (16)
Dennis Paulson (532)

Photo Classics
M. Woodbridge Williams (329)

Greg Pic'l (352, 472)
Jan Erik Pierson (533, 587)
John Pitcher (513, 569)
Rod Planck (572)
Robert Potts (464)
Harold Wes Pratt (188, 384, 392, 395, 400, 408, 410, 420, 427, 445, 476, 484, 495, 506)
Betty Randall (358, 366, 473, 613)
John Ratti (514)
J. V. Remsen, Jr. (551)
John N. Rinne/U.S. Forestry Service, Rocky Mountain Station (284)
Richard J. Rosenthal (305)
Edward S. Ross (601, 606)
Jeffrey L. Rotman (385, 446, 481)
Leonard Lee Rue III (223, 555)
Kenneth P. Sebens (448)
Ervio Sian (524, 527, 565, 590)
Arnold Small (23, 516, 517, 570, 583, 598)
Bruce A. Sorrie (544, 548, 573)
Southwest Fisheries Center (282)
Richard Spellenberg (611, 616)
Joy Spurr (487, 488, 496, 499, 509)

Tom Stack and Associates
Howard Hall (252, 258) Keith L. Murakami (224) Nadine Orabona (232) Kenneth Read (388) Tom Stack (18) Bill Tronca (250, 315) Bruce M. Wellman (198)

Charles Summers (594)
Ian C. Tait (557)

INDEX

FIELD NOTES

FIELD NOTES

THE AUDUBON SOCIETY

The National Audubon Society is among the oldest and largest private conservation organizations in the world. With over 518,500 members and more than 500 local chapters across the country, the Society works in behalf of our natural heritage through environmental education and conservation action. It protects wildlife in more than seventy sanctuaries from coast to coast. It also operates outdoor education centers and ecology workshops and publishes the prizewinning AUDUBON magazine, AMERICAN BIRDS magazine, newsletters, films, and other educational materials. For further information regarding membership in the Society, write to the National Audubon Society, 950 Third Avenue, New York, New York 10022.

CHANTICLEER STAFF

Publisher: Paul Steiner
Editor-in-Chief: Gudrun Buettner
Managing Editor: Susan Costello
Series Editor: Mary Beth Brewer
Text Editor: Ann Whitman
Associate Editor: Marian Appellof
Assistant Editors: David Allen, Constance Mersel
Editorial Assistant: Karel Birnbaum
Production: Helga Lose, Amy Roche, Frank Grazioli
Art Director: Carol Nehring
Art Associate: Ayn Svoboda
Art Assistant: Ellen Pugatch
Picture Library: Edward Douglas, Dana Pomfret
Maps and Symbols: Paul Singer
Senior Editor: Jane Opper
Natural History Consultant: John Farrand, Jr.
Design: Massimo Vignelli